Dr Stephen P. Kershaw h̲
of the Ancient Greeks, bo
been a Classics tutor for som̲ ̲̲̲̲̲̲̲̲̲̲̲̲̲̲̲ ̲ᵢᵥels from
beginner to PhD, currently c̲ ̲ ̲ ̲ ̲ ̲ᵤᵢ the Oxford University
Department for Continuing ᴇducation, authoring and teaching
undergraduate courses, and tutoring on the Masters in Literature
and Art. Steve has also created Oxford University's online courses
on 'Greek Mythology', 'The Fall of Rome' and 'The Minoans and
Mycenaeans'. He lectures at the Victoria and Albert Museum and, as
Professor of History of Art, runs the European Studies Classical
Tour for Rhodes College and the University of the South. In addi-
tion to titles published by Constable & Robinson, he has edited *The
Penguin Dictionary of Classical Mythology*. Steve was an expert
contributor to the History Channel's *Barbarians Rising* series; former
students include the Princess of Jordan; he translated the Greek
inscription on Matthew Pinsent's fourth Olympic gold medal for
him after his victory in Athens; and he is a guest speaker for Swan
Hellenic Cruises and the Royal Academy (through Cox & Kings). He
lives in the Oxfordshire village of Deddington with his wife, the
artist Lal Jones.

A Brief History of Atlantis

Plato's Ideal State

STEPHEN P. KERSHAW

ROBINSON

ROBINSON

First published in Great Britain in 2017 by Robinson

1 3 5 7 9 10 8 6 4 2

Copyright © Stephen P. Kershaw, 2017

The moral right of the author has been asserted.

A CIP catalogue record for this book
is available from the British Library.

ISBN: 978-1-47213-699-2

Typeset in Scala by Hewer Text UK Ltd, Edinburgh
Printed and bound in Great Britain by CPI Group (UK), Croydon CRO 4YY

Papers used by Robinson are from well-managed forests and other responsible sources.

MIX
Paper from
responsible sources
FSC® C104740

Robinson
An imprint of
Little, Brown Book Group
Carmelite House
50 Victoria Embankment
London EC4Y 0DZ

An Hachette UK Company
www.hachette.co.uk

www.littlebrown.co.uk

For Hebe

Contents

....

	Acknowledgements	xi
	Introduction	1
CHAPTER 1:	Ancient Mythical and Semi-Mythical Lands	3
	The Island of Atlas	
	Homer's Odyssey: Ogygia and Scherie	
	Erytheia, the Red Land	
	Hesperia	
	Hyperborea	
	Britannia	
CHAPTER 2:	Plato in Context – the Athens of His Ancestors	27
	Solon	
	Peisistratus	
	Herodotus: Invaders and Fabulous Cities	
	Persian Wars	
	The Pentekontaetia: Imperialism Out of Control?	
	The Peloponnesian War	
CHAPTER 3:	Plato the Philosopher	49
	Young Plato: Athens at War and a Natural Disaster	
	The Sicilian Expedition	
	Plato's Early Travels and the Founding of the Academy	
	The Second Athenian Empire: Failed Imperialism and a Natural Disaster	
	Plato's Later Trips to Sicily and Death	

CHAPTER 4: Plato's *Timaeus*   66
Socrates' Summary of the Ideal State
Socrates' Request – Tell Us About
   the Ideal State in Action
Critias' Response to Socrates' Request
The *Timaeus*

CHAPTER 5: Plato's *Critias*   86
Timescale and Catastrophe
Primaeval Athens: Landscape,
   People and Political Institutions
Atlantis: Names, Mythology and the
   Physical Features of the Island
The Capital City and Its Buildings
The Island Beyond the Capital City
Military Arrangements
The Political Structure of Atlantis
Decline and Punishment

CHAPTER 6: Plato's Atlantis in Classical Antiquity   108
Theopompus of Chios
Aristotle and Pseudo-Aristotle:
   Invention and Obliteration
Crantor of Soli: *Historia* and Myth
Atlantis: A Tale from Egypt?

CHAPTER 7: Plato's Atlantis in the Hellenistic and Roman Periods   128
The Hellenistic Age: Poseidonius of Apamea;
   Strabo; Diodorus Siculus
Atlantis in the Roman Empire – si *Platoni credimus* . . .
Allegorical Atlantis
Atlantis at the Fall of Rome: Proclus

CONTENTS

CHAPTER 8: Atlantis in the Age of Discovery   157
            Mapping Atlantis
            Marsilio Ficino
            The 'Columbus Effect'
            Atlantis and Syphilis
            The Ten Tribes
            The 'Theatre of the World'

CHAPTER 9: The Seventeenth Century: A New Atlantis   183
            New Atlantis
            Science and Scripture
            Atlantis in Sweden

CHAPTER 10: Enlightenment Atlantis   196
            Atlantis and the Bible
            Gian Rinaldo Carli: Atlantis in Italy
            Jean-Sylvain Bailly: Atlantis in the Arctic
            Atlantis in the Atlantic: The Madeiras, Canaries and Azores
            Cataclysms and Rituals
            The Athenians, Always the Athenians,
                Ever the Athenians

CHAPTER 11: Romanticism and Atlantis   214
            Occultist Atlantis
            William Blake
            Britain and Atlantis

CHAPTER 12: The Later Nineteenth Century: Atlantis Unleashed
            Continental Drift   226
            Thomas-Henri Martin – Heavyweight Platonic Scholar
            Brasseur de Bourbourg and Le Plongeon:
                Back to Central America
            Twenty Thousand Leagues Under the Sea
            Ignatius Donnelly: The Supreme Atlantist

CHAPTER 13: The Occult, Pseudoarchaeology and the Nazis 248
Madame Blavatsky: The Fourth Root Race
Edgar Cayce: The 'Sleeping Prophet'
Lewis Spence: Cro-Magnon Atlantis
Nazi Atlantis: Those Who Can Make You Believe
Absurdities Can Make You Commit Atrocities

CHAPTER 14: Post Second World War Atlantis: Catastrophism, Etc. 270
World Ice Theory (*Welteislehre*)
Immanuel Velikovsky: Worlds in Collision
Earth/Crustal Displacement Theory
Erich von Däniken: Was God an Astronaut,
and was Atlantis at Troy?

CHAPTER 15: Minoan Atlantis: Crete and Santorini 296
Cretan Mythology
Knossos and the Minoans
Atlantis on Crete
Atlantis on Santorini

CHAPTER 16: Plato's Atlantis: Where, What and Why? 319
'Utterly Extraordinary, but Totally True' Atlantis?
Search Criteria
Mythical Atlantis
Allegorical Atlantis
A Wonderful Story

Appendix: The Flood Myths of Deucalion, Noah,
Gilgamesh, Atrahasis and Hathor 334

Further Reading 339

Notes 349

Index 409

Acknowledgements

There are many individuals, groups and institutions without whose help and inspiration this book could never have been written. I must express my deepest thanks to many of my fellow students, and the brilliant teachers, from Salterhebble County Primary School, Heath Grammar School and Bristol University, without whose enthusiasm, dedication and expertise I would never have been able to engage with the Ancient Greeks and their language and culture; the fine people at Swan Hellenic, whose itineraries have allowed me to explore the physical world of the Greeks in so much style; my colleagues and students (both 'real' and 'virtual') at Oxford University Department for Continuing Education, European Studies and the V & A, for sustaining my interest and facilitating my professional development on our explorations of the ancient world together; Duncan Proudfoot, Amanda Keats, Howard Watson, Kate Truman, and Stephen Dew at Robinson for their professional excellence in putting this book together; Philip and Dorothy Kershaw for all their unconditional, rock-solid support throughout my career; Hebe for the unwavering canine companionship she always gave me; Lal Jones, whose constant love and understanding makes all this possible; and all the inhabitants of Atlantis in the past, present or future, be they real or imaginary.

Introduction

....

Myths are good to think with. Plato's myth of Atlantis has exercised a fascination on the imagination since the fourth century BC, when the story first appears in two Platonic dialogues, the *Timaeus* (*Timaios*) and the *Critias* (*Kritias*). But, when we read these dialogues, presented in this book in new translations by the author, we are treated to a wonderful story that is told in order to explore some important philosophical and political ideas: what is the the Ideal State? How might it cope under the pressure of external invasion? In posing these questions, Plato makes very ancient Athens embody the Ideal State, while Atlantis, a mighty island power located in the Atlantic Ocean, is cast as a decadent, imperialist aggressor. When palaeo-Athens has beaten back the marauding Atlanteans, Zeus decides to punish Atlantis for its *hybris*, and the island along with Athens, is inundated by earthquakes and flooding. Both states sink beneath the waves.

Plato's tale (*logos* in Greek) is vivid and memorable, but when we read about Atlantis in the *Timaeus* and *Critias*, are we looking at a real island and a real geological event filtered through a mythical lens? Is some other type of myth-making taking place? Is Atlantis the fountain-head of all civilisation? Is there a basis of fact, which Plato has embellished for his own purposes? Is Plato's tale derived from earlier mythological traditions? What is Plato's tale really about? How has the tale been used by historians, archaeologists, pseudoarchaeologists, mystics, politicians and religious thinkers from antiquity through to the twenty-first century? Is it true that Atlantis once existed?

This book will explore some of those questions by translating and analysing Plato's texts, and by examining philosophical, geophysical, archaeological and historical theories that range from the academically credible to the downright bizarre to the chillingly dangerous. On the way we will move from the depths of the Atlantic to the islands of Santorini and Crete, visiting locations as diverse as Scandinavia, the Caribbean, Britain, Central America and Antarctica, and look at the theories and motives of the people who have tried to unravel the 'mystery of Atlantis' ever since Plato first introduced it to his students in the fourth century BC.

CHAPTER 1

Ancient Mythical and Semi-Mythical Lands

....

THE ISLAND OF ATLAS

Atlantis makes its first appearance in the work of the fourth-century BC Athenian philosopher Plato in a story that is one of the most haunting and enigmatic to come out of Ancient Greece. It is a tale that still resonates very deeply, and perhaps too readily, with the modern imagination. As the characters in his *Timaeus* and *Critias* philosophise about 'life, the Universe and everything', Socrates says that he'd like to hear an example of the Ideal State in action, struggling against adversaries, and proving its virtue in a time of conflict. This prompts the old man Critias[1] to recollect a story that he heard when he was very young, and he treats the great thinker and his friends to a stunning description of *hē Atlantis nēsos* – the Island of Atlas: *Atlantis* in Greek actually means *of Atlas/Atlas'/belonging to Atlas*, so calling it 'the Island of Atlantis' is tantamount to saying 'the Island *of* Atlas'. It should be emphasised that the Atlas of Atlantis has nothing to do with the more famous mythological Atlas who holds up the sky: the latter, 'Very Enduring', is a Titan, the son of Iapetus and either Clymene or Asia; the former is the eldest son of Poseidon and Cleito.

Critias' story tells of a people who inhabit a wondrous paradise island, but who degenerate into imperialist aggressors. Their expansion brings them into conflict with the warriors of antediluvian Athens,[2] which in many ways is an embodiment of Plato's Ideal

3

State, and which heroically and single-handedly repels the mighty Atlantean forces, before a cataclysmic natural disaster (*kataklysmos* in Greek = 'flood') destroys both Atlantis and Athens.

Plato often used and invented myths to provoke thought and debate, and if the great philosopher was seeking to do this with his Atlantis story, he succeeded in the most spectacular fashion: it has been (mis)interpreted and (ab)used from antiquity through to the medieval, Renaissance and more modern times. The impulse to try to locate the island has proved to be a strong one, as has the drive to use the story to further the ideas and activities of people from a wide range of cultures and eras for diverse motives. These various responses to Plato's writings often say as much, if not more, about the beliefs and preoccupations of the people who are responding to Plato as they do about Atlantis itself, adding an extra layer of interest to the study of the texts.

And an amazing tale it is: it has wondrous descriptions of extraordinary things, it has drama, mystery and pathos, and it is full of challenging moral issues. But equally amazing is the fact that the story comes as a complete surprise to the people that Critias first tells it to, Socrates included. None of them have never heard this tale before. In fact, neither had anyone else: this is the first time in the entire Greek mythological tradition that any mention has been made of 'the Atlantis Island'.

Atlantis does not appear in Homer's *Iliad* or *Odyssey*, committed to writing in the eighth century BC after a long tradition of oral transmission prior to that; not in Hesiod (*c.* 700 BC), whose *Theogony*, dealing with the origins of the gods, *Works and Days* and the fragmentary *Catalogue of Women* contain important mythical material; not in the epic-style *Homeric Hymns* (seventh/sixth centuries BC), which honour some of the major Greek deities, including key players in the Atlantis story such as Poseidon, Athena, Zeus and Hephaestus,[3] and relate important stories from their mythologies; not in Pindar (518–438 BC), a lyric poet whose work is replete with mythological allusions; not in Herodotus (c. 484–425 BC), 'The Father of History',[4] who recorded a great many mythological tales on his travels and whose itinerary might have led us to expect information about Atlantis; not in Aeschylus (525–456 BC), Sophocles (496–406 BC) or Euripides (485–406 BC), the 'Big Three' Athenian tragic dramatists, who drew heavily on the mythical tradition, and often reworked it for sensational theatrical effect; not in Aristophanes (c. 445–385 BC), the Athenian comic playwright who often parodied or subverted mythological stories in his plays; not in the surviving fragments or references to historical writers such as Hecataeus of Miletus, Acusilaus of Argos, Pherecydes of Athens, Hellanicus of Lesbos or Antiochus of Syracuse, who probably wrote the first history of the Greeks in the West; not in any other author; and not in vase painting, sculpture or any of the visual arts. There is nothing whatsoever before Plato introduces it, first with a small tease in the *Timaeus* and then more fully in the *Critias*. It is hardly surprising, then, that Critias' audience are desperate to hear all about it.

One of the reasons that Critias' listeners are so excited is because the Greek mythology they grew up with is very well endowed with marvellous mythical lands and islands: a new one that no other Greek has ever heard of is obviously quite astonishing. There are places beyond this world – Olympus, the abode of the gods; Hades, the subterranean Underworld where the ordinary dead reside, whose entrance, according to Homer, was in the far west beyond the Ocean; Elysium, sometimes referred to as the White Isle, a region within Hades where a few blessed mortals lived a happy existence; Tartarus, where famous evil wrongdoers were punished, located the same distance underneath the earth as the earth is from the sky[5] – as well as others that belong in the more physical areas of the mythical world like Ogygia, Scherie, Erytheia, Hesperia and Hyperborea, and others that are strange, but which can be definitively identified as being real places, such as Britannia. These all carry a great deal of fascination, but none of them has generated quite the consistent level of interest as their late-born companion Atlantis.

HOMER'S ODYSSEY: OGYGIA AND SCHERIE

Homer's *Odyssey* takes us through the fabulous world of Odysseus' travels, and the first time we encounter him at first hand he is on Calypso's island of Ogygia. She is a daughter of the Titan Atlas, and she has already kept Odysseus with her for seven years. It is an exquisite place:

> Round about the cave grew a luxuriant wood, alder and poplar and sweet-smelling cypress, wherein birds long of wing were wont to nest, owls and falcons and sea-crows with chattering tongues, who ply their business on the sea. And right there about the hollow cave ran trailing a garden vine, in pride of its prime, richly laden with clusters. And fountains four in a row were flowing with bright water hard by one another, turned one this way, one that. And round about soft meadows of violets and parsley were blooming. There even an immortal, who chanced to come, might gaze and marvel, and delight his soul.[6]

Ogygia is sometimes associated with Atlantis. Although trying to find the whereabouts of many of the places mentioned in Homer is fraught with difficulty, there is a tradition, which goes back to the late fourth century BC (and maintained by contemporary tradition in Malta), that Ogygia is the island of Gozo. However, other authors make links with Egypt or the Ionian Sea, while the ancient geographer Strabo puts it in the Atlantic Ocean:

Homer says also: 'Now after the ship had left the river-stream of Oceanus' and 'In the island of Ogygia, where is the navel of the sea,' going on to say that the daughter of Atlas lives there; and again, regarding the Phaeacians, 'Far apart we live in the wash of the waves, the farthermost of men, and no other mortals are conversant with us.' Now all these incidents are clearly indicated as being placed in fancy in the Atlantic Ocean.[7]

The biographer, author and Delphic priest Plutarch (c. AD 46– after 119) gives a slightly differently nuanced version of Ogygia's whereabouts:

First I will tell you the author of the piece [. . .] who begins after Homer's fashion with, an isle Ogygian lies far out at sea, distant five days' sail from Britain, going westwards, and three others equally distant from it, and from each other, are more opposite to the summer visits of the sun [. . .] The great continent by which the great sea is surrounded on all sides, they say, lies less distant from the others, but about five thousand *stadia*[8] [1,000 km] from Ogygia, for one sailing in a rowing-galley; for the sea is difficult of passage and muddy through the great number of currents, and these currents issue out of the great land, and shoals are formed by them, and the sea becomes clogged and full of earth, by which it has the appearance of being solid.[9]

Clearly there is plenty of scope for discussion when it comes to locating mythical islands.

Having left Ogygia on a raft, Odysseus is then wrecked by a mighty storm sent by Poseidon, but is washed up on the island of

Scherie, where he meets the beautiful Nausicaa, princess of the Phaeacians, and her parents Alcinous and Arete. Their island is located 'far from men that live by toil' and has a walled city, temples, and plough lands. As Nausicaa puts it:

> We are about to enter the city, around which runs a lofty wall,
> – a fair harbour lies on either side of the city and the entrance
> is narrow, and curved ships are drawn up along the road, for
> they all have stations for their ships, each man one for
> himself. There, too, is their place of assembly about the fair
> temple of Poseidon, fitted with huge stones set deep in the
> earth.[10]

Odysseus is impressed by all of this; he is utterly staggered when he arrives at Nausicaa's parents' palace. There they live in luxurious paradise conditions, perpetually supplied with abundant fruit, vines and vegetables by a miraculous garden:

> Odysseus went to the glorious palace of Alcinous. There he
> stood, and his heart pondered much before he reached the
> threshold of bronze; for there was a gleam as of sun or
> moon over the high-roofed house of great-hearted Alcinous.
> Of bronze were the walls that stretched this way and that
> from the threshold to the innermost chamber, and around
> was a cornice of cyanus. Golden were the doors that shut in
> the well-built house, and doorposts of silver were set in a
> threshold of bronze. Of silver was the lintel above, and of
> gold the handle. On either side of the door there stood gold
> and silver dogs, which Hephaestus had fashioned with
> cunning skill to guard the palace of great-hearted Alcinous;
> immortal were they and ageless all their days. Within, seats
> were fixed along the wall on either hand, from the threshold

to the innermost chamber, and on them were thrown robes of soft fabric, cunningly woven, the handiwork of women. On these the leaders of the Phaeacians were wont to sit drinking and eating, for they had unfailing store. [. . .] But without the courtyard, hard by the door, is a great orchard of four acres, and a hedge runs about it on either side. Therein grow trees, tall and luxuriant, pears and pomegranates and apple-trees with their bright fruit, and sweet figs, and luxuriant olives. Of these the fruit perishes not nor fails in winter or in summer, but lasts throughout the year; and ever does the west wind, as it blows, quicken to life some fruits, and ripen others; pear upon pear waxes ripe, apple upon apple, cluster upon cluster, and fig upon fig. There, too, is his fruitful vineyard planted, one part of which, a warm spot on level ground, is being dried in the sun, while other grapes men are gathering, and others, too, they are treading; but in front are unripe grapes that are shedding the blossom, and others that are turning purple. There again, by the last row of the vines, grow trim garden beds of every sort, blooming the year through, and therein are two springs, one of which sends its water throughout all the garden, while the other, over against it, flows beneath the threshold of the court toward the high house; from this the townsfolk drew their water. Such were the glorious gifts of the gods in the palace of Alcinous.[11]

The overall effect, and a good number of the details in this description, are well worth bearing in mind when examining Plato's description of Atlantis: one thing that is for certain is that although the great philosopher seriously disapproved of Homer's poetry – he regards him as an 'imitator of phantoms of virtue'[12] – he knew it inside out.[13]

Again, the location of this island (if it is anything other than a mythological invention) is in dispute: Strabo, in the passage quoted above, places it in the Atlantic, whereas the fifth-century BC historian Thucydides records a tradition that Scherie was Corfu (Corcyra). The Corcyraeans

> could not repress a pride in the high naval position of an island whose nautical renown dated from the days of its old inhabitants, the Phaeacians.[14]

Locating mythical isles is fraught with difficulty: the ancient geographer Eratosthenes said that he would believe in Odysseus' travels when someone found the leatherworker who made the bag that Aeolus put the winds in. Apollodorus censured those who placed Odysseus' wanderings in the neighbourhood of Sicily, since in that case, 'one should go on and say that, although the wanderings took place there, the poet, for the sake of mythology, placed them out in Oceanus'.[15] In Odysseus' case the big problem is that once the North Wind blows him off course and drives him past Kythera, we never get clear information. The wind directions that Homer mentions are only approximations, and when we factor in the considerable problems of making sense even of those places that do seem to have some historical reality, there is a very strong case for calling off the search for Odysseus' 'real' route, and for the islands that he visits.[16]

Both Ogygia and Scherie will enter the debate about Atlantis on numerous occasions, as will the Land of the Hyperboreans, although we might note that Apollodorus was prepared to forgive 'writers in general' for seeking these islands, but not Callimachus, because he 'makes a pretence of being a scholar'[17] and calls Gaudos [Gozo] the 'Island of Calypso', and Corcyra 'Scheria'.[18]

Erytheia, the Red Land

Even within the well-established 'mainstream' traditions of Greek mythology, the quest for mythical islands can be a Herculean task, and one land associated with Greek mythology's greatest hero Heracles is Erytheia, the sea-circled 'Red Land' located out in the far west beyond the mighty earth-encircling river Oceanus. Oceanus, which gives us our word ocean, is an important element in Greek geography: he/it can be both a deity and a river, and Homer speaks of

> the enormous strength of Oceanus with his deep-running waters, Oceanus, from whom all rivers are and the entire sea and all springs and all deep wells have their waters of him.[19]

For his tenth Labour, Heracles was detailed to steal the cattle of Geryon, who is usually described as a triple-bodied monster who owned great herds of red-coloured livestock, from Erytheia. Prior to his arrival on the island, Heracles cleared Crete of wild beasts, made Libya fertile and prosperous, and visited Tartessus in Spain, where he erected two pillars opposite each other at the boundaries of Europe and Libya: the so-called Pillars of Heracles, which defined the Strait of Gibraltar.[20] Finding himself oppressed by the heat, Heracles shot arrows at the sun god Helios, who then gave him the golden bowl, which, after sunset, carried Helios and his horses through Oceanus back to the east in time for sunrise. Oceanus became stormy until Heracles menaced him into calmness with his bow.

On reaching Erytheia, the great hero slew the cattle's herdsman and their double-headed guard dog 'out in the murky meadow beyond glorious Oceanus',[21] but another herdsman who was tending the cattle of Hades saw the incident and reported it to Geryon, who ambushed Heracles as he was driving the cattle away. A tanta-lising set of papyrus fragments now survives, which gives snatches of a poem called the *Geryoneis* by Stesichorus (seventh to sixth century BC) describing the ensuing combat, in which Heracles seems to smash one of Geryon's heads with his club, knock the helmet off another with a stone, and shoot him with one of his venom-soaked arrows.[22] Having despatched Geryon, Heracles herded the cattle into the bowl and sailed back to Tartessus, which has also become a site mentioned in Atlantis speculation.[23]

Because of Heracles' itinerary, various classical writers also iden-tified Erytheia with the region of southern Spain. Herodotus informs us that Geryon lived 'west of the open sea, settled in the island called by the Greeks Erytheia, on the shore of Oceanus near Gadeira, outside the pillars of Heracles;'[24] Apollodorus makes similar connec-tions, telling us that 'Erytheia was an island near the Ocean; it is now called Gadeira;[25] and the geographer Strabo (64 or 63 BC–*c.* AD 24) tells us that

> the ancient writers seem to call the River Baetis[26] 'Tartessus', and Gadeira[27] and the nearby islands 'Erytheia'. This is supposedly why Stesichorus spoke as he did about Geryon's herdsman – that he was born 'almost opposite famous Erytheia by the limitless silver-rooted[28] waters of the river Tartessus in the hollow of a rock'[29] [. . .] Furthermore, Eratosthenes says that the country next to Calpe [Gibraltar] is called 'Tartessis', and that Erytheia is called 'The Happy Island'.[30]

Clearly, rather like with Atlantis in the modern world, there was a great deal of discussion in antiquity concerning the whereabouts of Erytheia. Strabo adds that by 'Erytheia', in which the myth-writers place the adventures of Geryon, Pherecydes seems to mean Gades. Others, however, think that Erytheia is the island that lies parallel to Gades and is separated from it by a strait 200 m wide.[31]

The true state of the confusion is made clear by Pliny the Elder, who himself perished in a major natural disaster at Pompeii in AD 79:

Towards Spain [*in the Atlantic Ocean*], at about 100 paces distance, is another long island, three miles wide, on which the original city of Gades stood. By Ephorus and Philistides it is called Erythia, by Timaeus and Silenus Aphrodisias, and by the natives the Isle of Juno. Timaeus says, that the larger island used to be called Cotinusa, from its olives; the Romans call it Tartessus; the Carthaginians Gadir, that word in the Punic language signifying a hedge. It was called Erythia because the Tyrians, the original ancestors of the Carthaginians, were said to have come from the Erythraean, or Red Sea.[32] In this island Geryon is by some thought to have dwelt [. . .] Other persons again think, that his island is another one, opposite to Lusitania, and that it was there formerly called by that name.[33]

The fact that the island also shared its name with the Erythraean (Red) Sea helps to create further confusion between them. Strabo comments that even Homer was ignorant about Egypt and Libya because he failed to mention the isthmus between the Erythraean and Egyptian (Mediterranean) Seas, although he excuses this lack of knowledge on the grounds that writers after him 'have been ignorant of many things and have invented marvellous tales'.[34] Nevertheless, the fact that in Plato's Atlantis story the younger twin

13

brother of Atlas, the first King of Atlantis, was called Gadeirus in the language of Atlantis, and was allotted the 'part of the island towards the Pillars of Heracles, facing the region that is now called Gadeira',[35] has stimulated a certain amount of excitement in the Atlantis-seeking community.

With the cattle of Geryon in his possession, Heracles moved through Spain to southern France, and then on to the forests north of the Black Sea, where, by a woman who was a snake from the waist downwards, he sired three sons, the youngest of which gave his name to Scythia. In Tyrrhenia, at the future site of Rome, he subdued Cacus, a fire-breathing monster who ate human flesh and nailed the heads of his victims to the doors of his cave. Further south, at Rhegium, one of the bulls broke away and swam over to Sicily, and Apollodorus says that Italy was so named because the Tyrrhenians called the bull *italos*.[36] Having finally tracked down the bull, Heracles was able to deliver the cattle to Greece, where Eurystheus, who had sent Heracles on his Labours, sacrificed them to Hera.

Hesperia

The Cattle of Geryon Labour fulfilled the Ten Labours that Heracles had originally been assigned, but Eurystheus then insisted on two more, because he refused to count the Labour of the Hydra (he had received help) or that of cleaning the Stables of Augeias (he had been paid). So Heracles now had to fetch the Golden Apples from the Hesperides. Strabo seems to have thought that his western exploits became overworked clichés:

> The poets who came after Homer keep dinning into our ears similar stories [i.e. myths set in Spain]: the expedition of Heracles in quest of the cattle of Geryon and likewise the

expedition which he made in quest of the Golden Apples of the Hesperides.[37]

The Hesperides, the 'Daughters of Evening', who were also sometimes said to be daughters of Night or of the heaven-bearing Titan Atlas, were nymphs who lived in a vaguely located place out in the far west, in a garden beyond the sunset, where Atlas held up the sky. The Golden Apples had been a wedding present for Zeus and Hera, and Hera loved them so much that she had them planted in the garden of the Hesperides. In order to prevent them being stolen, the goddess stationed Ladon, an immortal serpent with a hundred heads, to watch over the tree. The Hesperides, whose numbers vary in the tradition from between two and seven, also shared guard duties.

Heracles' first problem vividly illustrates how difficult it is for scholars accurately to pinpoint mythical places: he had to locate the land of the Hesperides. The ancient shape-changing sea god Nereus knew the way, but Heracles had to subdue him before he would divulge the information. Armed with the directions he needed, the hero crossed Libya, which was at that time ruled by Antaeus, son of Poseidon and Earth, who used to kill strangers by forcing them to wrestle, and, according to Pindar,[38] decorated the temple of Poseidon with the skulls of his victims. Antaeus was invincible provided he stayed in contact with his mother Earth, so in the bout Heracles lifted him aloft and crushed him to death above his head. From Libya he traversed Egypt, which was under the rule of Busiris, another son of Poseidon, who was in the habit of sacrificing strangers to Zeus ever since Egypt had suffered a nine-year famine and the seer Phrasius said that it would stop if they adopted this practice. Busiris started with Phrasius himself and continued to kill any foreigner who landed. Herodotus narrates what happened next in the myth, but then adds his own sceptical comments – not all Greeks believe their own myths, and, interestingly in the light of the fact that Plato's Atlantis story is said to originate in Egypt, they have a very poor understanding of Egypt:

> The Greeks have many stories with no basis of fact. One of the silliest is the story of how Heracles came to Egypt and was taken away by the Egyptians to be sacrificed to Zeus, [. . .] and how he quietly submitted at the altar, when he exerted his strength and killed them all. For me at least, such a tale is proof enough that the Greeks know nothing whatever about Egyptian character and custom. The Egyptians are forbidden by their own religion to kill animals for sacrifice [with a few exceptions]: is it likely, then, that they would sacrifice human beings? Besides, if Heracles was a mere man (as they say he was) and single-handed, how is it conceivable that he should have killed tens of thousands of people? And I hope that both gods and heroes will forgive me for saying what I have said on these matters![39]

Heracles resumed his travels and again utilised the bowl of Helios to cross Oceanus. En route, in the Caucasus Mountains, he shot the great eagle that had been devouring the eternally renewed liver of Prometheus for the last 30,000 years, and liberated him. Prometheus advised Heracles not to go after the apples himself, but to send Atlas to do it after relieving him of the job of holding up the sky. Acting on this advice, he arrived in the land of the Hyperboreans and shouldered the heavens, while Atlas collected three apples from the Hesperides. Atlas did not want to carry on supporting the sky, so he offered personally to deliver the apples to Eurystheus. However, Heracles tricked Atlas by asking him to hold the heavens while he put a cushion on his head. Atlas agreed, put the apples on the ground and took the sky from Heracles, who simply picked up the apples and walked off.

It is important to be aware that Greek mythology is not a fixed and immutable 'system' – it is full of variants and alternative versions, told by different myth-tellers at different times, in different places and for different reasons. For instance, Apollodorus locates the Garden of the Hesperides near to the land of the Hyperboreans in the north,[40] while a different tradition places it in Libya, close to the Atlas Mountains, and makes Heracles kill the serpent Ladon with his poisoned arrows and pick the apples himself. In Apollonius Rhodius' *Argonautica*,[41] Jason and the Argonauts carry their ship, the *Argo*, on their shoulders overland to Lake Tritonis, near to the Garden of the Hesperides, and find the snake dead apart from its twitching tail, and the Hesperides in mourning: Heracles had performed his Labour only the day before. Orpheus sang to the Hesperides and they turned into trees; Ladon was immortalised as the constellation Draco; and Heracles ultimately delivered the Golden Apples to Eurystheus. Eurystheus inspected them and gave them back to him; Heracles passed them on to Athena; and Athena returned them to the Hesperides because it was not lawful for a mortal to own them.

In none of these tales of mythical islands in the west is any mention made of Atlantis.

HYPERBOREA

Up in the Greek mythological north we find the Hyperboreans. They were a blessed race who spent their long lives singing, dancing and sacrificing to Apollo, who spent his winters with them. Hyperborea, 'the Land Beyond the North Wind', was an earthly paradise inaccessible to ordinary mortals: only the greatest heroes could go there, and its inhabitants knew nothing of war, age or disease. They were a byword for happiness:

Your wish is better than gold. It surpasses great good fortune, even that of the Hyperboreans.[42]

Hyperborea's southern border was protected by the mythical Rhipaean Mountains, which were the abode of the North-Wind god Boreas. The mountains were guarded by griffins and one-eyed Arimaspians, and Hyperborea was further isolated from the rest of humanity by a land of perpetual winter called Pterophoros ('Winged'). To the north was Oceanus, from which Hyperborea's main river, the south-flowing Eridanus, drew its waters. The land enjoyed an eternal springtime: most of its territory, known as 'the Garden of Apollo', was covered with abundant forests, but the cultivated areas produced two grain crops every year. The capital city contained a circular temple of Apollo.

Apollodorus was highly sceptical about historians who speak of the 'Rhipaean Mountains' and of the settlement of the Gorgons and Hesperides;[43] Strabo put the fact that any heed has been given to those who created the mythical Rhipaean Mountains and Hyperboreans down to ignorance of these regions,[44] and Herodotus also had some interesting comments to make regarding people's ideas about the Hyperboreans, and the geography of the earth:

I have said this much of the Hyperboreans, and let it suffice [. . .] But if there are men beyond the North Wind (Boreas), then there are others beyond the South. And I laugh to see how many have before now drawn maps of the world, not one of them reasonably; for they draw the world as round as if fashioned by compasses, encircled by the Oceanus river, and Asia and Europe of a like extent. For myself, I will in a few words indicate the extent of the two, and how each should be drawn [see Fig. 1].[45]

Fig. 1:

THE GREEK WORLD AS
DESCRIBED BY HERODOTUS

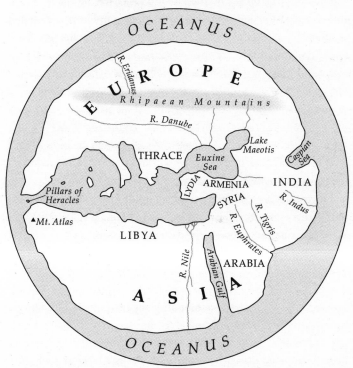

What is absent from these maps, and from Herodotus' description of world geography as he saw it, is any reference to Atlantis.[46]

Hyperborea makes regular appearances in Greek myths, most notably in the story of Phaethon, son of Helios (the Sun). The myth itself is a fascinating one, perhaps best known from the Roman poet Ovid's brilliant account of it in his *Metamorphoses*,[47] where we hear that Helios promised to give Phaethon anything his heart desired. Phaethon asked for his father's chariot, and permission to control its 'wing-footed horses', just for a day. It was a crazy request. Driving the chariot of the Sun needed specialist divine skills, but Phaethon was adamant, Helios could not renege on his promise, and disaster was inevitable.[48] With convoluted instructions from his father ringing in his ears, Phaethon mounted the chariot pulled by Fiery, Dawnsteed, Scorcher and Blaze, and almost instantly lost control: the chariot set the heavens alight and created the Milky Way, before searing the earth with heat so intense that forests burned, rivers dried up, the seas contracted, the skins of the Ethiopians were turned black and North Africa became a desert. With the world on the brink of total destruction, Zeus stepped in. He fought fire with fire, hurling a thunderbolt at Phaethon, and the boy's flaming body fell like a comet into the Hyperborean River Eridanus. His sisters, the Heliades, mourned so intensely that they turned into poplar trees, and their tears became drops of amber exuding from the trees. It is a myth that will feature in Plato's Atlantis tale,[49] and a great deal has been made of comets in relation to the destruction of Atlantis.[50]

BRITANNIA

The extreme vagueness surrounding mythical lands like Ogygia, Scherie, Erytheia, Hesperia and Hyperborea makes it challenging, if not impossible, to locate them. It is also interesting to note that these intriguing places have attracted far less interest in finding them than Plato's Atlantis, where an enormous amount of energy has been expended over the centuries analysing the minutiae of the description in terms of its geography, size, agriculture, architecture, military prowess, location and very existence. But it is as well to be aware that ancient geography is not an exact science, and that even when there is good, detailed knowledge of real places, misconceptions can easily persist. Taking Roman knowledge of Britain as an example reveals some very illuminating practices and attitudes.

When Julius Caesar was planning his first expedition to Britain in 55 BC, he complained that he wasn't able to get reliable information about the island from merchants engaged in trade with it. But once he had actually been there he provided a fascinating and very influential description:

> The interior of Britain is inhabited by people who claim, on the strength of their own tradition, to be indigenous. The coastal areas are inhabited by invaders who crossed from Belgium for the sake of plunder [. . .] The population is extremely large, there are very many farm buildings, [. . .] and the cattle are very numerous.
>
> There is timber of every kind, [. . .] but no beech or fir. They think it wrong to eat hares, chickens, or geese, keeping these creatures only for pleasure and amusement. The climate is more temperate than in Gaul, the cold season being less severe.
>
> The island is triangular in shape, with one side facing Gaul. One corner of this side points east and is on the coast of Kent, the landing point for almost all ships from Gaul; the lower corner points south. The length of this side is some 800 km. The second side of the island faces westward, towards Spain. In this direction lies Ireland, which is thought to be half the size of Britain and is the same distance from Britain as Gaul is. Midway between Ireland and Britain is the Isle of Man, and it is believed that there are several smaller islands too, where, some writers say, there is continual darkness for 30 days in midwinter. We made numerous inquiries about this, but found out nothing [. . .] This western side of Britain is, in the opinion of the natives, 1125 km long. The third side of the island faces north; there is no land opposite this side, but the eastern corner of it points roughly towards

Germany. The length of this side is reckoned to be 1300 km, which means that the whole island is some 3225 km in circumference.[51]

Perhaps the most striking aspect of this is the supposed orientation of the island: the west side of Britain does not, of course, point towards Spain.

The geographer Strabo is an often-quoted source when it comes to discussions about Atlantis,[52] and he too has things to say about Britain:

Britain is triangular in shape. Its longest side lies parallel to Gaul, and neither exceeds nor falls short of it in length. Each measures about 860–880 km.[53] [The British shore] extends from Kantion [Kent] (which is directly opposite the mouth of the Rhine), as far as the westerly end of the island which lies opposite Aquitania and the Pyrenees.

Again, the west side of Britain is made to face Spain. Then he includes some information about the resources of the island and the way of life of its inhabitants:

It produces corn, cattle, gold, silver and iron. These things are exported along with hides, slaves and dogs suitable for hunting [. . .] The men of Britain are taller than the Gauls and not so yellow-haired. Their bodies are more loosely built [. . .] They live much like the Gauls but some of their customs are more primitive and barbarous. Thus for example some of them are well supplied with milk but do not know how to make cheese; they know nothing of planting crops or of farming in general. They are ruled by their own kings. For the most part they use chariots in war [. . .] Their cities are

22

the forests, for they fell trees and fence in large circular enclosures in which they build huts and pen in their cattle, but not for any great length of time. The weather tends to rain rather than snow. Mist is very common, so that for whole days at a stretch the sun is seen only for three or four hours around midday.[54]

Some of this is accurate, but some of it is just plain wrong, notably the alleged British ignorance about agriculture. But Strabo had never travelled to Britain, so he had to derive all his information at second hand. Neither had Britain been definitively conquered in Strabo's time, but just before Claudius' invasion of AD 43, Pomponius Mela expressed hopes that the mysteries of the damp, misty island would be revealed at last:

It will soon be possible to describe the nature of Britain and the character of the people she produces with greater certainty and knowledge gained from exploration; for indeed the closed book of Britain is being opened by the greatest of Emperors, victor over peoples not only unconquered, but before him absolutely unknown.[55]

Yet Pomponius Mela's confidence seems somewhat misplaced. The historian Tacitus, who was writing after Roman armies had penetrated to the northern part of Scotland and Britain had been circumnavigated by a Roman fleet, proudly proclaims that his predecessors 'had to fill out their lack of information with tricks of style: I can offer fact'. He gives a description of Britain along these lines, written in around AD 98:

Be this as it may, the question who were the first inhabitants of Britain and whether they were indigenous or immigrant is one which, as one would expect among barbarous people, has never received attention. The physique of the people presents many varieties, whence inferences are drawn: the red hair and the large limbs of the inhabitants of Caledonia [modern Scotland] proclaim their German origin; the swarthy faces of the Silures [from South Wales], the curly quality, in general, of their hair, and the position of Spain opposite their shores, attest the passage of Iberians in old days and the occupation by them of these districts; those peoples, again, who adjoin Gaul are also like Gauls, whether because the influence of heredity persists, or because when two lands project in opposite directions till they face each other the climatic condition stamps a certain physique on the human body; but, taking a general view of the case, we can readily believe that the Gauls took possession of the adjacent island.[56]

Again, after some fifty years of Roman occupation during which the Romans acquired a certain amount of very detailed knowledge about Britain, building roads whose long-distance alignments prove that routes between places far apart were accurately surveyed, the Romans still believed that the west of Britain faced south. It is also very wet and shows the characteristics of a very northerly latitude:

The sky is overcast with continual rain and cloud, but the cold is not severe. The length of the days is beyond the measure of our world: the nights are clear and, in the distant parts of Britain, short, so that there is but a brief space separating the evening and the morning twilight. If there be no clouds to hinder, the sun's brilliance – they maintain – is visible throughout the night: it does not set and then rise again, but simply passes over. That is to say, the flat extremities of the earth with their low shadows do not project the darkness, and nightfall never reaches the sky and the stars.

Britain produces gold and silver and other metals: conquest is worthwhile.[57]

Tacitus' final statement is probably the key to his discussion, but even a further fifty years after his work, when Claudius Ptolemaeus ('Ptolemy') compiled his *Geography* in Greek, there are still anomalies in the details. Because Ptolemy attempted to provide precision to his data by including coordinates for many of the locations he discusses, we can construct maps from his text. However, when we do this, we find that St Albans was placed on the same latitude as Leicester (it is well to the south), and Silchester is placed north of both Cirencester and London (it is south of both of them). Scotland is rotated through ninety degrees so that its main axis runs west–east instead of south–north, and Hadrian's Wall, the Antonine Wall, the legionary fortress at Caerleon and the towns of Gloucester, Dorchester and Caerwent are all conspicuous by their absence. Again, Ptolemy never visited Britain and so he was entirely dependent on the quality of other people's work.

The point here is that whether we are dealing with descriptions of the mythical Scherie, the real Britannia or of Plato's Atlantis, ancient geographical knowledge can be vague and contradictory. The reason for this is that in our sources we are dealing with a *literary tradition*: the writers tended to repeat what others have said, and in Britain's case a conventional picture was quite quickly created, which often only bore a tangential relation to reality. Many of the authors, be they writing about Atlantis, Britannia or any other legendary place, are doing so for a primarily political, moral, philosophical or biographical purpose. So Britain is presented as a distant, mysterious, semi-mythical land across the Ocean, near the end of the world – the poet Horace spoke of Britain as 'the furthest nation of the world',[58] and of 'the whale-burdened sea that bursts on the exotic British coast'[59] – but also as a place that is rich in precious metals, minerals, pearls, corn, slaves and potential tribute. This makes it both prestigious and profitable to conquer, and those who write about it included geographical detail in order to add colour and authenticity to their accounts, and/or to enhance or denigrate the reputations of the people they are writing about. We often learn far more about what was *thought* to be interesting or important to the writers and readers than we do about the true facts. It is crucial to bear this in mind when we set off in search of a mysterious island across the Ocean.

CHAPTER 2

Plato in Context – the Athens of His Ancestors

················

SOLON

The Island of Atlas had never been mentioned anywhere in the whole of world literature until, in a fictional conversation in Plato's dialogue *Timaeus*, the character Critias tells Socrates that their discussion has just reminded him about an odd tale that was attested by Solon, who was a friend and relative of Critias' great-grandfather.[1]

Solon came to be regarded as one of the Seven Sages of Greece. He was a man of good birth, widely respected for his integrity and moderation, and expressed his political views in his poems, small fragments of which still survive. Around 594 or 593 BC, he was appointed by the noble families at Athens to reconcile some difficult social tensions, which in other states had led to the ousting of aristocratic regimes by people known as *tyrannoi*, 'tyrants'.[2] Solon put through a package of reforms that stimulated the economy, and by granting the people what Aristotle dubbed 'a necessary minimum of power',[3] he set the Athenians on the road to democracy. His laws were published on revolving wooden beams called *axones*, and tablets/pillars with a pointed top known as *kyrbeis*,[4] but Solon was acutely aware of how controversial his measures would be: too many people wanted to quiz him about points of detail, ask for clarification, criticise or offer unwanted advice, and he was 'anxious to disengage himself from these complications'.[5] So, having required all Athenians to take an oath to observe his laws for 100 years, he left

Athens for a decade for the combined purposes of trade and travel.[6] One of the places on his itinerary was Egypt.

Approximately 450 years after Plato, Plutarch wrote a biography of Solon, in which he tells us that Solon spent some of his time in Egypt studying with some highly erudite priests called Psenophis of Heliopolis and Sonchis of Saïs, and that this is where he first heard the Atlantis story, which he then tried, unsuccessfully, to introduce to the Greeks in a poetic form.[7] Plutarch had studied Plato very deeply, but he disagreed with him as to why Solon never completed his Atlantis poem:

> Now Solon, after beginning his great work on the story or fable of the lost Atlantis, which, as he had heard from the learned men of Saïs, particularly concerned the Athenians, abandoned it, not for lack of leisure, as Plato says, but rather because of his old age, fearing the magnitude of the task. For that he had abundant leisure, such verses as these testify:
>
> 'But I grow old ever learning many things;'
>
> and again,
>
> 'But now the works of the Cyprus-born goddess are dear to my soul,
>
> Of Dionysus, too, and the Muses, which impart delights to men.'
>
> Plato, ambitious to elaborate and adorn the subject of the lost Atlantis, as if it were the soil of a fair estate unoccupied, but appropriately his by virtue of some kinship with Solon,[8] began the work by laying out great porches, enclosures, and courtyards, such as no story [logos], tale [mythos], or poetic composition ever had before. But he was late in beginning, and ended his life before his work.[9] Therefore the greater our delight in what he actually wrote, the greater is our distress in view of what he left undone. For as the Olympieium in the

28

city of Athens, so the tale of the lost Atlantis in the wisdom of Plato is the only one among many beautiful works to remain unfinished.[10]

It should be noted that no trace of any such work of Solon's now survives: no fragments in quotations from any ancient author, and no ancient source predating Plato makes any reference to it. This clearly raises the question of whether or not the whole story is in fact Plato's invention, rather than Solon's factual report.

Plutarch goes on to outline Solon's travels to Cyprus, and to the court of the fabulously rich King Croesus of Lydia. He is aware that the meeting between Solon and Croesus might well be fabricated, but he still *wants* to believe it:

As for his interview with Croesus, some think to prove by chronology that it is fictitious. But when a story is so famous and so well-attested, and, what is more to the point, when it comports so well with the character of Solon, and is so worthy of his magnanimity and wisdom, I do not propose to reject it out of deference to any chronological canons, so called, which thousands are to this day revising, without being able to bring their contradictions into any general agreement.[11]

But despite Plutarch's assertions, which resemble those of numerous more recent authors on the Atlantis tale, there has to be a question mark over their meeting: the tradition is at least as old as Herodotus,[12] but if Solon died *c.* 560/559 BC he is unlikely to have met Croesus, who reigned *c.* 560–546 BC.

On his return to Athens, the aged Solon still commanded great respect. We hear that more than ever before he indulged himself in leisurely amusement, wine and song.[13] Evidently completing his important Atlantis poem was not at the top of his 'to do' list, maybe because Athens was being torn apart by factional strife. His reforms had been designed to prevent a takeover by a tyrant, but in fact he lived just long enough to witness his failure when Peisistratus, himself distantly related to Solon,[14] orchestrated a *coup d'état* in 561/560 BC, although it took him three attempts to establish himself on a permanent basis.[15] Solon, in one tradition, died in the archonship of Hegestratus (560/559 BC), although other versions give him a few more years.[16]

PEISISTRATUS

Peisistratus' power was absolute,[17] enforced by using foreign mercenaries, murdering or exiling many of his opponents, taking hostages from the leading families, and tolerating no party policy except his own. Yet he also bestowed various benefits on the lower classes, supported trade and industry, gained overseas territory, made important alliances, embarked on a large programme of public works, was a significant patron of the arts and, to a large degree, respected Athens' civil and constitutional legal protocols. His rule became known as 'The Age of Cronos' (a mythical Golden Age), and Plato's pupil Aristotle seems to have approved:

> Peisistratus administered the city's affairs moderately, and more like a citizen than a tyrant.[18]

When Peisistratus died in 527 BC, his sons Hippias and Hipparchus 'took over the regime and continued the management of affairs in the same way'.[19] But their honeymoon period soon degenerated into a homosexual love-triangle; Hipparchus was assassinated; Hippias became tyrannical in the modern sense; and the Athenians expelled him in 510 BC.[20] Hippias spent the next twenty years cultivating friendly relations with Darius I, the King of Persia (ruled 521–486 BC), but in the meantime, under an aristocratic reformer called Cleisthenes, Athens became the world's first democracy.[21] Cleisthenes' Athenian democracy (*dēmokratia*) was based on the creation of ten new tribes for political purposes: most of the political offices and institutions operated in decimal units – ten generals, ten *prytaneis* (tribe-based sub-committees of the Council, who operated for one of the ten months of the year), various 'Boards of Ten', and so on. The political structures of Plato's Atlantis will also show a notable liking for units of ten.

HERODOTUS: INVADERS AND FABULOUS CITIES

Athens' dealings with Darius I's mighty Persian Empire over the next generation were crucial to the course of the history of the Western world, and also, undoubtedly, to Plato's Atlantis story. Discussing ancient history at the beginning of his work, Thucydides calls the ensuing conflict between Persia and the Greeks 'the greatest war of the past', thereby making it trump the Trojan War,[22] which he mentions, and the Atlantis versus Athens conflict, which he does not.

Our main source for the Persian Wars is Socrates' contemporary Herodotus, who was born in the cosmopolitan but culturally Greek city of Halicarnassus (modern Bodrum in Turkey) sometime between 490 and 480 BC. He produced a wonderfully engaging account of his *historia* ('inquiry') into the origins and events of these hostilities, in a book that is also replete with geographical and ethnographical material. He tells us that during the course of this often first-hand research, he visited Egypt (probably sometime after 454 BC, but possibly earlier), and that one of the places he visited was Saïs, where Plato says Solon heard the Atlantis story. There, Herodotus, who could not speak Egyptian, although he does mention interpreters,[23] says he talked to the scribe who kept the register of the treasures of Athene in the Temple.[24] The historian reports a great deal of interesting information that he gleaned at Saïs, but if the priest told him anything about Atlantis, he didn't include it in his work.

Solon's conversations at Saïs, as recorded by Plato, also look rather like Herodotus' story of the Greek historian Hecataeus of Miletus, who tells some Egyptian priests that he was descended from a god in the sixteenth generation, only to be upstaged by an Egyptian genealogy extending for 345 generations.[25] Like many authors on the topic of Atlantis since, Herodotus is keen to stress the antiquity of Egypt and its customs:

> It would seem, too, that the Egyptians were the first people to establish solemn assemblies, and processions, and services; the Greeks learned all that from them. I consider this proved, because the Egyptian ceremonies are manifestly very ancient, and the Greek are of recent origin.[26]

This is, of course, not true, and the reliability of Herodotus in relation to Egypt has been challenged since the time of Thucydides, who although not specifically name-checking his predecessor, probably refers to him in his opening remarks:

> And it may well be that the absence of the fabulous [to mythōdes] from my narrative will seem less pleasing to the ear; but whoever shall wish to have a clear view both of the events which have happened and of those which will some day, in all human probability, happen again in the same or a similar way – for these to adjudge my history profitable will be enough for me. And, indeed, it has been composed, not as a prize-essay to be heard for the moment, but as a possession for all time.[27]

The 'prize-essay' comment is a dig at Herodotus, who according to Lucian (c. AD 125–after 180), premiered his *Histories* to a standing ovation at the Olympic Games.[28] Herodotus' writings are crammed with *to mythōdes*, fabulous stories which he records, sometimes circumspectly, but often uncritically.

Modern scholarly opinion about Herodotus' visit to Egypt is divided and nuanced. On the sceptical/critical side, opinion escalates from arguing that his writing has serious defects as an historical work and operates with inadequate sources,[29] to commenting that 'though we cannot entirely rule out the possibility of Herodotus having been in Egypt, it must be said that his narrative bears little witness to it',[30] to questioning whether Herodotus ever travelled up the Nile and regarding pretty much everything he says about Egypt as dubious:[31] for him, Egypt, like its main river which floods in high summer, not in winter, is simply an inversion of Greek normality.

Herodotus does not operate like a modern historian. He unquestionably wants to give his audience an accurate account of events, but this also includes the type of mythological material that both he and his audience feel helps him to express the truth behind his narrative. Our distinctions between 'myth' and 'history' would baffle Herodotus: for him, brought up in the cultural milieu of the fifth-century BC Greeks, the way events are remembered and retold is through myths. These tales generate a valid kind of understanding, even when this retelling is not entirely factual.[32] Plato also uses *mythos* ('myth') to get at the truth: *understanding* is more important than *facts*.[33]

Having left Egypt, assuming he really went there, Herodotus probably travelled via Tyre to the River Euphrates and down to Babylon, from where he produced a memorable description of the city:

It lies in a great plain, and is in shape a square, each side 120 *stadia* [24 km] in length; thus 480 *stadia* [96 km] make the complete circuit of the city. Such is the size of the city of Babylon; and it was planned like no other city whereof we know. Round it runs first a moat deep and wide and full of water, and then a wall of fifty royal cubits' thickness [about 25 m],[34] and two hundred cubits' height [i.e. 100 m]. The royal cubit is greater by three fingers' breadth than the common cubit.[35]

The walls of Babylon were clearly wondrous: our first list of the Seven Wonders of the Ancient World, which occurs in a poem *On the Temple of Artemis at Ephesus* attributed to either Antipater of Sidon or Antipatros of Thessalonica,[36] includes them instead of the lighthouse at Alexandria:

I have set eyes on the wall of lofty Babylon on which is a road for chariots, and the statue of Zeus by the Alpheus, and the hanging gardens, and the colossus of the Sun, and the huge labour of the high pyramids, and the vast tomb of Mausolus; but when I saw the house of Artemis that mounted to the clouds, those other marvels lost their brilliancy.[37]

Yet despite this, Herodotus' description is manifestly absurd: 96,000 x 25 x 100 m = 24 million m of material in the walls.[38] This raises the issue of whether he had actually seen them, and certainly underlines the dangers of the literal interpretation of ancient evidence, especially when it comes to the dimensions of things. But Herodotus continues with his description:

On the top, along the edges of the wall, they constructed buildings of a single chamber facing one another, leaving between them room for a four-horse chariot to turn. In the circuit of the wall are a hundred gates, all of bronze, with bronze lintels and side-posts [. . .] The city is divided into two portions by the river which runs through the midst of it. This river is the Euphrates [. . .] The city wall is brought down on both sides to the edge of the stream: thence, from the corners of the wall, there is carried along each bank of the river a fence of burnt bricks. The houses are mostly three and four stories high; the streets all run in straight lines, not only those parallel to the river, but also the cross streets which lead down to the water-side. At the river end of these cross streets are low gates in the fence that skirts the stream, which are, like the great gates in the outer wall, of bronze, and open on the water.

The outer wall is the main defence of the city. There is, however, a second inner wall, of less thickness than the first, but very little inferior to it in strength. The centre of each division of the town was occupied by a fortress. In the one stood the palace of the kings, surrounded by a wall of great strength and size: in the other was the sacred precinct of Zeus Belus, a square enclosure two *stadia* [400 m] each way, with gates of solid bronze; which was also remaining in my time. In the middle of the precinct there was a tower of solid masonry, a *stadion* [200 m] in length and breadth, upon which was raised a second tower, and on that a third, and so on up to eight [. . .] On the topmost tower there is a spacious temple, and inside the temple stands a couch of unusual size, richly adorned, with a golden table by its side. There is no statue of any kind set up in the place, nor is the chamber occupied of nights by anyone but a single native woman [. . .]

Below, in the same precinct, there is a second temple, in which is a sitting figure of Zeus, all of gold. Before the figure stands a large golden table, and the throne whereon it sits, and the base on which the throne is placed, are likewise of gold. The Chaldaeans told me that all the gold together was eight hundred talents' weight. Outside the temple are two altars, one of solid gold [. . .] the other a common altar, but of great size [on which] the Chaldaeans burn the frankincense, which is offered to the amount of a thousand talents' weight, every year, at the festival of the God. In the time of Cyrus there was likewise in this temple a figure of a man, twelve cubits high, entirely of solid gold. I myself did not see this figure, but I relate what the Chaldaeans report concerning it [. . .]

The whole of Babylonia is, like Egypt, intersected with canals. The largest of them all, which runs towards the winter sun, and is impassable except in boats, is carried from the Euphrates into another stream, called the Tigris, the river upon which the town of Nineveh formerly stood. Of all the countries that we know there is none which is so fruitful in grain. It makes no pretension indeed of growing the fig, the olive, the vine, or any other tree of the kind; but in grain it is [so abundant that] the fruitfulness of Babylonia must seem incredible to those who have never visited the country.[39]

Plato's Atlantis resounds with echoes of Herodotus' Babylon, and another major city in the Persian Empire that Herodotus describes, and which might have had a bearing on Plato's Atlantisville, was Ecbatana (modern Hamadan in Iran):

Deioces[40] bade them build for him a palace worthy of the royal dignity and strengthen him with a guard of spearmen. And the Medes did so: for they built him a large and strong palace in that part of the land which he told them [. . .]. He

built large and strong walls, those which are now called
Ecbatana, standing in circles one within the other. And this
wall is so contrived that one circle is higher than the next by
the height of the battlements alone. And to some extent, I
suppose, the nature of the ground, seeing that it is on a hill,
assists towards this end; but much more was it produced by
art, since the circles are in all seven in number. And within
the last circle are the royal palace and the treasure-houses.
The largest of these walls is in size about equal to the circuit
of the wall round Athens; and of the first circle the battlements are white, of the second black, of the third crimson, of
the fourth blue, of the fifth red: thus are the battlements of
all the circles coloured with various tints, and the two last
have their battlements one of them overlaid with silver and
the other with gold.[41]

Fact and fantasy are hard to disentangle in this description –
most of the site now lies under the modern city – although the Late
Babylonian Nabonidus Chronicle in the British Museum[42] speaks of
Cyrus of Persia marching against 'the country Agamtanu' [i.e.
Ecbatana] in 550/549 BC and seizing the royal residence along with
the 'silver, gold, other valuables of the country Agamtanu', and the
Greek historian Xenophon (c. 430–c. 355 BC) tells us that Ecbatana
subsequently became the summer residence of the conquering
Achaemenid Persian kings.[43] Likewise Polybius, writing after Plato's
death, tells us that the city was richer and more beautiful than all
other cities in the world; although it had no wall, the palace, built on
an artificial terrace, had impressive fortifications; the circumference
of the citadel was seven *stadia* (about 1.4 km); the builders used
cedar and cypress wood, which was covered with silver and gold; the
roof tiles, columns and ceilings were plated with silver and gold;
and that the palace was stripped of its precious metals during the

invasion of Alexander the Great (Alexander's dear friend Hephaestion died there in 324 BC), and also in the reigns of his successors Antigonus and Seleucus. Aspects of the city could well have served as templates for the city of Atlantis with its circular layout, variegated stone constructions and metal-coated fortifications.[44]

When Herodotus' travels were over he migrated to Athens, possibly around 447 BC. His work doesn't mention anything that we can date to later than 430 BC, and it is generally assumed that he died shortly after that date, perhaps before he reached the age of sixty.

PERSIAN WARS

The Persian Empire, which Herodotus described so evocatively, was one of the most powerful in the ancient world, and as it expanded under Cyrus and his successors it had come to control the sophisticated Ionian Greek communities of Asia Minor, Herodotus' native Halicarnassus included. But in 499 BC, when Darius I was on the throne, some of these cities rebelled, and Athens sent ships to help them. The ultimate failure of this 'Ionian Revolt' was never in doubt, though, and once the rebels had been overwhelmed, the Great King (as the Greeks called him) sought revenge. Athens was at the top of his list.

Armed with a list of 'just grievances', Darius moved to subjugate Greece in a seaborne invasion, despatching a force said to number 600 ships. The invaders crossed the Aegean Sea, and in the summer of 490 BC they landed at Marathon, about 40 km north-east of Athens. The Athenians sought help from Sparta, but this was not forthcoming. Effectively on their own, with just 1,000 Plataean allies at their side, the hoplites (heavy infantrymen) of Athens, led by their swashbuckling general Miltiades, confronted the overwhelming barbarous/barbarian seaborne might of the Persian

Empire, and, to general astonishment, they won one of the most significant battles in the history of the Western world.[45] The Marathon-men and Athens revelled in the glory; the Persians yearned for revenge.

Miltiades died the year after his triumph at Marathon. But in 483 BC the Athenians struck a rich vein of silver in their mining district of Laurium. Ten years prior to this the anti-Persian politician Themistocles had instigated fortification projects at Piraeus, 5 km from Athens, in order to create a new naval base and commercial harbour. Plutarch observes that, 'it was his ambition to unite the entire city to the sea',[46] and now Themistocles persuaded the Athenians to spend their silver windfall on a large fleet of state-of-the-art warships called triremes. He actually exploited the hostility of the Athenians towards their neighbours on the island of Aegina, rather than against the Persians, but as Herodotus commented, this animosity saved Greece by forcing Athens to become a maritime power.[47] It was one of the most significant decisions the Athenians ever made: their transition from the land-fighting era of Marathon to their sea-based imperialist dominance of the Aegean world, which coincided with the peak of their democracy, was absolutely crucial, and these developments were not lost on Plato when he was composing the Atlantis narrative.[48]

Over in Persia, when Darius I died in 486 BC the vengeance project fell to his son Xerxes, who assembled a vast invasion force drawn from forty-six different nationalities,[49] which grew to 5,283,320 soldiers, sailors and logistics back-up, if we believe Herodotus' calculations.[50] And if we believe Plato, the Atlanteans will deploy similarly overwhelming numbers in their military assault on Athens.[51]

Xerxes' preparations for the invasion also involved some extraordinary feats of engineering, one of which was to spend about three years digging a canal through the Mount Athos peninsula in northern Greece, because he had previously lost a number of ships when they attempted to sail round it:

> All sorts of men in the army were compelled by whippings to dig a canal [. . .] At the mountain's landward end it is in the form of a peninsula, and there is an isthmus about twelve *stadia* [2.4 km] wide; here is a place of level ground or little hills [. . .] The foreigners dug as follows, dividing up the ground by nation: they made a straight line near the town of Sanē; when the channel had been dug to some depth, some men stood at the bottom of it and dug, others took the dirt as it was dug out and delivered it to yet others that stood higher on stages, and they again to others as they received it, until they came to those that were highest; these carried it out and threw it away. For all except the Phoenicians, the steep sides of the canal caved in, doubling their labour; since they made the span the same breadth at its mouth and at the bottom, this was bound to happen. But the Phoenicians showed the same skill in this as in all else they do; taking in hand the portion that fell to them, they dug by making the topmost span of the canal as wide again as the canal was to be, and narrowed it as they worked lower, until at the bottom their work was of the same span as that of the others. [. . .] As far as I can judge by conjecture, Xerxes gave the command for this digging out of pride,[52] wishing to display his power and leave a memorial; with no trouble they could have drawn their ships across the isthmus, yet he ordered them to dig a canal from sea to sea, wide enough to float two triremes rowed abreast.[53]

This is incredibly impressive, and archaeological traces of it still remain,[54] but the moral of Herodotus' story is Xerxes' high-minded arrogance, and the same applies to the bridging of the Hellespont, over which the Persian army crossed from Asia into Europe:

> The men who had been given this assignment made bridges starting from Abydus across to that headland; the Phoenicians one of flaxen cables, and the Egyptians a papyrus one. From Abydus to the opposite shore it is a distance of seven *stadia* [1.4 km]. But no sooner had the strait been bridged than a great storm swept down, breaking and scattering everything. When Xerxes heard of this, he was very angry and commanded that the Hellespont be whipped with three hundred lashes, and a pair of fetters be thrown into the sea. I have even heard that he sent branders with them to brand the Hellespont. He commanded them while they whipped to utter words outlandish and presumptuous, 'Bitter water, our master thus punishes you, because you did him wrong though he had done you none. Xerxes the king will pass over you, whether you want it or not; in accordance with justice no one offers you sacrifice, for you are a turbid and briny river.' He commanded that the sea receive these punishments and that the overseers of the bridge over the Hellespont be beheaded.[55]

A new batch of workers then completed the construction of the project, using 674 ships to support the causeway over the sea. Again, Herodotus is showing us the combination of ambitious engineering projects with out-of-control arrogance.

When the Great King sent envoys to Greece demanding earth and water as tokens of submission, many states sided with him, remained neutral or dithered. So again, it fell to Athens to stand in the forefront of the resistance, since although Sparta was given the high command in both the military and naval spheres, it was ultimately the Athenians, under the brilliant Themistocles, who forced the issue. While the King Leonidas' 300 Spartans were winning immortal fame by their heroic last stand in the pass of Thermopylae, the Athenians conducted indecisive naval actions at Cape Artemisium nearby. However, the setback at Thermopylae compelled the Greek forces to retreat south; the Persians sacked Athens in September 480 BC; Themistocles convinced the Greek allies that the best place to fight was in the narrow waters by the island of Salamis; Xerxes sent his mammoth fleet into the confined space between the island and the mainland; the Persians lost formation; Themistocles exploited local knowledge of weather and sea conditions to devastating advantage; and, as the Athenian playwright Aeschylus dramatised it in his tragedy *The Persians*, 'the sea was hidden, carpeted with wrecks and dead men; all the shores and reefs were full of dead.'[56]

Athens, at least as far as their own view of history saw it, had once again successfully led the resistance to a hostile invasion from the barbarian world. Xerxes himself returned to Persia, although his land forces remained in Greece until the Spartans led a combined Greek army into battle near the Boeotian town of Plataea in 479 BC, and won a conclusive victory that effectively put an end to the Persian menace for several generations. Freed from external menace, the Greeks would now begin to fight one another.

THE PENTEKONTAETIA: IMPERIALISM OUT OF CONTROL?

The period from 479 to 431 BC – the end of the Persian Wars to the outbreak of the Peloponnesian War between Athens and Sparta – is called the *Pentekontaetia* ('Fifty Years', even though it isn't exactly fifty years). It was a period in which ascendant Athens effectively rejected Sparta's traditional hegemony of the Greek world. In some regards, the two states were polar opposites: Athens was an Ionian democratic sea-power known for its energy, artistic innovation and creativity; Sparta was a Dorian oligarchic land-power with a reputation for austerity and lack of initiative. However, there was no immediate direct clash of interests, since Sparta's formidable alliance (the Peloponnesian League) was not geared up for extensive overseas activity, and Sparta remained focused on the Greek mainland, while Athens' interests lay in the Aegean Sea.

After Xerxes had been driven from Greece, the Athenians led a new Greek coalition, known to modern scholars as the Delian League, in counter-offensive against Persia. Formed in the winter of 478/477 BC on the island of Delos, the League's immediate aim was to recoup their losses and to liberate various states still under Persian control, although the longer-term objective had to be the preservation of Greek freedom from any future Persian aggression. Sparta was not part the League, and neither were any mainland Greek states founder members, but under Miltiades' son Cimon the Delian League scored some impressive successes, to the point where it is possible that a treaty known as the Peace of Callias[57] was signed between Athens and Persia in 449 BC, effectively ending hostilities.

The absence of any Persian threat allowed Athens to concentrate on the Delian League, which by now was looking more like an Athenian empire than a free alliance – something that the Athenians seem to have felt little guilt about:

> We have done [said Pericles, who ultimately superseded Cimon as Athens' leading politician] nothing contrary to human nature in accepting an empire when it was offered to us and then in refusing to give it up. Three very powerful motives prevent us from doing so – security, honour and self-interest.[58]

Athens' bullishness in this era was also accompanied by some astounding cultural achievements across a wide range of disciplines, however, and one of her most famous sons, Plato's teacher Socrates, was born during this period of expansion in 469 BC. Athens became the focus for some vibrant intellectual activity: Plato describes the young Socrates avidly acquiring the books of the early philosopher Anaxagoras;[59] depicts him holding conversations with the great visiting philosophers Parmenides and Zeno of Elea in the *Parmenides*; and in the *Protagoras* of 433/432 BC he shows him debating the most effective ways to educate Athens' young generation in the company of Protagoras, Prodicus and Hippias, who were the celebrity teachers of the day. Also prominent in Athens' cultural scene was Hippodamus of Miletus, described by Aristotle as the first non-statesman to explore the ideas of the 'Ideal Constitution'. This had a somewhat Platonic flavour,[60] but Hippodamus was also heavily involved in practical projects, most notably the layout of Athens' port of Piraeus. This was done, despite the challenges posed by the terrain, on the basis of a chequerboard streetplan that was applied regardless of whether the city's natural landscape suited it or not. Piraeus flourished, however, and as the hub of Athens' empire it became a busy, vibrant, noisy, well-fortified commercial and military centre equipped with hundreds of ship sheds, warehouses, banks, shops, brothels and other ancillary facilities.[61]

Snapshots of life at Piraeus would undoubtedly fire Plato's imagination as he contemplated the activities of the maritime inhabitants of his Atlantis,[62] and so would the way in which Athens' relationship with the Delian League shifted inexorably away from an equal partnership between the *hēgemon* ('leader') and her allies towards an authoritarian rule *(arkhē)* over subjects. Thucydides, who was also the first historian ever to analyse the causes of a war seriously, felt that it was this (over)confident imperialism that led Athens into the catastrophic Peloponnesian War with Sparta:

> The real reason (*alēthestatē prophasis*) for the war was [. . .] the growth of Athenian power and the fear which this caused in Sparta.[63]

Plato knew his Athenian history. It was good to think with.

THE PELOPONNESIAN WAR

The Peloponnesian War (431–404 BC) was a ghastly conflict, eloquently recorded by Thucydides, who served as a general on the Athenian side, but who was ultimately sent into exile as a result of his military failures, and it has been well said that 'in order to understand the [Atlantis] myth, you need first to read Thucydides'.[64] The year before the conflict broke out, Socrates served as a hoplite with the Athenian forces who suppressed a revolt at Potidaea, reducing the hapless population to cannibalism before they surrendered.[65] On the homeward march, he distinguished himself in a battle near Spartolus,[66] saving the life of the wounded Alcibiades.[67]

The war has frequently been described as a clash between an elephant and a whale: the Athenian whale sought to avoid direct confrontation with Sparta on land, keep the sea lanes open, harass the enemy from the sea and maintain its grip on the empire; the Spartan elephant felt that it simply had to invade and devastate Athens' territory, which would either force the Athenians into surrendering or offering battle, which the Spartans were confident of winning. Neither of these scenarios happened, but in 430 BC a devastating plague was transmitted[68] from Ethiopia into Egypt and Libya, on into Persian territory, and then, via Piraeus, to Athens. Lasting several years, and exacerbated by the crowded conditions caused by country-dwellers sheltering in the city from the Spartans, the plague may have killed 30 per cent of Athens' population.

Thucydides, who caught the plague and survived, wrote a closely observed description in order to allow future generations to identify the disease should it break out again,[69] but despite this, scholars and physicians, deploying forensic anthropology, demography, epidemiology and paleopathogy, including DNA analysis of skeletons from the plague years in an Athenian cemetery, still disagree: bubonic plague, influenza, typhoid fever, smallpox, epidemic typhus, measles and ebola are just some of the suggestions.[70] But that, in one sense, is secondary to Thucydides' purpose. The precise nature of 'Thucydides syndrome' is irrelevant because ethics matter more than science here: the focus is primarily on a carefully structured story about moral degradation at Athens.

The plague narrative functions as a deliberate contrast to Pericles' Funeral Oration, where the great leader eulogises the virtues of the Athenians at the end of the first year of the war. 'I shall speak first of our ancestors,' he says, 'for it is right and at the same time fitting, on an occasion like this, to give them this place of honour in recalling what they did.'[71] This would be a perfect opportunity to refer to ancient Athens' defeat of the Atlantean aggressors, but Pericles makes no reference to it. However, he does use all the right emotive vocabulary: we don't imitate other people – they imitate us; we are a democracy; our laws afford equal justice to all; class doesn't interfere with merit; poverty is no obstacle to advancement; we obey the magistrates and the laws; we have an inclusive attitude towards foreigners; we cultivate refinement without extravagance; we employ wealth for use more than for show; we are generous; and so on.[72] But now, because of the overwhelming disaster of the plague,

men, not knowing what was to become of them, became careless of all law, sacred as well as profane [. . .] The plague first introduced into the city a greater lawlessness. For where men hitherto practised concealment, that they were not acting purely after their pleasure, they now showed a more careless daring. They saw how sudden was the change of fortune in the case both of those who were prosperous and suddenly died, and of those who before had nothing but in a moment were in possession of the property of the others. And so they resolved to get out of life the pleasures which could be had speedily and would satisfy their lusts, regarding their bodies and their wealth alike as transitory. And no one was eager to practise self-denial in prospect of what was esteemed honour, because everyone thought that it was doubtful whether he would live to attain it, but the pleasure of the moment and whatever was in any way conducive to it came to be regarded as at once honourable and expedient. No fear of gods or law of men restrained; for, on the one hand, seeing that all men were perishing alike, they judged that piety and impiety came to the same thing, and, on the other, no one expected that he would live to be called to account and pay the penalty of his misdeeds. On the contrary, they believed that the penalty already decreed against them, and now hanging over their heads, was a far heavier one, and that before this fell it was only reasonable to get some enjoyment out of life.[73]

Thucydides is actually far less interested in providing a medical account than in telling a moral story *masquerading* as a medical account, and his 'Funeral Speech + medical description' pairing is clearly designed to make his readers analyse crucial questions about human behaviour in times of great stress. This is exactly what Socrates says he wants to explore in the *Timaeus*,[74] and which prompts Critias to tell the Atlantis story, and although the plague

47

isn't specifically mentioned in his Atlantis-related dialogues, the horror of tens of thousands of Athenian deaths might well have shaped Plato's ideas about natural disasters and the sudden destruction of humanity. Like Thucydides, he was less interested in the science (of plagues or sunken islands) than in the morality (of decadent Athenians or Atlanteans) that this gave the opportunity to examine.

The most high-profile victim of the plague was Pericles himself, who died in 429 BC. But around the same time as Pericles' soul descended to Hades, and 'bodies of dying men lay one upon another, and half-dead people rolled about in the streets and, in their longing for water, near all the fountains',[75] a new soul entered the world – that of Plato.

CHAPTER 3

Plato the Philosopher

....

The Ancient Greek language has several different 'moods', which include: the indicative, where you assert or present something as being real or certain ('Plato speaks Greek'); the subjunctive, where you represent something as uncertain but probable, express wonder and/or uncertainty, question what you should do, or make a doubtful assertion ('shall I?'; 'what are we to do?'; 'when/if Plato goes to Athens, he'll talk about philosophy'); and the optative, which is used when you want to say that something is possible (but no more than that), or to express a future possibility ('should Plato go to Sparta [but I don't really think he will], then he would talk about philosophy'). The subjunctive and the optative moods seems particularly apt both for investigating Plato's life, and for examining his Atlantis story.

The man that we know as Plato was, apparently, called Aristocles. 'Plato' (*Platōn* in Greek) seems to have been a nickname (*platos* = 'breadth'; *platys* = 'broad'):

> He learnt gymnastics under Ariston, the Argive wrestler. And from him he received the name of Plato on account of his robust figure, in place of his original name which was Aristocles, after his grandfather, as Alexander informs us in his *Successions of Philosophers*. But others affirm that he got the name Plato from the breadth of his style, or from the breadth of his forehead, as suggested by Neanthes.[1]

As far as the details of Plato's life are concerned, we only have frustrating snippets of biographical information in his own

49

writings, and it takes over twelve generations for us to get any coherent standalone accounts.[2] We cannot date his birth with 100 per cent certainty because Diogenes Laertius, the notoriously unreliable third-century AD[3] biographer who wrote the *Lives of Eminent Philosophers*, tells us that

> Apollodorus in his *Chronology*[4] fixes the date of Plato's birth in the 88th Olympiad, on the seventh day of the month Thargelion, the same day on which the Delians say that Apollo himself was born.[5]

This puts his birthday on 21 or 22 May 427 BC by standard scholarly calculations. However, the link with Apollo sounds suspicious, and that day is also the day after Socrates' birthday. We also have a potential dating calculated in relation to Socrates' death in 399 BC,[6] when Plato was said to be twenty-eight years old at the most:

> When Socrates was gone, he attached himself to Cratylus the Heraclitean, and to Hermogenes who professed the philosophy of Parmenides. Then at the age of twenty-eight, according to Hermodorus, he withdrew to Megara to Euclides, with certain other disciples of Socrates.[7]

Again, this implies, although not with 100 per cent certainty, that Plato was born in 427 BC. But then things get more confusing:

> He died, according to Hermippus,[8] at a wedding banquet, in the first year of the 108th Olympiad, at the age of eighty-one.[9]

Clearly there is something awry here: the first year of the 108th Olympiad is 348 BC, which means that if he was born in 427 BC he wouldn't live to be eighty-one – he'd only be seventy-nine or eighty, depending on whether he died before or after his birthday. Elsewhere, Diogenes tells us:

> His death [. . .] took place in the thirteenth year of the reign of King Philip [II of Macedon], as stated by Favorinus[10] in the third book of his *Memorabilia*, and according to Theopompus[11] honours were paid to him at his death by Philip.[12]

Philip II ascended to the throne in 359 BC, again strongly suggesting that Plato's birthday was in 427 BC.

We might also raise suspicions concerning Plato living to the age of eighty. That is the standardised age of death in the Alexandrian tradition that Apollodorus belongs to: if the person's details are somewhat obscure, they have their *akmē* (the pinnacle of their career) at forty (Plato meets Dion and founds the Academy); die at eighty; and experience important life-events at twenty (Plato meets Socrates) and sixty (Plato meets Aristotle). In Plato's case, this all looks rather glib and convenient.

A further tradition has him dying on his eighty-first birthday.[13] To die on your birthday marks you out as unusually important, and the number eighty-one can be seen as highly significant and mystical: $3 \times 3 \times 3 \times 3 = 81$; $3 \times 3 = 9$ (also the number of the Muses) and $9 \times 9 = 81$.

Then again, though, Diogenes says that

> Neanthes [. . .] makes him die at the age of eighty-four. He is thus seen to be six years the junior of Isocrates. For Isocrates was born in the archonship of Lysimachus, Plato in that of Ameinias, the year of Pericles' death.[14]

The archonship of Lysimachus was 436/435 BC; Diogenes is simply wrong about the archonship of Ameinias, which was

423/422 BC; and Pericles succumbed to the plague in the autumn of 429 BC. So in this version Plato seems to live from 429 to 345 BC.

These are by no means the only chronologies available in the ancient sources,[15] and current scholarship remains divided, albeit with a broad consensus of 428 or 427 to 348 or 347 BC, with Plato aged eighty or eighty-one:[16] the discrepancies might seem small, but the information is discussed here to illustrate the real difficulties in extracting and interpreting accurate chronological information from our ancient sources, even when dealing with one of the best known names from antiquity. Classical scholars would like to live in a world of indicative certainty, but they have to spend the majority of their time in subjunctive and optative uncertainty.

YOUNG PLATO: ATHENS AT WAR AND A NATURAL DISASTER

Plato's birthplace is also disputed. Athens is the default location, but the nearby island of Aegine is also mentioned:

> He was born, according to some, in Aegina, in the house of Phidiades, the son of Thales, as Favorinus states in his *Miscellaneous History*, for his father had been sent along with others to Aegina to settle in the island, but returned to Athens when the Athenians were expelled by the Lacedaemonians [i.e. Spartans], who championed the Aeginetan cause.[17]

However, we have no record of any Spartan expulsion of Athenians from Aegina between 431 and 411 BC.

When it comes to Plato's ancestry (see Fig. 2), we get unity on his father's identity, varying names for his mother, a rape, an intervention by Apollo, and descent from Poseidon on both sides of the family.

Fig. 2:
PLATO'S FAMILY TREE

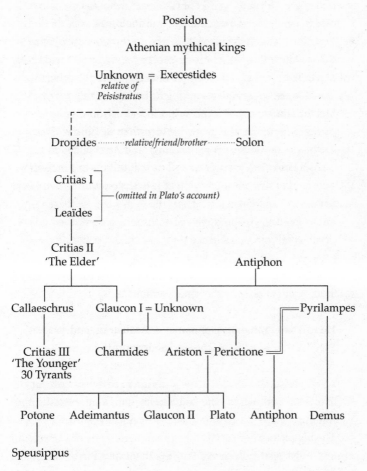

Plato was the son of Ariston and a citizen of Athens. His mother was Perictione (or Potone), who traced back her descent to Solon. For Solon had a brother, Dropides; he was the father of Critias [II, the Elder], who was the father of Callaeschrus, who was the father of Critias [III, the Younger], one of the Thirty, as well as of Glaucon[18], who was the father of Charmides and Perictione. Thus Plato, the son of this Perictione and Ariston, was in the sixth generation from Solon. And Solon traced his descent to Neleus and Poseidon. His father too is said to be in the direct line from Codrus, the son of Melanthus, and, according to Thrasylus,[19] Codrus and Melanthus also trace their descent from Poseidon.[20]

Speusippus in the work entitled *Plato's Funeral Feast*, Clearchus in his *Encomium on Plato*, and Anaxilaïdes in his second book *On Philosophers*, tell us that there was a story at Athens that Ariston made violent love to Perictione, then in her bloom, and failed to win her; and that, when he ceased to offer violence, Apollo appeared to him in a dream, whereupon he left her unmolested until her child was born.[21]

We can be confident that Plato also had two (probably older) brothers,[22] and a sister by the same parents:

He had two brothers, Adeimantus and Glaucon, and a sister, Potone, who was the mother of Speusippus.[23]

After Ariston's death, Plato's mother married her uncle, Pyrilampes,[24] with whom she had another son, Plato's half-brother Antiphon.[25]

The big picture here is clear: Plato came from one of the wealthiest and most politically active families in Athens;Plato's oligarchic uncle Charmides was listed among the dead after the battle on Mounychia between the notorious Thirty Tyrants, who overthrew the Athenian democracy in 404 BC, and the forces seeking to re-establish it the following year; Charmides' cousin Critias III the

Younger was the leader of the Thirty; Critias III admired, and wrote about, Sparta's way of life; Xenophon portrays Critias III as a violent, unscrupulous extremist,[26] although that is not how Plato shows him; and we should also notice that not all Plato's relatives were linked to oligarchic politics – his stepfather Pyrilampes was apparently a close associate of Pericles, when the latter led Athens' democratic faction. Overall, the family influence seems to have left Plato dissatisfied with governmental systems in general.

After Pericles' death in 429 BC, the Athenians pursued a much more aggressive, but less coherent, strategy in their conflict with Sparta, and in the midst of the fighting an event took place in 426 BC that some scholars think might have come to influence Plato in his Atlantis story. Peloponnesian forces advanced towards Athens,

> but a great many earthquakes occurred, causing them to turn back again, and no invasion took place. At about the same time, while the earthquakes prevailed, the sea at Orobiae in Euboea receded from what was then the shoreline, and then coming on in a great wave overran a portion of the city. One part of the flood subsided, but another engulfed the shore, so that what was land before is now sea; and it destroyed of the people as many as could not run up to the high ground in time. In the neighbourhood also of the island of Atalante, which lies off the coast of Opuntian Locris, there was a similar inundation, which carried away a part of the Athenian fort there, and wrecked one of two ships which had been drawn up on the shore [. . .] And the cause of such a phenomenon, in my own opinion, was this: at that point where the shock of the earthquake was greatest the sea was driven back, then, suddenly returning with increased violence, made the inundation; but without an earthquake, it seems to me, such a thing would not have happened.[27]

Strabo and Diodorus Siculus also mention tsunamigenic earth-quakes in this region,[28] with the former basing his account on a lost catalogue of ancient earthquakes by Demetrius of Callatis (c. 200 BC), and the latter simply mashing up Strabo with Thucydides. Inconsistencies between the accounts, along with evidence from recent archaeological excavations, suggest Strabo could be describing a more powerful seismic event from the third century BC,[29] but from Plato's perspective what matters is earthquakes, tsunamis and the inundation of a town called Atalante: it hardly needs emphasising that this passage of Thucydides might well have resonated with him.

In between his philosophising, Socrates fought heroically at the battle of Delium, where Athenian forces under the command of Laches were defeated in 424 BC.[30] Plato's dialogue *Laches*, whose dramatic setting is that same year, explores the nature of courage, and makes Socrates a friend of the Athenian general Nicias. Socrates' celebrity status at Athens is indicated by the fact that he featured in two of the plays performed there at the Great Dionysia festival of 423 BC: *Connus* (the name of Socrates' music teacher) and Aristophanes' *Clouds*.

In 422 BC Socrates was on military service again, participating in another Athenian setback, this time at Amphipolis. As far as we know, this was the last time he went to war, and when a period of uneasy peace was ushered in under the terms of the Peace of Nikias in 421 BC, he was able to return to philosophy, this time with a particular emphasis on exploring the nature of erotic love,[31] and to marry Xanthippe, who bore him sons named Lamprocles (possibly after her father) and Sophroniscus (after Socrates' father).

The fortunes of both sides in the Peloponnesian War ebbed and flowed; treaties and peace deals were agreed to and flouted; commanders on the battlefield and demagogues in the political arena came and went; and Athenian imperialism reached a particu-lar nadir in 416 BC when the Athenians demanded that the neutral (though probably pro-Spartan leaning) island of Melos should join the Delian League. The Melians refused. The Athenians gave a chilling insight into the 'might is right' ethic of their imperialism – 'This is no fair fight, with honour on one side and shame on the other. It is rather a question of saving your lives and not resisting those who are far too strong for you'[32] – and proceeded to slaughter the adult males and enslave the women and children.

THE SICILIAN EXPEDITION

The following year, the adolescent Plato's life would have been dominated by the experience of the Athenians launching a massive naval invasion of Sicily. Whipped up into a frenzy of irrational fear that the rich and powerful city of Syracuse posed a security threat to them, the Athenians voted to send an enormous naval force to conquer it. The whole episode turned out to be an example of Greek democracy at its chaotic worst, and it may well have influenced the young philosopher's future political attitudes, as well as his Atlantis narrative.

No sooner had the fleet sailed than Alcibiades, the main advocate for the invasion, was recalled to face accusations of profaning the Eleusinian Mysteries and being involved in the 'mutilation of the *Herms*' – rectangular stone pillars with a bust of Hermes on the top, feet on the bottom and a set of erect male genitals in the middle. Whether as an act of sacrilege (Hermes was the god of travel), political subversion or just as a 'student prank', someone had hacked off the statues' phalluses. The reaction was hysterical – imprisonment, torture, exile and executions followed, adversely, if not fatally, affecting a number of people who were close to Socrates, and Plato's uncle Charmides, and Charmides' cousin Critias III the Younger. Alcibiades was not prepared to risk facing trial, so he defected to Sparta before the assault force even got to Sicily. The first wave of

Athenian attacks ran into serious difficulties; the commander Nicias, who had been opposed to the entire project from the outset, asked for massive reinforcements and to be relieved of the command, hoping that the scale of his request would induce the Athenians to abandon the expedition altogether; but they gave him even more than he asked for; a night attack on the Syracusan positions went catastrophically wrong; the Syracusans defeated the Athenian forces, crushing them in the harbour on 9 September 413 BC; Nikias was forced to surrender; and some 7,000 POWs were incarcerated for months in Syracuse's stone quarries.

One of the key players on the Syracusan side was their statesman and general Hermocrates, who duly appears as one of the participants in Plato's dialogues about Atlantis. He had warned the Sicilians about the potential Athenian menace as far back as 424 BC, and specifically alerted his fellow Syracusans in the years immediately preceding the main invasion, before going on to play an effective role in the defeat of the Athenian expedition, both as an advisor and commander.

Sicily was a shattering defeat for Athens, with devastating consequences for both external and internal politics. In 411 BC, Athens' democratic machinery was briefly replaced by the rule of 'the Four Hundred', until this oligarchic regime was superseded first by a 'moderate democracy/mixed oligarchy and democracy' dubbed the Five Thousand Legislators, and then by a restored democracy. The Athenians still managed to win an amazing victory off the islands of Arginousae in 406 BC, but then it all went horrendously wrong: adverse winds prevented the rescue of some crews; a blame-culture arose; politicians got involved; popular hysteria took hold; Socrates tried to stand up for correct legal procedures in the trial, but all eight Athenian commanders were condemned to death;[33] and when the Spartans offered peace the Athenians rejected it. Athens' *hybris* was 'rewarded' the following year, when their fleet at Aegospotami was taken by surprise and destroyed practically without a fight. Athens' surrender came in the spring of 404 BC, at which point Plato, who was by this time a full citizen of Athens, may well have feared for his life. But rather than doing to the Athenians what they had done to Melos, the Spartans installed a collaborationist regime of anti-democratic Athenian aristocrats. Repressive and unpopular, they became known as the Thirty Tyrants. Prominent among them was Critias III the Younger, who some scholars think is the character who introduces Atlantis to the world,[34] although he was killed in the fighting when Athens' pro-democracy supporters overthrew the hated regime in 403 BC.

Post-war Athens remained a centre of intellectual creativity, although it was not always tolerant of its creative intellectuals. In 399 BC Socrates was impeached on nebulous charges of 'refusing to honour the gods honoured by the state, introducing new divinities, and corrupting the youth', found guilty, and met his end by drinking the *Conium maculatum* variety of hemlock. Revolutionising Greek thought had cost him his life, and, with the death of the man described in Plato's work as 'the best man of his time in wisdom and justice',[35] we come to the end of an era.

PLATO'S EARLY TRAVELS AND THE FOUNDING OF THE ACADEMY

After Socrates' execution, Plato left Athens and went to Megara.[36] We don't know how long he stayed there, but as he was still eligible for military service he would probably have been called up when Athens was fighting in the 'Corinthian War' from 395 BC. Without specifying precisely when, Diogenes informs us that,

> next he proceeded to Cyrene on a visit to Theodorus the mathematician, thence to Italy to see the Pythagorean philosophers Philolaus and Eurytus, and thence to Egypt to see

those who interpreted the will of the gods; and Euripides is said to have accompanied him thither.[37]

Again, our sources disagree on the itinerary and order of his travels. The Roman orator Cicero doesn't mention Cyrene and puts the visit to Egypt before the ones to Italy and Sicily,[38] while a papyrus from Herculaneum only mentions the journeys to south Italy and Sicily and makes them happen immediately after Socrates' death, when Plato was twenty-seven.[39] Overall the visit to Egypt is hard to rule in or rule out: there was a thriving Greek trading centre at Naucratis, connected to Saïs by a canal; Plutarch says that Plato funded his stay in Egypt by selling oil;[40] Plato had a deep interest in Egypt and its culture and mythology, although that, of course, is neither evidence for nor against him going there; Plato never reveals anything of any consequence when he does mention Egypt;[41] there is no reference to voyages to Cyrene or Egypt either in Plato's dialogues or in the Platonic *Letters*;[42] Strabo claims to have been shown where Plato hung out when he visited Heliopolis in Egypt,[43] which testifies to a strong Egyptian tradition that Plato had been there, albeit one being related by tourist guides over three centuries after the event, and Strabo undermines his own story with the impossible assertion that Plato stayed in Egypt for thirteen years; and similarly impossible is Diogenes' statement that Euripides accompanied Plato – Euripides had died in Macedonia in 406 BC. If the great philosopher had indeed been to Egypt, it invites the question of why he didn't follow in the footsteps of Solon and Herodotus, and visit the priests at Saïs himself.

Plato's visits to Italy and Sicily have much stronger evidence, especially in the Seventh Letter:

I made my first visit to Sicily, being then about forty years old.[44]

Why he went, and how long he stayed, he never says, although he might have wanted to meet a philosopher-statesman called Archytas of Tarentum.[45] He stayed at Syracuse, where he taught Dion, the young brother-in-law of the tyrant Dionysius I. Plato liked Dion a great deal – intellectually, morally, politically and possibly erotically – but the Sicilian penchant for *la dolce vita*[46] disturbed him, and various rather dubious stories tell of Dionysius I getting irritated with Plato and arranging for him to be sold into slavery.[47]

In any event, Plato was duly ransomed, returned to Athens and founded a school, known as the Academy. Although this gives us our word 'academic', the Academy actually got its name from its location, a grove of trees sacred to the hero Academus – or Hecademus – about a mile outside the walls of Athens.[48]

The Second Athenian Empire:
Failed Imperialism and a Natural Disaster

Plato was badly disillusioned with politics at this time – 'all cities at the present time are without exception badly governed'[49] – and well he might have been. Greek history in the generations after the Peloponnesian War sees Sparta fail to exploit the victory over Athens, Persia once again start to establish some influence in the Aegean area, Thebes enjoy a brief hegemony, and Macedon start to rise to ascendancy in the Hellenic world. Athens also sought to bounce back and to reassert something of its former power. Rather like in the situation after the Persian Wars, the Greek states started to fight among one another, and the so-called Corinthian War was waged from 395 to 387 BC between Corinth, Athens, Thebes and Argos on one side and Sparta on the other: Sparta won the battles but, aided by Persian funding, Athens started to recover some of her naval power and rebuilt many of her fortifications, including at Piraeus. Ultimately the Persians became worried about how well Athens was doing, and so formed an alliance with Sparta and defeated the Athenians in the Hellespont in 387 BC, before terminating the conflict and imposing the King's Peace in 386 BC.[50]

In 382 BC Sparta treacherously captured the citadel of Thebes, although the Thebans managed to recover it by 378 BC, which was the same year that the Athenians established a military alliance under their hegemony that modern historians call the Second Athenian Confederacy/League, and the ancient sources 'the Athenians and their allies'.[51] It was initially quite popular, and an Athenian inscription dating to 377 BC set out its 'mission statement':

> If any of the Greeks or of the barbarians dwelling on the mainland, or of the islanders, except such as are subjects of the King, wish to be allies of the Athenians and their allies, they may become such, while preserving their freedom and autonomy, using the form of government that they desire without either admitting a garrison or receiving a commandant or paying tribute upon the same terms as the Chians, Thebans and other allies.[52]

The overall aim was mutual defence against Sparta, and the joining terms sought to reassure potential members that the Second Athenian League would not be a 'Delian League Mark II'.

As the Second Athenian Confederacy went about its business, a disastrous event occurred in 373 BC that could have inspired Plato's thinking regarding his Atlantis story. Helice, a city on the Corinthian Gulf, was destroyed by a tsunami:

> The sea was raised by an earthquake and it submerged Helice, and also the temple of the Heliconian Poseidon, whom the Ionians worship even to this day, offering there the Pan-Ionian sacrifices. And, as some suppose, Homer

recalls this sacrifice when he says: 'but he breathed out his spirit and bellowed, as when a dragged bull bellows round the altar of the Heliconian lord.'[53] [A discussion about bull-sacrifices now occurs.] Helice was submerged by the sea two years before the battle at Leuctra.[54] And Eratosthenes says that he himself saw the place, and that the ferrymen say that there was a bronze Poseidon in the strait, standing erect, holding a hippocampus in his hand, which was perilous for those who fished with nets. And Heracleides says that the submersion took place by night in his time, and, although the city was twelve *stadia* [2.4 km] distant from the sea, this whole district together with the city was hidden from sight; and two thousand men who had been sent by the Achaeans were unable to recover the dead bodies; [. . .] and the submersion was the result of the anger of Poseidon.[55]

A temple of Poseidon, bull-sacrifices, a wrathful deity, and a city sunk beneath the waves: all these figure prominently in Critias' account of Atlantis.

As far as the Second Athenian League was concerned, the Muse of History played theme-and-variations with herself after the Thebans, under their brilliant general Epaminondas, unexpectedly, but comprehensively, defeated the Spartans at the Battle of Leuctra in 371 BC. This effectively made the alliance redundant, but Athens was reluctant to let her new-found power go. While the power of Thebes rose and fell and Macedon began to flourish under its new king, Philip II, Athens faced escalating ill-feeling that ultimately led to the Social War of 357–355 BC. Chios, Rhodes, Cos and Byzantium rebelled from the Confederacy; inept and disunited generalship on the Athenian side incurred naval defeats; Philip II exploited the situation to his maximum advantage, as did the Persian king, Artaxerxes III; and Plato was left to ruminate on the negative effects of imperialism – a theme that figures prominently in his Atlantis dialogues.

PLATO'S LATER TRIPS TO SICILY AND DEATH

The first of Plato's remaining two Sicilian adventures came after Dionysius I died in 367 BC and his young son, Dionysius II, ascended to the throne. The new tyrant's uncle/brother-in-law Dion persuaded him to invite Plato to help him become a philosopher-king along the lines described in the *Republic*. Plato, now in his sixties, was not entirely confident as to the outcome, but he still agreed to go.[56] And he was right to be pessimistic: before long Dion had been sent into exile,[57] and Plato was under house arrest as the tyrant's 'personal guest'.[58]

Plato eventually managed to secure permission to return to Athens, where he and Dion were reunited at the Academy.[59] Dionysius II agreed to invite Plato and Dion back to Syracuse 'after the war' – possibly the Lucanian War of 365 BC.[60] It seems that Dion and Plato remained philosophising in Athens until around 361 BC, when Dionysius II summoned Plato, but wanted Dion to wait a year longer. Dion seemed amenable to this arrangement,[61] but Plato dug his heels in.[62] Dionysius II kept up the pressure, tried hard to convince Plato that he was making good philosophical progress, and finally sent a ship carrying Plato's Pythagorean friend Archedemus, himself a friend of Archytas, to play on their mutual respect and friendship, and get Plato to go back to Syracuse.[63] The scheme worked, but on arrival in Syracuse Plato found Dionysius II to be cocksure of his own philosophical excellence, but actually wallowing in his own ignorance without knowing he *was* ignorant. Plato never even got to finish outlining his curriculum, and once again ended up effectively imprisoned in the palace grounds. Ultimately, he managed to escape thanks to the involvement of Archytas and his friends at Tarentum.[64]

The whole affair soured Plato's relationship with Dion, who subsequently gathered an army of mercenaries and invaded his own homeland. But his success was short-lived: he was assassinated and Sicily was reduced to chaos. Plato wrote an epitaph:

> By thee, O Dion, great deeds done
> New hopes and larger promise won.
> Now here thou liest gloriously,
> How deeply loved, how mourned by me.[65]

There would be no more forays into practical politics for Plato. He returned to Athens and the Academy, where Aristotle was now a star student, and spent his final thirteen years there. Diogenes Laertius says that he was buried in the Academy, and that all the students there joined in the funeral procession.[66] We know little about this last phase of Plato's life, but it is highly likely that it was during this time that he composed the *Timaeus* and *Critias*, and so introduced the world to the amazing story of Atlantis.

CHAPTER 4

Plato's *Timaeus*

....

Without Plato there would be no Atlantis. If the *Timaeus* and then the *Critias* hadn't been written, or if, like so much Ancient Greek literature, they had been lost, nobody would ever talk about Atlantis or go looking for it today: no other ancient author of any kind ever mentioned the story until Plato did, even though a number of them might have had good reason to do so, had the story been well known. So, since the existence of the Atlantis story depends on Plato, and Plato alone, any exploration of the island must start from his texts.

In the first of these, the *Timaeus*, Plato is keen to analyse the idea that 'man is not alone in the Universe with his moral concerns'.[1] Goodness is represented in the Universe, Plato believes – the Universe is formed by the joint operation of Intelligence (*nous*) and Necessity (*anankē*); Intelligence, operating in pursuit of the Good, persuades Necessity – and therefore we can learn useful lessons about Goodness by studying the cosmos. Cosmology will teach us how to live our lives, and by 'learning the harmonies and revolutions of the Universe' it will make us better people and allow us to attain 'that goal of life which is set before men by the gods as the most good both for the present and for the time to come'.[2] Although the Atlantis story is a crucial element of the discussion in the *Timaeus*, it is important to be aware that it is not Plato's prime focus: it is a vehicle through which he explores the idea of Goodness in the cosmos.

The *Timaeus* dialogue is essentially Plato's attempt to describe how the world came into being, an account of the creation of the world by the *dēmiourgos* ('Demiurge'/'divine craftsman'). But he also tells us that it is no more than a 'likely account' (*eikōs logos*) or a 'likely story' (*eikōs muthos*).[3] So we should not have high expectations for it: the speaker Timaeus merely claims that he will try to give an account that is 'inferior to none in likelihood',[4] and that while it will merit our *pistis* ('confidence')[5] it cannot be grasped by *nous* ('understanding'/'the faculty for apprehending unchanging truths').[6] So Plato's account is reasonable and invites our confidence, but it isn't definitive and it isn't complete,[7] which means it could always be revised.[8] Any quest for the 'truth about Atlantis' should take this into consideration, along with the fact that Plato insists that any definitive account of these matters is elusive to humans:[9] 'the principles which are still higher than these are known only to God and the man who is dear to God'.[10]

Despite Plato's caveats, the *Timaeus* is still a fascinating example of how far the imagination can stretch in an effort to understand the mysteries of the Universe, and to modern readers it exhibits a bizarre blend of 'immature science and mature invention'.[11] But the work was extremely influential in later antiquity and, thanks to a translation into Latin by Cicero, became highly influential during the Middle Ages.

The dramatic setting of the dialogue is at the Athenian festival of the Apatouria, probably in the year 429 BC or shortly afterwards,[12] and as the dialogue begins, Socrates reminds Timaeus about a conversation they were having the day before about the various kinds of citizens that were needed in an Ideal State. Socrates then rehearses the main points of Books 2 to 5 of the *Republic*: the basic institution of the Ideal State is the class of Guardians, a cohesive group who have no private property or individual family life, and who have absolute control over the government and over defence. Although Socrates refers to the elementary education that the Guardian class receives, he makes no mention of the elite group of Philosopher Kings that appears in the *Republic*.

The *Timaeus* and *Critias* were composed quite a lot later than the *Republic*, and Plato's thinking has clearly changed in certain respects: he seems to have lost confidence in the idea that anyone, no matter how wise, could hold absolute power without falling prey to the temptations to immorality that power brings with it; and the narrative of the moral decline of the Kings of Atlantis,[13] which ultimately brings down the wrath of Zeus and the destruction of their island, seems designed to illustrate his modified ideas that unchecked political power leads to moral degeneration, which leads to political disunity, which leads to disaster for the entire state. Plato also makes it clear that the imaginary conversation that he outlines here, although it is similar, is not the same one that happened in the *Republic*: it takes place 'yesterday' at a festival of Athena, not Bendis like in the *Republic*,[14] and the location and participants are different.

It is in the introductory part of the *Timaeus* where Atlantis emerges for the first time. The Atlantis myth is unique in the corpus of Greek mythology in that it has no antecedents, and it has no genealogical relationship to any earlier myths: the Greek myths are not 'standalone' stories that exist in isolation, but form an intimately interconnected web of stories, but the Atlantis tale is entirely self-contained – it sprang fully formed from the head of Plato rather like the birth of Athena from the head of Zeus. The fact that it appears from nowhere differentiates it from the rest of Greek mythology: as T. Wyatt points out, 'If *Atlantis* had preclassical roots comparable to other myths, then one would expect some hints of them to have emerged from linguistic studies',[15] but they have not done so. Plato's Atlantis tale stands in splendid isolation.

What follows in this chapter and the next is the author's translation of Plato's works, with a commentary in the notes from pp. 357–85.

SOCRATES' SUMMARY OF THE IDEAL STATE

SOCRATES:[16] [17a] One, two, three ... but hang on, my friend Timaeus, where's the fourth[17] of yesterday's diners, who were going to be today's feast-providers?[18]

TIMAEUS: He's poorly in some way, Socrates. He wouldn't have missed this meeting voluntarily.

SOCRATES: Then the job of filling the absentee's place comes down to you and these guys, doesn't it?

TIMAEUS: [17b] Absolutely. And we'll do our utmost not to leave anything undone. After all, it wouldn't be fair, after the friendly gifts of hospitality that we received from you yesterday, if those of us who remain didn't eagerly give you a full feast in return.

SOCRATES: All right then. Do you remember the quantity and quality of the subjects that I directed you to talk about?

TIMAEUS: We remember some of them, but you'll be here to remind us about any we don't. Better still, if it's not boring for you, go back over them again briefly from the beginning, so that they stick in our minds better.

SOCRATES: [17c] Okay. Yesterday the main point of my discourse was about politics – what kind of constitution,[19] composed of what kind of citizens, would make it seem likely to me to be the very best.

TIMAEUS: Yes, Socrates, and as far as we're all concerned, it was entirely as intelligence requires.

SOCRATES: Didn't we start by dividing off in it the class of farmers, and all other craftspeople, from the class of those who will fight on its behalf?[20]

TIMAEUS: Yes.

SOCRATES: And when, according to each person's nature, [17d] we'd assigned to them their one-and-only suitable occupation, just one craft to each, we said that those whose job it was to fight on everyone's behalf must be guardians of the city and nothing more than that – whether someone were to come from outside to damage it, or from those people inside it – and that they should pass judgement humanely on those who are under their authority [18a] and who are their natural friends, but get tough with their enemies when they encounter them in battle.[21]

TIMAEUS: Absolutely.

SOCRATES: Yes, because I think we said that the nature of the soul of the guardians ought to be simultaneously spirited and philosophic to an outstanding degree, so that it could treat each group humanely or toughly as the situation dictated.

TIMAEUS: Yes.

SOCRATES: And what about their upbringing? Didn't we say that they were to be trained in athletic exercises, and music, and every other subject which is proper for them?[22]

TIMAEUS: Oh yes!

SOCRATES: [18b] And it was also said, I think, that the people brought up in this way should never regard gold or silver, or any other possession for that matter, as their own private property. But like mercenary soldiers taking payment for the protection they provided from those they safeguard – at a rate suited to people of moderate needs – they were both to spend their money and live communally with one another, having total regard for excellence and enjoying leisure from all other occupations.[23]

TIMAEUS: Yes, as you say. That's what was said.

SOCRATES: [18c] And we made further mention of the women[24] as well, and said that their natures must be harmonised into near equality with those of the men,[25] and that all common business should be assigned to all of them, both in wartime and in other aspects of life.

TIMAEUS: Again, as you say. That's what was said.

SOCRATES: And what about the procreation of children? Or was this pretty easy to remember because of the novelty of what we said? We stipulated that all marriages and children should be in common, contriving that nobody should ever recognise a child as their own, but that everybody should regard everyone [18d] as being of the same family – those within a suitable age-limit as their brothers and sisters; those of the older generation as their parents and grandparents; and those of the younger generation as their children and children's children.[26]

TIMAEUS: Yeah! As you say, that's really memorable!

SOCRATES: Then again, so that they might, as far as possible, instantly become excellent in their natural characters – don't you remember? – we said that when it came to sexual relationships the male and female rulers had to use secret lotteries to devise a way in which [18e] the bad men and the good men should each be paired up [by lot] with women of a similar nature, and in which no ill-feeling should break out among them because of this, seeing that they'd attribute the allotment process to chance?[27]

TIMAEUS: I remember that.

SOCRATES: [19a] And do you also remember that we said that the children of the good parents were to be brought up, but those of the bad should be secretly distributed to other parts of the community; and while these children were all growing up the rulers were to be continually on the lookout, so that they could reinstate the worthy ones, and transfer the unworthy ones in their own ranks to the places of the promoted ones?[28]

TIMAEUS: That's what we said.

SOCRATES: Okay then, Timaeus, my friend, have we gone over yesterday's conversation, at least as far as covering the main points is concerned? Or are we still missing anything? Has anything been omitted?

TIMAEUS: [19b] Not at all, Socrates; it was exactly like you've said.

SOCRATES' REQUEST – TELL US ABOUT THE IDEAL STATE IN ACTION

SOCRATES: And now you might like to hear how I happen to feel about the State that we've described. Well, my gut feeling is a bit like someone who's been looking at beautiful animals, either in a work of painting or at ones that are actually alive but which are motionless, and who is seized with desire to see them moving or competing in a contest in one of the ways that appears to suit their bodily forms. [19c] That's my emotion about the city that we've described. I'd dearly like to hear someone giving an outline of our city competing in the contests that cities compete in, struggling against others, going to war in a way that fits her, and in that war displaying qualities that match her education and upbringing, both in military action and in negotiations with various other cities.[29]

Anyhow, Critias and Hermocrates, [19d] as far as these things are concerned, I'm aware that I personally wouldn't ever be able to eulogise our city and her citizens in an appropriate way.[30] As far as I'm concerned, this isn't surprising in the least.[31] But I've arrived at the same opinion about the poets, both those of the past and those of today – not that I'm disrespecting poets in general, but it's obvious to everyone that the whole tribe of imitators[32] will imitate best and most easily the surroundings in which they are brought up, while what is beyond the range of anyone's education is hard to imitate in works of art,[33] and harder still to put into words. [19e] I've always thought that the whole tribe of the Sophists[34] is highly experienced in making all sorts of beautiful speeches on other topics, but I fear that perhaps, because they wander from city to city and don't have their own fixed abode, they may miss the scale and quality of the actions and statements that men who are both philosophers and statesmen would make in their various dealings with their enemies both in war and on the battlefield, be this in the actual fighting or the negotiations.

So, by process of elimination, that leaves only the people of your sort, who are equipped both by nature and nurture for politics *and* philosophy. [20a] For example, Timaeus[35] here comes from the outstandingly well-governed city of Locris[36] in Italy. He is second to none of the people there either in property or ancestry, and he hasn't just had a share in the greatest offices and civic honours of his own state, but in my opinion he's also attained the absolute pinnacle of all aspects of philosophy; as for Critias, all of us Athenians know that *he* doesn't lack professional knowledge of the subjects we're talking about. And as far as Hermocrates' nature and nurture are concerned, we must trust the many people who testify that he is up to the job in these respects.

[20b] So it was for this reason that yesterday, after giving it some thought, when you'd requested me to describe the constitution, I gladly agreed, knowing that, if you were willing, no one else would be more likely to provide the sequel. For, of the people alive today, you alone could give an account of our State engaging in a conspicuously fitting war, and displaying all its proper qualities. So, once I'd said what I was supposed to, I demanded these things that I'm speaking about now from you in return. You agreed that, after putting your heads together, you would pay me back today with a feast of words. So here I am, dressed up in my party outfit, and nobody's more up for receiving this promised banquet than I am!

CRITIAS' RESPONSE TO SOCRATES' REQUEST

HERMOCRATES: [20c] Right then, indeed, Socrates![37] As Timaeus here said, we won't be lacking enthusiasm in any respect, and there isn't the slightest excuse for us not to do what you want. As a result, only yesterday, we began looking into it as soon as we arrived at the guest-suite at Critias' place where we're staying. More precisely, we were doing this even earlier, on the way there. [20d] Critias then related a story (*logon*)[38] from ancient tradition. Actually, Critias, why don't you tell it to Socrates now? That way he can assess, as can we, whether or not it's appropriate to the assignment he's given us.

CRITIAS: Okay. I ought to do that, if it also seems like a good idea to our third partner. Well, Timaeus?

TIMAEUS: Yes, it does.

CRITIAS: Then listen up, Socrates, to a story (*logou*)[39] which is utterly extraordinary, but totally true, as once-upon-a-time Solon, the wisest of the Seven Sages of Greece, said.[40] [20e] He was a relative and a very close friend of my great-grandfather, Dropides, as Solon himself often says in his poetry; and he [*Dropides*] told it to my grandfather Critias,[41] as the old man in his turn used to relate from memory to us.[42] [See Fig. 3] What he said was that there were ancient deeds of this city – great and amazing ones – which had been obliterated by time and the destruction of humanity.[43] But there was one exploit that was the greatest of all, [21a] and thinking about this now would be a suitable way both to repay our debt of gratitude to you and justly and truly to sing the praises of the goddess Athena on her national festival day, as though in a hymn.[44]

Fig. 3:

THE TRANSMISSION OF THE ATLANTIS STORY

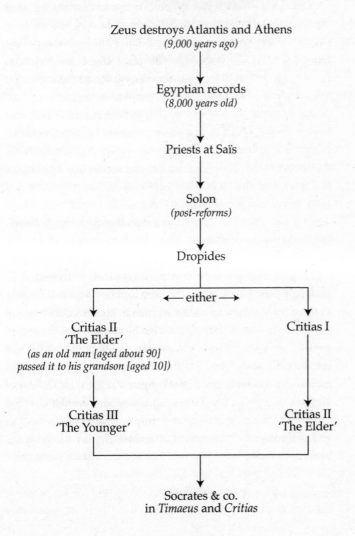

Zeus destroys Atlantis and Athens
(9,000 years ago)

Egyptian records
(8,000 years old)

Priests at Saïs

Solon
(post-reforms)

Dropides

← either →

Critias II
'The Elder'
*(as an old man [aged about 90]
passed it to his grandson [aged 10])*

Critias I

Critias III
'The Younger'

Critias II
'The Elder'

Socrates & co.
in *Timaeus* and *Critias*

75

SOCRATES: Splendid! But what sort of ancient exploit was this that Critias set out in detail as being not a mere story but actually performed by this city, according to Solon's story?

CRITIAS: I will tell you: the story is old, and I heard it from a man who wasn't young. For at that time, as he said himself, [21b] Critias was already nearly ninety years old, while I was somewhere around ten.[45] It happened to be Children's Day in the Apatouria festival,[46] at which there were always customary ceremonies for the boys: our fathers offered us prizes for reciting poetry. Many poems by many poets were recited, and many of us children sang Solon's poems, which were quite a novelty at that time.[47] And one of our fellow brotherhood members, either because he really thought so at the time or just because he was doing a favour [21c] to Critias, said that in his view Solon was not only the wisest of men in other matters, but also the most free-spirited of all the poets.[48] The old man – I remember it really well – was absolutely delighted, and said, with a smile on his face, 'Amynander, I wish that he hadn't treated his poetry as a side-line but had taken it seriously like others did. If he'd completed the story that he brought back here from Egypt, and hadn't been forced to neglect it because of the class struggles and other evils he found here when he got home, [21d] I don't think Hesiod or Homer or any other poet would have been more celebrated than Solon.'[49] 'And what was the story, Critias?' asked Amynander. 'It was about the greatest exploit,' Critias said, 'and it would rightly be the most famous of all those ever performed by our city, except that the story has not endured until our day because of the lapse of time and the destruction of those who were involved in it.' 'Tell it from the beginning,' said Amynander, 'what was this true account which Solon gave? How did he get it? And who told him it was true?'[50]

[21e] Critias replied, 'In Egypt, at the apex of the Delta, where the stream of the River Nile divides, there is an administrative

district called the Saïtic. The biggest city of the district, from which King Amasis[51] came, is called Saïs. The founding ancestral goddess of the inhabitants is called Neïth[52] in the Egyptian language; in Greek (according to their account) she's called Athena: and they like the Athenians very much, and say that they are related to them in some way. Solon said that when he went there on his travels[53] he was very highly honoured by them, [22a] and furthermore, that when he quizzed the priests who were most knowledgeable about ancient times on that topic, he discovered that neither he nor any single other Greek knew practically anything about antiquity. On one occasion, when he wanted to lead them into a dialogue about ancient history, he set out to give an account of the earliest events known here, telling them about Phoroneus, said to be the first man, and Niobe, and he went on to tell the mythical tale of Deucalion [22b] and Pyrrha after the Great Flood, and how they survived it, and to provide a genealogy of their descendants, and by recording the years since the events of which he was speaking, he tried to work out their dates.[54] And Solon said that a really old one of the priests said, 'Oh Solon, Solon, you Greeks are always children: Greek old men don't exist.'[55]

On hearing this Solon asked, 'What mean you by that?'

'You are young in your souls,' replied the priest, 'every one of you. You see, in those souls you don't have one single belief that is ancient and based on old tradition; nor do you have any knowledge that is grey-haired with age.[56] And this is the reason why: [22c] there have been, and will continue to be, many different destructions of humanity, the greatest ones by fire and water, but also other somewhat insignificant ones by a myriad of other causes. For instance, the story that's told among you about how Phaethon, the son of Helios the Sun god, harnessed his father's chariot, but wasn't able to drive it along his father's course, incinerated things that were on the earth, and was himself destroyed by a thunderbolt[57] – this story is told in a way that gives it the appearance of a myth, but the truth[58] is [22d] that there is a deviation of the bodies moving in the heavens around the earth, and a destruction, which recurs after long periods of time, of the things on the earth in a massive conflagration.[59]

'At those times, the mountain-dwellers, and those who live in high and dry places, are destroyed more comprehensively than those who live near rivers or by the sea; but in our case, the Nile, who is our Saviour in other ways, also saves us at such times from this emergency when he is set free.[60] But when, on the other hand, the gods cleanse the earth with a deluge of waters, it's the herdsmen and shepherds on the mountains who survive,[61] [22e] whereas those who inhabit cities in your part of the world are swept into the sea by the rivers. In this land of Egypt, though, the water doesn't come down onto the fields from above – not then nor at any other time – but on the contrary it all tends to rise up naturally from below.

'So for those reasons the stories that are preserved here are the most ancient to be told.[62] The fact of the matter is, that wherever extreme cold or burning heat doesn't prevent it, the human population always exists in greater or smaller numbers. [23a] But whatever happens, whether it takes place in your country or in ours or in some other place that we gather from hearsay (at least if it's something noble or great or has something exceptional about it), has all been written down since ancient times and has been kept safe in the temples. On the other hand, every time it happens, your lifestyle and that of the others has only recently come to be furnished with writings and everything else that civilised communities need, when again, after the usual number of years, the flood from heaven comes pouring down on them like a plague, and leaves only the illiterate [23b] and uncultured ones of you, so that you have to start again from the beginning, like children, in total ignorance of what existed in our country or in yours in ancient times.

'At least, these legendary genealogies of your own people, which you ran through just now, are hardly any different from children's stories.[63] For a start, you only remember one inundation of the earth, although there have been many earlier ones,[64] and what's more you don't know that the finest and noblest race in all mankind existed in your land, and that you and your fellow citizens are descended from a slender remnant of their seed. [23c] But you don't know anything about it because for many generations the survivors died without expressing themselves in writing. You see, Solon, there was a time, before the greatest of all destructions by water,[65] when the city that is now Athens was the most excellent in war and exceptionally well governed in all respects: to that city were said to belong the finest exploits and the finest political institutions of any under the heavens that we heard word of.'

[23d] When he heard this, Solon said that he was astonished and that he keenly begged the priests to go through everything about those ancient citizens in detail and in order.[66]

'I'll willingly do that, Solon,' said the priest, 'both for your sake and for that of your city, but principally as a favour to the goddess who obtained by lot both your land and ours, and nurtured and educated them – she took over yours 1,000 years earlier,[67] after she received your [23e] seed from Earth and Hephaestus;[68] she took over ours later. The date of our civilisation is recorded in our sacred writings as being 8,000 years old. Regarding your fellow-citizens, then, who lived 9,000 years ago, I shall briefly describe to you their laws and the noblest exploit that they performed; we'll go through the precise details of [24a] everything in sequence at leisure some another time, with the writings in front of us.[69]

'Consider their laws in relation to ours:[70] you will find here among us today many parallels to your institutions of the old days.

In the first instance, our class of priests has been separated from the others, as has our manufacturing class – each type sticks to its own task and doesn't get involved with the rest – and so have the classes of the shepherds, hunters and farmers.[71] [24b] And of course you've doubtless noticed that the military class in Egypt is separated from all the others, being required by law to devote itself exclusively to military activities. And besides, the style of their weaponry consists of shields and spears,[72] which we were the first people in Asia to arm ourselves with, because the Goddess instructed us to do so, just as she did in your part of the world first. And again, as far as wisdom is concerned, you see what great care the law has devoted from the beginning to the divine principles of cosmology. It has derived [24c] all the arts that aim at human health from these, even down to divination and medicine.[73] And it has mastered the other subsidiary studies that are connected with these.

'So at that time the goddess founded this whole arrangement and system when she established your state first, and she chose the place in which you were born, seeing that the well-balanced nature of its seasons[74] would produce exceptionally intelligent men. Being herself a [24d] lover of war and a lover of wisdom she chose a location that would produce men most similar to herself in character, and settled that one first.

'So you lived there under laws like these,[75] and still better ones, and exceeded all men in every kind of virtue, as you'd expect of people who were produced and educated by the gods. Many great achievements of your city are recorded and admired here,[76] but one of them surpasses all the others in greatness and virtue: [24e] our inscribed records say that once upon a time your city checked a mighty power which advanced full of *hybris*[77] to attack all of Europe and Asia. They started from outside; they came from the Atlantic Ocean. You see, at that time, the sea there could be crossed:[78] it used to have an island[79] in front of the mouth that you call, as you say, the

'Pillars of Heracles'.[80] The island was bigger[81] than Libya[82] and Asia put together, and from here it was possible for travellers in those times to make a passage to the other islands, and from the islands [25a] to the whole of the opposite continent which surrounds that genuine ocean.[83] For all these parts that lie within the mouth that I'm talking about,[84] resemble a harbour with a narrow entrance: that outer sea is the real ocean, and the land entirely surrounding it may most accurately be called the true continent. [See Fig. 4]

Fig. 4:
THE WORLD OF PLATO'S ATLANTIS

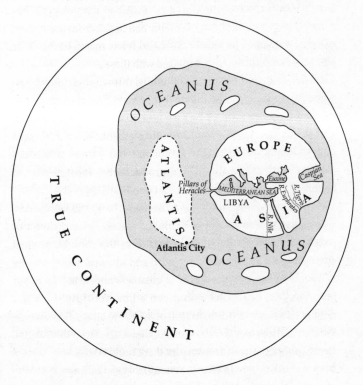

'Now, a mighty and wondrous power had arisen on this island of Atlantis, under kings who ruled not just the entire island but many other islands and parts of the continent; and as well as those, of the lands here within the Pillars of Heracles, this power ruled [25b] Libya as far as Egypt and Europe as far as Tyrrhenia.[85] All this strength, concentrated into one, once attempted to enslave your country, our country, and every place within the mouth, in one single assault. But then, Solon, the power of your city became conspicuous among all humanity in respect of its excellence and strength.[86] Her courage and military expertise were outstanding above everyone; [25c] sometimes she led the Greeks; sometimes, when the others deserted her, she fought alone out of sheer necessity; she encountered the most extreme dangers; she defeated the invaders and set up a trophy; she prevented those who hadn't yet been enslaved from losing their freedom; and she ungrudgingly liberated all the others who were dwelling inside the Pillars of Heracles.[87]

'But at a later time when extraordinarily violent earthquakes and floods had taken place, and one [25d] awful day and night had suddenly occurred, the entire warrior class in your land sank beneath the earth *en masse*, and in the same way[88] the island of Atlantis sank beneath the sea and disappeared.[89] That's the reason why the sea in that region is now impassable and impossible to find your way through, because there is mud just below the surface[90] that impedes your progress, which the island produced as it subsided.'

So, Socrates, you've now heard in brief what was said by the old man [25e] Critias according to what he heard from Solon.[91] And yesterday, when you were talking about your State and the citizens you were describing, I was amazed as I remembered these things that I'm talking about now, observing how closely, by some miraculous chance, you agreed for the most part with what Solon said. But I didn't [26a] want to speak on the spur of the moment, because after such a long lapse of time I didn't remember well enough.[92] So I reflected that it was necessary for me to go back over it all properly in my own mind first, and only then to speak. That's why I quickly consented to what you required of me yesterday. I reckoned – and this is the hardest thing in all matters like these – that we should be fairly well off for proposing a story fit for our purposes.

So, as Hermocrates has told you,[93] the instant I left your place yesterday I began repeating the story to these guys here as I remembered it, and when I got back home [26b] I recovered pretty well all of it by thinking it over during the night. How true it is, as the saying goes, that the lessons of our childhood cling strangely to our memory. You know, I'm not sure whether I could remember everything that I heard yesterday, but I'd be completely amazed if any of these things which I heard so very long ago have slipped my mind in any detail.[94] I listened at the time with immense [26c] childish pleasure: the old man was very keen to teach me, seeing that I constantly kept on asking questions, with the result that it has become permanently fixed in my mind, like the indelible picture on an encaustic painting. And moreover, I immediately told all this to these guys at the crack of dawn, so that they might have plenty to talk about in common with me.

So now, Socrates, to get to the point of this preamble, I'm ready to tell you the story, not just under general headings but in each individual detail, just as I heard it. We will now transfer[95] the city and citizens which you described to us yesterday as in a myth [26d] into historical fact,[96] placing it here and assuming it to be that real city of antediluvian Athens. And we shall posit the citizens you theorised about as[97] being those genuine ancestors of ours that the priest spoke about. They'll harmonise perfectly, and we won't be singing out of tune if we say that those ideal citizens of your State are the citizens of ancient Athens. So, dividing the subject between us, we will all try to the best of our ability to do justice to the theme that you've [26e] imposed on us. Therefore, Socrates, it's necessary to consider whether this story is fit for our purpose, or whether we should seek another one in place of it.

SOCRATES: What topic should we take up that'll be better than this one, Critias? It's a story which would be well suited to the festival of the goddess which is being held right now, and the fact that it is true history and not an invented myth[98] is massively[99] important, I suppose. How and where shall we find other stories, if we reject these? It's not possible. You must speak, and Good Luck be with you, while I, in return for my discourse of yesterday, must now [27a] relax and listen in turn.[100]

CRITIAS: Consider the arrangement of the entertainment which we've made for you, Socrates. It seemed like a good idea to us that Timaeus should speak first. He is the best astronomer among us and he has made understanding the nature of the universe his special job, and he'll start with the beginning of the universe and end with the origin of mankind. I'll go after Timaeus, taking over mankind from him, which he will have already created in his speech, and taking over a number of men who have been [27b] exceptionally well-educated by you.[101] Then, on the basis of Solon's story and his law-code we agreed to lead them into our 'virtual court' and make them citizens of our city, and treat them as if[102] they were those ancient Athenians whose disappearance was revealed by the report of the sacred writings. From then on I will go ahead with my discourse as if[103] they were indeed Athenians and our fellow-citizens.

SOCRATES: It looks like I'm going to be repaid with a complete and brilliant banquet of words. So now, it'll be your job, Timaeus, to

make the next speech, once you have invoked the gods according
to the law.

THE *TIMAEUS*

Timaeus now starts to speak, and we now have wait until the next
dialogue in the sequence, the *Critias*, to learn more about Atlantis.
The rest of the *Timaeus* presents an elaborate account of the formation of the Universe. Timaeus is deeply impressed with the order
and beauty that he sees in the world around him, and so he tries to
explain it. His proposal is that the Universe is the product of a
rational, purposive and beneficent power, and is put together by a
Divine Craftsman (often referred to as the 'Demiurge', *demiourgos*,
Timaeus 28a6), who turns pre-existent chaos into mathematical
order and generates the ordered Universe (*kosmos*) in the process.
This Universe is arranged so as to produce an enormous array of
good effects, which Plato feels is the result of the conscious intent of
Intellect (*nous*), embodied in the Demiurge, who both plans and
constructs a world that is as excellent as its nature allows it to be.
The *Timaeus* is widely regarded as one of the most important, and
one of the most philosophically challenging, of all Plato's works, but
Atlantis is not mentioned in it once Critias has stimulated our desire
to know more. There are more important philosophical issues to be
resolved first.

CHAPTER 5

Plato's *Critias*

....

Once the intense discussions of the *Timaeus* are over, its eponymous
speaker welcomes the chance to have a rest. He prays to the *Cosmos*
(Universe), and, as they've all agreed, he hands on the task of speaking next to Critias, who applauds the excellence of Timaeus' speech,
asks for indulgence from his comrades, and accepts what he regards
as a more difficult assignment.

> It is easier, Timaeus, to appear to speak satisfactorily to men
> about the gods, than to us about mortals. For when the listen-
> ers are in a state of inexperience and complete ignorance
> about a matter, such a state of mind affords great opportuni-
> ties to the person who is going to discourse on that matter;
> and we know what our state is concerning knowledge of the
> gods.[1]

To illustrate his point, Critias uses an analogy of a painter:

> The accounts given by us all must be, of course, of the nature
> of imitations[2] and representations; and if we look at the
> portraiture of divine and of human bodies as executed by
> painters, in respect of the ease or difficulty with which they
> succeed in imitating their subjects in the opinion of onlook-
> ers, we shall notice in the first place that as regards the earth
> and mountains and rivers and woods and the whole of
> heaven, with the things that exist and move therein, we are
> content if a man is able to represent them with even a small

degree of likeness; and further, that, inasmuch as we have no
exact knowledge about such objects, we do not examine
closely or criticise the paintings, but tolerate, in such cases,
an inexact and deceptive sketch. On the other hand, whenever a painter tries to render a likeness of our own bodies, we
quickly perceive what is defective because of our constant
familiar acquaintance with them, and become severe critics
of him who fails to bring out to the full all the points of similarity. And precisely the same thing happens, as we should
notice, in the case of discourses.[3]

Timaeus has been talking about the gods, but Critias reckons it's
harder to talk about mortals: he thinks that because we don't know
very much about what is celestial and divine, we examine it with less
precision than what is mortal and human, which we are more familiar with:

To an account given now on the spur of the moment[4] indulgence must be granted, should we fail to make it a wholly
fitting representation; for one must conceive of mortal
objects as being difficult, and not easy, to represent
satisfactorily.[5]

Socrates grants Critias' request very graciously, and says that he
will also treat Hermocrates in the same way when his turn comes to
speak (even though Hermocrates never gets the chance because the
trilogy is unfinished). Hermocrates then tells Critias to get on with
it. He should invoke Apollo and the Muses, and show them the
excellence of the ancient citizens that he's already spoken about.
Revealingly, the aged Critias says that in addition to the deities
mentioned by Hermocrates, he must call upon Mnemosyne, the
goddess of Memory. This might make us pause for thought in any

assessment of how true what he is about to say might be. He is aware that pretty well all the most important parts of his speech will depend on how well he remembers the details, and thinks that *if* he can remember and report the tale told by the Egyptian priests and passed on to Solon, he will have done his job well. The question is how well he remembers. He is talking about things that happened a very long time ago indeed.

Finally, Critias says it is time to stop procrastinating. He starts his amazing story . . .

TIMESCALE AND CATASTROPHE

CRITIAS: [108e] Okay, then. First of all, we need to remember that, as it has been disclosed, the total number of years that has gone by since the war that took place between the people living outside the Pillars of Heracles and all those within them, was 9,000.[6] I must now describe this war thoroughly. It was said that this city of ours was the leader of the one side and fought throughout the entire war, while the other side were commanded by the kings[7] of the island of Atlantis, which we said was, once upon a time, an island[8] bigger[9] than Libya and Asia. But now that it has been sunk by earthquakes, it has created a barrier of impenetrable mud that hinders people from sailing out from here to any part of the Ocean, [109a] with the result that they can't go any further.[10] With regard to the many barbarian tribes and peoples of the Greeks which existed then, the course of the narrative will unroll, point by point, so to speak, the facts as they appear on each occasion; but first of all I have to give the facts about the Athenians of that day, and about the enemies that they fought against, and also the respective military capabilities and forms of government of the two sides. We ought to give priority in our account to Athens.[11]

[109b] Once upon a time the gods were dividing up the whole earth between them according to its regions. And there was no strife:[12] I mean, it wouldn't be reasonable to believe that the gods didn't know what was appropriate for each of them, or that, knowing this, they would try to get for themselves things that more rightfully belonged to others by quarrels. So, by the allocations of justice they obtained what they wished for as their own portion, and established communities in their lands. And when they had set up these communities, they reared us like shepherds rear their flocks, as their possessions and nurslings, except they didn't control our bodies with bodily force like shepherds do with their flocks, [109c] guiding them with blows from their sticks, but rather, like a helmsman steering from the prow, from where the animal is most manageable – but using persuasion as a rudder – they took hold of our minds as they thought best, and in this way they steered the whole human race.

Now, the various gods set the various territories which they had been allocated in order. But Hephaestus and Athena, who, as brother and sister sprung from the same father have an inherited nature in common, and also pursue the same goals in their love of wisdom and technical skill, both obtained this land, which was naturally suitable and adapted for excellence and wisdom, [109d] as their joint allocation.[13] And there they implanted in the earth some good men of the soil,[14] and put into their minds the organisation of the government. The names of these people have been preserved, but their deeds have been lost sight of because of the repeated destruction of the people who received the tradition, and because of the long lapse of time.

You see, as was said before,[15] the people that always survived were illiterate mountain dwellers who had only heard the names of the rulers, but very little about their actions apart from that. They were delighted to [109e] pass on these names to their children, but they knew nothing of the virtues and laws of their predecessors, apart from some obscure bits of hearsay about them. And in any case, because they and their children [110a] lacked the bare necessities of life for many generations, they focused their attention on the things they didn't have, and talked about those; they didn't really care about things that had happened in the distant past. For myth-telling and investigating the past come to communities in company with leisure-time, whenever they see that some people are equipped with the necessities of life, but not before that.[16] This is why names of the early kings have been preserved but not their achievements.

I say this on the grounds that Solon said that in their narrative of the war the priests mentioned the names of Cecrops, and Erechtheus, Erichthonius and Erysichthon,[17] [110b] plus most of the things that are recorded about each of the names of the other heroes who come before Theseus, and similarly the names of the women.[18] And what's more, Solon said that as far as the form of the statue of the goddess Athena was concerned, it was because military activities at that period were common to both women and men that, following that custom, the image of the goddess-in-full-armour was set up at that time.[19] And this is evidence that with all [110c] animals that feed together in herds, both male and female alike, the entire species is naturally capable, as a group, of practising its own appropriate type of excellence.

PRIMAEVAL ATHENS: LANDSCAPE, PEOPLE AND POLITICAL INSTITUTIONS

Now, various classes of citizens inhabited the territory of Athens in those days: those involved in manufacture; people who grew food on the land; and the warrior class, who at the beginning had been set apart by divine men, and who lived by themselves.[20] The warriors had everything that was necessary for their maintenance and education: none of them had any private property; [110d] they regarded

everything they had as communal to everyone; they did not require
that they should receive anything from the other citizens apart from
their basic sustenance; and really they practised all the ways of living
that we talked about yesterday when we were discussing our hypo-
thetical 'Guardians'.[21]

And indeed what used to be said about our country is both plausible and true, namely that, in the first place, its boundaries at that
time were delimited by the Isthmus of Corinth, and in relation to
the rest of mainland Greece they reached as far as [110e] the peaks
of Mount Cithaeron and Mount Parnes, coming down and encompassing the region of Oropus on the right and the River Asopus as
the limit on the left facing the sea.[22] It surpassed every other land in
terms of its fertility, and for that reason it could, in those days,
support a large army that was free from the demands of agricultural
work.[23] There is strong proof of its fertility: the remnant of it that
now exists is on a par with any other in the all-productive abundance
of its fruits and in the richness of its pasture for all manner of
beasts.

But in those days the high quality was matched by great quantity.
How can this be made credible? And on what basis might we say
that it is a remnant of the land that then existed?[24] The whole territory lies like a long promontory[25] stretching out from the rest of the
continent into the sea, and the basin of the sea which surrounds it
is, as it happens, extremely deep. Many great floods have occurred
during the 9,000 years[26] – because that is the number of years
which have gone by from that time until the present day [111b] – and
during that time and through so many calamities, there has not
been any significant accumulation of soil coming down from the
high land as in other places, but the earth has always slipped away
all round and disappeared into the depths. And, just like happens
with small islands, you are left with something rather like the bones
of a sick person's body: the fat and soft parts of the soil have wasted

away, and only the skinny body of the land is left behind.[27] But at that time, when the country was still unravaged, [111c] it had high hills instead of mountains, and what are now called the Plains of Stony Ground were full of rich soil, and there was plenty of wood in the mountains, of which there are still visible traces today. For although some of the mountains now only provide sustenance for bees, it's not long since trees were chopped down from that area to make roof-timbers for the largest building projects, and the roofs are still standing.[28] And there were also lots of other high trees of the cultivated type, which bore inconceivable amounts of food for the cattle. In addition [111d] to that, the soil reaped the fruits of the annual rainfall from Zeus, which was not lost, as it is now, by it flowing off the bare land into the sea. The rain was abundant, and was absorbed and stored in the impervious clayey earth, so that the water that was gulped down by the higher ground was discharged into the hollows, providing abundant springs and flowing rivers everywhere. You can still see sacred shrines in the places where springs once existed, which proves that my present description of the land is true. [111e] This, then, was the natural state of the rest of the country, and it was tended, as you'd expect, by trusty farmers who were completely focused on their work. They were lovers of honour and naturally suited to the job,[29] and they had the finest land, more than enough water[30] and, in the skies above, a climate that was extremely well-balanced.[31]

As far as the city is concerned, at that time it was laid out like this. For a start, the Acropolis wasn't like it is now. [112a] The fact is that one single night of extraordinary rain dissolved it away and denuded it of soil, and earthquakes happened simultaneously with the third of the violent floods that happened before the great destruction in the time of Deucalion.[32] But prior to that, in earlier days, in terms of its size it went down towards the Eridanus and Ilissus Rivers, embraced the Pnyx Hill within it, had Mount Lycabettus as its border on the side opposite the Pnyx, and was all rich in soil and almost completely level on the top.[33] [112b] Outside the Acropolis, right underneath its sides, lived the craftsmen and the workers who farmed the land nearby. Up above, alone by themselves, around the Temple of Athena and Hephaestus, lived the warrior class,[34] who had surrounded those parts with one enclosing wall, like a garden of a single dwelling.[35]

On the north side of it they inhabited their communal dwellings and constructed winter mess-rooms, plus everything that was necessary for their [112c] common way of life in respect of their houses and temples. But there was no gold and silver – they didn't use this for anything whatsoever.[36] On the contrary, in the modest houses they constructed, they pursued a middle way between arrogant ostentatiousness and tight-fistedness, and they and their children's children grew old in them before handing them down unaltered[37] to others who were like themselves. In the summertime, as is natural, they abandoned their gardens and gymnasia and mess-rooms, and used the southern side of the Acropolis for the same purposes. In the region where the Acropolis is now, there was a single spring,[38] which [112d] was blocked up by the earthquake, and has left only a few trickling streams that still exist in the area, but in the past it provided an abundant flow for everyone, at an even temperature in both winter and summer. So this was the fashion in which they lived:[39] they were both the guardians of their own citizens and the leaders of the other Greeks, who followed them consentingly.[40] And they took special care to ensure that as far as possible there was at all times the same number[41] of men and women who were of military age and capability – [112e] i.e. about 20,000.

So this was the kind of people they were, and this is how they justly administered their own affairs and those of Greece. They were renowned across all of Europe and Asia for the beauty of their bodies and the multifarious virtues of their souls, and they were the most eminent of all the people who lived in those times. But now, if I haven't been deprived of the memory of what I heard when I was a kid,[42] I will publicly divulge the characteristics and origins of the people who made war against them. Friends should share everything in common.

ATLANTIS: NAMES, MYTHOLOGY AND THE PHYSICAL FEATURES OF THE ISLAND

[113a] But briefly, before I start my narrative, I need to explain something, in case you're surprised at hearing Greek names applied to barbarian people. You'll now learn the reason for this. Solon was intending to use the story in his own poem, and when he asked about the meaning of the names, he found out that when the Egyptians wrote them down they had translated the originals into their own language. So he reversed the process: when he learned the meaning of each name, [113b] he wrote it down in Greek.[43] My grandfather had possession of the original manuscript, and I still have it now.[44] I often studied it when I was a child. So don't be surprised if you hear names like the ones we use here. I've told you the reason why. The story that was told then was a long one, and it started like this . . .

I've already mentioned, when I was speaking about the allocations of the gods,[45] that they distributed the whole earth into portions – some larger [113c], some smaller – and established temples and sacrifices for themselves. Poseidon was allotted the Island of Atlantis,[46] and he settled the children that he sired by a mortal woman in a specific area of the island. And this is what it was like. On the coast, in the middle of the whole island,[47] there was a plain which, of all the plains that exist, was said to be the most beautiful and plentiful in its fertility. Near the plain again, also in the centre of it, at a distance of about 10 km,[48] there was a mountain that was low on every side. Here on the mountain lived one of the original [113d] earth-born inhabitants[49] called Euenor, along with his wife Leucippe. They had an only daughter called Cleito.[50] When Cleito had just reached marriageable age, both her mother and father died. But Poseidon fell in lust[51] with her. Then he had sex with her. And he fortified the hill where she lived by enclosing it, like a man using a lathe, in a circle with alternate concentric rings of sea and land, two of land and three of sea, equidistant from the middle of the island,[52] [113e] so that it was inaccessible to men (for neither ships nor sailing existed in those days).[53]

And as is natural for a god, Poseidon easily put the central island in order: he made two springs of water flow up from under the earth, one hot and the other cold,[54] and provided all kinds of abundant produce from the earth. He sired five pairs of male twins, raised them, and divided the whole Island of Atlantis into ten[55] portions which he assigned to each them: the elder of the eldest pair of twins [114a] got his mother's residence and the allotted portion around it, which was the biggest and best, and Poseidon made him King over the others:[56] they were each made governors of many people and a large tract of land.

He named all of them. To the eldest, their king, he gave the name from which the whole island and the ocean took their title 'Atlantic': Atlas, [114b] the first ruler at that time; to his younger twin brother, who was allotted the furthest point of the island towards the Pillars of Heracles, facing the region that is now called Gadeira after that place, he gave the name Eumelus in Greek but Gadeirus in the language of Atlantis,[57] which is the very name which presumably provided the current title; of the second pair he called one Ampheres[58] and the other Euaimon;[59] the elder of the third pair was called Mneseus,[60] [114c] the one who followed him was named Autochthon;[61] the elder of the fourth pair was Elasippus,[62] the

95

younger was Mestor;[63] and the name bestowed on the elder of the fifth pair was Azaes,[64] and Diaprepes[65] on the younger. So, all these and many generations of their descendants lived and governed many other islands[66] throughout the Ocean and, as was previously said,[67] they also ruled the people inside of the Strait of Gibraltar as far as Egypt and Tyrrhenia.

[114d] Atlas created a long line of honourable descendants. Across many generations the eldest son always handed power over to his eldest sons, and in that way they preserved the kingdom.[68] They also possessed the kind of massive wealth that had never before been seen in any royal dynasty, and which will never easily occur in the future,[69] and they were provided with everything they could possibly need, be this in the city or in the rest of the countryside.

Because of their empire many things were imported [114e] from outside, although the island itself provided most of what they needed for day-to-day life:[70] in the first place they extracted whatever metals were in the earth, both solid as well as fusible,[71] including one that is now only a name. Then, though, it was much more than a name: it was '*oreikhalkon*' or 'mountain bronze'.[72] It was dug out of the earth in many areas of the island, and in those days it was the most precious metal apart from gold. There was a plentiful supply of timber from the woodlands for carpenters to work with, and ample resources to support both domesticated and wild animals. Moreover, there was a great profusion of elephants[73] on the island. For there was ample pasturage, not just for all the other animals which live in the lakes and marshes and rivers, [115a] or in the mountains or on the plains, but also for this beast – the biggest and most voracious of them all.

In addition to this, the earth freely produced all the aromatic essences that it does today, and brought them to perfection: roots, herbs, bushes, fruit extracts and floral essences. There was cultivated produce, cereals which we use for basic nutrition, [115b] pulses (that's the generic name that we give them) which we use to feed ourselves as well; and there were the fruits of orchard trees, hard to store but which provide liquid and solid food and oils which give us amusement and pleasure, and which we serve as a delightful dessert to stimulate people's appetites and counteract fullness[74] – the sacred island produced all these, beautiful and amazing and boundless in their quantity, when it still lay beneath the sun.[75]

The Capital City and Its Buildings

The Atlanteans received all these products from the earth, and they went on constructing [115c] temples, royal residences, harbours and dockyards, and they organised the entire country in the following manner.[76] [See Fig. 5]

The first thing they did was to bridge the rings of sea that surrounded the ancient mother-city, creating a road towards and away from the royal palace. And straight away they built this palace in the district where their god Poseidon and their ancestors had lived, and as each king received it from his predecessor, he embellished the embellishments, [115d] always doing his utmost to outdo the king before him, until they completed a residence that was staggering to behold in terms of size and the beauty of its workmanship.[77]

And beginning from the sea, they excavated a canal 100 m wide, 33 m deep and 10 km long,[78] which united it with the outermost ring, thereby creating access to it by ship, as though to a harbour. They left an opening in it wide enough for the biggest ships to sail into. At the bridges, they made gaps in the rings of land that separated the rings [115e] of sea, wide enough to allow the passage of one trireme at a time from one circle to the next, and roofed the gaps over to make a subterranean sea-way; for the rims of the land-rings were raised a sufficient height above sea-level.[79]

Fig. 5:
CITY PLAN OF ATLANTIS

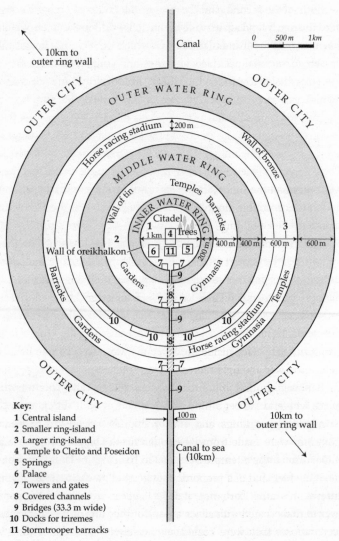

10km to
outer ring wall

Canal

0   500 m   1km

OUTER CITY

OUTER CITY

OUTER WATER RING

Horse racing stadium   ‡200 m

Wall of bronze

MIDDLE WATER RING

Wall of tin

Temples   Barracks

INNER WATER RING

Citadel
1
1 km   4   Trees
2   200 m   400 m   400 m   600 m   600 m
6   11   5
3

Wall of oreikhalkon   7   7

Gardens   9   Gymnasia

Barracks   8   7

Gardens   7

10   9

10   10   Horse racing stadium   Gymnasia

10   8   Temples

7   7

9

OUTER CITY   OUTER CITY

100 m

10km to
outer ring wall

Canal to sea
(10km)

Key:
1 Central island
2 Smaller ring-island
3 Larger ring-island
4 Temple to Cleito and Poseidon
5 Springs
6 Palace
7 Towers and gates
8 Covered channels
9 Bridges (33.3 m wide)
10 Docks for triremes
11 Stormtrooper barracks

Now, the largest of the rings, which was linked to the sea by the canal, was 600 m[80] wide, and the ring of land inside it was of equal breadth; of the second pair, the ring of water was 400 m[81] wide, and the ring of dry land again was equal to it; the ring of water [116a] that surrounded the central island itself was 200 m[82] across. This island, on which the royal palace stood, was 1 km[83] in diameter.[84]

Now, they surrounded the island, and the rings and the bridge (which was 33.3 m[85] in width) with a stone wall all the way round, placing towers and gates at the bridges on either side where they crossed the water.[86] The stone used in the construction of these was white, black [116b] and red.[87] It was quarried from underneath the central island, all around it, and from the two rings of land, on both the outer and the inner side, and as they extracted it they hollowed out interior double dockyards, roofed over by the native rock.[88] Some of their buildings were simple, but others were patterned,[89] mixing different types of stone for the sake of pleasure, giving the buildings an inherent attractiveness. And they smeared the entire circuit of the wall that encompassed the outer ring with bronze, as though with paint, melted tin all over the inner wall, and [116c] applied *oreikhalkon*, sparkling like fire, to the one which went round the acropolis itself.[90]

The royal palace inside the acropolis was arranged like this. In the centre was a temple sacred to Cleito and Poseidon, consecrated as hallowed ground and encircled by a golden wall. This was the place where at the beginning they had conceived and begotten the family of the ten kings, and it was there that year by year seasonal offerings were made from the ten districts as sacrifices to each of them. There was a temple of Poseidon [116d] himself, 200 m long, 100 m wide[91] and of a proportionate height to look at, albeit having something rather barbaric[92] about its appearance. The outside of it was entirely coated with silver, apart from the topmost architectural decorations: they were coated with gold. As for the interior, the visible parts of the ceiling were entirely made of ivory, embellished with gold, silver and *oreikhalkon*, and they coated all of the walls, columns and floor with *oreikhalkon*.[93] And they set up golden statues in it: the god standing in a chariot – the driver of six winged [116e] horses – and of such a size that he touched the ceiling with his head; 100 Nereids – in those days they thought that was their number[94] – in a circle around him, riding on dolphins;[95] and many other statues dedicated by private individuals.

And outside, around the temple, stood golden images of all the rulers who were descended from the ten kings, plus their wives, and many other large dedications made by kings and private people both from the city itself and from the foreign ones over which they ruled. There was an altar [117a] as well, which matched its setting in terms of its size and workmanship, and likewise the palace suited the greatness of the kingdom and the magnificence of the temples.

The two springs, flowing cold and hot,[96] provided an unlimited supply of water, wonderfully suited by nature, in its pleasantness and quality, for the use to which it was put. They erected buildings around the springs along with plantations of trees that were appropriate [117b] to the waters, and all around they constructed cisterns, some of them open-air, others roofed over for use in the winter as hot baths.[97] There were separate suites for royalty and for private individuals, and also for women, and others for horses and other beasts of burden, all of which were allocated their own appropriate type of decoration.[98] They led the outflowing water into the grove of Poseidon, which, because of the richness of the soil, contained all kinds of trees that were of extraordinary beauty and height, and also channelled it to the outer ring-islands by means of aqueducts down along the bridges.[99] [117c] Here they had constructed many temples for many gods, many gardens and many exercise areas,[100] some for men and some for horses in both of the ring-islands. And as well as these, there was a space reserved in the middle of the larger island[101] as a race-course,

200 m wide and as long as a complete circuit of the island,[102] for equestrian competition. Round it, on this side and on that, were the barracks [117d] of the main contingent of the stormtroopers;[103] a more trustworthy garrison was stationed on the smaller ring-island closer to the citadel; and those who were the most trustworthy of all had quarters assigned to them inside the acropolis, near the kings themselves. And the dockyards were full of triremes and all the tackle that triremes require.[104] Everything was properly equipped.

So that's how everything was organised around the residence of the kings. Heading away from there, as you went past the outer harbours, three of them, you came to a wall that went round in a circle starting at [117e] the sea at a constant distance of 10 km from the largest ring and harbour, and which completed its circuit by coming back on itself at the mouth of the canal by the sea.[105] The whole of this wall was packed with many densely built houses, and the canal and large harbour were full of ships and merchants arriving from everywhere, who from out of their vast numbers caused shouting and all kinds of racket and clattering in the day and throughout the night.[106]

THE ISLAND BEYOND THE CAPITAL CITY

So, as far as the city and the environs of the ancient dwelling are concerned, I have now recorded it more or less as it was originally recounted.[107] But I must also try to remember[108] the nature and the type of organisation of the rest of [118a] the country.[109] To start with, the entire country was said to be extremely high and to rise precipitously above the level of the sea,[110] but the territory immediately about and surrounding the city was a plain, which was in turn enclosed by mountains which stretched down as far as the sea. This plain was smooth and even and was rectangular in shape, extending 600 km on either side, and 400 km wide at the centre, measuring from the sea.[111] [118b] This entire area of the island faced towards the south, and was sheltered from the north.[112] The mountains that surrounded it at that time were famous for being more numerous, bigger and more beautiful than any which still exist now; and they had in them many rich villages of country dwellers, not to mention rivers and lakes and meadows, which provided abundant nutrition for all kinds of domesticated and wild animals, and woodland which, both in quantity and in the variety[113] of its types, was abundant for each individual requirement of every kind of work.

This is what the plain was like, [118c] as it had been modified by the natural environment and the work of many kings over a long period of time. [See Fig. 6] It was originally, as I said, mostly rectangular, with straight sides, and elongated. Where it deviated from this shape they made it straight by digging a ditch round about it.[114] Its depth and breadth and length might sound unbelievable for a man-made project, especially when it was in addition to all the other operations, but I must report them as I was told them, whether they are true or not:[115] it was excavated to a depth of 33.3 m; it was 200 m wide[116] everywhere; [118d] and, because it was dug right round the entire plain, its length was 2,000 km.[117] It received the streams, which came down from the mountains, and after circling around the plain, and converging on the city from both sides, it was allowed to discharge into the sea at that point.[118] Further inland, straight canals 33.3 m wide[119] were cut through the plain, and again they discharged into the ditch on the seaward side, with the distance between them being 20 km.[120] They cut transverse channels from one canal into another and also to the city, and by this means [118e] they transported timber down from the mountains into the town, and also seasonal produce by boat.[121] They reaped the produce of the land twice a year, exploiting the rains from Zeus in the winter and the waters which the earth brought forth in the summer, bringing the streams in from the ditches.[122]

Fig. 6:

THE PLAIN OF ATLANTIS

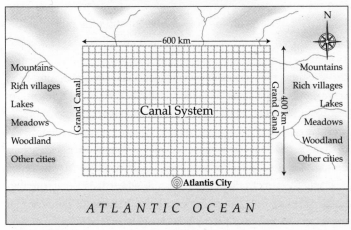

MILITARY ARRANGEMENTS

As far as their manpower was concerned, it had been prescribed that [119a] each allotment should provide one leader of all the men in the plain who were fit for military service. The size of the allotments was 2 x 2 km, and there were 60,000 of them in total.[123] The number of the men in the mountains and in the rest of the country was said to be infinite, and they were all assigned to these allotments and their leaders on the basis of their districts and villages.

It was prescribed that for war each leader should provide: a sixth part of the equipment of a war chariot, so as to make a total complement of 10,000, plus two horses and [119b] riders for them; and additionally a pair of horses without a chariot, equipped with a fighter with a small shield[124] who dismounts to fight, and a charioteer to drive them both and to stand behind him; two hoplites; archers and slingers – two of each type; light-armed stone throwers and javelin men – three of each type; and four sailors to make up the crew of 1,200 ships.[125] Such then were the military dispositions of the royal city; those of the other nine varied in detail and it'd take a long time to describe them.

THE POLITICAL STRUCTURE OF ATLANTIS

[119c] From the outset, their magistracies and honours were arranged like this. Each of the ten kings had absolute authority, in his own individual region and in his own city, over citizens and, in most cases, over the laws, and could punish or execute whoever he wished.[126] But the distribution of power among them, and their mutual relations, were subject to the orders of Poseidon, handed down to them by the law and by the records inscribed by the first kings on a pillar of *oreikhalkon* which was situated at the centre of the island in the [119d] temple of Poseidon. There they gathered together alternately every fifth and then every sixth year (thereby assigning equal value to the even and to the odd[127]), and when they had done so, they deliberated on matters of common interest and carefully examined whether anyone was transgressing, and gave judgement. And when they were about to give judgement they first gave pledges to one another that were like this. There were free-range bulls in the temple of Poseidon, and the ten kings, on their own by themselves, prayed to the god that they might capture a victim that was gratifying [119e] to him, and hunted after the bulls, not with iron weaponry but with sticks and lassoes.[128] And they led the bull that they caught up to the pillar and slaughtered it by slitting its throat over the top of the pillar, so that its blood ran down the inscription.[129] On the pillar, besides the laws, there was inscribed an oath invoking mighty curses upon anyone who disobeyed them.

Then, when they had finished sacrificing [120a] according to their laws and were consecrating all the limbs of the bull, they mixed a bowl of wine and threw in one clot of blood on behalf of each of them, and they carried the rest of the blood to the fire after they had purified the pillar. After this, they drew wine from the bowl using golden dishes, and, pouring a libation over the fire, they swore: to give judgement according to the laws on the pillar; to exact punishment if anyone happened to have been an offender in the past; that they would not willingly transgress any of the writings on the pillar; and that they would neither give orders nor [120b] obey anyone who issued orders unless they were in line with the laws of their father Poseidon. Each of them swore this oath on behalf of himself and his descendants, drank, and dedicated his bowl in the temple of the god. They spent some time over dinner and necessary matters, and then, when darkness fell and the sacrificial fire had died down, they all donned the most gorgeous dark blue[130] robes and sat on the ground by the embers of fire where they had sworn the oath, by night, [120c], extinguishing all the fire that was around the temple. And if any one of them accused them of some transgression, they gave and received judgement. Afterwards, when they had pronounced judgement, once dawn had broken they inscribed their judicial decisions on a golden tablet and dedicated it along with their robes as a record.

Among many other specific laws governing the prerogatives of the several kings the most important were: that they should never take up arms against each other; that they should come to each other's help if any one of them tried to overthrow the royal family in any city; that, like their ancestors before them, they should have communal discussions [120d] concerning war and other matters, conceding the hegemony to the descendants of Atlas; but that a king should not have the right to execute any of his kinsmen unless he had the consent of the majority of the ten.

Decline and Punishment

This was the nature and extent of the power which existed in those regions at that time, and which Zeus organised in battle array and brought against our lands for something like the following reason, so the story goes.[131]

[120e] For many generations, as long as the divine part of their nature was sufficiently strong, they were obedient to the laws and friendly towards their innate divinity. They possessed spirits that were true and great in every way, responding with moderation and good sense not only to the various fortunes that came their way but also to one another. For that reason, they despised everything but virtue, thought little [121a] of their current prosperity, and bore the 'burden' of their gold and other possessions easily. Neither did they get drunk on luxury – on account of their wealth – and nor did they lose control of themselves and stagger around; on the contrary, they were sober, and saw clearly that all these good things grow out of common friendship and moral excellence, whereas too much enthusiasm and respect for them diminishes the material possessions and destroys virtue along with them.

As a result of this kind of reasoning, and as long as their divine nature stayed with them, everything that I've just been talking about continued to grow. But when the portion of divinity in them began to become faded through [121b] frequently being mixed up with a large element of mortality, and their human side gained the ascendancy, then they weren't able to bear the good things which they had, and they began to disgrace themselves. To those who could see it, they became visibly shameful, because they had lost the most beautiful things from their most valuable assets; but to those who are unable to see the true life that leads to happiness, that was the moment when they seemed to be at their happiest and most beautiful, filled as they were greed and a lawless sense of power.[132]

Zeus, the god of gods, who reigns according to law, and is able to see such things, perceived that a fine race had degenerated into a miserable state and made a decision to discipline them, [121c] so that they might be brought to their senses and become morally harmonious.[133] So, he summoned all the deities to his own most glorious residence, which stands at the centre of the cosmos and looks out over everything which participates in creation. And when they had assembled, he said—

The dialogue cuts off in mid-sentence, and there is no evidence at all that Plato wrote any more than this.[134] The prospective trilogy has come to a dead end, and, for whatever reason – loss of patience? Loss of confidence? – this dialogue remains unfinished and the *Hermocrates*, which the interlocutors have promised us, was never written. The entire purpose of the trilogy, to explore the functioning of the Ideal State in wartime, is therefore, never really dealt with. It is, however, interesting to observe that Zeus' words up to this point imply that Atlantis is only going to be taught a very severe lesson in order to make it see good moral sense. Although the island is sunk in the *Timaeus*, there could be a possibility that Plato might have resurrected it at some future point. Zeus was seeking to restore the order which the Atlanteans have violated, and once that has been done, Atlantis might have had an opportunity to rise again. It would not do so in Plato's work – he had never mentioned Atlantis before, and he never mentions it again – but over the ensuing millennia, there would be a plethora of other writers who would seek to locate it and bring it back from the depths.

CHAPTER 6

Plato's Atlantis in Classical Antiquity

....

Plato's story of Atlantis did not make the impression on the ancients that it has made on us. There are no extant treatises about Atlantis: but if they did exist, they have vanished without a trace, and there are no references to them in any other works. Neither were there any dramatic, poetic or historical works inspired by the tale, leaving us dependent on random references from a variety of ancient writers, which can be extremely dismissive of the story or very accepting, but not always reliable. Atlantis lies on the road less travelled.

THEOPOMPUS OF CHIOS

The historian Theopompus of Chios, a younger contemporary of Plato, born in 378/377 BC, was 'an eye-witness of many events and conversed with many of the eminent men and generals of his day because of his profession as a historian, and also with popular leaders and philosophers'.[1] It is not inconceivable that Plato was one of those people, although their relationship may have been fractious. Theopompus is alleged to have slandered Plato at the court of Philip II of Macedon, possibly when Philip was in the process of hiring a tutor for his son Alexander (the Great), although if Theopompus thought this would help him get the job, he was mistaken: Philip hired Plato's student, Aristotle. Theopompus' *Against Plato's School*[2] claimed that most of Plato's dialogues were useless or full of lies, and that the majority of them were actually by other authors.

However, this seems ironic given that Aelian, a Roman teacher of rhetoric (*c.* AD 175–*c.* 235), exposes how Theopompus quite flagrantly ripped off the *Timaeus* and the *Critias*:[3]

> Theopompus describes a meeting between Midas the Phrygian and Silenus[4] [. . .] Silenus spoke to Midas on the following themes.
>
> Europe, Asia, and Libya are islands, around which the ocean flows, and the only continent is the one surrounding the outside of this world. He explained how infinitely big it is, that it supports other large animals and men twice the size of those who live here. Their lives are not the same length as ours, but in fact twice as long. There are many large cities, with various styles of life, and laws in force among them are different from those customary among us. He said there were two very big cities, not at all like each other, one called Warlike [*Makhimos*] and the other Pious [*Eusebēs*]. The inhabitants of Pious live in peace and with great wealth; they obtain the fruits of the earth without the plough and oxen, and they have no need to farm and cultivate. They remain healthy and free of disease, he said, and end their lives full of laughter and contented. They are indisputably just, so that even the gods frequently deign to visit them. The citizens of Warlike are for their part very bellicose; they are born with weapons, they are always fighting, and they subdue their neighbours; this one city controls a great many nations. The inhabitants are not less than twenty million. Sometimes they die of illness, but this is rare, since for the most part they lose their lives in battle, wounded by stones or wooden clubs (they cannot be harmed by iron). They have an abundance of gold and silver, so that to them gold is of less value than iron is to us. He said they had once tried to cross over to these

islands of ours, and sailed over the ocean with a force of ten million until they reached the Hyperboreans. Learning that the latter were the richest of our peoples, they felt contempt for them as inferior beings of lowly fortunes, and for that reason dismissed the idea of travelling further.

He added an even more remarkable fact. He said that some men called Meropes live among them in numerous large cities, and on the edge of their territory is a place named Point of No Return, which looks like a chasm and is filled neither by light nor darkness, but is overlaid by a haze of a murky red colour. Two rivers run past this locality, one named Pleasure, the other Grief. Along the banks of both stand trees the size of a large plane. Those by the river Grief bear fruit, which has this quality: if someone tastes it he sheds so great a quantity of tears that he melts into laments for all the rest of his life and dies in this condition. The other trees, growing by the river Pleasure, produce a fruit that is quite the opposite. The person who tastes it loses all his previous desires; and if he had any love, he forgets it as well, and is slowly rejuvenated, recovering the previous stages of life that he has passed through. Casting off his old age he returns to his prime and finds his way back to the years of adolescence; then he becomes a child and an infant, after which he dies.[5]

There is little that is original here: the land of the Meropes is a version of the land of the Cimmerians in Homer's *Odyssey*; the contrast between imperialistic Warlike and peace-loving Pious, show that Theopompus knew Plato's *Critias* very well; Warlike's intended overwhelming seaborne assault on the Hyperboreans resembles Atlantis' on Athens; and the Meropes are lifted straight out of Plato's *Statesman*. This might be plagiarism, but at least

Theopompus recognised Plato's tale as an allegory, and got the point of it.

There are those who have argued that Theopompus' narrative could indicate an Atlantis tradition that does not go back to Plato. Robert Graves suggested that 'Silenus' sounds like 'Solon', and that Aelian 'seems to have had access at second or third hand to a comedy by Thespis, or his pupil Pratinas, ridiculing Solon for the Utopian lies told in the epic poem [i.e. Solon's Atlantis poem], and presenting him as Silenus, wandering footloose about Egypt and Asia Minor.'[6] If this is the case, Theopompus and Aelian would certainly not be transmitting an independent tradition, but it could conceivably suggest that Plato's tale came down from Solon. But in either case, Graves' suggestion is the purest speculation: there is not the slightest evidence to back up his assertion. There is only one source for the Atlantis story, and that is Plato.

Apollodorus was also deeply sceptical about 'Meropis [sic]', which he includes in an entertaining list of weird and wonderful made-up places and people that includes Hesiod's 'men who are half-dog'; Alcman's 'web-footed men'; Aeschylus' 'men with eyes in their breasts'; the settlement of the Gorgons and Hesperides; Euhemerus' 'Land of Panchaea'; and the 'City of Dionysus', which it is impossible for the same man ever to find twice.[7]

There is also a bizarre comment made by Aelian that

the male Ram-fish has a white band running round its forehead (you might describe it as the tiara of a Lysimachus or an Antigonus or of some other king of Macedon[8]), but the female has curls, just as cocks have wattles, attached below its neck [. . .] Those who live on the shores of Ocean tell a fable of how the ancient kings of Atlantis, sprung from the seed of Poseidon, wore upon their head the bands from the male Ram-fish, as an emblem of their authority, while their wives, the queens, wore the curls of the females as a proof of theirs.[9]

Unfortunately, Aelian doesn't give the source of this information, but the fact that the tiaras remind him of those worn by the Macedonian successors to Alexander the Great suggests that his source was no earlier than about 300 BC. But, in any case, he is incredibly dismissive of Theopompus:

> If someone is prepared to believe the author from Chios, let this tale be credited; but to me he seems a clever inventor of stories,[10] both in this and in other cases.[11]

ARISTOTLE AND PSEUDO-ARISTOTLE: INVENTION AND OBLITERATION

Theopompus was by no means Plato's only critic, and there seems to have been a certain amount of controversy about Atlantis after his death. As usual, we are hampered by the lack of contemporary sources and have to rely on information provided by authors who lived centuries later, but the two figures on whom the discussion centres are Plato's pupil Aristotle (c. 384–c. 322 BC) and Crantor of Soli in Cilicia (approximately 335–275 BC), who is credited with writing the first commentary on the dialogues. Conventional opinion holds that Aristotle thought that the Atlantis tale was entirely Plato's invention, whereas Crantor believed the story completely.

Our key source here is the fifth-century AD neo-Platonist Proclus (AD 410/2–85), who was the head or 'successor' (of Plato) of the Academy for almost fifty years. He wrote a commentary on the *Timaeus* (*In Timaeum*), where he discusses the early debate about the Atlantis tale, albeit at a distance of almost 700 years after Plato. In respect of the moment where the earth swallows Athens and the sea engulfs Atlantis, Proclus says:

Hence one should not say that the one who obliterated the evidence undermines his subject matter, just like Homer in the case of the Phaeacians or of the wall made by the Greeks. For what has been said has not been invented, but is true.[12]

With these examples, just as with Atlantis, we witness destruction perpetrated by Poseidon and water. In the *Odyssey*, Poseidon turns the Phaeacian ship that carried Odysseus home into stone, in order to stop the Phaeacians escorting seafarers in future, and also expressed a wish to envelop their city with a high mountain. Whether he does the latter is not made clear, but the Phaeacians now completely disappear from the Greek radar.[13] 'The wall made by the Greeks' is their camp at Troy, which was totally obliterated by Poseidon and Apollo (flooding by rivers plus destruction by earthquakes) and Zeus (flooding by rain) after the sack of Troy.[14]

The Greek/Achaean[15] wall is also mentioned in a discussion about Atlantis by Strabo:

[Poseidonius, a second/first-century BC Stoic philosopher] does well to cite the statement of Plato that it is possible that the story about the island of Atlantis is not a fiction.[16] Concerning Atlantis Plato relates that Solon, after having made inquiry of the Egyptian priests, reported that Atlantis did once exist, but disappeared – an island no smaller in size than a continent; and Poseidonius thinks that it is better to put the matter in that way than to say of Atlantis:[17]

Its inventor obliterated it, just like the Poet obliterated the wall of the Achaeans.[18]

The overall point here is that Solon/Plato sidestepped the historical ramifications of his fiction by sinking the island that he had created, exactly like Homer did by destroying the Achaean wall. Interestingly, both Proclus and Strabo use the same Greek verbs for 'invent' and 'obliterate' (*plassō* and *aphanizō* respectively), which Critias uses when Atlantis disappears (*ēphanisthē*, the passive of *aphanizo*[19]) and when Socrates talks about invented (*plasthenta*[20]) stories.[21] Plato is effectively being said to follow 'best practice' by working the destruction of the evidence for his invention into the actual story: you can't ask for proof of imaginary things like the Phaeacian ship, the Achaean wall or the Island of Atlantis, because Homer and Plato wrote them out of existence.

Strabo also informs us about where the phrase 'its inventor obliterated it' came from. While discussing Troy, he expresses astonishment that Achaeans failed to fortify their naval station until late in the Trojan War, because

> [Homer] says the wall had only recently been constructed (or else it wasn't constructed at all, but having invented it, the poet then obliterated it, as Aristotle says).[22]

Again, the same words are used for 'invented' [*plasas*] and 'obliterated' [*ēphanisen*].

Aristotle was accepted into Plato's academy as a teenager, and spent twenty years or so studying there until Plato died, so it seems reasonable that he should know a considerable amount about the Atlantis dialogues from their creator at first hand. Aristotle obviously regarded the inundation-motif as Plato's explanation for the lack of evidence that Atlantis ever existed: Atlantis was a literary construct used to make a philosophical point.

Aristotle's stance on Atlantis must be given considerable weight, and it is noticeable that although he had numerous excellent and useful chances to make reference to Atlantis throughout his work, he never took them. For instance, his *On the Heavens*, written while Plato was still alive, and which influenced Christopher Columbus' 'India project',[23] argues that the earth is spherical, in which case

> one should not be too sure of the incredibility of the view of those who conceive that there is continuity between the parts about the Pillars of Hercules[24] and the parts about India, and that in this way the Ocean is one. As further evidence in favour of this they quote the case of elephants, a species occurring in each of these extreme regions, suggesting that the common characteristic of these extremes is explained by their continuity.[25]

The elephants present a golden opportunity for him to deploy Plato's Atlantis, which Critias says could support large numbers of them,[26] and indulge in discussions of the island in the Ocean beyond the Pillars of Heracles. But he lets it go by.

In fact, Aristotle shows barely any interest in Atlantis. Again, in his *Meteorology*, he tells us that 'the sea outside the Pillars of Heracles is shallow thanks to the mud, but calm because it lies in a hollow'.[27] Plato, of course, said that it was the submersion of Atlantis that produced the mud that makes the sea in that region impassable,[28] but although Aristotle replicates his tutor's geographical mistakes, he pointedly ignores the island that he 'invented and then obliterated', and which was used to explain them.

There are other islands in the Atlantic Ocean that appear in the corpus of works attributed to Aristotle, and sometimes enter the 'Atlantis-real-or-imaginary' debate. One such appears in the bizarre *On Marvellous Things Heard*, which scholars strongly agree is not by Aristotle, but which contains much material derived from Theopompus. In this we are told that in the sea outside the Pillars of Heracles they say that a desert island was found by the Carthaginians, having woods of all kinds and navigable rivers, remarkable for all other kinds of fruits, and a few days' voyage away; as the Carthaginians frequented it often owing to its prosperity, and some even lived there, the chief of the Carthaginians announced that they would punish with death any who proposed to sail there, and that they massacred all the inhabitants, that they might not tell the story, and that a crowd might not resort to the island, and get possession of it, and take away the prosperity of the Carthaginians.[29]

The location and prosperous nature of this island can make it interesting to Atlantis-hunters, but Pseudo-Aristotle does not name it as such, and it obviously isn't under water.

Western islands that are semi-submerged do occur elsewhere in *On Marvellous Things Heard*, however:

They say that Phoenicians who live in what is called Gades, on sailing outside the Pillars of Heracles with an east wind for four days, came at once to some desert lands, full of rushes and seaweed, which were not submerged when the tide ebbed, but were covered when the tide was full, upon which were found a quantity of tunny-fish, of incredible size and weight when brought to shore; pickling these and putting them into jars they brought them to Carthage.[30]

'Desert lands, full of rushes and seaweed' are not prime candidates for Atlantis, though, and the author makes nothing of any possible connection.

CRANTOR OF SOLI: *HISTORIA* AND MYTH

Aristotle's remark about invention and obliteration shows that he thought Atlantis was a made-up place. But on the other hand, Crantor of Soli is frequently cited as having the diametrically opposite view. Proclus informs us that

> some say that all this tale about the Atlantines is straightforward *historia*, like the first of Plato's interpreters, Crantor. He says that [Plato] was mocked by his contemporaries for not having discovered his constitution himself, but having translated[31] the [ideas] of the Egyptians. He took so little [or 'so much'[32]] notice of what the mockers said that he actually attributed to the Egyptians this *historia* about the Athenians and Atlanteans, which says how the Athenians had at one time lived under that constitution. The prophets of the Egyptians, Crantor says, also testify [for him], saying that these things are inscribed on pillars that still survive.[33]

Proclus thinks that Crantor felt the Atlantis story was historical, and he uses the word *historia* like we use 'history' – 'a written account of your inquiries; narrative; history' – rather than like Herodotus' 'inquiry'.[34] But this raises the issue of what, for the Ancient Greeks and Romans, *historia*/history really is, or isn't. They certainly didn't demand that writers of *historia* should tell 'the truth'; they believed it was a branch of literature very close to oratory and that style was more important than substance;[35] ancient historians seldom write without a motive, put fictional speeches into the mouths of their main personalities, and have no objection to 'sexing up' the narrative if this suits their purposes. So *historia* doesn't necessarily imply truth, although it doesn't necessarily exclude it. Part of what makes Herodotus' *historia* so readable is its non-historical material, particularly the myths and travellers' tale he has picked up. Similarly, the story that Plato's Critias relates is really just Solon's traveller's tale, but travellers' tales themselves can still count as *historia*. A prime example of this is Lucian of Samosata's ironically titled second-century AD *Alēthes Historia* (True [Hi]story), which satirises the whole genre of ancient travel-writing by making the narrator travel to the moon and meet aliens.[36]

The conversation about the myth of Phaethon that appears in the Atlantis episode also sheds light on how we might interpret Crantor's use of *historia*. In his commentary on the *Timaeus*, Proclus says that he will analyse the Phaethon story *historikōs*, i.e. as *historia*:

> The *historia* asserts that Phaethon, the son of Helios and Clymene daughter of Ocean, veered off course when driving his father's chariot, and Zeus, in fear for the All, struck him with a thunderbolt. Being struck, he fell down upon Eridanus, where the fire coming from him, fuelling itself on the ground, set everything alight [. . .] It is a basic requirement that the conflagration should have happened (for that is the reason for the story's being told).[37]

This is a myth, not a narrative of real events,[38] but Proclus still calls it a *historia*. He feels that stories like this are created to explain events, and so he argues that the event which needs explaining (a world-wide conflagration that set the heavens alight, created the Milky Way, incinerated forests, dried up rivers, contracted the seas, turned the skins of the Ethiopians black and turned North Africa into a desert) really happened. So, for Proclus, the *historia* is the basic *narrative* (the Phaethon story), not the *events* (the conflagration): Proclus' *historia* is not our 'history'; it is our 'myth'.[39] The Ancient Greeks have had such an enormous influence on modern society that it is easy to think of them as being very much 'like us', but there are aspects of their thinking that can also seem very wrong-footing and alien.

So, when Crantor says that the Atlantis story is 'straightforward *historia*' this doesn't mean that he thought it was true. For Proclus that phrase really means 'a narrative that doesn't have an allegorical meaning', but he does say that, unlike Crantor, some interpreters do read the Atlantis story allegorically:

> Others say that it is a myth and an invention,[40] something that never actually happened but gives an indication of things which have either always been so, or always come to be, in the cosmos.[41]

By 'myth' these unnamed 'others' mean a story that has been purposely written to reflect eternal truths, so for them the Atlantis tale is 'false on the surface and true in its hidden meaning'.[42]

Then Proclus introduces another group of interpreters who sit halfway between Crantor and the 'others':

> Some do not rule it out that this could have happened in this way, but think that it is now adopted as [a set of] images of pre-existing rivalry in the universe. For [they say that] 'War is the father of all' as Heraclitus puts it.[43]

This third group are not claiming that the Atlantis story is historically true. They are simply not ruling out the possibility that it might have happened, and Proclus adds a comment whose sentiments many seekers for the lost island would concur with:

> We shouldn't be sceptical about it, even if one were to take what is being said as *historia* only.[44]

Here again *historia* doesn't imply truth, because if it did, Proclus would effectively be saying, 'we shouldn't disbelieve the story, even if one were to take it as true only', which obviously makes no sense.

ATLANTIS: A TALE FROM EGYPT?

The discussion of *historia* highlights the need for a knowledge of the Greek language and its nuances of usage if we are fully to understand Plato's Atlantis tale: we need to understand his culture in order to understand his words and ideas. And in this respect we encounter a further significant problem. There is not the slightest hint in Crantor either that Plato's Atlantis narrative was derived from a generations-old family story, or that Plato wanted the truth about Atlantis preserved for the future. Far from it: Crantor said that Plato was reacting to being ridiculed by his contemporaries for borrowing Egyptian ideas when he was constructing the Ideal State in the *Republic*. Some modern ideological interpretations do argue that the *Republic* has Egyptian roots,[45] but these misunderstand the methods of ancient biographers, who regularly, and without evidence, link specific works to significant events in their authors' lives. Furthermore, the chief mockers would have been the comic poets, for whom prominent contemporary politicians, poets, musicians, scientists, philosophers, plus any general manifestation of cultural change, were prime targets. For instance, in Aristophanes' *Assembly Women*, Praxagora plans to set up an Ideal State run exclusively by women. To the Athenian males in the audience this is both hilarious and outrageous, and her scheme is characterised as being extremely high-brow, and features ideas obviously derived from some early fourth-century philosopher, and which we also find in the *Timaeus*: communal property, communal sex-partners, communal eating, communal living and so on, all of which make excellent material for parody.[46]

The priest from Saïs in the *Timaeus* mentions parallels between Egyptian culture, with its clearly defined social classes and specialist soldiers, and that of Palaeo-Athens.[47] He also talks about some totally unremarkable similarities in weaponry (Egyptians and Greeks both use shields and spears) as if they were highly significant, and to the 'care that Egyptian law has devoted to various divine principles cosmology', from which the Egyptians 'derived all the arts that aim at human health [. . .] even down to divination and medicine of learning [and] other subsidiary studies that are connected' with them.[48] But this hardly matches the Ideal State that Socrates was talking about at the start of the *Timaeus*,[49] and the priest says nothing about communal property, communal wives or the procreation and upbringing of children.

Essentially, when Plato's critics claimed that he'd ripped-off Egyptian institutions to create the *Republic*, their point was not that he was being unoriginal (there wasn't much comic potential in that, and creative artistic borrowing wasn't necessarily seen as a bad thing[50]), but that he'd got the ideas *from Egypt*, which to Athenian thinking was both ridiculous and hilarious. It is true that the Athenians, like many modern Atlantis-seekers, respected the immense antiquity of Egypt's civilisation and had a 'mysterious faith in Egyptian wisdom',[51] even though the Egypt of Herodotus' and Plato's time was ruled by the Persians, who were superseded by the Macedonian Ptolemies after Alexander the Great conquered it, and then by the Romans after the defeat of Cleopatra. It is also true that the Egyptians used the antiquity of their culture to massage their national pride and assert their superiority to the Greeks. ('My culture is older than, and therefore superior to, yours' is a common theme in internet-based Atlantis exchanges, too.) But far more pertinent is the fact that the Athenians stereotyped the Egyptians as duplicitous, dishonest and dishonourable. This image is what matters here: no 'normal' Athenian would ever think that Egypt's institutions were worth copying, and so Plato's interest in Egyptian culture was an open goal to comedians, who could allege that his political ideas were stolen from people that he himself denigrated as unenlightened, greedy, deceitful and just like the Phoenicians, who themselves had been synonymous with cheating, stealing, lying and mischief-making for centuries.[52]

In the twentieth century, the idea of Greek philosophy being influenced by Egypt moved one stage further. The black separatist leader Marcus Garvey (1887–1940), for instance, not only bought into the myth that utopian Egypt was the root of Greek and Roman civilisation, but also that the ancient Egyptians were black Africans and that the Greeks had stolen, not borrowed, their culture:

> Every student of history, of impartial mind, knows that the Negro ruled the world, when white men were savages and barbarians living in caves; that thousands of Negro professors at that time taught in the universities in Alexandria, then the seat of learning; that ancient Egypt gave to the world civilization and that Greece and Rome have robbed Egypt of her arts and letters, and taken all the credit to themselves. It is not surprising, however, that white men should resort to every means to keep Negroes in ignorance of their history, it would be a great shock to their pride to admit to the world today that 3,000 years ago black men excelled in government and were the founders and teachers of art, science and literature.[53]

There is much about Garvey's assertion that is problematical, if not plain wrong,[54] but ideas like this continue to be expressed.[55] For example, Cheikh Anta Diop (1923–86) proposed a highly speculative and unsubstantiated account of the Egyptian 'university curriculum' followed by Greek philosophers: 'every Greek initiate or pupil had to write a final paper on Egyptian cosmogony and the mysteries, irrespective of the curriculum that he had followed'.[56] To fit his thesis, Diop wanted the *Timaeus* to be based on Egyptian ideas that Plato assimilated at Heliopolis. Diop used the highly suspect methodology, also much favoured by many Atlantis-seekers, of treating apparent resemblances as proof of connection and influence: Plato says the world was created by the Demiurge; Ra, the god of Heliopolis, also created the world; therefore, Plato stole the idea from Egypt. The erroneous principle 'after which = on account of which' was also deployed to assert that because both Plato and the Egyptians were interested in law and order, he must have got his ideas from them.[57] Without providing any details to support his claim, Diop also said that Plato's astronomy was a copy of Egyptian theory, albeit a 'mediocre, degraded and mystical' one, and, in an extraordinary piece of racial stereotyping, he further claimed that another obvious sign of Egyptian influence on Plato was his 'optimism', which was 'a heritage of the African school' because Indo-Europeans are generally pessimistic.[58]

In fact, the chances of the whole of Plato's Ideal State of the *Republic* being stolen or borrowed from Egypt are beyond negligible. Of course, Egyptian priests were more than happy to tell tourists that Plato and many of Greece's greatest literary and philosophical figures did derive their ideas from visits to Egypt. In the first century BC, Diodorus Siculus was told that everything that these writers and thinkers were admired for by the Greeks was exported from Egypt.[59] And, in a process not unlike that which happens in certain modern 'Atlantological' publications, some ancient biographers seized on even the faintest whiff of anything vaguely Egyptian in their works to find 'evidence' of direct personal contact: the slightest interest in Egypt became hard evidence for studying there. For example, because 'Plato tells how the god taught mankind to reckon by the stars and calculate the length of a year',[60] it was automatically assumed that he got this interest in mathematics from Egypt, even though Plato himself doesn't say anything in the *Timaeus* to substantiate the claim.[61] We have seen that Strabo went to Heliopolis and was shown where Plato allegedly spent thirteen years acquiring knowledge about the heavenly bodies and leap-years, despite the fact that 'the barbarians concealed most of the information',[62] and that Diogenes Laertius also made Plato go to Egypt to study,[63] while other writers even name the man who supposedly told Plato the story of Theuth that appears in the *Phaedrus* – Sechnupis of Heliopolis.[64] The further away in time from Plato that the source is, the more detailed it often claims to be.

Greek thinkers could not have learned what became 'Greek philosophy' in Egypt: the ancient biographers present them as going there to learn 'Eastern wisdom', which is something very different, and among the vast amount of literary and archaeological material that has emerged from Egypt over the last century or so there is no evidence of similar philosophical writings coming from there: the thousands of documents that we now have show that Egypt's civilisation and modes of thought are vastly different from those of the Ancient Greeks. Furthermore, given the Greeks' fascination with all things Egyptian, there is no possibility that a massive collection of Egyptian philosophical material, resembling what we think of as Greek, has simply disappeared into oblivion. If there had been, we'd have heard about it from Greek sources. Plato's work is full of references to Egyptian learning, but crucially he presents this wisdom in the form of moral tales, and does so in continuous narratives delivered by just one speaker, rather than in question-and-answer dialogues that comprise the majority of his work. This strongly suggests that these stories, including Critias' Atlantis tale, are Plato's own creations.

But even if Plato *did* follow Diop's Egyptian 'university curriculum', he must have been a lousy student or it must have been a lousy course: our knowledge of Egyptian theology from genuine Egyptian sources shows that Plato didn't learn anything definitively Egyptian: his Egyptian professors could only have been offering superficial, stereotyped, second-hand knowledge that he could have acquired in Greece. Essentially Plato's ideas about Egypt are those of a normal fourth-century BC Athenian, fictionalised, idealised and glamorised in order to compare and contrast it with Athens for politico-philosophical purposes. Plato is a philosopher, not a historian.

Plato's use of 'tales from Egypt' has provided multiple possibilities for misunderstanding by modern commentators, and opened him up to multiple possibilities for ridicule from his Greek contemporaries. But his response to the latter is interesting: 'he took so little/much notice of what the mockers said that he actually attributed [the Atlantis story] to the Egyptians [including the idea that] the Athenians had at one time lived under that constitution'[65] (i.e. the Ideal State). He even embraces his critics' allegations by having the Egyptian priest say:

> consider the [antediluvian Athenians'] laws in relation to our [Egyptian ones]: you will find here among us today many parallels to your institutions of the old days.[66]

However, Socrates' recap of the Ideal State at the start of the Timaeus[67] shows that these 'parallels' are extremely restricted, and by making the Egyptians tell Solon that the Ideal State actually went back to the archaeo-Athenians, Plato is in effect asserting that there isn't anything alien about it: it is a genuine piece of Athens' history, obscured by the mists of time, but ultimately traceable directly to the Athenians' patron deity, Athena.

In saying that Plato attributed the *historia* about the Athenians and Atlanteans to the Egyptians in response to mockery, Crantor was ruling out any possibility that the Atlantis story was 'just an attempt to write plausible history'.[68] As Harold Tarrant rightly comments, it is all about putting the Ideal State in its proper context, not about any supposed historical truth, and furthermore, 'if Plato had been working from within his mockers' assumptions and accepting here the stereotype of the unreliable Egyptian, then he was himself subtly undercutting Critias' story'.[69] Tarrant also observes that we should 'distinguish between the view that *Plato* was trying to engage in historical inquiry and the view that Plato represents *Critias* as trying to do so [. . .] Crantor could legitimately have been suggesting that *Critias* was offering his story as *historia* rather than as *mythos*, while explaining *Plato's* purpose in offering the story as quite independent of its genre or its truth-status'.[70]

Our evidence about Crantor ends on a tantalising note with his statement that the Egyptian priests said that these things have been inscribed on pillars (*stēlais*) that still survive.[71] Might this prove that the story is true after all? No. Firstly, Crantor could simply be repeating the part of Plato's story where the Egyptian priest tells Critias that noble, great or exceptional events that happen in Athens, Egypt and elsewhere 'have all been written down since ancient times and kept safe in the temples'.[72] Secondly, as Tarrant cogently points out,[73] even if Crantor *was* saying that priests of his day would affirm that the story is recorded, that does not guarantee that he accepted the information at face value: there is a good deal of scope for irony in what he says, and because the Greeks can regard the Egyptians as notoriously unreliable, his comment would be more about Egyptian untrustworthiness than the truth of the story. Thirdly, Plato's account doesn't specify the medium on which the information was recorded – he doesn't mention 'pillars/steles' with the Atlantis story on them, and neither does any other commentator after Crantor. In 2001, underwater archaeologists at the sunken city of Thonis-Heracleion in Egypt found the Stele of Saïs,[74] a black granodiorite stone hieroglyphic inscription that advertises a royal decree of

Nectanebo I, who was pharaoh during Plato's lifetime.[75] It is almost the identical twin to one unearthed in 1899 at Naukratis:[76] both steles mention donations to the Temple of Saïs and depict Nectanebo I carrying offerings to Neïth, 'Mistress of Saïs', who is also 'Mistress of the Flood' and equated to Athena at *Timaeus* 21e. But this is the beneficent Nile flood, and there is no mention of Atlantis on these pillars. As far as Crantor is concerned, the Atlantis narrative was 'straightforward *historia*', a story, and nothing more than that.

CHAPTER 7

Plato's Atlantis in the Hellenistic and Roman Periods

....

Plato had lived under the rise of Philip II of Macedon, and Aristotle had tutored Philip's son Alexander III 'the Great', whose conquests changed the entire nature of the Greek world. With Alexander's death in 323 BC we enter the Hellenistic Age, in which his 'Successors' carved out individual kingdoms from his empire, which lasted until they were gradually picked off by the rising power of Rome, with Cleopatra VII of Egypt being the last Hellenistic ruler to fall, defeated at the Battle of Actium in 31 BC.

The Hellenistic Age is characterised by a great liking for scholarship and 'library culture'. But Plato's Atlantis tale remained relatively unimportant in this intellectual environment: the material on Atlantis at the beginning of the *Timaeus* was often regarded as an insignificant, if not irrelevant, introduction to the far weightier cosmological material that follows it, and the fact that the *Timaeus–Critias–Hermocrates* trilogy ends in mid-sentence made it tricky to assess why Plato included it at all.

THE HELLENISTIC AGE: POSEIDONIUS OF APAMEA; STRABO; DIODORUS SICULUS

New philosophies such as Cynicism, Epicureanism, Stoicism, Scepticism and neo-Platonism grew as thinkers tried to respond to the new world order, and the Stoic Poseidonius of Apamea (*c.* 135–*c.* 50 BC), one of the towering intellects of the Hellenistic Age who tutored both the great Roman orator Cicero and Strabo, reputedly endorsed the existence of Plato's Atlantis. Roughly 350 years after Plato, Strabo suggested that his teacher was correct to quote Plato about it being possible that the story about the island of Atlantis is not a fiction. Poseidonius also refers to Plato's information about the existence and destruction of Atlantis coming from Egyptian priests, and concludes that this is a better solution than Aristotle's sceptical 'its inventor obliterated it'.[1] Evidently the issue was still being discussed in Hellenistic times, with Poseidonius at odds with Aristotle.

The great centre of scholarship in the Hellenistic world was the Library at Alexandria, established after Ptolemy I Soter had taken control of Egypt in the power-struggles following Alexander's death.[2] In addition to developing its extensive Greek collections, which were the primary focus of the Library's interests, the Ptolemaic dynasty supposedly coaxed Egyptian priests like Manetho, who spoke Greek fluently, into collecting the records of their traditions and heritage and making them available to Greek scholars like Hecataeus of Abdera.[3] Both authors wrote works entitled *On the Egyptians*, but if their source material included any of the Atlantis-related information that Solon supposedly got from the priests of Saïs, no trace of it has filtered through. We might add that modern assertions about Aristotle stealing Egyptian learning from the Library at Alexandria[4] obviously fall down at the first chronological hurdle: he had been dead for at least twenty-five years before it was put together. And if his ghost had gone to the 'Atlantis' section of the Library, it would only have found two works – Plato's *Timaeus* and *Critias*. There is zero evidence for the Library holding scrolls with information about Atlantis in them: if it had, the argument between Poseidonius and the late Aristotle would have been conclusively settled well before any of the events that resulted in the destruction of the Library's collections.[5]

There is, however, one tantalising hint that there might conceivably have been an Atlantis tradition that didn't go back to Plato. This involves a certain Marcellus, who Proclus mentions when he asserts the existence of Atlantis and quotes 'certain travellers' to prove his point. These people talk about seven islands sacred to Persephone located in 'the Outside Sea' (i.e. the Atlantic Ocean), plus three huge other ones including one sacred to Poseidon, the length of which was 1,000 *stadia* (200 km), whose inhabitants preserved the memory of 'the Atlantis that actually came into being'.[6] However, Marcellus, who later appears as the author of an *Enquiry on Ethiopia*,[7] is never mentioned by any other ancient author. Proclus might be confusing him with Marcianus of Heraclea, a Greek geographer who possibly wrote a *Periplous of the Outside Sea* just before Proclus' time, although scholars still accept that this Marcellus probably existed, perhaps in the first century BC. But the title of his work should make us wary: it sounds like the kind of travel writing that Lucian satirised in his *Alēthes Historia*.[8] First-century BC writers were well aware that there were islands off Africa and Europe, so it is hardly unusual for them to make connections with Plato when they heard about them. What is more curious is how little use they made of them: presumably sailors' tales were seen for what they were. The possibility of there being a non-Platonic source for the Atlantis tale is nil.

Around the time that Cleopatra, 'gazing on her desolated palace with a calm smile, unflinchingly laid hands on the angry asps until her veins had drunk the deadly poison deep',[9] a Sicilian-born Greek historian known as Diodorus Siculus was putting the finishing touches to his *Library*, a forty-book universal history from mythological times to his own day, which he started researching on a visit to Egypt in around 60–56 BC. His work is both valuable, because it is extensively preserved, and frustrating, because it is full of errors and confusions.

In Book 3[10] Diodorus tells us that once upon a time there lived a race ruled by warrior women, who lived in western Africa, and followed a lifestyle that was a complete inversion of the 'normal' Greek one. Because they were deprived of their breasts for military reasons, the Greeks called them 'Amazons'.[11]

> Their home was on an island which, because it was in the west, was called Hespera, and it lay in the marsh Tritonis. This marsh was near the Ocean which surrounds the earth [. . .] and this marsh was also near Ethiopia and that mountain by the shore of the Ocean which is the highest of those in the vicinity and impinges upon the Ocean and is called by the Greeks Atlas. The island [. . .] was of great size and full of fruit-bearing trees of every kind, from which the natives secured their food. It contained also a multitude of flocks and herds, namely, of goats and sheep, from which possessors received milk and meat for their sustenance; but grain the nation used not at all because the use of this fruit of the earth had not yet been discovered among them.[12]

The Amazons conquered all the cities on the island apart from one, which was inhabited by Ethiopian 'Fish-Eaters', prone to eruptions of fire, and rich in precious stones. After that, they subdued many of the neighbouring Libyans, founded a city called 'Peninsula' (*Kherronēsos*) in the Tritonis marsh, and set out on various imperialistic ventures. Their first victims were the very vaguely located, non-island-dwelling Atlantioi ('Atlanteans'), 'the most civilized men among the inhabitants of those regions, who dwelt in a prosperous country and possessed great cities'.[13] The terrifying Amazon army, 33,000 strong, wearing the skins of incredibly large snakes as body armour, and using 'Parthian shot' tactics, defeated the Atlantioi so violently that they surrendered unconditionally. Peaceable relations were then established, to the point where the Amazons attacked the Atlantioi's bellicose neighbours the Gorgons, and put them firmly in their place.

> But the Gorgons, grown strong again in later days, were subdued a second time by Perseus, the son of Zeus, when Medusa was queen over them; and in the end both they and the race of the Amazons were entirely destroyed by Heracles, when he visited the regions to the west and set up his Pillars in Libya, since he felt that it would ill accord with his resolve to be the benefactor of the whole race of mankind if he should suffer any nations to be under the rule of women. The story is also told that the marsh disappeared from sight in the course of an earthquake, when those parts of it which lay towards the Ocean were torn asunder.[14]

It is possible to find echoes of Plato here: an island in the west of great size and fecundity; aggressive invaders; Libya; people called Atlantioi – although it is notable that Plato never gives the inhabitants of Atlantis a name; and a major seismic event. But there the parallels cease, and many of the motifs are inverted. Nevertheless, Diodorus then informs his readers that these Atlantioi, who dwell in fertile territory on the edge of the Ocean, also show extraordinary reverence towards the gods and outstanding humanity towards strangers. In fact, the Atlantioi's mythical tradition has it that the gods were born among them. Diodorus then gives an analysis of these myths in the style of Euhemerus of Messene, who c. 300 BC, wrote an interesting text called the *Hiera Anagraphe*, 'Sacred Record', which described a column that recorded the achievements of ancient kings such as Uranus, Cronus and Zeus. Popular admiration made these kings into celebrities, but as time went by they came to be thought of as gods. So essentially 'euhemerism', as the method is called, reduces all mythology to distorted history. Uranus is just another man, albeit one who, in Diodorus' account, put an end to the lawless ways and bestial lifestyle of his subjects, who, suitably impressed by his knowledge of astronomy, proclaimed him King of the Universe.

In this mythical tradition, Uranus' daughter Monarchy married her brother Hyperion, who was murdered by her jealous other brothers. The Atlantean kingdom was then divided among Uranus' other sons, with Atlas receiving the regions on the Ocean coast. He then gave his name both to the Atlantioi (= 'The People of Atlas') and to Mount Atlas. A further euhemeristic interpretation explains that Atlas perfected the science of astronomy and was the first to publish the doctrine of the sphere, which is the 'reality' behind the myth of Atlas supporting the world on his shoulders.[15] In this mythical account, Atlas had seven daughters (Greek *Atlantides* = 'Daughters of Atlas'), who slept with the most famous gods and heroes and so became the first ancestors of most of the human race. Many of their offspring, again via the euhemerist process, came to be called gods and heroes, and various Atlantides also gave birth to children who founded different cities or nations. Consequently, Diodorus concludes, the vast majority of the most ancient heroes trace their descent back to the Atlantides.[16] One of the Atlantides also gives birth to ten sons in Crete by a Zeus, albeit not *the* Zeus of the normal Greek tradition.

The existence of ten sons, even though they are fathered by a Zeus and not by Poseidon, could be interpreted as a link between Diodorus' story and Plato's Atlantis tale, but Diodorus clearly has no interest in whether Atlantis ever existed or not: all he wants to do is to relate the inhabitants of an area with connections to Atlas to various other mythological inhabitants on the fringes of the world. There is also great potential for confusing Diodorus' Atlantides with other daughters of Atlas who appear in the Greek tradition, such as the Hesperides, the Hyades, the Pleiades, Calypso, Maera and Dione. Overall, this is very strange mythology, but it is only linked to Plato by the most tenuous of filaments, if at all: as Pierre Vidal-Naquet pertinently says, 'in Diodorus Siculus's *Library of History*, there is no Atlantis, in the Platonic sense of the word'.[17]

ATLANTIS IN THE ROMAN EMPIRE – *SI PLATONI CREDIMUS . . .*

After Cleopatra's suicide in 30 BC, the Romans acquired total dominance of the Mediterranean world and shortly moved to one-man rule under an emperor.[18] In the imperial period, we still get sporadic mentions of the Atlantis story, but these always go back to Plato. In this highly multi-cultural world the Hellenised Jewish philosopher Philo of Alexandria, aka Philo Judaeus, who lived at the same time as Jesus,[19] tried to reconcile the words of Moses the Lawgiver with Greek philosophy. His treatise *On the Eternity of the World* discusses how land is often swallowed up by the sea. This is important to him: his opponents say that the sea is receding, which therefore proves that the cosmos is destructible. To disprove this, he cites the inundation of the Peloponnesian towns of 'Aegira, Bura, lofty Heliceia [i.e. Helice], Whose walls would soon be clad with thick sea-moss',[20] and the catastrophe that engulfed Atlantis:

> The island of Atlantis, 'greater than Libya and Asia put together', as Plato says in the *Timaeus*, 'in a single day and night, through extraordinary earthquakes and floods, sank below the sea and suddenly disappeared', turning into a sea which was not navigable but full of abysses.[21]

The quotation marks used by the translator here are slightly misleading, because Philo is not quoting Plato with 100 per cent

accuracy (he doesn't use 'suddenly'). The 'abysses' are also a new
feature (they replace Plato's mud), but Philo obviously accepts
Plato's story, if only because it suits his argument to do so.

The whole of this passage is sometimes attributed to
Theophrastus[22] (c. 371–287 BC), the colleague of Aristotle who took
over as head of the Lyceum after he died. Theophrastus is regularly
named as being at loggerheads with Aristotle about Plato's Atlantis
tale,[23] but it's much more likely that Philo just added the Plato (mis)-
quotation to material that was already in the source he was using,
and apart from this passage we have no hard evidence of
Theophrastus' view about the historicity of Plato's Atlantis story.
However, Theophrastus was a student of Aristotle, so on balance it's
far more likely that he followed his professor's opinion that Atlantis'
inventor obliterated it.[24]

There was a reasonable amount of scientific interest in Atlantis-
like natural events at this time. Between AD 60 and his death in AD
65, Lucius Annaeus Seneca, one of the towering figures of Roman
philosophy, wrote his *Natural Questions*, which discusses floods and
earthquakes, including the various well-known examples of the
disaster at Atalante in the Peloponnesian War and the inundations
of Helice and Buris in 373 BC.[25] Yet Plato's Atlantis is conspicuous by
its absence – astonishing in this context, at least if he thought the
story told the literal truth.

Seneca also wrote about the earthquake of *c.* AD 60 that caused
considerable damage to Pompeii and Herculaneum. Pliny the Elder,
who died when the eruption of Mount Vesuvius engulfed those two
towns in AD 79, made a brief reference to Atlantis in his *Natural
History*. The context of his discussion has similarities to Philo's, in
that he's talking about islands that have been united to the mainland, lands that have been separated by the sea, including Atalante
from Euboea, and lands that have been totally changed into seas.
His first example of land that nature has entirely stolen away by the

sea is '(if we are to believe Plato), the immense area covered by the Atlantic'.[26] Now, two things emerge from this: firstly, he takes it for granted that his readers know Plato's Atlantis tale pretty well; and, secondly, 'if we are to believe Plato' (*si Platoni credimus*) shows that he is sceptical. Pliny appears to be in the awkward position of being dubious about a story, but having to include it because it has become part of mainstream scientific belief. Quite revealingly, though, when he discusses islands round Africa elsewhere in his work, he mentions one called Atlantis, but doesn't link it to Plato's story.[27]

As we have already seen, one of the key sources for our knowledge of the Atlantis tale, particularly in relation to Solon, is Plutarch, who died in AD 120. He himself testifies to the power which the Atlantis story still had, some 450 years after Plato:

> Reflect how keenly we are stirred as we read Plato's tale of Atlantis and the last part of the *Iliad*.[28]

Yet quite what he thought about the reality of the island itself is harder to judge. We know that he used both Crantor and Poseidonius in his other work, so if there had been a raging debate going on about the status of the story we might expect it to filter through. But it doesn't. Although Atlantis makes an important appearance in his *Life of Solon*, the *Moralia* has no mention of the Atlantis-section of the *Timaeus*, and just three mentions of the *Critias*, one of which is about how Timaeus conceives the universe, and the others are about the moral values of proto-Athens:[29] they don't have anything to do with the status of the Atlantis story.

Plutarch also gives information that is at odds with Plato's account, and adds bits to it: he makes Solon's trip to Egypt happen *after* his laws, but in Plato it happens *before* the 'class struggles and other evils he found here when he got home', which made the legislation necessary;[30] the Egyptian priests are anonymous in Plato, but not in Plutarch, who calls them Psenophis of Heliopolis (there is no mention of Heliopolis in Plato) and Sonchis of Saïs[31] (his name could be derived from Shoshenq or Sheshonq, a pharaoh who reigned *c.* 943–922 BC), but this is of no historical significance; and Plutarch says that Solon abandoned his Atlantis-poem project because of old age, whereas, in Plato, Critias says he couldn't find the time.[32]

In Plutarch's version, Plato was not motivated by a driving urge to preserve a lost historical tale. Rather, it was kinship obligation to Solon, and ego: he 'began the work by laying out great porches, enclosures, and courtyards, such as no *logos*, *mythos*, or poetic composition ever had before'.[33] Plutarch thinks that Critias' Atlantis story has been padded out with made-up material simply designed to 'elaborate and adorn' his fictional tale. As Tarrant neatly sums up, 'Plutarch does nothing to alter our picture of a scholarly world without any notable advocate of the view that the story of Atlantis was strictly and literally true'.[34] At best Plutarch hedges his bets regarding the credibility of what he describes as either a *logos* or a *mythos*.[35] He seems happy enough to accept that its links with Solon are pretty genuine, and that Solon picked it up from Egyptian priests. But he shows barely a flicker of interest in discovering any real historical content in the material about antediluvian Athens, Atlantis and their conflict. His words '*logos* or *mythos*' ('story or tale') might sound neutral, but in fact they challenge Socrates' honesty towards the end of the discussion in the *Timaeus* where he says 'the fact that it is true history [*logos*] and not an invented myth [*mythos*] is massively important'.[36] Not to Plutarch it isn't.

The first Christian writer that we know to have made reference to Atlantis was Tertullian, whose *Apology* was produced in Carthage during the reign of Septimius Severus, possibly in AD 197. He argued that to make the Christians responsible for the wrath of the pagan gods, and hence for natural disasters, is simply absurd:

If the Tiber reaches the walls, if the Nile does not rise to the fields, if the sky doesn't move or the earth does, if there is famine, if there is plague, the cry is at once: 'The Christians to the lion!' What, all of them to one lion?

I ask you – [. . .] before Christ came, what great disasters smote the world and the city? We read that Hiera, Anaphe, and Delos and Rhodes and Cos, whole islands with thousands of inhabitants went to ruin. Plato tells of a land greater than Asia or Africa swept away by the Atlantic. [. . .] I hardly suppose these things could have happened without hurt to the inhabitants.[37]

In *On the Mantle*, Tertullian brings the disappearance of Atlantis into a discussion about change in the world:

There even was a time that the whole earth changed and was covered by all the water that exists [. . .] Even now she locally changes her look, when a region incurs damage; when among the islands Delos is nothing anymore, and Samos is just a heap of sand, and the Sybille proves to be no liar; when land the size of Africa or Asia goes missing in the Atlantic . . .[38]

Around the years AD 198–203, Clement of Alexandria, who was steeped in classical literature and philosophy but converted to Christianity, produced his *Patchwork* all about Christian life. Early Christian writers were generally brought up in the midst of pagan myth, history and philosophy, and found it difficult to reconcile this deeply embedded cultural heritage with their new faith. One way that they often dealt with the problem was to read pagan myths allegorically,[39] which is how Clement interprets the Atlantis–Athens war:

Even those myths in Plato (in the *Republic*, that of Hero the Armenian; and in the *Gorgias*, that of Aeacus and Rhadamanthus; and in the *Phaedo*, that of Tartarus; and in the *Protagoras*, that of Prometheus and Epimetheus; and besides these, that of the war between the Atlantini and the Athenians in the *Atlanticum*) are to be expounded allegorically, not absolutely in all their expressions, but in those which express the general sense. And these we shall find indicated by symbols under the veil of allegory.[40]

For Clement, Atlantis is not the tale of a hidden island, but a tale with a hidden meaning.

ALLEGORICAL ATLANTIS

Allegorical or semi-allegorical interpretations of the Atlantis myth were popular with ancient commentators in Late Antiquity. In discussing Crantor, we saw that Proclus referred to several writers who said that the Atlantis story was a myth and an invention, and made it clear that he thought that anyone who adopted a totally allegorical approach was not reading Plato properly.[41] Proclus added that others preferred a *primarily* allegorical interpretation. One of the latter is Numenius of Apamea, a Platonist philosopher (*fl.* AD 150–76), whose work only survives in fragments preserved by later sources like Proclus, who says that Numenius' approach to Atlantis is to

interpret it as a dispute between the finer souls – the foster-children of Athena – and others who work at generation and who belong to the god presiding over generation.[42]

The 'others' here are the Atlanteans; in this context 'the god presiding over generation' is Poseidon.

It is possible that Numenius could have categorically denied Atlantis' literal truth. Proclus, bringing him into the narrative in the wrong chronological sequence, says that Origen[43] 'agreed with Numenius' party' in stating that the Atlantis story was an invention. Numenius probably wouldn't have been looking for literal truth here anyway, since he had a penchant for reading myths allegorically, as he did with the Cave of the Nymphs in the *Odyssey* (the cave = the cosmos);[44] with Odysseus (someone travelling through successive generations until he escapes to a people beyond the waves and the sea, things of which they have no knowledge);[45] with the Myth of Er in the *Republic* (connecting Plato's words with horoscopes and these to mystic rites);[46] and with the soul's prison in the *Phaedo* (the Good is pleasure).[47] So Numenius found a great deal of hidden meaning in the story of Atlantis: for him the war represented the conflict between the finer souls and the inferior souls.

Strange, esoteric and obscure as this is, Numenius' response to Plato's tale illustrates a clear rejection of any literal/historical interpretation at a superficial level, and a desire to seek deeper truths within the narrative.

Another proponent of reading Plato's tale allegorically was the great Christian neo-Platonist Origen of Alexandria (AD 185/6–254/5). Origen was a fierce critic of pagan philosophy, but he also learned a lot from it, and adapted many of its teachings to suit his own purposes.[48] He read the Atheno-Atlantean war as symbolising a conflict between *daemons*:

> Others interpret [the Atlantis war] as a conflict of *daemons*, with some being better and others worse, the one side superior in numbers, the other in power, with the one being victorious and the other vanquished, as Origen supposed.[49]

Proclus adds that

Origen claimed that the narrative had been invented, and to this extent he agreed with Numenius' party, but not that it had been invented in the interests of artificial pleasure, in the manner of Longinus. Yet he did not add a reason for the invention.[50]

The word twice translated 'invented' here is a form of the verb *plassō*, which, as we have seen, is frequently used in relation to made-up stories, and which comes from the same root as the noun *plasma* (= 'invention'), which Proclus used when discussing allegorical interpretations.[51] It also references Plato's *plasthenta mython* ('invented myth').[52] So for Origen, the Atlantis story has no historical basis – it would never fit with the way he understood Plato's work for him to think it did.

One of the features of allegorical interpretation is that it can allow myths to broadcast very different messages, depending on who is analysing them, and why. And so it is with Amelius, another neo-Platonist philosopher of the second half of the third century AD, who arrived at yet another solution. Proclus informs us that some analysts of the Atheno-Atlantean war

> look upwards for the solution to the fixed stars and planets, supposing the Athenians to be analogous to the fixed stars and the Atlanteans to the planets, with the conflict arising from the counter-revolution, and the one side winning because of the single turning-motion of the cosmos. The goodly Amelius is certainly of this opinion putting up such a fight to support its being so, because of the island of Atlantis being clearly divided into seven circles in the *Critias*.[53]

So for Amelius, Atlantis is essentially a map of the universe, although it's tricky to work out quite how he visualised it as 'clearly divided' into seven circles. It isn't: Poseidon 'divided the whole Island of Atlantis into ten parts'.[54] One might add up Cleito's central island, the two rings of land, the three of water and the surrounding territory to make, if not seven circles, at least seven areas, although quite how these can then be directly linked with the seven planets – the seven 'wandering' heavenly bodies that now give us the names of the days of the week: the Sun, the Moon, Mars, Mercury, Jupiter, Venus and Saturn – remains obscure. Amelius' imaginative solution is really no better or worse than any other allegorical approaches: it fits quite neatly with the wider subject matter of the *Timaeus*, but it also raises the question of why Plato couldn't have explained all this in a clear and straightforward way.

For over twenty years, Amelius was the secretary of Plotinus (AD 204–70), who is often regarded as the founder of neo-Platonism. Plotinus uses allegory as an analytical tool,[55] but says nothing about Atlantis. However, the literary critic Cassius Longinus (AD c. 213–73), who taught at Athens for thirty years prior to becoming the advisor of Queen Zenobia of Palmyra,[56] seems to have spurned Plotinus' neo-Platonism in favour of old-school Platonism, and regarded the Atlantis tale as true.

There was clearly some considerable debate about Atlantis in the third century AD, and although Longinus regarded the tale of Atlantis as literally true, Proclus also implies that he felt Plato's story was designed to give 'artificial pleasure',[57] and that Plato was trying to 'hook' his reader at the beginning. Proclus also tells us that Longinus didn't like allegory:

We should again remind ourselves about this entire business concerning the Athenians, that it is neither a myth [*mythos*] that is being related nor a straightforward historical study [*historia*]. Some understand the account only as history [*historian*] others as a myth [*mython*]. And some [i.e.

Longinus] say that, firstly, the allegorical unveiling of these and similar tales appears to Plato to be 'for a hard-working person who is somewhat wide of the mark'.[58] Secondly, Plato's communicative method is not of the [. . .] riddling sort [. . .] but gives clear teaching on very many points of doctrine [. . .] Thirdly, that an allegorical unveiling of the story is not necessary in the present circumstances, since there is an acknowledged reason for the presentation of this narrative – the seduction of the listeners. And further, fourthly, if we explain away everything, then we shall suffer the same fate as those who waste time with tricky minutiae of Homer.[59]

As we saw in the discussions of Crantor above, *historia* doesn't mean 'factual history' in our sense. It means a normal narrative which doesn't contain hidden meanings, as opposed to a *mythos*, which does. The fact that Longinus rejects the allegorical approach doesn't mean that he accepts the story is true history.

While Longinus was teaching in Athens, one of his students was Porphyry of Tyre (AD *c.* 234–*c.* 305), the neo-Platonist philosopher who published Plotinus' *Enneads*. Porphyry did favour an allegorical interpretation of the Atlantis v. Athens war:

Others [. . .] say that it is a conflict between souls and *daemons*, with the *daemons* being a down-dragging force and the souls trying to come upwards. [*Daemons of the*] corrupt kind – the soul polluters [. . .] strike up this war with souls on their descent into generation. And they claim that, just as the ancient theologians refer this to Osiris and Typhon or to Dionysus and the Titans, Plato attributes it to Athenians and Atlanteans out of reverence. For he hands down the tradition that, before they come into three-dimensional bodies, there is rivalry between souls and the enmattered *daemons* that he assigned to the west;[60] for the west, as the Egyptians say, is the region of harmful souls. The philosopher Porphyry is of this view, and one would be surprised if he is saying anything different from the view authorized by Numenius.[61]

Again, it looks like there was a vigorous debate about the interpretation of the details of individual passages in the late third century AD, both within the allegorist camp, and between the allegorists and the literalists. Porphyry certainly appears to be attacking the literalist stance when he introduces the story of Phaethon into the mix:

> Others, however, base their views on the story of Phaethon, of which Plato says that it 'takes the shape of a myth, whereas its true reference' is to something else, one of the things that happens in the natural world; and they think it right to trace this story back to its connection with nature.[62]

So Plato explicitly says that the Phaethon myth is allegorical. Porphyry then adds that Egyptian teaching practice also prefers the allegorical use of myths, and comments that Plato didn't approve of openly revealing everything to people who were ignorant about philosophy. And when he concludes by saying that Plato regularly transmits truth via riddles, Porphyry explicitly rejects the literal interpretation of the Atlantis tale. Indeed, Porphyry's own analysis of Atlantis is far from literal. For him, the moon represents Athens because it is closely associated with Athena, Asclepius and Hephaestus. Souls with technical expertise are sown into the moon, after which they descend with a 'war- and wisdom-loving' nature like Athena's, engage with daemonic forces, and perform wondrous deeds.[63]

One of Porphyry's most influential students was an affluent Syrian who traced his descent to the priest-kings of Emesa, called Iamblichus (c. AD 242–327). Iamblichus went on to exert considerable influence over the way that later neo-Platonist philosophy developed, despite strongly disagreeing with his tutor about a number of issues, including Atlantis.

As we have seen, prior to Iamblichus the main debate concerning the war between Athens and Atlantis was about whether it was a straightforward narrative or an allegory: there was precious little interest in whether or not it was a genuine historical event. The types of questions concerning the detailed truth of the Atlantis story that exercise many modern interpreters were, at this stage, largely irrelevant. However, one of the modern areas of interest is Plato/ Critias' statement that the story is 'utterly extraordinary, but totally true',[64] and in the fifth century AD Proclus said that there were those who didn't rule out the possibility that it could have happened in that way.[65] And in any case, a true story can still carry a metaphorical meaning. Numenius, Origen, Amelius and Porphyry would all have rejected the literal truth of the story, but, Proclus tells us,

> these people at any rate were in my view given a really splendid caning by Iamblichus. Both he and my own teacher [Syrianus] prefer to explain this conflict not at [the expense of] setting aside the surface meaning, but on the contrary in the conviction that these things have happened *in every sense*.[66]

Iamblichus believes that the surface meaning is important. For him, Plato has taken the true story of the war between Athens and Atlantis and used it to symbolise conflicts in the cosmos, which makes it *totally* true. So, if a symbolic truth doesn't exclude a literal one, Iamblichus can have his cake and eat it: antediluvian Athens'

Ideal State = the unifying elements in the cosmos; the Athens versus Atlantis war = the divisive elements in the cosmos. Read in this way, the Atlantis story makes a crucial contribution to understanding the natural world, and given that it does, Iamblichus has to believe that events like it really can happen. However, we might also observe that (a) Iamblichus doesn't try to prove that the literal meaning of the Atheno-Atlantean war is historically true, and (b) that the focus of all these interpreters is very much on the war, not on the inundation of Atlantis.

For much of the lifetimes of Origen, Plotinus, Longinus, Porphyry, Amelius and Iamblichus, the Roman Empire was in a state of omnishambles. Following the succession of Maximinus Thrax in AD 235, Rome had embarked on five decades of chaos, which, amidst a seemingly endless list of emperors, usurpers, rebels and outlaws, nearly all of whom were assassinated, the empire confronted challenges from barbarians outside its borders and economic meltdown within them. Ultimately Rome's 'broken society' recovered the stability that it craved in the person of Diocletian (ruled AD 284 to 305), and one of his primary tasks was to maintain the *pax deorum*, the peace of/with the gods: piety guaranteed the security of the state, but conversely there was zero tolerance for any religious subversiveness that might alienate the gods. And for Diocletian, the Christians were subversive, so in AD 303 he unleashed his notorious Great Persecution. One early Christian apologist who lived through the atrocities was Arnobius of Sicca, who wrote a work entitled *Against the Pagans*, tackling the pagan justifications for the persecution. Rather like Tertullian, he catalogues various catastrophes that afflicted the world before the existence of the Christians, and asks a series of indignant questions:

When was the human race destroyed by a flood? was it not before us? When was the world set on fire, and reduced to coals and ashes?[67] was it not before us? When were the greatest cities engulphed in the billows of the sea? was it not before us? [. . .] For, inasmuch as you are wont to lay to our blame the cause of frequent wars, the devastation of cities, the irruptions of the Germans and the Scythians, allow me, with your leave, to say, – In your eagerness to calumniate us, you do not perceive the real nature of that which is alleged.[68]

And then he introduces Plato's Atlantis, not as the location of one of these natural disasters, but as an example of uncontrolled imperialism:

Did we bring it about, that ten thousand years ago a vast number of men burst forth from the island which is called the Atlantis of Neptune [i.e. Poseidon], as Plato tells us, and utterly ruined and blotted out countless tribes?[69]

The Atlantis invasion stands at the head of a list of similar conflicts – the Trojan War (certainly thought to be historical), Xerxes' invasion of Greece, Alexander the Great's conquests, Rome's domination – which strongly suggests that Arnobius regarded the Atlantis war as a genuine historical occurrence.

Diocletian's Great Persecution failed to stem the tide of Christianity, and around the time that Arnobius died, we get the birth of Ammianus Marcellinus,[70] a pagan author widely regarded as the last of the great Roman historians. His lively, elegant and informative work is our prime source for events in the third quarter of the fourth century AD, and it features a grisly description of an earthquake storm that struck Asia, Macedonia and Pontus, and shattered the city of Nicomedia on 24 August AD 358. This prompts him into a digression about various types of seismic event:

They are either *brasmatiae*,[71] or upheavings, which lift up the ground from far within, like a tide and force upward huge masses, as in Asia Delos came to the surface, and Hiera, Anaphe, and Rhodes [. . .]; also Eleusis[72] in Boeotia, Vulcanus in the Tyrrhenian Sea, and many more islands. Or they are *climatiae*[73] which rush along to one side and obliquely, levelling cities, buildings, and mountains. Or they are *chasmatiae*, or gaping, which with their intensive movement suddenly open abysses and swallow up parts of the earth; as in the Atlantic Ocean an island more extensive than all Europe, and in the Crisaean Gulf, Helice and Bura; [. . .] these were all sunk into the deep abysses of Erebus, and lie hidden in eternal darkness.[74]

It is interesting that Ammianus makes what is presumably Atlantis larger than Europe, rather than Libya and Asia as it is in Plato, but there is no scepticism here about the reality of the event, which features in a catalogue of other well-known, if not entirely accurately recorded, disasters, such as the one at Helice.

The Atlantis story was undoubtedly popular enough for it still to be interesting in the later years of the Roman Empire, and after the era so beautifully recorded by Ammianus Marcellinus, the philosophy teacher Syrianus 'the Great' became the head of the Athenian Platonist school. There, as an old man, he taught the youthful Proclus, who succeeded him as head of the school on his death in AD 437. Proclus makes it clear that Syrianus' interpretation of the Atlantis war was closely aligned with that of Iamblichus.[75]

Atlantis at the Fall of Rome: Proclus

It has doubtless become apparent from the discussions up to this point that if we didn't possess Proclus' extraordinarily conscientious work, we would have scant information about how the Atlantis tale was received in the Roman Empire. Proclus rounds off his discussion of the *Timaeus'* Atlantis section saying that although the Middle Platonist Severus didn't write a commentary on it, and Longinus felt that it was superfluous, Porphyry and Iamblichus had showed that it was worth looking at in detail.[76]

Proclus was a great fan of Plato, and a great believer in Atlantis. He tried to wring every last drop of meaning from Plato's text, painstakingly analysing almost every word or phrase, and as he does so he expresses unhappiness with people who argue that Atlantis is an invention,[77] because it challenges Critias' famous assertion that the Atlantis story is true:

> These people pay no attention to Plato when he exclaims that the account is very unusual, yet certainly true in all respects. For what is true in all respects is not true in one way and untrue in another, nor false on the surface and true in its hidden meaning. No such thing could be true in all respects.[78]

For Proclus, 'true in all respects' requires both literal *and* symbolic truth. And he is so desperate to confirm the existence of the Atlantis episode that, like many Atlantis-seekers since, he seizes on absolutely anything that might prove its literal truth. He knows full well that much of Critias' account is suspect, but still strives to prove that it isn't completely impossible. Harking back to Homer's Achaean wall and the Phaeacians,[79] he argues that (a) many parts of the earth are washed over by the sea, (b) nothing Homer said happened was impossible, and so (c) the Atlantis story is true.[80] The logic of 'it's not impossible so it must be true' is deeply flawed.

Proclus' next move is to show that Atlantis really did exist, and pretty well as Critias described it. He knows it is an enormous task, but takes it on manfully, and one of the awkward passages he confronts is Critias' statement that outside the Pillars of Heracles there had been an island bigger than Africa and Asia combined, from where you could access other islands, and ultimately the continent that surrounds the Ocean.[81] There *is* evidence for an island as big as this, he says: 'some of those who give the story of the region of the outside sea' say that there is.[82] These travellers mention ten islands in the Atlantic, one of which was sacred to Poseidon and 200 km in length. Whether these islands might reflect knowledge of the Canary Islands, the Madeira Islands, the Cape Verde Islands, the Azores or none of the above is hard to tell, but Poseidon's sacred island is way too big for any of those islands, and far too small for Atlantis, whose plain alone was 600 x 400 km, even before one got to the mountains. That said, ancient reports and measurements tend to be inaccurate, flexible, exaggerated or just plain wrong, even in the case of real and very well-known islands like Britain.[83]

Quoting the elusive Marcellus who wrote the *Enquiry on Ethiopia*, Proclus adds that inhabitants of the central island have kept alive an ancestral memory of 'the Atlantis that actually came into being', which was the hugest island there, and which ruled all the islands in the Atlantic Ocean over many cycles of time, and was sacred to Poseidon.[84] But then a hint of doubt enters his discussion, suggesting that the question of Atlantis' existence is less important than that it is good to think with:

> But, even if this is right and some such island did arise, it is still possible to take the story about it both as *historia* and as an image of something that arises naturally within the whole universe, both explaining this [island] in terms of what it resembles, and gradually accustoming those who hear of such spectacles to the whole study of encosmic things.[85]

Essentially, Proclus thinks that Atlantis' philosophical usefulness outweighs its existence in travellers' tales. But even so, he wants the size of the Island of Atlantis to be believable, so he turns to Critias' statement that the Atlantean kings didn't just rule their own island but many others, plus parts of the continent, and vast tracts of land within the Pillars of Heracles right up to Egypt and Italy.[86] Commenting on this, Proclus references Plato's *Phaedo*, where assumptions about the earth do not accord with calculations of the mathematicians: there Socrates says he thinks the earth is bigger:

> I believe that the earth is very large and that we who dwell between the Pillars of Hercules and the river Phasis live in a small part of it about the sea, like ants or frogs about a pond, and that many other people live in many other such regions.[87]

Socrates is actually going to relate a myth about underground rivers here, so this doesn't really do Proclus any favours, but he is prepared to ignore the quotation's context because he wants to show that it is not inconceivable that Atlantis was as big as Critias said. Proclus then proceeds, in a way that has parallels with the methods of some of the more extreme Atlantis-speculators, to reject the expert calculations of the mathematicians and introduce unproven and unprovable anecdotal material instead:[88] 'there is a story that' Heracles reached Mount Atlas, whose height, according to 'those who wrote *Ethiopica*'[89] enabled it to touch the ether and cast a shadow 900 km long; Mount Athos casts its shadow as far as Lemnos, 130 km away (it is actually about 90 km); Ptolemy says that the Mountains of the Moon have an enormous height (the relevance of this is very unclear); and Aristotle says the Caucasus is illuminated by the sun for a third of the night after sunset and a third before sunrise.[90] Calculations based on high places like this make the earth big enough to fit Atlantis in, and therefore we shall have no need of any mathematical methods to suit our interpretation regarding the earth, nor shall we try to refute them. [Satisfied with the outcome, Proclus concludes his discussion by saying] so much for the alleged size of Atlantis; we should not be sceptical about it, even if one were to take what is being said as *historia* only.[91]

Interestingly, when Proclus wants to assert that Atlantis' final fate is believable, he *is* prepared to turn to the experts, in this case to Aristotle:

That what is said is consistent with physics is clear to those who are not entirely unversed in physical science. That an earthquake should occur of such a size as to destroy an island of that size, is not remarkable, since the earthquake that took place a little before our time shook Egypt and Bithynia in one day.[92] And that an inundation should follow the earthquake is nothing unexpected, since this always accompanies large earthquakes as Aristotle reports,[93] giving the reason for it at the same time. Wherever an inundation occurs along with an earthquake, a wave is the cause of this phenomenon. [A somewhat erroneous explanation of seismically created tsunamis follows.] This is the manner in which the earthquake occurred in the region of Achaea at the same time as the onset of the wave that flooded the coastal cities of Boura and Helice.[94]

The last example is the famous inundation from Plato's time,[95] and although 'the level of [Proclus'] reliance on the Peripatetics is a sad reflection on the progress of ancient geophysics',[96] Proclus ends with a flourish: how could an expert on physics possibly reject this account?[97]

When it comes to Critias' description of navigational difficulties in the Atlantic, Proclus again deploys the experts to support his ideas:

Furthermore, that the same place could be passable and impassable on land and sea is one of the things agreed by physicists, as Aristotle too thinks and as the narrative shows. And the same man tells that there is mud [*pēlos*] in the outside sea [the Atlantic] beyond the mouth [i.e. the Pillars of Heracles], and that that place is full of shoals,[98] so if mud [. . .] just below the surface signifies 'full of shoals' it is not remarkable. For even now they call submerged rocks with water over the top 'surface-reefs'. So why would anybody be bothered making out a detailed case for this?[99]

In fact, despite Proclus' slightly exasperated ending remark here, detailed cases for explaining the shoals and/or reefs have figured prominently in more recent attempts to locate the Island (or Peninsula) of Atlantis.

In philosophical interpretations like this, the location of places can have a great bearing on their symbolic meaning. So, the fact that Atlantis is 'in the outside sea' is crucial: for Proclus, the Pillars of Heracles define the boundary between the Same and the Other; 'outside' signifies far from the gods; forces from outside represent everything that is unstable, material, impure and not unified; the Atlantic Ocean is a 'sea of dissimilarity', and it relates to matter itself; matter is described in terms derived from the bad side of the Pythagorean table of opposites[100] – 'limitlessness', 'darkness', 'irrationality', 'measurelessness', 'otherness', etc.; and this 'outside' Atlantic Ocean gets its name from Atlantis, whose people, Proclus tells us, are aligned with all the negative terms of the table of opposites.[101] So Atlantis and its inhabitants do not represent some kind of ancient 'super-civilisation'. On the contrary, the Athenians do: they live inside the Pillars of Heracles and so represent the better, while the Atlanteans outside represent the worse.[102] Inferior Atlantis needs to be put in its place by superior Athens. What matters here is not where Atlantis actually was, but where it was imagined to be.

So, overall, 800 years or so after Plato, Proclus gives us a fascinating blend of history/*historia* (in the ancient sense) and symbolism. But for him, the history must not get in the way of the philosophy. He is quite happy to make historical analogies when it suits him, and it is illuminating that he makes a connection between the Atlantis v. Athens war and the Persians v. Greeks war:

> Since the Persian invasion force set out against the Greeks, and the Athenians in particular, from the east, [Plato] himself brought the Atlantic war from the west, so that you could picture the Athenians' city, as if in the centre, chastising the barbarian forces that moved in a disorderly fashion on either side.[103]

The fact that these 'barbarian' invaders from outside are 'disorderly' has a philosophical nuance: order is better than chaos; in the *Timaeus* the Demiurge leads everything to order from chaos;[104] and Athenians at the centre, fighting against Persians or the Atlanteans from the eastern and western fringes, do the same. What matters above all is order out of chaos, not historical veracity. This seriously undermines any idea that Plato's Atlantis war reflected genuine historical places or events.

Proclus lived through the period that saw the deposition of Romulus Augustulus, the last Western Roman Emperor, in AD 476. As the Roman Empire in the west was being transformed into medieval Europe, the Eastern Empire lived on in the form of the Greek-speaking Byzantine Empire, based in Constantinople, until the city fell to the Ottoman Turks under Mehmet II the Conqueror in AD 1453. During that transitory period, in the middle of the sixth century AD, a Christian Greek traveller and geographer known to us as Cosmas Indicopleustes, wrote his *Christian Topography*. Atlantis enters his work in the context of a discussion of Noah's flood, which he says the Chaldeans knew about, but not the Greeks (except Timaeus):

> The philosopher Timaeus also describes this earth as surrounded by the Ocean, and the Ocean as surrounded by the more remote earth. For he supposes that there is to westward an island, Atlantis, lying out in the Ocean, in the direction of Gadeira (Cadiz), of an enormous magnitude, and relates that the ten kings having procured mercenaries from the nations in this island came from the earth far away, and conquered Europe and Asia, but were afterwards conquered by the Athenians, while that island itself was submerged by God under the sea. Both Plato and Aristotle praise this philosopher, and Proclus has written a commentary on him. He himself expresses views similar to our own with some modifications, transferring the scene of the events from the east to the west. Moreover he mentions those ten generations as well as that earth which lies beyond the Ocean. And in a word it is evident that all of them borrow from Moses, and publish his statements as their own.[105]

It is interesting that the story has been appropriated by a Christian author who thinks it has been stolen from the biblical tradition, and who attributes it to a philosopher called Timaeus (not to Plato or even Critias), and says that God, not Zeus, inundated the island. Cosmas also says that Solomon was the Egyptian priest who told Plato (not Solon) that 'you Greeks are always children', and finally dismisses the whole Atlantis story as 'a most manifest invention [*plasma*], for as he could not point out the island, he gave out that God had consigned it to a watery grave'.[106]

So although Plato's Atlantis has now moved out of its original pagan context into a Christian one, we have also, in a sense, come back to Aristotle's view that 'its inventor obliterated it': Cosmas Indicopleustes regarded Atlantis as fictitious (*plasma* yet again), and its destruction by God was a neat way of disposing of it. And that, so far as the ancient world is concerned, was pretty well the last thing that was said about Atlantis.

CHAPTER 8

Atlantis in the Age
of Discovery [1]

....

After God had submerged Atlantis in Cosmas Indicopleustes'
Christian Topography, it stayed hidden for quite some time. Plato's
Timaeus and the *Critias* continued to be studied by Byzantine scholars, but until the Renaissance the medieval West really had access
only to the *Timaeus*, primarily through just one translation of the
early sections, plus a sketchy commentary, by the philosopher
Calcidius, dating from *c.* 400.[2] We get no hint of any raging debate
about the existence, whereabouts or philosophical significance of
Plato's island for several centuries.

MAPPING ATLANTIS

Between the fall of Rome in the West and the Renaissance there was
plenty of discussion about the Atlantic Ocean and about mythical
western islands on the fringes of the known world. It is occasionally
suggested that echoes of Plato's Atlantis can be heard in the legend
of the Irish monk Saint Brendan the Voyager (*c.* 484–577).[3] We first
hear of him in connection with an island in the ninth-century *Voyage
of Saint Brendan the Abbot*, in which, after a seven-year voyage where
he encounters demons, dragons, sea-serpents and volcanoes, some
of which clearly echo Homer's *Odyssey*, he arrives at a paradise
island where the sun never sets, called *Terra Repromissionis*. As with
so many narratives of this sort, there is wide scope for pinpointing
the island's location, if anyone can find it at all: the cartographer of

the Ebstorf *Mappamundi* (1234) puts an empty rectangle off the west coast of Africa to mark 'the lost island'; on the Hereford *Mappamundi* (1275) the island becomes an entire archipelago described as 'The Isles of the Blessed and the Island of St Brendan'; on the *Catalan Atlas* (1375) it is fairly close to south-west Ireland; and elsewhere it is identified with the 'Fortunate Isles' of the ancients and located much further south:[4] Plutarch had placed two Fortunate Isles/ Elysian Fields in the Atlantic 10,000 *stadia* (2,000 km) from Africa in his *Life of Sertorius*,[5] who wanted to retire there, and they also appear in Lucian of Samosata's satirical *Alēthes Historia*.

These Fortunate Isles were influential in a variety of contexts. In his *History of the Kings of Britain*, Geoffrey of Monmouth (*c.* 1100– *c.* 1155) tells us that King Arthur's sword Excalibur was forged on Avalon, where Arthur retired after being wounded in the Battle of Camlann. Geoffrey's description of the island in his *Life of Merlin* is strongly influenced by Isidore of Seville (*c.* 560–636), who wrote an account of the Isles of the Fortunate in his *Etymologies*.[6] However, even though Geoffrey and Isidore's islands are Atlantisesque in their fecundity, neither author makes any connection between them.

A close contemporary of Geoffrey of Monmouth was the Arab geographer and advisor to King Roger II of Sicily, Ash-Sharif al-Idrisi (1100–1165/6). He wrote one of medieval geography's greatest works, *Kitāb nuzhat al-mushtāq fī khtirāq al-āfāq* (*The Entertainment for He Who Longs to Travel the World*) – or *Kitā Rujār* (*The Book of Roger*) for short – and produced a very splendid world map.[7] Al-Idrisi mashed up material from Greek, Christian and Islamic texts with first-hand observation and eyewitness accounts, and the book, completed in January 1154, gives a wonderful account of a voyage of discovery in the 'Sea of Darkness' (the western Atlantic) by eighty *mugharrirun* ('intrepid explorers'). They left Lisbon, then a Muslim city, to find out what was in the Sea of Darkness, and where it finished. For about eleven days they ran before a gentle easterly wind, at which point they came to a foul-smelling sea with heavy waves, reefs and very little light. So they headed south.

Al-Idrisi says the *mugharrirun* visited thirteen Atlantic islands plus one unnamed one, before reaching Morocco. The intrepid explorers could genuinely have visited Madeira, the Canaries and even the Azores, but they also have some fantastic encounters: on the island of al-Su'ali the inhabitants, who are not sexually differentiated, are shaped like women, have protruding canine teeth, eyes that flash like lightning, thighs like logs, fight with sea-monsters, and dress in leaves; the population of the mountainous island of Hasran are short, brown people with broad faces, big ears, beards to their ankles, who live on a diet of grass; on Qalhan, animal-headed people swim in the sea to catch their food; Alexander the Great spent the night on Sawa, 'near the Sea of Darkness'; and on the Atlantisesque al-Mustashkin, with its mountains, rivers, fruit trees, cultivated fields and high-walled town, there used to be a dragon that the people were forced to feed with bulls, donkeys and humans, until Alexander the Great arrived and fed it with high explosive. The Arabic-speaking world transferred a number of Heracles' feats to Alexander, and al-Idrisi's Alexander-and-the-dragon story looks like an echo of Heracles despatching the dragon Ladon as he acquires the Golden Apples of the Hesperides. Given that various Greek mythographers located the Isles of the Hesperides off the coast of North Africa,[8] and that al-Idrisi knew his Greek mythology, the reefs encountered by the *mugharrirun* may well reference the mud in the Atlantic where Atlantis sank in Plato's *Timaeus*.

Itinerant bishops also appear in a Portuguese legend in which the Archbishop of Porto, six other bishops and their congregations fled from the Moorish invasion in 734. They sailed west and landed on a large rectangular island where they founded seven cities that became utopian models of agricultural, economic and cultural bliss.

This island is quite frequently identified with one called Antilha, Antilia, Antillia or Antigla ('the Opposite Island'; 'the Island of the Other'), which appears opposite Portugal, and about the same size and shape, on various fifteenth-century maps by Zuane Pizzigano of Venice (1424) – the first to name Antilia – Battista Beccario of Genoa (1435), Andrea Bianco of Venice (1436), Bartolomeo Pareto of Genoa (1455), Grazioso Benincasa of Ancona (1463), Pedro Roselli of Majorca (1463), etc.[9] Even though Plato explicitly says that Atlantis disappeared, it may still have impinged on the consciousness of the medieval map-makers, and theories that 'Antillia' is a badly transcribed version of 'Atlantis' still crop up: Alexander von Humboldt and M. D'Avezac briefly flirted with the idea in the nineteenth century,[10] and it still remains popular with 'alternative' Atlantological theories.[11] Also, because it was felt to correspond fairly closely in size, shape and direction to Cuba, that island and its neighbours were duly dubbed the Antilles when European voyagers first found them.

MARSILIO FICINO

The Italian Renaissance philosopher, translator and commentator Marsilio Ficino (1433–99) is now famous mainly for coining the phrase 'platonic love', but he also played a key role in reviving Plato and Platonism, and in transmitting Plato's Atlantis story to the Renaissance world and beyond. His translations of all of Plato's dialogues into Latin, *Platonis Opera Omnia*, were published in 1484, and his commentary makes it explicit that he thought Plato's Atlantis was real.[12] Summarising the *Critias*, Ficino says that whenever Plato imagines something, he calls it a fable [*fabulam*], but in this case he has no hesitation in calling it history; and he highlights *Timaeus* 20d, where Critias says the story is 'indeed amazing, but totally true'.[13]

Ficino's opinion became highly influential. The Spanish bishop, historian and social reformer Bartolomé de las Casas (*c.* 1484–1566) was one who accepted Plato on the basis of Ficino:

> I would have to call Plato's stories regarding the marvels of that island fable rather than history, were they not confirmed by Marsilio Ficino in his compendium of the *Timaeus*, and in his argument on Plato's next dialogue, *Critias*, or *Atlantis*, in which he speaks of the antiquity of the world. Marsilio affirms this as true history, not fable, and he proves it with the judgements of many who have studied Plato's works.[14]

When las Casas discusses the date and location of Atlantis, he also relies on Ficino:

> It is clear that in Plato's day – which was 423 years before the coming of our saviour Jesus Christ, thus a little less than 2000 years ago, as Marsilio notes at the beginning of the works of Plato, the ocean, from the Straits of Gibraltar or just about the mouth of the same, from whence Atlantis began, was non-navigable due to the existence of sunken islands, like those we now find in these Indies.[15]

We can also see the influence that Ficino's ideas were exerting from a comment made in 1567 by Francisco Cervantes de Salazar (1514?–75), the Spanish rector of the Royal and Pontifical University of Mexico, who testifies to the way in which the debate was moving:

> All those who write on Plato say that his history is certain and true to such an extent that the majority of them, especially Marsilio Ficino [. . .], do not even admit a possible allegorical reading although there are others who do so aver, as

Marsilio himself writes in his *Annotations on the Timaeus*. So accepting the supposition that this history is true, who would deny that the island of Atlantis began at the Straits of Gibraltar, or just after Cadiz, then continued and extended through this great gulf, from where to the north and south, as well as the east and west, it had space to be perhaps larger than Asia and Africa?[16]

One of Cervantes de Salazar's Spanish contemporaries, the explorer, astronomer, historian and scientist Pedro Sarmiento de Gamboa (1532–92), also wrote about a 'marvellous history that is full of truth [told by] the divine Plato',[17] even though one gainsayer in the shape of Antonio de Herrera y Tordesillas (1559–1625), the Head Chronicler of the Indies, expressed himself concisely in the margin of Cervantes de Salazar's manuscript: '*es fábula*' (= 'it's a fable').[18] But in spite of dissenting voices, many later writers accepted Ficino's position, and Atlantis started to be seen as the origin of the pre-Columbus inhabitants of the New World.[19]

THE 'COLUMBUS EFFECT'

Christopher Columbus (1451–1506), 'the man who discovered America' in 1492 (even though it might be better to say that he ultimately 'discovered' various islands including the Bahamas, Hispaniola, Cuba, and the Central and South American coasts), unintentionally altered the course of world history. He has been credited with, and pilloried for, opening up the Americas to European colonisation, but in so doing he altered the trajectory of Plato's Atlantis story. The appearance of Antil(l)ia on pre-Columbian maps[20] has generated considerable debate about the possibility of voyages to that area, particularly Cuba, before Columbus, often discussed with a vigour that is inversely proportional to the quality of the available evidence.[21] As we have seen, by the end of the fifteenth century all manner of weird and wonderful mythical islands had 'appeared' in the Atlantic to supplement those of the classical tradition. In a sense, as European knowledge moved further westwards, Atlantis, as an island located on the edge of the known world, moved westwards with it.

It is suggested that Columbus was inspired by Aristotle, or by Seneca's *Medea*, where the Chorus sing about new lands possibly being discovered in the future:

> There will come an epoch late in time
> when Ocean will loosen the bonds of the world
> and the earth lie open in its vastness,
> when Tethys will disclose new worlds
> and Thule not be the farthest of lands.[22]

From the sixteenth century onwards, these lines were sometimes read, with benefit of hindsight, as prophesying the discovery of the Americas by Europeans. But if these texts influenced Columbus' thinking, it seems that Atlantis didn't. Alexander von Humboldt noticed that Atlantis was conspicuous by its absence from any of Columbus' writings and, although he asserted that Columbus 'liked to remember Solon's Atlantis',[23] Columbus' son Ferdinand explicitly stated that his father never showed any interest in Plato's tale.[24]

Columbus might not have been interested in Plato's Atlantis, but his discoveries radically changed the way it was received. Rather like the challenges faced by the Christians of the Roman Empire in reconciling their Graeco-Roman pagan cultural heritage with their new faith, whose biblical tradition they regarded as the truth, the sixteenth-century Europeans now had to interpolate the New World into the classical and biblical traditions that underpinned their lives.

As the great French structural anthropologist Claude Lévi-Strauss put it,

> [A continent], hardly touched by mankind, lay open to men whose greed could no longer be satisfied in the other [continent]. A second Fall was about to bring everything into question: God, morality, and the law [. . .] The Garden of Eden was found to be true, for instance; likewise the ancients' Golden Age, the Fountain of Youth, Atlantis, the Gardens of the Hesperides, and the Fortunate Islands. But the spectacle [. . .] made the European sceptical of [the existing notions of] revelation, salvation, morality and law.[25]

It was immediately realised that there was a New World to respond to, and Peter Martyr d'Anghiera (1457–1526), an Italian historian working for the Spanish, is widely credited with creating that term, which he used in a letter written on 1 November 1493, prior to publishing his *On the New World*, which was first translated into English in 1555.[26] William Shakespeare took it up a level in describing it as a 'brave' new world in *The Tempest*:

> MIRANDA: O, wonder!
> How many goodly creatures are there here!
> How beauteous mankind is! O brave new world,
> That has such people in't!
> PROSPERO: 'Tis new to thee.[27]

Miranda's words aptly apply to the way Plato's Atlantis now came to be perceived. Rather like the way that speculation outweighs empirical data in some of the more wayward Atlantis-theorising today, for the people of the fifteenth and sixteenth centuries the authority of the classical texts still outweighed what they were actually observing. This made it very difficult for scholars to accept that the Americas were in fact a 'New World', and had never been mentioned in the Bible, Plato or Aristotle. So the fact that Plato's *Timaeus* and *Critias* had spoken of a great lost land in the western sea was helpful. Finding a place for Atlantis in the brave new world would be a great challenge, but one that would propel the story forward with increased energy: an intense search for the island began, which has shown little sign of abating.

ATLANTIS AND SYPHILIS

One character who certainly propelled the Atlantean debate forward, and also sought to reconcile the new discoveries of the previously unsuspected and quite alien cultures of the New World with classical antiquity was Girolamo Fracastoro (c. 1478–1553). He was a colleague of the astronomer Copernicus at the University of Padua, and operated a private medical practice in Verona. He is particularly famous for his 1530 poem *Syphilis or the French Disease*. In contrast to its subject matter, the poem is rather beautiful, and somewhat unexpectedly it includes references to Atlantis.

The poem starts by echoing Virgil's 'I sing of arms and the man':[28] 'I sing of that terrible disease', and how an 'intrepid flotilla' leaves Spain 'in search of another world' in the west. There they witness some strange rituals performed by a priest for some victims of 'the hideous ravages of a disease that was unknown to them'. When the leader of the Spaniards asks the priest for an explanation, the priest proceeds to describe the disasters and how they came about:

> An issue of Atlas, of Atlas our father, whose name no doubt
> is not unknown to thee, our nation lived for a long time
> happily and cherished of the sky, as long as it honored the

gods and remained faithful to their worship. But a time came, alas! in which corruption and impiety slipped in among us, in which the sacred altars of our fathers were devoted to contempt. The punishment of such a crime did not take time to come, for from that period dates for us a series of misfortunes which I would be unable to recite. It was, at first, that famous island to which Atlas had given his name, that queen of the seas, Atlantic, that a fearful cataclysm shook to its very foundations, and which threw itself in the bosom of those waves which were formerly subject to its empire. Then the anger of heaven turned itself against our flocks, and [. . .] as a result, we have nothing to offer to our gods but the blood of foreign victims, born under a sky which is not ours. Later on yet, the anger of the gods and the vengeance of Apollo unchained upon us the terrible scourge of which thou hast seen the ravages. This disease has spread itself in all our cities.[29]

The priest's words are very obviously based on Plato's *Timaeus*, but in suggesting that the Indian cultures of the New World are the survivors from Atlantis, Fracastoro is setting Plato's story on a new track, which many subsequent authors would follow, and which some still do.

Syphilis or the French Disease is densely populated with pagan mythical figures, some from the Greek tradition and others that Fracastoro creates, notably the shepherd Syphilus whose sacrilege triggered the entire epidemic. At this time, imitation of Greek and Roman authors was entirely normal in literature, history, rhetoric, the visual arts and, crucially, politics, where classical references could provide glib justifications for annexing land in the New World. It was in fact a process that went back to classical times, where mythical propaganda was exploited in regional disputes to reinvent people's origins, disparage opposing regions and influence public opinion.[30] So in 1535, the Spanish historian Gonzalo Fernández de Oviedo y Valdés (1478–1557) published the first nineteen books of his monumental *General and Natural History of the Indies*, which contained material imitating Pliny the Elder's writings about the Hesperides.[31] To the evident pleasure of the Spanish King Charles V, Valdés explained that the Antilles were the Isles of Hesperides, which had been discovered by the legendary Spanish King Hesper, which meant that their annexation was actually a God-endorsed *re-conquest* of people who had once been Spanish subjects in the first place.

Another tale with Atlantean ramifications that was influential in this context was the one carried by Diodorus Siculus and Pseudo-Aristotle's *On Marvellous Things Heard*,[32] in which Carthaginian seafarers had exited the Pillars of Heracles and settled an uninhabited land, prompting the Carthaginian authorities to fear an emigration crisis and/or of a hostile takeover of the new colony, and so execute the discoverers and ban further voyages. Valdés floated the idea that this was the origin of the American Indians, but although the possibility of Carthaginians crossing the Atlantic (and returning) cannot be ruled out, there is, as yet, no archaeological evidence to support this theory.

THE TEN TRIBES

Alongside the Graeco-Roman elements, there is also a biblical aspect, which again had far-reaching ramifications for Atlantis interpretation, and in his important study of the Atlantis story, the great French 'activist historian' (his own description) Pierre Vidal-Naquet points out that while Plato provided one pole of reference here, the Bible provided at least three more.[33] Firstly, the Atlantis tale is a flood myth of sorts: the central figure in the biblical Flood is Noah; every branch of the human race sprang from his sons; but it was incredibly difficult to assimilate the American Indians into Noah's descendants; yet, because they were human beings, this problem had to be solved. Secondly, there were the Ten Lost Tribes of Israel in IV Esdras:[34]

> Those are the ten tribes, which were carried away prisoners out of their own land in the time of Osea the king, whom Salmanasar the king of Assyria led away captive, and he carried them over the waters, and so came they into another land. But they took this counsel among themselves, that they would leave the multitude of the heathen, and go forth into a further country, where never mankind dwelt. That they might there keep their statutes, which they never kept in their own land. And they entered into Euphrates by the narrow places of the river. For the most High then shewed signs for them, and held still the flood, till they were passed over. For through that country there was a great way to go, namely, of a year and a half: and the same region is called Arsareth. Then dwelt they there until the latter time; and now when they shall begin to come, The Highest shall stay the springs of the stream again, that they may go through: therefore sawest thou the multitude with peace.[35]

The New World very quickly became somewhere that the Ten Lost Tribes might be found, and their story was felt to dovetail quite nicely with Atlantis.[36] Thirdly, we encounter a notion that Atlantis was in fact Palestine before the Flood. The French historian Jean de Serres (Latinised as Serranus, 1540–98), whose 2,000-page-long work on all Plato's dialogues was published in Geneva in 1578, felt that this accorded well with Cosmas Indicopleustes' *Christian Topography*, and his ideas remained quite influential in the eighteenth century, and theories that Palestine/Sinai = Atlantis are still aired today.[37]

Nevertheless, in the mid-sixteenth century, the Americas still remained the favourite candidate for the 'real Atlantis', and there were compelling reasons why people should want that to be the case. As G. M. Sayre puts it,

> the relevance to the origin question is that the identity of Atlantis with America is only possible because 'America' was a signifier with no referent. It has been the prerogative of Europeans to constitute 'America' and its peoples within historical discourse. Hence the myth of Atlantis has been taken seriously as evidence for a pre-Columbian migration, whereas American Indian myths, even if no more fantastic, are not considered historically valid.[38]

Yet one Spanish historian who did deploy American Indian material to support his ideas was Francisco López de Gómara. In his *General History of the Indes* of 1553 he cited the *Timaeus* and the *Critias*, skated over the problem that what Plato said was destroyed still survives, and suggested that Plato's Atlantis and the New World were one and the same, or at the very least Plato had heard of it and interpolated it into his work. The idea of the Atlanteans escaping from their sinking island and populating the New World gained traction because it was felt to account for the great wealth of some of the peoples there, particularly in Mexico. What was particularly interesting here was an Aztec legend that they migrated from a paradise-like place called Aztlan or sometimes Aztalan ('The Land of Whiteness'; 'The Land of the Heron'), albeit in the twelfth century AD, and that in the Nahua language '*atl*' was the word for 'water'. Gómara and his followers took this as evidence for an Atlantis/flood connection. The idea was popular,[39] and indeed in 1561 the French scholar Guillaume Postel suggested that either North or South America should be named 'Atlantis'.

In the context of the 'Atlantis + the Ten Tribes' speculations, one of the key figures is Diego de Landa (1524–79), the Spanish Franciscan bishop of Yucatán, who is particularly known for writing an account of Mayan culture, a great deal of which he helped to destroy, and for presiding over a horrendous catalogue of atrocities against the Mayan peoples. The Maya thought that his interest in their culture was positive, and they showed him their precious books about their history and astronomy. He, on the other hand, felt that the books

> contained nothing in which there were not to be seen super-stition and lies of the devil, [so] we burned them all, which they regretted to an amazing degree, and which caused them much affliction.[40]

However, Diego de Landa's zeal to eradicate the contents of the books was matched by his curiosity about the script they were written in, and after he was recalled to Spain to face charges of exceeding his authority, he wrote a seminally important work on Mayan culture entitled *Account of the Affairs of Yucatán* (1566), which included transcriptions, and a woefully misguided 'decipherment', of the Mayan writing system. In it he wrote:

> Some of the old people of Yucatán say that they have heard from their ancestors that this land was occupied by a race of people, who came from the East and whom God had deliv-ered by opening twelve paths through the sea. If this were true, it necessarily follows that all the inhabitants of the Indes are descendants of the Jews.[41]

In due course, Landa's writings were picked up by the proponents of theories relating to the Ten Lost Tribes of Israel, and to other ideas linking the Maya to Atlantis, notably those put forward in the nineteenth century by Charles-Étienne Brasseur de Bourbourg,[42] who constructed a bizarre history of Atlantis based on Mayan myths, saw parallels between those myths and Egyptian ones, and assumed that these came from a common source on Atlantis.

Overall Diego de Landa unleashed a torrent of pseudoscientific speculation that still recurs quite regularly, and it is striking how much some current pro-Atlantis speculation owes to the ideas to which he and his sixteenth-century contemporaries subscribed.

THE 'THEATRE OF THE WORLD'

Once explorers had acquired a taste for new lands, they started to find them everywhere, whether they existed or not. Abraham Ortelius (1527–98), the Flemish cartographer who is generally recognised as the creator of the first modern atlas, included a world map in his *Theatrum Orbis Terrarum* (*Theatre of the World*) of 1570[43] which featured a number of fictitious places including the Isle of Brazil, St Brendan's Isle, the Isle of the Seven Cities (i.e. Antillia), the Isle of the Demons and numerous others. The Isle of Brazil (not to be confused with the South American country) possibly gets its name from the Irish tribe Ui Breasail (not the Portuguese *pa-brazil* of the brazilwood tree) and has certain similarities to Atlantis in Celtic folklore: it was a circular island lying to the west of Ireland, sometimes said to be inhabited by enormous rabbits and an evil necromancer but also depicted as a paradise whose immortal and eternally happy islanders were ruled by King Breasal. The island itself emerged from, and swiftly returned to, the depths on a seven-year cycle, and regularly appeared on maps until the geographer

Alexander G. Finlay finally put an end to the frantic search for it and wiped it off the map in the nineteenth century.

Like its predecessor, the Piri Re'is map of 1513,[44] the *Theatre of the World* has been influential in stimulating more recent speculation about Atlantis, since it depicted *Terra Australis Incognita*, a massive southern continent like Antarctica, only ten times as big, which the ancient geographers had been speculatively placing in the southern Indian and South Pacific Oceans:[45] Theopompus of Chios, Crates of Mallus, Hipparchus and Ptolemy had all speculated about the possible existence of continents to the west or the south of the Graeco-Roman world. However, the existence of truly accurate knowledge of the frozen regions of *Terra Australis* on Ortelius' map seems to be called into question by a label that designates a 'region of parrots' (*psytacorum regio*) where the 'beautiful' (*formosi*) inhabitants go naked (*nudi*).

If Ortelius was off the mark in Antarctica, he should be credited with an insight that turned out to be very much on the mark in the Atlantic, even though it took over 300 years to verify. The continents on the opposite sides of the Atlantic Ocean look like they might fit together quite neatly (especially Africa and South America), and Ortelius posited a somewhat more vigorous version of what was later called 'Continental Drift'. For him, the Americas were

> torn away from Europe and Africa [. . .] by earthquakes and floods [. . .] The vestiges of the rupture reveal themselves, if someone brings forward a map of the world and considers carefully the coasts of the three [continents].[46]

This has been another potential area of exploration in the quest for Atlantis, and it is interesting that, in 1572, the Spanish explorer Pedro Sarmiento de Gamboa had produced a *Historia general llamada Indica – Historia de los Incas* in which he told Philip II of Spain

that, long ago, Atlantis, in other words America, had been next to
Europe, and so it belonged to him by divine right. Atlantis had
become highly politicised.

A further similar politicisation of Atlantis, along with another
addition to the repertoire of locations for a potential discovery that
still attracts the modern Atlantis-hunters, also goes back to the
sixteenth century. Johannes Goropius Becanus, aka Jan Gerartsen
van Gorp (1519–72), has given his name to a type of activity that
many Atlantis-speculators have been guilty of over the centuries –
'goropism' (= inventing absurd etymologies) – but he is also responsible for putting Tarshish into the mix. His posthumously published
Hispanica (1580) argued that ancient Tarshish was (a) both the biblical Tarshish and the Tartessus of Herodotus;[47] (b) the forerunner of
modern Spain; and (c) the capital of Atlantis. Furthermore, in a neat
mash-up of the classical, the biblical and the contemporary political,
Goropius asserted that Tarshish had been founded by two brothers
who were grandsons of Noah's son Japheth, namely Atlas-Tartessus
and Odysseus-Hesperus. Atlas was the elder, so he took precedence,
and therefore his successors, the kings of Spain, could obviously
claim authority over the Atlantic seaboard of Africa and America.[48]
Myths are seldom neutral.

It should be said, though, that in the midst of this burgeoning
Atlantis speculation, there were dissenting voices. One such was
Father José de Acosta (1539–1600), a Jesuit theologian and
missionary to the New World, whose *Natural and Moral History of
the West Indies* attacks the veracity of the Atlantis tale in a number
of pertinent ways. Chapter 22 carries the title 'That the lineage of
the Indians hath not passed by the Atlantis Iland as some do
imagine':

> Some (following Plato's opinion, mentioned before) affirme
> that these men parted from Europe or Affricke to go to that

famous and renowned Iland of Atlantis, and so passed from one Iland vnto anothor, vntill they came to the maine land of the Indies, for that Cricias of Plato in his Timeus discourseth in this maner. If the Atlantis Iland were as great as all Asia and Affrike together, or greater, as Plato saies, it should of necessitie containe all the Atlantike Ocean, and stretch even vnto the Ilands of the new world. And Plato saieth moreover that by a great and strange deluge the Atlantis Iland was drowned, and by that meanes the sea was made vnnavigable, through the aboundance of banckes, rockes, and roughnesse of the waves, which were yet in his time. But in the end the ruines of this drowned Iland were setled, which made this sea navigable. This hath been curiously handled and discoursed of by some learned men of good judgement, and yet, to speak the truth, being well considered, they are ridiculous things, resembling rather to Ovid's tales then a Historio or Philosophie worthy of accompt. The greatest part of Platoe's Interpreters affirme that it is a true Historie, whatsoever Cricias reports of the strange beginning of the Atlantis Iland, of the greatnes thereof, of the warres they had against them of Europe, with many other things. That which gives it the more credite of a true Historie, be the wordes of Cricias (whom Plato brings in in his Timeus), saying that the subject be means to treat of is of strange things, but yet true. The other disciples of Plato, considering that this discourse hath more show of a fable then of a true Historie, say that we must take it as an allegorie, and that such was the intention of their divine Philosopher. Of this opinion is Procles and Porphire, yea, and Origene, who so much regardes the writings of Plato as when they speake thereof they seeme to bee the bookes of Moses or of Esdras, and whereas they thinke the writings of Plato have no shew of truth; they say they are to be vnderstood mystically, and in allegories. But, to say the truth, I do not so much respect the authoritie of Plato (whom they call Divine), as I wil beleeve he could write these things of the Atlantis Iland for a true Historie, the which are but meere fables, seeing hee confesseth that hee learned them of Critias, being a little childe, who, among other songs, sung that of the Atlantis Iland. But whether that Plato did write it for a true Historie or a fable, for my part I beleeve that all which he hath written of this Iland beginning at the *Dialogue of Timeus* and continuing to that of Critias, cannot be held for true but among children and old folkes. Who will not accoumpt it a fable to say that Neptune fell in love with Clite, and had of her five paire of twinnes at one birth. And that out of one mountaine hee drew three round balles of water and two of earth, which did so well resemble as you would have judged them all one bowell. What shall Wee say, moreover, of that Temple of a thousand paces long and five hundred broade, whose walles without were all covered with silver, the seeling of gold, and within ivorie indented and inlaied with gold, silver, and pearle. In the end, speaking of the ruine thereof, he concludes thus in his time: 'In one day and one night came a great deluge, whereby all our souldiers were swallowed by heapes within the earth, and in this sort the Atlantis Iland being drowned, it vanished in the Sea.' Without doubt it fell out happily that this Iland vanished so suddenly, seeing it was bigger than Asia and Affrike, and that it was made by enchantment. It is in like sort all one to say that the ruines of this so great an Iland are seene in the bottome of the sea, and that the Mariners which see them cannot saile that way. Then he addes: 'For this cause vnto this day that Sea is not navigable, by reason of the bancke, which by little and little has growne in that drowned Iland.' I would willingly demand what Sea could swallow vp so infinite a continent of land, greater then Asia and Affrike, whose confines stretched vnto the Indies, and to swallow it vp in such sort as there should at this day remaine no signes nor markes thereof whatsoever) seeing it is well knowne by experience that the Mariners finde no bottome in the Sea where they say this Iland was [. . .] The argument they make to prove that this Atlantis Iland hath been really and indeede, saying that the sea in those parts doth at this day beare the namo of Atlantike is of small importance, for that wee knowe. Mount Atlas, whereof Plinie says this sea tooke the name, is vpon the confines of the Mediterranean Sea. And the same Plinie reportes that joyning to the said Mount there is an Iland called Atlantis, which he reports to be little and of small accompt.[49]

Having dealt with Atlantis, José de Acosta then goes on in Chapter 23 to distance himself, point by point, from the idea derived from IV Esdras 40–7, that the race of the Indians comes from the Jews:

Some will apply this text of Esdras to the Indies, saying, they were guided by God, whereas never mankinde dwelt, and that the land where they dwelt is so farre off, as it requires a yeere and a halfe to performe the voyage, beeing by nature very peaceable. And that there are great signes and arguments amongst the common sort of the Indians, to breed a beleefe that they are descended from the Iews; for, commonly you shall see them fearefull, submisse, ceremonious, and subtill in lying. And, moreover, they say their habites are like vnto those the Iewes vsed; for they weare a short coat or waste-coat, and a cloake imbroidered all about; they goe

176

bare-footed, or with soles tied with latchets over the foot, which they call ojatas.[50] And they say [. . .] that this attire was the ancient habite of the Hebrewes, and that these two kinds of garments, which the Indians onely vse, were vsod by Samson, which the Scripture calleth *Tuniciam et Syndonem*; beeing the same which the Indians terme waste-coat and cloake. But all these coniectures are light, and rather against them then with them; for wee know well, that the Hebrewes vsed letters, whereof there is no shew among the Indians; they were great lovers of silver; these make no care of it; the Iews, if they were not circumcised, held not themselves for Iewes, and contrariwise the Indians are not at all, neyther did they ever vse any ceremionie neere it as many in the East have done. But what reason of coniecture is there in this, seeing, the Iewes are so careful to preserve their language and Antiquities, so as in all parts of the world they differ and are known from others, and yet at the Indies alone, they have forgotten their Lineage, their Law, their Ceremonies, their Messias; and, finally, their whole Indaisme [. . .] Esdras (if wee shall beleeve the Scriptures that bee Apocrypha) [. . .] saith [. . .] that the ten tribes went from the multitude of the Heathen, to keepe their faith and ceremonies, and we see the Indians given to all the Idolatries in the world. And those which holde this opinion, see well if the entries of the River Euphrates stretch to the Indies, and whether it be necessary for the Indies to repasse that way, as it is written. Besides, I know not how you can name them peaceable, seeing they be alwaies in warro amongst themselves. To conclude, I cannot see how that Euphrates in Esdras Apocrypha should be a more convenient passage to goe to the new world, then the inchanted and fabulous Atlantis Iland of Plato.[51]

José de Acosta was not a lone voice. In France, the philosopher Michel de Montaigne (1533–92), one of the most learned humanists of the sixteenth century, was seeking to exert his 'natural judgement' in displaying his erudition, popularising the essay as a literary genre, and writing 'On Cannibals':

> We grasp at everything but clasp nothing but wind. Plato brings in Solon to relate [the entire Atlantis story, which Montaigne summarises]. It is most likely that that vast inundation should have produced strange changes to the inhabitable areas of the world; it is maintained that it was then that the sea cut off Sicily from Italy [. . .], as well as Cyprus from Syria and the island of Negropontus [Euboea] from the Boeotian mainland [. . .] Yet there is little likelihood of that island's being the new World which we have recently discovered, for it was virtually touching Spain; it would be unbelievable for a flood to force it back more than twelve hundred leagues to where it is now; besides, our modern seamen have already all but discovered that it is not an island but a mainland contiguous with [. . .] lands lying beneath both the Poles.[52]

Montaigne doesn't say that he thinks Plato's Atlantis is a fiction, but he is very clear that the story has nothing to do with America, and although he doesn't explicitly discuss any Atlanto-Palestinian theories, he shows that he is aware of them, and tells us he wants historical and geographical credibility:

> What we need is topographers who would make detailed accounts of the places which they had actually been to. But because they have the advantage over us of having seen Palestine, they want to enjoy the right to tell us tales about all the rest of the world![53]

Montaigne then suggests that if the inhabitants of the New World had been conquered by Greeks or Romans, rather than by the Conquistadors, they would be far more 'civilised', and the whole process would have been considerably less traumatic:

> Oh, why did it not fall to Alexander and those ancient Greeks and Romans to make of it a most noble conquest; why did such a huge transfer of so many [. . .] peoples not fall into hands that would have gently polished those peoples, clearing away any wild weeds while encouraging and strengthening the good crops that Nature had brought forth among them, not only bringing to them their world's arts of farming the land and adorning their cities (in so far as they were lacking to them) but also bringing to the natives of those countries the virtues of the Romans and the Greeks?[54]

Another forthright critic of the Conquistadors with an opinion about Atlantis was the Belgian classical philologist and humanist Justus Lipsius (1547–1606). He wrote a number of works which aimed at reconciling ancient Stoicism with orthodox Christianity in order to create a new philosophy that could help people negotiate the difficulties posed by their own historical circumstances. Constancy became his key virtue, and in his dialogue *De Constantia* (1584), he used Atlantis to illustrate how a Stoic might deal with the horrors of war:

> Neither grudge thou to see war among men, there is likewise between the elements. What great lands have been wasted, yea wholly swallowed up by the sudden deluges, and violent overflowings of the sea? In old time the sea overwhelmed wholly a great island called Atlantis (I think not the story

fabulous [i.e. fictitious]) and after that the mighty cities Helice and Bura.[55]

So Lipsius took Plato at face value, and also knew his ancient history. The correspondence of Charles Darwin also shows that Lipsius speculated about whether the existence of Atlantis might have facilitated the migration of animals from Africa to America, an idea that the naturalist Edward Forbes had picked up on, and which attracted Darwin's good friend, the botanist J. D. Hooker: 'was [Forbes'] the first *scientific* proposition of Atlantis?', he wondered.[56] But Darwin was sceptical:

> I cannot admit the Atlantis connecting Madeira & Canary Islands without the strongest evidence & all on that side: the depth is so great; there is nothing geologically in the islands favouring the belief; there are no endemic mammals or batrachians; did not Bunbury shew that some orders of plants were singularly deficient?[57]

In early November 1572, a new star, B Cassiopeiae or SN 1572, appeared in the sky. Astronomers categorise it as a Type Ia supernova, and it is often named Tycho's Nova, after the Danish astronomer Tycho Brahe, who published his observations of it in *On the Star, new and never before seen in the life or memory of anyone* in 1573. It was visible during daylight for seventeen months, and one of the other highly interested observers was Queen Elizabeth I's court astrologer Dr John Dee (1527–1608). Many observers thought the star heralded the end of the world, but Dr Dee felt it indicated the start of a British Empire – a phrase which he coined. In his unpublished manuscript entitled *The Limits of the British Empire*,[58] he used legendary material to justify British claims on

Sondrye foreyne Regions, discovered, inhabited, and partlie Conquered by the Subjects of this Brytish Monarchie.[59]

These 'foreign regions' included North America, and the Queen's royal title also extended

to all the coasts, and lands beginning at or about Terra Florida, and so alongst, or neere unto Atlantis goinge Northerly: and then to all the most northern Islands great and small.[60]

So Atlantis had been relocated from the Spanish-controlled Caribbean to North America and claimed by the British. Then, in order further to substantiate the case, Dee quoted a wide range of real and legendary voyages made by, among others, King Arthur[61] (Dee fancied himself as Merlin to Elizabeth I's Arthur), Saint Brendan and the Welsh prince Madoc:

The Lord Madoc, sonne of Owen Gwyndd prince of North Wales, leaving his brothers in contention, and warre for their inheritance sought, by sea (westerlie from Irland), for some forein, and – Region to plant hymselfe in with soveranity: wth Region when he had found, he returned to Wales againe and hym selfe wth Shipps, vituals, and men and women sufficient for the coloniy, wth spedely he leed into the penin-sula; then named Farquara; but of late Florida or into some of the Provinces, and territories neere ther abouts: and in Apalchen,[62] Mocosa, or Norombera:[63] then of these 4 beinge notable portions of the ancient Atlantis, no longer – nowe named America.[64]

The point is that if the Welshman Madoc had colonised 'Atlantis' 300 years prior to Columbus, then the British claim to the New

World obviously would trump Spain's. So, in 1583 George Peckham duly produced *A True Reporte of the late discoveries and possession taken in the right of the Crowne of Englande, of Newfound Landes*, in which it was claimed in print for the first time that Madoc had indeed reached America.

The only sticking point in the plan was that the Queen herself was not 100 per cent committed to it. So it never really materialised. But the myth of the 'Welsh Indians' stuck: tales of blue-eyed, blond-haired Indians speaking something that sounded Welsh sprang up. These Welsh Indians were never discovered, and no verifiable connection to Madoc or the Welsh was ever made, but, as with the Atlantis story that they so strangely became a part of, not everyone entirely stopped believing in them, and some 'alternative historians' still champion their cause even now.

CHAPTER 9

The Seventeenth Century: A New Atlantis

....

By the turn of the seventeenth century, Plato's Atlantis had come a very long way from its origins in the story delivered by Critias in the *Timaeus* and *Critias*, be this in its location, ethos, the reasons for relating the tale or its continuing existence. In particular, Plato's Atlantis had become a neat 'explanation' for the Indian cultures of the Americas. It was almost taken for granted that these cultures couldn't have developed on their own, but on the other hand it was hard to trace them back to any civilisation from the Old World. So Atlantis became the perfect solution, so long as people were prepared to distance their version of it from Plato's, and argue that it hadn't been sunk completely without trace, and that its cultural heritage could still be observed, albeit in a highly degraded form, in the native peoples of the Americas.

NEW ATLANTIS

The Atlantis = America equation was developed by Sir Francis Bacon (1561–1626) in his unfinished novelistic essay *New Atlantis*, published posthumously in 1627. It resembles a cross between Plato's Atlantis dialogues and Thomas More's *Utopia* (1516), and in it Bacon shows us a virtually forgotten Golden Age. This ancient wisdom has been lost; mankind does not remember its past glories; and current philosophies are debased. However, *New Atlantis* wants that knowledge, and hence that high level of civilisation, to be retrieved. Bacon, like Plato, uses fictional material in order to make his philosophical and political points but whereas Plato's decadent Atlantean civilisation is eradicated by the literally cataclysmic destruction of the entire island, Bacon combines Old-Atlantean Platonic flooding with New-Atlantean ideal living, although his island ultimately feels less like an Ideal State, and more like an Ideal Institute of Science and Technology.

Bacon's New Atlantis also has a new location. Again, as had happened with the New World, and is still wont to happen in more recent interpretations, Atlantis has been moved into the space occupied by hitherto *terra incognita*: it is a characteristic of Atlantis that the search for it moves outwards as knowledge of the world moves outwards, with the island often remaining on the furthest fringes of the known area. So Bacon keeps the Old Atlantis in America, but locates his New one in the South Sea (i.e. the Pacific Ocean), which had been traversed in Bacon's lifetime by Sir Francis Drake in the *Golden Hind* (1597).

Bacon clearly knew his Plato, as the commentary of the Governor of the House of Strangers clearly shows:

At the same time, and an age after, or more, the inhabitants of the Great Atlantis [America] did flourish. For though the narration and description, which is made by a great man with you [i.e. Plato]; that the descendants of Neptune [i.e. Poseidon] planted there; and of the magnificent temple, palace, city, and hill; and the manifold streams of goodly navigable rivers, (which as so many chains environed the same site and temple): [. . .] yet so much is true, that the said country of Atlantis, as well that of Peru, then called Coya, as that of Mexico, then named Tyrambel, were mighty and proud kingdoms in arms, shipping and riches: so mighty, as at one time (or at least within the space of ten years) they both made two great expeditions; they of Tyrambel through the Atlantic to the Mediterrane Sea; and they of Coya through the South Sea upon this our island: and for the former of these, which was into Europe, the same author amongst you (as it seemeth) had some relation from the Egyptian priest whom he cited. For assuredly such a thing there was. But whether it were the ancient Athenians that had the glory of the repulse and resistance of those forces, I can say nothing: but certain it is, there never came back either ship or man from that voyage.[1]

So the Mexicans are really Plato's Atlanteans, and having been defeated by the Athenians in the traditional Platonic manner, they suffer a similar, but not quite identical fate:

But the divine revenge overtook not long after those proud enterprises. For within less than the space of one hundred years, the Great Atlantis was utterly lost and destroyed: not by a great earthquake, as your man saith; (for that whole tract is little subject to earthquakes;) but by a particular deluge or inundation [. . .] But it is true that the same inundation was not deep; not past forty foot, in most places, from the ground; so that although it destroyed man and beast generally, yet some few wild inhabitants of the wood escaped. Birds also were saved by flying to the high trees and woods. For as for men, although they had buildings in many places, higher than the depth of the water, yet that inundation, though it were shallow, had a long continuance; whereby they of the vale that were not drowned, perished for want of food and other things necessary.[2]

This semi-destruction of the Great Atlantis accounts for the current 'backwardness' of the Americans:

So as marvel you not at the thin population of America, nor at the rudeness and ignorance of the people; for you must account your inhabitants of America as a young people; younger a thousand years, at the least, than the rest of the world: for that there was so much time between the universal flood and their particular inundation. For the poor remnant of human seed, which remained in their mountains, peopled the country again slowly, by little and little; and being simple and savage people, (not like Noah and his sons, which was the chief family of the earth;) they were not able to leave letters, arts, and civility to their posterity; and having likewise in their mountainous habitations been used (in respect of the extreme cold of those regions) to clothe themselves with the skins of tigers, bears, and great hairy goats, that they have in those parts; when after they came down into the valley, and found the intolerable heats which are there, and knew no means of lighter apparel, they were forced to begin the custom of going naked, which continueth at this day [. . .] So you see, by this main accident of time, we lost our traffic with the Americans.[3]

So the 'Great Atlantis', which was inundated but subsequently drained, is now America; the New Atlantis is an island called Bensalem.

In *New Atlantis*, the people being told his information are travellers who have landed on Bensalem after their ship was blown off course as they were sailing from Peru to China. Their hosts are generous and provide all the information about the island that they need: the islanders are Christians, having been converted 'through the apostolical and miraculous evangelism of Saint Bartholomew', who also helped them to survive the flood by using an ark; a college of scholars, known as the House of Solomon, seeks 'the knowledge of causes, and secret motions of things; and the enlarging of the bounds of human empire, to the effecting of all things possible'; their marriages are strong, and 'there are no stews, no dissolute houses, no courtesans, nor any thing of that kind'; the productivity of their land, fishing and local trade means that they are completely self-sufficient; and they even have 'houses of deceits of the senses; where we represent all manner of feats of juggling, false apparitions, impostures, and illusions; and their fallacies.' In short, they have everything for a beautiful life.

On the whole, the Bensalem islanders keep themselves to themselves, although they do keep abreast of developments across the world. They have much to lose, and rather than risking everything on Plato-style Atlantean imperialistic ventures, which we know ultimately ended in defeat and divine destruction, they seek their own intellectual enrichment by peaceful means. Indeed, they are keen that others should benefit from their example, since once the Governor has concluded his narrative, he says,

God bless thee, my son; and God bless this relation, which I have made. I give thee leave to publish it for the good of other nations; for we here are in God's bosom, a land unknown.[4]

And in a final homage to Plato, Bacon ends the work in the style of the *Critias*:

[The rest was not perfected.][5]

SCIENCE AND SCRIPTURE

Sir Francis Bacon favoured reading ancient myths allegorically. He felt that this allowed him to get beyond crazy narratives and access the wisdom of antiquity.[6] But other thinkers were more inclined to take the historicist line, at least with Atlantis, as the idea of Atlantis-in-America persisted. One of these was the English doctor and clergyman John Swan (died 1671), who wrote the rather bizarre *Speculum mundi: Or A glasse representing the face of the world shewing both that it did begin, and must also end: the manner how, and time when, being largely examined. Whereunto is joyned an hexameron, or a serious discourse of the causes, continuance, and qualities of things in nature; occasioned as matter pertinent to the work done in the six dayes of the worlds creation.*[7] First published in 1635, and true to its title, Swan's book approaches natural history within the framework of theology, and tries to make an encyclopaedic representation of seventeenth-century scientific knowledge, arranged on the basis of the six days of the Creation. It confronts contemporary conflicts between science and scripture, and in doing so deals with Atlantis:

> this I may think may be supposed, that America was some-
> times part of that great land which *Plato* calleth the Atlantick
> island, and that the Kings of that island had some inter-
> course between the people of Europe and Africa [. . .] But
> when it happened that this island became a sea, time wore
> out the remembrance of remote countreys: and that upon
> this occasion, namely by reason of the mud and dirt, and
> other rubbish of this kind. For when it sunk, it became a sea,
> which at first was full of mud; and thereupon could not be
> sailed, untill a long time after: yea so long, that such as were
> the sea-men in those dayes, were either dead before the sea
> came to be clear again, or else sunk with the island. [So the]
> memorie perished [. . .] Yet that such an island was, and
> swallowed by an earthquake, I am verily perswaded: and if
> *America* joyned not to the West part of it, yet surely it could
> not be farre distant, because *Plato* describes it as a great

island: neither do I think that there was much sea between
Africa and the said island.[8]

So we have Atlantis in America; Atlantis as a bridge between the
two sides of the Atlantic; the inundation of the island; navigational
problems caused by mud; fading memories; and an earthquake, all
of which Swan is happy to accept. This is fascinating, given that he
was prepared to criticise the ignorance that characterised spontane-
ously combusted swamp gases being taken for walking spirits, and
that he also rejects tales of many fantastic creatures, although he
also accepts the existence of fish with feet and mermaids among the
'strange fish' of the waters.

The potential truth of Plato's Atlantis story, and specifically the
dating given by the Egyptian priest, was always going to have ramifications for biblical studies. In the second quarter of the sixteenth
century, Bishop James Ussher had worked out from the genealogies of Genesis that the Creation took place on Sunday, 23 October
4004 BC. But if that was correct, how could it be reconciled with
'the divine' Plato's Egyptian records, which extended back several
millennia prior to that? It was in fact an issue that was over 1,000
years old, since back in the fifth century, in *The City of God*,
Augustine had entered the controversy with a chapter headed, 'Of
the falseness of the history that the world hath continued many
thousand years', followed later by confronting 'The Egyptians'
abominable lyings, to claim their wisdom the age of 100,000
years'.[9]

Classical paganism and Genesis could not easily coexist, and
seventeenth-century discoveries about the natural world were also
raising serious and persistent questions. For instance, the Dane
Niels Stensen (1638–86), better known by the Latinised forms of his
name Nicholas Stenonis or Nicolas Steno, whose work is still influential among modern geologists and palaeontologists, challenged

the prevailing explanations of rock formation. And as far as Atlantis was concerned, he was a believer:

> I would not like to be won over too easily by the fabulous tales of the Ancients, but they do contain many things that I believe to be true. Consider, for example, a series of assertions whose falsity rather than truth seems to me questionable. For instance, the separation of the Mediterranean from the western ocean [the Atlantic], the existence of a link between the Mediterranean and the Red Sea, and the submersion of the island of Atlantis.[10]

The scientific explorations being pursued by Steno and others represented a major challenge to Christian chronology, even though Steno himself subsequently converted to Roman Catholicism in 1667 and pretty well abandoned science after that, to the chagrin of his colleagues. But one solution to the problem, or one of the most dangerous heresies ever to make it into print, depending on one's standpoint, came from Isaac La Peyrère (1596–1676). His 'pre-Adamite' theory was expounded in *Praeadamitae, sive Exercitatis super versibus duodecimo, decimotertio, & decimoquarto, capitis quinti Epistolae D. Pauli ad Romanos. quibus inducuntur primi homines ante Adamum conditi*, published in Amsterdam in Latin in 1655, and in English translation as *Men Before Adam* the year after. The gist of his argument was that the spread of human beings across all the regions of the world implies that there must have been human beings before Adam and Eve. So La Peyrère set out to prove that Adam was not the father of the entire human race, but only of the Jews: the Chosen People come from Adam and Eve; the Gentiles are the descendants of humans created before Adam – the 'pre-Adamites'. Arguments supporting this could come from Genesis, where Adam and Eve's son Cain takes a wife (who presumably has to come from somewhere other than Adam and Eve), or from Plato, where Solon say that Atlantis existed 9,000 years before he went to Egypt. Plato's testimony carried a lot of weight with La Peyrère: if the 'divine' philosopher said that Atlantis existed *c.* 9600 BC, then the human race existed long before Adam.[11] QED.

In 1665, also in Amsterdam, La Peyrère's older contemporary Athanasius Kircher (1602–80) released a publication that contained one of the most famous, and subsequently most discussed, maps of *Insula Atlantis*. The book in question was *Mundus subterraneus (The Subterranean World)*,[12] which expounded all sorts of theories (sometimes quite extraordinary) about various geological and geographical topics – water and fire cycles; aquifers; magma chambers; speleology, etc. – and contained some fascinating engravings showing the earth's interior, Mount Vesuvius and Mount Etna erupting, a dragon, some giants, and *Situs Insulae Atlantidis, a Mari olim obsorptae ex mente Aegyptiorum et Platonis discriptio* ('the Site of the Island of Atlantis, once-upon-a-time swallowed up by the Sea, a description from mind of the Egyptians and of Plato').[13] The illustration in question, which has north at the bottom as indicated by an arrow pointing downwards, shows Plato's Atlantis more or less in the middle of the Atlantic Ocean, much smaller than Europe and Africa put together, with a large expanse of sea between it and the clearly labelled Africa and Hispania on the left, and two unnamed islands between it and America on the right. There are six rivers on Atlantis Island, plus a large mountain in the centre, but there is no city, no rings of water, walls, canals, etc. It is essentially a vague and imaginative sketch, but it has not been without its influence in the vague and imaginative musings of more recent seekers of the island.

ATLANTIS IN SWEDEN

Up until around the end of the seventeenth century, the primary texts in the various searches for Atlantis and its influence were Plato and the Bible, and the island, or its inhabitants, were generally moving westwards and/or southwards, or to Judaea, in line with the discovery of new lands and/or nationalist, religious and imperialist ideologies. But then the Swedish scholar Olaüs or Olof Rudbeck (1630–1702) introduced a radically new approach to Atlantis, its whereabouts and its place in the history of the world. He became Rector of the University of Uppsala, where he created a botanical garden and an anatomy theatre, in addition to discovering lymphatic circulation, but although botany and anatomy were his true areas of expertise, he also had an interest in etymology and archaeology, for which he found an outlet in his *Atlantica, sive Manheim, vero Japheti posteriorum sedes ac patria*, published in Uppsala in several volumes between 1679 and 1702.

As the title of the work makes explicit, Rudbeck's thesis was that Atlantis was the home of Mankind (*Manheim*), 'the seat and land of the descendants of Noah's son Japheth'. There was nothing too original about that, but where he departed radically from his predecessors, although there is no hint of it in the title of the book, is where he located Atlantis. He started with the medieval Icelandic texts known as the *Eddas*, which are a valuable source for Norse mythology. These in turn led him to 'discover' that this 'seat and land' of Atlantis was in Sweden, with the main city situated quite close to Uppsala. He had based this on the assumption that Plato's Atlantis and Calypso's Isle of Ogygia in the *Odyssey* were identical. Then he used the wind directions given in the *Odyssey*, supplemented by some comments by Plutarch about the shape of the earth, and decided that Atlantis could be found between the latitudes of Mecklenburg in Germany and Vinililand in Sweden. The deft manipulation of some Viking poetry then allowed him to come down in favour of the latter.

There is much in here that is nationalistic. Rudbeck was following a kind of 'Gothic supremacism', tracing Swedish power back to the Gothic tribes whose relations with the Late Roman Empire in the West saw them able to defeat Roman armies, dictate the terms of treaties and, indeed, under Alaric, to sack Rome itself in 410.[14] Sweden was a significant power in the seventeenth century, especially under King Gustavus Adolphus (reigned 1611–32), but in Rudbeck's lifetime the Swedes had suffered some serious military setbacks, and his 'Atlanto-nationalism' needs to be understood in the context of seventeenth-century conflicts, which frequently had a Catholic v. Protestant edge to them. *Atlantica, sive Manheim* was written while Lutheran Sweden was still coming to terms with the abdication in July 1654 of Queen Christina, 'Queen of the Swedes, Goths and Vandals', and her conversion to Roman Catholicism. For the Protestant Rudbeck, the Atlantis project was part of an attempt to champion Swedish nationalism, both politically and religiously: annexing Atlantis, which the Catholic/Mediterranean world had so often used to assert its own supremacy, and moving it to Protestant Sweden was an ingenious move.

Although Rudbeck was Christian, his theory needed to blend in some Greek paganism, too. In *Atlantica, sive Manheim*, Atlas is said to be the son of Japheth, and to have settled in Scandinavia, out of which all the very early European and Asian peoples, ideas and traditions developed. Rudbeck argued that his highly sophisticated Swedish culture predated that of the Mediterranean, and in order to achieve this extraordinary cultural relocation he relied heavily, amidst other intellectual gymnastics, on goropism[15] – invented etymologies. Among his claims were: that Scandinavian runes came before the Phoenician and Greek alphabets; that Plato's 'years' were a misunderstanding/mistranslation of the much shorter Egyptian 'lunar cycles', which meant that the date of Atlantis' destruction could be brought forward to around 1500 BC – an idea ultimately derived from Francisco Cervantes de Salazar, and before him Plutarch, Diodorus Siculus and ultimately Eudoxus of Cnidus

(408–355 BC);[16] that the Pillars of Hercules should be relocated to the Øresund Strait between Sweden and Denmark;[17] that the Baltic Sea was the location of the voyages of Odysseus, Aeneas and Jason and the Argonauts (the latter 'proved' by dragging three ships Viking-style for 70 km between two rivers to show that the Argonauts could have done the same between the rivers that disgorge into the Black Sea and the Baltic;[18] that the Sibyl of Cumae lived in the Gulf of Bothnia; that the Greek word *nēsos* ('island'), used by Plato to describe Atlantis, should actually be translated 'peninsula' (the context of Plato's references conclusively rule this out[19]); that explanations of all the names of the Greek deities can be found in the Gothic/Swedish language, because the Greek gods ultimately came from Scandinavia (although the pre-Olympian Titans stayed behind to become the ancestors of the Hyperboreans);[20] that the Greek 'Hyperborean' has an etymological connection with the Scandinavian *Yfwerborne* (= 'high born'), and/or that '-borean' references the Norse god Buri; that finds of large skeletons in burial mounds provide archaeological evidence for the mythically giant Hyperboreans; that the Temple of Janus in Rome was modelled on the old temple in Uppsala, and that there had never been two temples in the entire world that resembled each other so closely; that Atlantis has nothing to do with Atlas, but everything to do with the mythical Swedish King Atle (hence Atland, the title of Rudbeck's work in Swedish – *Atland eller Manheim*); that the Swedish *Atlefjell* (= 'Atle's Mountain') signifies a link to the Atlas Mountains; and so on.

On the frontispiece of *Atlantica, sive Manheim*, volume one, there is a map. This shows the Eurasian continent with three biblico-symbolic trees on it. The root of Ham's tree gets lost in the African desert; the vine tree of Shem grows up to the name of Jesus; and the apple tree of Japheth has a root that runs from Noah to Sweden. Its trunk carries the name ATLAS, the copious fruit on the tree is labelled with the names of real and legendary Swedish kings, and the fruit on the ground shows the names of European nations. The meaning is obvious: the Swedes, not the Jews are God's chosen people. Israel has become Atlantis; Atlantis has become Sweden.

Rudbeck's publication also carries a fine engraving that shows him surrounded by Hesiod, Plato, Aristotle, Apollodorus, Tacitus, Odysseus, Ptolemy, Plutarch and Orpheus, although pointedly not Herodotus, who hadn't made the Gothic-Atlantean connection. Rudbeck uses a scalpel to point out his Atlantis (Sweden) on a globe.

Some of the greatest minds of Rudbeck's day certainly bought into his ideas, as did Isaac Newton and Samuel Pepys, and theories of a Scandinavian Atlantis are still in evidence; others were sceptical, notably Denis Diderot in his *Encyclopaedia, or a Systematic Dictionary of the Sciences, Arts, and Crafts* (1751–72), where the entry 'Etymologie' uses Rudbeck's work as an example of linking etymology with mythical history in a misleading way. Rudbeck's old university seems ambivalent about its former rector's *Atlantica*: their website tells us that

Olof Rudbeck [. . .] is one of Uppsala University's most outstanding figures throughout the centuries [. . .] Otherwise Rudbeck became best known for his book *Atlantica*, an extremely patriotic account of ancient history, today largely regarded as learned fantasies. But many other aspects of Rudbeck's work have been of lasting value.[21]

CHAPTER 10

Enlightenment Atlantis

....

By the beginning of the eighteenth century, Plato's Atlantis had entered the world of the Enlightenment. Building on the scientific advances of the sixteenth and seventeenth centuries, Western thought and culture started to undergo dramatic changes in science, philosophy, art and society, which would ultimately generate the transition away from the medieval world-view to that of the modern Western world. It was also an age of political revolutions, notably in America and France. The mathematician and philosopher Jean Le Rond d'Alembert (1717–83), who was a significant figure in what the French called the *siècle des Lumières* ('Century of the Enlightened'), described this period as 'the century of philosophy *par excellence*',[1] because of the astonishing intellectual and scientific progress that was going on all around him, and which brought with it the hope and expectation of this 'age that philosophy' (in the widest, Greek sense of *philosophia* = 'love of wisdom') would genuinely make human life better. The ancient Greek philosophers, even those before Plato, had explored powers and uses of reason, and in the eighteenth century reason acquired considerable importance, while many aspects of received authority came under intense intellectual scrutiny. It is possible to detect a great sense of optimism in much (although certainly not all) of Enlightenment thought, which manifested itself in the notion that unlike in the model of decline from a mythical Golden Age that we find in Greek writers like Hesiod, human history follows a trajectory of general progress. In this context, Plato obviously had a significant role to play, even if some of the towering figures of the Enlightenment – Montesquieu and

Rousseau, for instance – showed not the slightest interest in his imaginary island.

In respect of Atlantis thought, the eighteenth and nineteenth centuries have been described as 'the heyday of the speculative mythologist, when any scholar is qualified to construct, on the basis of some jejune late-Roman poetaster or obscure Byzantine annotator, a whole new cosmos-shaking theory of the origins of mankind and of civilization'.[2] Or put another way, there were now so many traditions and avenues of exploration available that it was always possible to have your Atlantean cake and eat it: 'Given that the world of fable was pronounced by the spiritual authorities to be a profane world with no truly sacred content, no blasphemy or treason was involved when it was misrepresented'.[3] So although the problem of reconciling the Bible with non-biblical traditions would not go away, writers were able to exploit the antithesis between the sacred (Christian) and the profane (which still had many mythological connections), either by playing on their irreconcilable differences, or by exploring the parallels between them. Ancient mythology became extremely 'good to think with'.

ATLANTIS AND THE BIBLE

The 'same-old-same-old' views of Plato's Atlantis continued to be recycled in the Enlightenment, as the island criss-crossed the Atlantic from Mexico to Palestine. Back in 1679, Pierre-Daniel Huet (aka Huetius, 1630–1721), the scholar, antiquary, scientist and Bishop of Avranches, had published a book entitled *Demonstratio Evangelica*, where he argued that all pagan history and mythology were based on the Old Testament, even though he encountered difficulties in persuading his contemporaries that the pagans really had included Moses in their pantheon. Huet brings Atlantis into his discussion, going back to Lopez de Gómara, and indeed to Cosmas

Indicopleustes before him, and arriving at the conclusion that the Mexicans were descended from the people of Atlantis.[4] This, though, was not an idea which appealed to a lawyer from Marseilles by the name of Claude Mathieu Olivier, who, in his *Dissertation sur the Critias de Platon* of 1726, dryly commented that it was 'more likely that Solon spoke with the Egyptian priests of the history of the Hebrews than that of Mexico'.[5] From there he moved on to posit the idea that because Plato's Atlantis had been divided into ten parts, they could be equated with the ten tribes of Israel who occupied the near side of the river Jordan (being on the other side, Ruben and Gad 'would have been less known among the Egyptians', and so could conveniently be ignored). This is a typical approach: in short, take a text of your choosing (Olivier choses *Critias*), and uncover a deeply buried secret of your choosing.

This was, of course, completely at odds with Rudbeck's Scandinavian nationalist musings, and the gloves came off: in 1733 Heinrich Scharbau weighed in on the side of Atlantis in the Holy Land;[6] so did J. Euremius in his *Atlantica Orientalis*, in Swedish and then Latin,[7] and F.-C. Baer,[8] whose *Essai historique et critique sur les Atlantiques* of 1762 turned the ten kingdoms of Atlantis into the twelve tribes of Israel, the Atlantic Ocean into the Red Sea, and the sons of Atlas-of-Atlantis into the Israelites. Baer also included a critique of Euremius, although by publishing his work in French he duly opened himself up to a scathing attack by Denis Diderot.[9] These authors were all Protestant, but some Catholic writers at least shared their views when it came to locating Atlantis in Palestine. One such was Abbé Jacques-Julien Bonnaud whose 'completely dotty book',[10] *Herodotus: The Historian of the Hebrew People Without Knowing It*, was published in The Hague (in a Protestant country) in 1786.[11] Bonnaud was satisfied that Baer really had proved that Plato's Atlantis never had actually existed, but was instead just a description of Judaea, albeit quite heavily camouflaged.

GIAN RINALDO CARLI: ATLANTIS IN ITALY

Another way in which Rudbeck's thesis was challenged was in a similarly nationalist interpretation, but one that made Italy the heir to Atlantis, and which introduced an astronomical phenomenon, which has frequently been introduced into Atlantis-speculation in more recent times, alongside the idea that Atlantis is the origin of all ancient wisdom. The author was Comte Gian Rinaldo Carli (1720–95), who combined Italian myths with musings on America, which had once again come on trend. Carli was deeply interested in, and admiring of, the Incas of Peru, and for him their society, which reached its zenith in the fifteenth and sixteenth centuries, embodied elements of Plato's Ideal State. So he put two and two together:

> I am committed to developing with you my thoughts, or dreams, about the ancient peoples of the Americas, which I believe are for the most part, descended from the most ancient inhabitants of Atlantis.[12]

He assumed that Plato's island used to link the Mediterranean with America, which duly allowed Italy to have links to both Greece and America. Carli believed that the dwellers of Atlantis

> had, in part, passed through Africa and Europe, where they brought their notions about astronomy and various usages and customs, and some of them even went to America.[13]

His explanation for the end of the island involved a close encounter with a large comet, which changed the earth's orbit from circular to elliptical. This, he said, lengthened the year by ten days, one hour and thirty minutes *per annum*, which in turn pulled the oceans up into an eight-mile-high flood tide, which together with condensation from the atmosphere, caused the flood: in short,

> a comet produced the last revolution of our globe [as a result of which] Atlantis may have sunk, as it was located in the middle of the Atlantic Ocean. From it sprang those populations that spread, in Americas as well as in Egypt and Europe, the first seeds of science, astronomy, the Atlantic writing – hieroglyphics – that was called sacred, customs and religion.[14]

There has been some recent speculation that a comet might have exploded over North America some 13,000 years ago, wiping out the larger mammals and human inhabitants of the region and triggering the cold phase of the Younger Dryas period. At this point, the research is tentative and the conclusions highly speculative, although the news media tends to present them in far more certain terms, and they are inevitably seized upon by writers of an Atlantological bent.[15]

In any case, Carli believed that the Canaries and Azores provided concrete evidence of the sunken island, and that the flood had also inundated various lands that were located/inhabited on the Atlantic and Pacific coasts:

> If then as shown, the Mediterranean is a new sea, and if the ancients preserved a constant, uninterrupted tradition handed down from generation to generation, of the ocean breaking over that strait and flooding Atlantis; and if the physical observations of the seabed made by the modern geographic philosophers, and the discoveries effected over the whole ocean and the Pacific sea all combine and conspire to prove that on that side also there was such a phenomenon,

I do not find it unreasonable to whisper in your ear that in ancient times, the globe was on this side for the most part dry, and that these spaces were cultivated and inhabited.[16]

In his quest to solve what he regarded as the enigma of the high level of Inca civilisation, Carli combined his readings of the ancient texts with the discoveries of the naturalists of his day, and concluded that the surprising similarities that he perceived between these very distant civilisations (both in time and space) could be explained by their common origin on Atlantis. Such ideas are still voiced,[17] often doing the rounds in memes on the internet, and like later Atlantis-speculators would also do, Carli argued his case on the base of apparent (although spurious) linguistic parallels. Practically any two words sounding vaguely alike were taken as evidence of connection:

Nothing was more common in America than the names *Atlas* and *Antaeus*. Next to the province of Meuchan [in Peru] was a city called Atlan. In that proximity were other cities with the same suffix, that is, Guatatlan, Cinatlan, Itz-atlan: all located between Mechuacan and Lelisco. The dwellers of these places were called Atlantids.[18]

This also dovetailed with the ideas of Carli's contemporary John Francis Gemelli Careri (1651–1725), an Italian adventurer and traveller who was making similar assumptions – in his case that the ancient Egyptians and the Amerindians were both descended from the inhabitants of Atlantis – on the basis of the assumed similarity of the meso-American pyramids with those of Egypt:

The building of these pyramids is attributed to the *Ulmecos*, the second planters of *New Spain*, who came from that island

Atlantis, Plato speaks of in his *Timaeus*. This conjecture is made because all the *Indian* histories unanimously agree, that these *Ulmecos* came by sea from the east; and on the other side, according to *Plato*, the inhabitants of the island *Atlantis* derived their original from the Egyptians, who had the custom of raising pyramids.[19]

Carli, though, was interested in Italy, not Egypt. His Atlantis is simultaneously American and Italian, and Roman mythology had a character who suited his purposes perfectly: the two-faced deity Janus, who, unusually for a Roman god, had no Greek equivalent. He was referred to as the 'god of gods' (*diuom deo*) and the myth of his origin that suited Carli best (as with many myths there are variant traditions) makes him a genuine person who had been exiled from Thessaly in northern Greece, who arrived in Rome with his wife Camise or Camasenea, had children, including Tiberinus (ultimately the god of the River Tiber), built a city named Janiculum on the bank of the Tiber, ruled Latium peacefully, and was deified after his death. During Janus' reign, Saturnus, a god closely associated with the Greek Cronus – the ex-Lord-of-the-Universe who had been expelled from Mount Olympus by his son Zeus – arrived in Italy, duly succeeded Janus, and presided over a Golden Age. Carli made one significant alteration to the tradition, though: Saturnus arrived in Italy as the ruler of the peoples of Atlantis.[20]

Carli's goal was a nationalistic one. Bringing in the Atlanteans as the heroes of Rome's mythical Golden Age was his way of eradicating undesirable 'foreign peoples' from the Italians' ancestry: he could eliminate the barbarians who overran Italy after the fall of Rome in 476; he could eliminate the Jewish tradition because the flood caused by his comet wasn't Noah's flood; he could eliminate the Greek tradition because Janus was unequivocally Roman; he could eliminate Rudbeck's Nordic nationalism; and having done all that, he could bring (the) Enlightenment (with or without a capital 'E') to humanity, admittedly indirectly via Atlantis-America, by way of the Italians.

There are three very big 'ifs' in Carli's thesis, as he acknowledges above, and he knew his assertions would be challenged, and on what grounds:

1. Many writers considered Plato's account a fable;
2. One should have fathomed the ocean in order to be able to believe in the existence of such a land;
3. A lowering of the sea level that would have left such a large part of the globe dry would have also meant that the Mediterranean basin, Adriatic and maybe even the Baltic and other seas would also have been dry;
4. As a result of 3, a great part of the face of the globe would have been different;
5. One would have to find a reason for such a great change and upheaval, independent of the Deluge, because this would postulate the survival of generations of men, on both sides of this new sea, where the memory and the knowledge of those prior times would have been preserved.[21]

Carli's hypothesis created a template for many that would come later: the range material and ideas is impressive; he tries to use credible documents and accounts to underpin his ideas; but the focus of his work lacks clarity; and although he is erudite he is easily lured into the realms of fantasy, possibly as a result of a lack of faith in the Enlightened society of his day.[22]

JEAN-SYLVAIN BAILLY: ATLANTIS IN THE ARCTIC

A further approach that planted further seeds for more modern speculations comes from the French astronomer and victim of the guillotine Jean-Sylvain Bailly (1736–93). His extensive writings on the history of astronomy[23] plundered the ideas of his predecessors, Rudbeck included, although without the nationalism, to produce a bizarrely eclectic theory that took Plato's island out of the Atlantic and placed it in the Arctic Ocean. He said that it was in fact Spitsbergen in the Svalbard archipelago, halfway between Norway and the North Pole. To accommodate the voracious Atlantean elephants of *Critias* 114e in this untouched Arctic wilderness, Bailly posited climate change. In ancient times, he asserted, Spitsbergen/Atlantis was nice and warm, as were Ogygia and Hyperborea, which he also located among the Svalbard islands. But then extreme global cooling forced the Atlanteans to migrate south.

Bailly built this theory of Arctic Atlantis out of what he felt were errors in astronomical data brought back by missionaries from India, south of the equator. To him, this data would only make sense if it had come from the northern hemisphere in Tartary, the vast area of northern and central Asia that stretches from the Caspian Sea and the Ural Mountains to the Pacific Ocean, and quite specifically at a latitude of forty-nine degrees north. So, he surmised, the data must have been acquired in Tartary, but then adjusted for the different latitude when it was taken to India. Bailly went on to explain this by stating that after the Atlanteans had migrated from the Arctic to Tartary, they inhabited the Caucasus in the region of the mythical Mount Qaf, before disseminating their culture to China, Phoenicia and the Mediterranean.

Bailly had his answers to the obvious objection that this has nothing to do with Plato. In a letter to Voltaire he suggested that

Plato's 'beguiling fable is [. . .] just a preserved memory of a land long abandoned but still beloved' or, alternatively, that an Atlantean Golden Age might lie in the future: 'If ever we find the country of the Atlantes, we shall know the land where our ancestors were so happy.'[24] Bailly's argument also underwent the type of protean contortions that become familiar in some later writers. His Plato lived in India,[25] and the story needs deciphering 'because he could not have expressed himself better had he wished to mislead posterity'.[26] So, Bailly argues, by situating Atlantis in the west, he really meant that it was in the east.

Nobody was really convinced at the time. The *Journal des savants* gave Bailly a critical mauling in February 1779. Others criticised him, but then proceeded to posit theories that were equally off the wall. Nicolas Fréret, the highly erudite secular scholar who was permanent secretary of the Académie des Inscriptions et Belles-Lettres in Paris when he died in 1749, was especially sceptical about all the theories of this type:

> Plato had to say what he did about these floods and their consequences in order to lend some credibility, in his fable of Atlantis, to the greatness and power of the ancient town of Athens and to the fertility of the land of Attica. Given that none of the events had taken place in his own time and that there remained not even any vestiges of the Atlantic island, he had to find some reply to objections on that score [. . .] The damage caused by the three successive floods that changed the face of Europe provided him with a solution. If the modern authors who have tried to find Plato's island of Atlantis in America had spared some thought for the general design of the *Timaeus* and the *Critias*, they would have realized that the whole thing should be regarded as a philosophical fiction.[27]

As Pierre Vidal-Naquet forcefully puts it, 'many misguided writers of his own time, of subsequent ages and also of today would have been very well advised to read Fréret before putting pen to paper',[28] but there were (and are) still plenty who cho(o)se to ignore Fréret.

ATLANTIS IN THE ATLANTIC: THE MADEIRAS, CANARIES AND AZORES

Fréret would presumably have approved of the straight-down-the-line view adopted by Jean Baptiste D'Anville. He was a geographer and cartographer who produced what Edward Gibbon thought was an 'incomparable map of Europe',[29] and he expressed the view that Plato was simply flattering the Athenians:

> Why not ascribe Plato's narrative to an Athenian who wished to celebrate his own land, and what he says about the organization of Atlantis to a philosopher indulging in speculation more magnificent than realistic?[30]

Voltaire, who was sceptical but polite in his correspondence with Bailly, stated his own views quite succinctly in his monumental 'universal history' *Essai sur les moeurs et l'esprit des nations*:

> The greatest of all these upheavals would be the loss of the land of Atlantis if it were true that such a part of the world ever existed. Most likely it was none other than the island of Madeira, which may have been discovered by the Phoenicians, the boldest seamen of Antiquity, but was then forgotten, eventually to be rediscovered in the fifteenth century AD.[31]

The Madeira-as-Atlantis hypothesis referred to by Voltaire here was nothing radically new. The Madeira islands, Canaries and

Azores commonly appeared (and still appear) in hypotheses for the interpretation of the *Timaeus* and the *Critias*. Carthaginian sailors might have visited the Madeiras, but there is no archaeological evidence to prove it, and the islands appear on the 1351 world-map produced by someone from the Liguria region of Italy (probably Genoese), known as the *Portolano Laurenziano Gaddiano*. However, when the Portuguese settled the Madeiras in the early fifteenth century they didn't find any human beings or even any land mammals. We know from Pliny and Plutarch that the Canary Islands (which are further south and closer to Africa's Atlantic coast than the Madeiras) were quite well known in Roman times, and European seafarers knew about them before Spain took the islands in 1479. Athanasius Kircher later suggested that the Guanches, the aboriginal Berber-speaking people on the islands, who had what was regarded as an extremely primitive lifestyle, might be survivors from Atlantis.[32] Further south and further off the African coast than the Canaries are the Cape Verde islands, which again might well have come into the orbit of Carthaginian mariners before the Moors, Venetians (possibly) and Portuguese made contact. Further away from Africa still, some 1,300 km west of Portugal, lie the Azores, 'discovered' in 1427 by the Portuguese, who found no traces of human presence on them. Naturally, sailors were quite capable of turning these into mythical islands of one sort or another, and they appear regularly as candidates for 'debris theory' about Atlantis.

'Debris theories', of which there are several, suggest that the islands in the Atlantic are the debris that now remains following Atlantis' inundation.[33] One proponent of this idea was a French naturalist called Jean Baptiste Bory de Saint-Vincent (1778–1846) whose *Essays on the Fortunate Islands and the ancient Atlantic*, complete with map, argued for a link with the Canaries. Again, his thinking wasn't entirely original, derived as it was from Joseph Pitton de Tournefort, professor of botany at the Jardin des plantes in Paris, who had suggested in his posthumously published *Relation d'un Voyage au Levant* (1717) that Atlantis was destroyed by seawater gushing out of the Mediterranean when, as a result of an older but similar event in which waters from the Black Sea created the Bosphorus, the Mediterranean sea level duly rose above that of the Atlantic, creating the Strait of Gibraltar in the process:

> Perhaps the horrifying eruption that occurred in the ocean at that time submerged or swept away the famous island of Atlantis that Plato described [. . .] The Canary Isles, the Azores and America may constitute what remains of it; so it would not be surprising to find that they are populated by descendants of Adam or Noah, nor that their peoples use the same weaponry as other peoples of Asia and Europe.[34]

Tournefort had himself derived this idea from the Greek Strato of Lampsacus, the head of the Peripatetic school after Theophrastus (died *c.* 270 BC), who back in Hellenistic times asserted that the quantity of mud brought down by rivers into the Black Sea had raised the level of its seabed, causing what was originally an inland sea to overflow into the Sea of Marmara near Byzantium:

> Strato [suggests] that the bed of the Black Sea is higher than that of the Sea of Marmara and the sea next after the Sea of Marmara, and at the same time adding the reason, namely, that the deeps of the Black Sea are being filled up by the mud which is carried down from the rivers, and are becoming shallow, and that, on this account, the current [at Byzantium] is outward. He applies the same reasoning to the Mediterranean Sea as a whole as compared with the Atlantic Ocean, since, in his opinion, the Mediterranean Sea is

making its bed higher than that which lies beneath the Atlantic Ocean; for the Mediterranean Sea, too, is being filled up with silt from many rivers, and is receiving a deposit of mud similar to that of the Black Sea. It should also be true, then, that the inflow at the Pillars and Calpe [the Rock of Gibraltar] is similar to the inflow at Byzantium.[35]

These processes still form the subject of quite a vigorous geological debate that mirrors that of the Enlightenment. Saint-Vincent's contemporary, the naturalist Georges-Louis Leclerc, Comte de Buffon (1707–88), also argued that Atlantis had been washed away by floodwater, but he had it flowing out of the Atlantic and into the Mediterranean, which had been largely dry land up to that point. This is a view favoured by many geologists today, who posit a process whereby around 15,000 years BP ('before the present') the melting of the ice-caps caused the Atlantic sea-level to rise until it broke through the Isthmus of Gibraltar, created the Straits, and filled the Mediterranean basin. Whether this was an instantly catastrophic event that could be mythologised into Plato's story is a further point of debate, but certainly one that is not proven.

CATACLYSMS AND RITUALS

Cataclysmic events appear in a somewhat differently nuanced manner in the work of Nicolas Antoine Boulanger (1722–59).[36] He developed a line of thought in which the entire prehistory of the world was punctuated by floods, including the biblical and Platonic ones. His ideas were summarised by Antoine Fabre d'Olivet,[37] the acknowledged founder of France's occultist religion, 'the Tradition', who wrote:

Boulanger, who undertook much research on this subject, believes with reason that after the loss of Atlantis, the peoples of our hemisphere who survived remained stupefied and continued for a long time to wander, without daring to settle; he believes that this life of savages grew out of the terror that that event had impressed upon them.[38]

Boulanger believed that following each periodical catastrophe, a despot-cum-religious-lawgiver (like Moses, for instance) would come along and take over the governance of traumatised humanity. These disasters also gave rise to religion and ritual:

Faced with the great spectacle of a universe destroyed and then restored before their eyes, men set up a Religion, the principal motive of which was to express infinite gratitude toward the Supreme Being who had saved them [. . .] To perpetuate the memory of the upheavals that had occurred, they instituted commemorative festivals which, through the details that they represented, were of a kind to remind the Nations constantly of the fragility of their existence on this earth and warn them, by representing the vicissitudes of the past, of all those to come.[39]

For Boulanger, this accounted for all ancient ritual:

The commemoration of nature's revolutions, either through water or through fire, was the original intention and earliest object of all the festivals of Antiquity, whatever form they took and among whatever peoples we find them.[40]

Interestingly, Boulanger's inundations are not punishments from the likes of God or Zeus, but periodically occurring natural events like the ones that Solon hears about in the *Timaeus* 22c–e. And as Boulanger reads the tales, this also means that

> the Egyptians and other peoples living near them maintained relations and dealings as far flung as we ourselves do and engaged in trading that the misfortunes of the world disrupted for thousands of years.[41]

If Boulanger saw 'water, water everywhere', his contemporary Louis Poinsinet de Sivry (1733–1804) saw fire, much to the amusement of Friedrich Melchior, Baron von Grimm. Grimm's cultural newsletter *La Correspondance littéraire, philosophique et critique*, distributed between 1753 and 1790, shines a wonderful light on the whole spectrum of Parisian cultural affairs, and features some biting criticism of contemporary literature, art and theatre, to which Poinsinet de Sivry fell victim for publishing his *Origins*:[42]

> The late Monsieur Boulanger [. . .] pursued all his investigations into the universe through the medium of water and at every step discovered evidence of a flood. The author of the work that I am now discussing operated everywhere with fire and could take not a single step without discovering traces of fire and its ravages. His perspicacity even extended to finding the word 'fire' in almost all the etymologies of geographical names. Could these gentlemen not have reached a compromise, the one making a little room for Monsieur Boulanger's water, the latter warming his water by means of the former gentleman's fire? The result might have been a rarefaction of the air that we could use to good effect.

> Between them they seem to have created lukewarm water . . .

THE ATHENIANS, ALWAYS THE ATHENIANS, EVER THE ATHENIANS

Boulanger was an amateur, in both the eighteenth- and twenty-first-century senses of that word. However, Giuseppe Bartoli (1717–88), the professor of Greek and Italian literature at the University of Turin and 'antiquarian' to the king of Sardinia, was a professional.[43] In 1779 he published a book pithily entitled *The speech with which His Majesty the king of Sweden opened the Diet, in Swedish, translated into French and into Italian verse, together with an essay on the historical explanation that Plato gave of his Atlantis, which has, until now, not been taken into consideration . . .*[44] It was published in Sweden, but was intellectually a very long way from Olof Rudbeck: as the title of Bartoli's book makes explicit his 'explanation' was 'historical'.

> Can our *philosophes*[45] really continue to be deceived by the political submersion of the isle of Atlantis, that is to say this image of the decadence suffered by the republic of Athens, abandoned by all and crushed by the domination of its enemies?[46]

The point that Bartoli was making was that Atlantis represented imperialist fifth-century BC Athens, brought to its knees by defeat in the Peloponnesian War.[47] And not only that. Bartoli surmised that the war between Athens and Atlantis also represented an internal struggle at Athens:

> We should certainly agree that this disunity in the Republic of Athens, this sedition whose unfortunate effects, according to Plato, stemmed from the fact that within the State there were several States, was marvellously represented by the image of two separate countries at war.[48]

In short,

It is all about one people, one town and one government that I am not yet sure whether to describe as all too well known or all too little known: namely the Athenians, always the Athenians, ever the Athenians.[49]

In going back to Plato, Bartoli was ahead of his time. He certainly came in for criticism and ridicule, with the great Plato-scholar Thomas-Henri Martin accusing him of deliberately mistranslating the texts to suit his argument,[50] but unlike his predecessors, and many who have come after him, he had realised that Plato wanted his readers to seek a vital political message, not a sunken island.

CHAPTER 11

Romanticism and Atlantis

....

As the eighteenth century made the transition to the nineteenth, new attitudes and/or intellectual orientations started to work their way into many works of literature, art, architecture, music, historiography and criticism. The people at the forefront of these changes are now known as the 'Romantics' although they wouldn't have used the term themselves: the label was only really attached retrospectively, from around the mid-nineteenth century. The Romantics were by no means unanimous in everything they said and did, but certain characteristic attitudes started to emerge:[1] some of them regarded themselves as prophetic figures who could (re)interpret reality; they highlighted the therapeutic effects of the imagination, which could empower people to transcend their everyday world; they believed that they could regenerate mankind spiritually; they rejected the calm, ordered, harmonious rationality of late eighteenth-century neoclassicism; they kicked against Enlightenment rationalism and emphasised the irrational, emotional, subjective, imaginative, spontaneous, personal, individual, visionary and transcendental; they felt that the imagination gave access to spiritual truth; they stood in awe of nature's beauty; they were fascinated by the genius, the hero, and his/her passions and inner struggles; they thought an artist's creativity outweighed any adherence to formal rules and traditional procedures; they were interested in folk culture, national and ethnic cultural origins; and some of them also developed a predilection for the exotic, the mysterious, the weird, the occult and the satanic. One might say that Atlantis could have provided them with a spiritual home.

Occultist Atlantis

One figure who straddles the transition from the Enlightenment to Romanticism is Jean-Baptiste Isoard (1743–1816), aka Delisle de Sales. He was not a man lacking self-confidence: he had a bust of himself engraved with the legend, 'God, man, nature: he explained them all', which he attempted to do in his forty-two-volume *A New History of all the Peoples of the World, or a History of Mankind*.[2] The people of Atlantis had a seminal role in this:

> Clearly, all that I write about the people of Atlantis can be accommodated with Genesis. Were that not the case, this part of my work would have to be rejected, for the authority of Moses is everything and mine is nothing.[3]

There is nothing very new in this, but Delisle de Sales then separates his Atlanteans from Plato's. Delisle de Sales' Atlantis was in the Caucasus Mountains, which are often said to divide Europe from Asia.[4] Then a cataclysmic flood forced them to migrate, with one group of refugees reaching the Atlas Mountains in Africa, which gave them their name, while, again on the assumption that Homer's Ogygia should be identified with Atlantis, Plato's Atlantis (not to be confused with Delisle de Sales') was situated in the Mediterranean between Italy and Carthage and originally encompassed great areas of Italy and North Africa. Sardinia is part of the debris.

Among Delisle de Sales' immediate circle of friends was Chateaubriand (1768–1848) who included some musings on American ruins in *The Genius of Christianity*:

> Man is suspended in the present, in between two abysses: behind him and before him, all is dark [. . .] But whatever the

conjectures on these American ruins may be, when combined with the visions of a primitive world and the chimera of an Atlantis, for the civilized nation that may have driven a plough through the plain where the Iroquois now hunt bears, the time needed in order to accomplish its destiny was no longer than that which swallowed up the empires of the likes of Cyrus, Alexander and Caesar.[5]

The allusion to 'visions of a primitive world' is aimed at Delisle de Sales.

Among Delisle de Sales' friends was the occultist Antoine Fabre d'Olivet (1767–1825), beautifully described as

a great mind lost in the dreams of the occult sciences and the mysteries of alchemy, and over-inclined to wrap himself in clouds of esotericism. In the middle of an ideally liberated world, he was determined to reconstruct a secret temple. He appointed himself its priest in the ancient manner, intermingling Egyptian beliefs with Christianity.[6]

However, Fabre d'Olivet regarded himself as a scholar, with access to what he described as knowledge held solely by the 'imperial theosophist' that had been revealed at the dawn of the ages.[7] Atlantis fitted his ideas nicely:

Who knows whether the *Athlantes* [sic] were not privileged to return [he uses *reçevoir*, but means *revenir*] more than once from the ice of winter to nature's springtime?[8]

Like a number of his predecessors, Fabre d'Olivet was obsessed with a combination of Plato's Atlantis and the Hebrews, which appeared in 1805 in his *Lettres à Sophie sur l'histoire*. Here, on

Atlantis, the young Adim (Adam), son of Neptune's (i.e. Poseidon's) high priest Eloim, is in love with Venus' priestess Evenha (Eve). Despite difficulties their romance achieves a happy ending after the Atlantis flood.[9] They end up in the Caucasus Mountains, which makes it clear enough that Fabre d'Olivet got the idea from his friend Delisle de Sales.

Fabre d'Olivet also regarded the peoples of 'primitive' times as comprising three groups:

1. the Atlanteans, who are the inventors of agriculture, and correspond to the Gods;
2. the Peris, who are the inventors of religions, and correspond to the Genies;
3. the Scythians, who are the inventors of warfare, and correspond to the Giants.

Then, after 'an upheaval similar to that which destroyed Atlantis',[10] the Hebrews become the heirs to the Atlanteans, the Chinese to the Peris, and the Celts to the Scythians. Then the races interbreed: Atlantean-Peri unions produce the trading peoples, while Scythian-Peri descendants include the Medes and the Aryans. As Vidal-Naquet rightly observes,[11] we have travelled a very long way from the Atlanto-nationalism of the likes of Rudbeck, or indeed the Spanish thinkers of the Age of Discovery.

The goal of Fabre d'Olivet's later *Hermeneutic Interpretation of the Origin of the Social State of Man and the Destiny of the Adamic Race*[12] was to bring together the sacred books of all nations, albeit without favouring 'an ignorant and poor small country called Judaea'. But the Bible was included, largely because Fabre – and only Fabre – claimed to have the only true key to it.[13] The book places great emphasis on a huge conflict between 'the White Race' and a more ancient 'Black Race' that 'dominated the earth and held the sceptre of power there'. Fabre d'Olivet openly concedes his debt to Rudbeck and Bailly:

> The vague memory of the [Nordic] origin of [the White Race] made the north pole the nursery of the human race [. . .] It gave rise to [. . .] the many traditions that led Olaus Rudbeck to place Plato's Atlantis in Scandinavia and authorized Bailly to discern the cradle of all the earth's sciences, arts and mythologies on the deserted rocks whitened by the frosts of Spitsbergen. [Fabre d'Olivet then adds an interesting foot-note . . .] In the writings of these two authors one may read the many testimonies with which they support their asser-tions. They are inadequate for their hypotheses as a whole. But they become irresistible in determining where the White Race first lived and its place of origin.[14]

However, Fabre d'Olivet relocates Atlantis away from Sweden and Spitsbergen. For him, the White Race of the North are going to become the Celtic or Scythian race; the Black Race live in the South, where the Atlantean 'masters of the universe', belong.[15] In the conflict, the Celts, led by the Druids, conquer the Atlanteans and somehow acquire 'a vague knowledge of writing', except that whereas the southern-hemisphere-dwelling Atlanteans wrote from right to left, the Celts chose the opposite direction because that is the way the sun moves across the sky in their northerly parts.[16]

Atlantis thought was clearly moving away from Plato's island at an extraordinary rate, and so it continued to do when Fabre d'Olivet asserted that the Atlanteans were monotheists, having derived that style of faith from the Hebrews. Atlantis has the curious property of constantly being relocated into areas of new discovery, and the epicentre of activity in Fabre d'Olivet's work became Egypt, whose culture was becoming far better known, particularly in France, as a result of Napoleon Bonaparte's activities there in the 1790s. Despite that, Fabre d'Olivet was happy to state that Egypt was the last country to remain under Atlantean domination. There is certainly a pleasingly neat circularity about Fabre d'Olivet's work: Plato's Atlantis had been born out of Solon's journey to Egypt, which is where Fabre d'Olivet destroyed it. For him, Egypt was where the interface contact between the Southern/Black Race and the ultimately dominant Northern/White Race took place.

> Through the former tradition, it even went back to an earlier tradition and preserved some idea of the 'Austral' race that had preceded the 'Southern' one. That first race, from which the primitive name Atlantis may have come, had totally perished in a terrible flood which, covering the earth, had ravaged it from one pole to the other and had submerged the immense and magnificent island that this race inhabited, beyond the seas.[17]

Fabre d'Olivet then proceeded to borrow the idea that only mountain-dwellers survive flood events like these from Plato's *Timaeus*, *Critias* and *Laws*. Needless to say, the Egyptian priesthood, which Fabre d'Olivet knew about from Plato's work, was guardian of these traditions.[18]

In full-flight by now, Fabre d'Olivet tells us that Moses grew up in Egypt but, after he'd killed an Egyptian,[19] he went to Ethiopia, met the Celto-Atlantean Hebrews, and became their priest. Moses' father-in-law Jethro, says Fabre d'Olivet, probably gave him some books about the Atlanteans.[20] Moses'

> sole mission [was] to preserve cosmogonic principles of every kind ['the most ancient tradition on earth', older even than the Atlanteans'] – and to store away the seeds of all

future institutions, as it were in a holy ark. The people to
which he entrusted the care of this ark was uncouth, but
robust, made the stronger by its exclusive laws.[21]

So essentially this version of Atlantis was the origin of everything that the Celto-Atlantes (i.e. the Jews) ultimately passed down
to posterity. In a nutshell, says Fabre d'Olivet,

to some extent [we, i.e. the White/Northern race] owe our
very existence to the disaster of Atlantis.[22]

Fabre d'Olivet's whole construct is obviously imaginary, although
it is very hard to ascertain what his own attitude to it was. But it
represents an important development in the way that Atlantis was
being used, and indeed sometimes still is. As Pierre Vidal-Naquet
put it, 'what is interesting and novel in Fabre d'Olivet is the fact that
his great fantasy is carefully set within a time-frame, unsupported
by any historical source of course but nevertheless presented as a
partly biblical, partly neo-pagan reconstruction of the history of
humanity'.[23] He had set the tone for many who would follow him.

WILLIAM BLAKE

A close contemporary of Fabre d'Olivet was William Blake (1757–
1827), a man whose childhood spiritual visions had a powerful
influence on both his personal and professional life. Blake never
found it easy to make a living from his work during his lifetime, but
his ideas ultimately became quite influential in the later nineteenth
century. In his mythology, the Giant Albion is the pre-Hebrew
ancestor of the Britons (Britain itself is also called Albion), and is
closely associated with 'the Atlantic continent'.[24] In *Jerusalem*,
subtitled *The Emanation of the Giant Albion* (1804–20, with later

additions, and not to be confused with the hymn 'Jerusalem'), Blake gives the Jews some extraordinary information about their ancestry:

TO THE JEWS.

Jerusalem the Emanation of the Giant Albion! Can it be? Is
    it a
Truth that the Learned have explored? Was Britain the
    Primitive Seat of
the Patriarchal Religion? If it is true, my title-page is also
    True, that
Jerusalem was & is the Emanation of the Giant Albion. It is
    True, and
cannot be controverted. Ye are united, O ye Inhabitants of
    Earth, in One
Religion: The Religion of Jesus: the most Ancient, the
    Eternal & the
Everlasting Gospel [. . .]
'All things Begin & End in Albion's Ancient Druid Rocky
    Shore.'

Your Ancestors derived their origin from Abraham, Heber,
    Shem, and
Noah, who were Druids: as the Druid Temples (which are
    the Patriarchal
Pillars & Oak Groves) over the whole Earth witness to this
    day.
[. . .]
Albion was the Parent of the Druids: & in his Chaotic State
    of Sleep
Satan & Adam & the whole World was Created by the
    Elohim.[25]

Albion's England, alongside America, is the heir to Atlantis, as well as being yet another homeland of the tribes of Israel:

Twelve-fold, here all the Tribes of Israel I behold
Upon the Holy Land: I see the River of Life & Tree of Life,
I see the New Jerusalem descending out of Heaven
Between thy Wings of gold & silver feather'd, immortal,
Clear as the rainbow, as the cloud of the Sun's tabernacle.
[. . .]
What do I see! The Briton, Saxon, Roman, Norman
    amalgamating
In my Furnaces into One Nation, the English: & taking
    refuge
In the Loins of Albion. The Canaanite united with the
    fugitive
Hebrew, whom she divided into Twelve, & sold into Egypt,
Then scatter'd the Egyptian & Hebrew to the four Winds:
This sinful Nation Created in our Furnaces & Looms is
    Albion.[26]

Blake was influenced by people who thought that the early Celts of the British Isles, and particularly the Druids, were the source of all ancient wisdom. He also took the legend that Britain was the domain of the Giant Albion, factored in that the Greek Atlas was associated with an island in the Atlantic Ocean, and so equated Albion with Atlas. In those ancient times Albion/Atlas' territory formed a link between Britain and America. But that changed:

Therefore remove from Albion these terrible Surfaces
And let wild seas & rocks close up Jerusalem away from
The Atlantic Mountains where Giants dwelt in Intellect:
Now given to stony Druids, and Allegoric Generation,

To the Twelve Gods of Asia, the Spectres of those who
    Sleep:
Sway'd by a Providence oppos'd to the Divine Lord Jesus:
A murderous Providence! A Creation that groans, living on
    Death,
Where Fish & Bird & Beast & Man & Tree & Metal & Stone
Live by Devouring, going into Eternal Death continually!
Albion is now possess'd by the War of Blood! the Sacrifice
Of envy Albion is become, and his Emanation cast out:
Come Lord Jesus, Lamb of God descend! for if, O Lord!
If thou hadst been here, our brother Albion had not died.[27]

Essentially Albion went into a moral decline, the Druids became
debased and the land bridge from Britain to the New World
disappeared.

The Atlantic Continent sunk round Albion's cliffy shore,
And the Sea poured in amain upon the Giants of Albion . . .[28]

In his earlier work *America a Prophecy* (1793), Atlantis lurks
beneath the sea, and Titanic powers erupt from it to inspire the
American and French revolutions, the latter of which was under way
when he wrote the poem:

On those vast shady hills between America and Albion's
    shore
Now barr'd out by the Atlantic sea, call'd Atlantean hills,
Because from their bright summits you may pass to the
    Golden world,
An ancient palace, archetype of mighty Emperies,
Rears its immoral pinnacles.[29]

We have no idea whether or not Blake was a literal believer in Plato's Atlantis, but he undoubtedly put it to very good use. Blake's Atlantis 'appeals to the revolutionary spirit that would raise the ideals, the palaces, and even the earth itself from the deep if necessary',[30] but because he borrowed Plato's name for the place, rather than inventing his own, Blake was able to play on a story with considerable historical and mythological impact.

BRITAIN AND ATLANTIS

Blake was not the only person of his day to be making connections between Britain and Atlantis. A contemporary of his, Captain Francis Wilford (1761–1822), published a series of articles about Hindu geography and mythology in the journal *Asiatic Researches*, which despite their staggering unreliability still had a significant influence on Romantic poets like Coleridge and Shelley. Deploying an extraordinary array of false etymologies, he claimed that all European myths were of Hindu origin. He did this by following 'the track, real or imaginary, of [Hindu] deities and heroes; comparing all their legends with such accounts of holy places in the regions of the west [. . .] preserved by Greek mythologists; and endeavouring to provide the identity of the places by the similarity of the names and remarkable circumstances'.[31] Among these Greek 'mythologists' was Marcellus,[32] and among the conclusions he drew were that the White Isles (the Islands of the Blessed[33]) were in fact Britain and Atlantis. Wilford noted that the Hindu religious texts known as the *Puranas* also state 'the White Isles to be the home of Vishnu, from whence Krishna brought the Vedas. Vyasa, the first who presumed to write the Vedas down in a book, resided so long in the White Isles that he was nicknamed *Dwaipayana*, He who Resided in the Islands.'[34] He went on to assert that 'the light of revelation came from the west, and the Vedas reside in the White Islands in human shape', because they are orally transmitted. In short, Wilford argued that the source of 'all fundamental and mysterious transactions of [the Hindu] religion' was the British Isles.[35]

Wilford had, in effect, constructed 'an orientalised [. . .] version of British national and imperial ideology',[36] but it was obvious that his informants had given him large-scale fake news. He ultimately came clean and admitted that his core material was based on vague recollections from the *Puranas*, which had resulted in three types of 'forgery': 1. where just a word or two was altered; 2. where the legends themselves had been significantly altered; and 3. where material had been written exclusively from memory.[37] In a way he had much in common with Critias in Plato's account, who prefaces his definitive description of Atlantis with an invocation of Mnemosyne, the goddess of Memory.

CHAPTER 12

The Later Nineteenth Century: Atlantis Unleashed

....

By around the middle of the nineteenth century, the range of theories about, and attitudes towards, Atlantis was enormous. Plato's narrative was accepted, rejected, allegorised, rationalised and even ignored, and his Atlantic island had been located in and under oceans, or on *terra firma* across an extraordinarily wide range of geographical areas and chronological time-frames, be these historical or mythological. On the way, Atlantis had been made to serve a wide variety of religious, nationalist and political viewpoints. But the interest so far was as nothing compared to what was about to happen from the latter half of the nineteenth century onwards.

CONTINENTAL DRIFT

The German naturalist and explorer Alexander von Humboldt (1769–1859) was an early pioneer of the idea of 'continental drift', an important precursor to the theory of plate tectonics. This posits the large-scale, very gradual, horizontal movements of continents (specifically relating to Atlantis, the movements of Africa and South America). Like others, including Ortelius, before him,[1] he observed the way South America apparently fits into Africa, and speculated about whether the continents now separated by the Atlantic Ocean might once have been joined. This is another area of science into which Atlantis has now been drawn, but von Humboldt himself was reluctant to make the connection:

The question, whether the traditions of the ancients respecting the Atlantis are founded on historical facts, is entirely different from this, whether the Archipelago of the Canaries and the adjacent islands are the wrecks of a chain of mountains, rent and sunk in the sea in one of the great convulsions of our Globe. I do not intend to form any opinion in favour of the existence of the Atlantis; but I endeavour to prove, that the Canaries have no more been created by volcanoes, than the whole body of the smaller Antilles has been formed by madrepores.[2]

Some fifty years later, in his work entitled *The Creation and its Mysteries Unveiled* (1858), the French geographer Antonio Snider-Pellegrini, argued that finds of identical fossilised plants in both European and North American coal deposits could be explained by a very ancient connection between the two continents, and went on to suggest that Noah's flood was caused by the break-up of this super-continent, which was rent asunder in order to restore equilibrium to the earth, which had become unbalanced. This would again prove seminal to a number of later Atlantis theories.

Meanwhile, the German poet Robert Prutz (1816–72) attempted to prove that the Phoenicians discovered America and found Atlantis in the process, thereby resurrecting ideas from the sixteenth century, when Gonzalo Fernández de Oviedo y Valdés argued that both Phoenician and Carthaginian settlers (the two often get erroneously conflated and confused) were responsible for populating the Americas. These ideas inevitably get entangled with theories about the Lost Tribes of Israel, who can be found voyaging with the Phoenicians and disembarking in the Americas. The Lost Tribes theme is now far less prominent with 'alternative archaeologists' than it was, but the idea of Phoenician/Carthaginian voyages to America still has its adherents and has generated some lively, if inconclusive, discussion into the twenty-first century. There are serious and valid objections to the idea of Phoenician and/or Carthaginian ships traversing the Atlantic in both directions, and so bringing news of an Atlantean-style society as described by Solon/Critias/Plato (but curiously no one else) back to the world of the Ancient Greeks. The Greeks themselves were deeply suspicious of 'Phoenician tales',[3] but the proponents of this particular scenario are less so. In 1872, a supposed Phoenician artefact came to light in Brazil: the Paraiba Stone, so-called because Joaquim Alves da Costa claimed to have found it near the Paraiba River. It contained an inscription, which was transcribed by da Costa and recognised as Phoenician by a naturalist called Ladislau Netto, who duly translated it. The text told how ten Phoenician ships sailed round Africa in 534 BC, got blown off course by storms, and ended up in Brazil. The French scholar Ernest Renan then recognised the Paraiba inscription for the hoax that it was; he received endorsement from other academics; Netto retracted his original conclusions; and da Costa disappeared, taking the stone with him, before any proper scholar had the opportunity to look at it. Yet, in a mindset that typifies much Atlantis-related speculation, some people still assert its authenticity.[4]

THOMAS-HENRI MARTIN – HEAVYWEIGHT PLATONIC SCHOLAR

One mid-nineteenth-century thinker who was implacably opposed to Atlantis speculation of this sort was the Platonic scholar Thomas-Henri Martin. His *Studies on Plato's Timaeus*, published in French in 1841, became the definitive commentary on what is often regarded as the most challenging of all of Plato's dialogues, and it includes a fascinating 'Dissertation on Atlantis'.[5] His intention was to kill off 'Atlantomania' for good, although he felt the whole process was an interesting topic for psychological study:

As I see it, Atlantis belongs no more to the history of events than it does to real geography; however, unless I am very much mistaken, it may contribute a very intriguing chapter to the no less interesting and no less instructive history of human opinions.[6]

He analysed many of the theories floated by scholars voyaging in the quest for Atlantis:

Many scholars, setting sail in quest of Atlantis with a more or less heavy cargo of erudition, but without any compass except their imagination and caprice, have voyaged at random. And where have they landed? In Africa, in America, in Australia, in Spitsbergen, in Sweden, in Sardinia, in Palestine, in Athens, in Persia, and in Ceylon, they say.[7]

Once Martin had analysed the speculation that had led these scholars to so many worldwide destinations, he responded with seven key points:

1. Plato's story is for all intents and purposes pure fiction.
2. It has an Egyptian, not a Greek origin.
3. The Egyptian priests made up this story involving the Greeks for their own political advantage.
4. If Atlantis did exist, it was in the Atlantic where Plato said it was, just outside the Strait of Gibraltar, thus making it impossible to put it in Africa, the seas to the north, America or Palestine.
5. It is impossible to believe that the sudden disappearance of an island as large as Atlantis would not have affected the geography of the world, and yet the fable of Atlantis

presupposes that Europe, Asia, and Africa are more or less where they always were.

6. There was no continent running along the edge of Oceanus over which the Atlanteans could have extended their power, and there are no shallows where the island used to be.

7. We had best stop looking for Atlantis; it is truly 'Utopia' ('No place').[8]

Martin's conclusion was decisive:

Some have thought that they recognized Atlantis in the New World. No, it belongs to a different world, one to be found not in the spatial domain but in that of thought.[9]

It was a line of attack that has won overwhelming support from within the scholarly community ever since. Pierre Vidal-Naquet approvingly quotes Jacques Brunschwig ('[Martin] was the first (but not the last) scholar who seems sober, after so many drunkards') and adds his weight to the sceptical side of the debate: 'I have long been of the opinion that the history of all these ramblings should have been brought to a close at the point where Martin reached his conclusion.'[10] However, Martin's viewpoint perhaps understandably attracts far less interest and excitement than the ideas it sought to demolish – mystical sunken paradise islands that are the origin of all human civilisation are far sexier to many than the thought processes of a dead Greek philosopher. If Thomas-Henri Martin was hoping to pour cold water over the 'Atlantomaniacs' and sink the speculation about the island for eternity, he would be deeply disappointed. Atlantis was about to emerge from the waves more dramatically than ever before.

Brasseur de Bourbourg and Le Plongeon: Back to Central America

Just over twenty years after Martin's publication, a Flemish ethnographer, historian and archaeologist named Charles-Étienne Brasseur de Bourbourg (1814–74) was taking Atlantis back to Mesoamerica. He travelled extensively in the region, learned some of the Amerindian languages, sought the origins of the Indian peoples and their culture, and generally contributed positively to the wider understanding of the Mayan and the Aztec civilisations. On the other hand, his interests in spiritualism and his speculations about the links between the Maya and the lost continent of Atlantis gave considerable impetus to the pseudo-science of Mayanism (which should not be confused with the scholarly specialism of the Mayanists who study the Maya civilisation).[11]

Abbé Brasseur de Bourbourg started writing about Atlantis in his *Grammaire élémentaire de la langue quichée* (1862).[12] There he argued that the high level of civilisation of Plato's Atlantis predated that of any of the cultures of Europe and Asia. In a familiar line of attack, he suggested that various European and Persian words originated in the Americas, and concluded that there had been regular contact between cultures on either side of the Atlantic Ocean.

One of Brasseur de Bourbourg's prime influences was Diego de Landa's *Account of the Affairs of Yucatán* (1566).[13] He came across an abridged edition of this in the Historical Academy of Madrid in 1864. This volume, which is also known as the Tro-Cortesianus Codex or the Troano Codex, featured a 'decipherment' of Mayan glyphs – highly imaginative and appallingly inaccurate – to which Brasseur de Bourbourg proceeded to apply his own – highly imaginative and appallingly inaccurate – translation techniques. Modern

Mayan scholarship conclusively confirms that the Troano Codex deals with astrology and divination, but in Brasseur de Bourbourg's mind it read like this:

The master is he of the upheaved earth, the master of the calabash, the earth upheaved of the tawny beast (at the place engulfed beneath the floods); it is he, the master of the upheaved earth, of the swollen earth, beyond measure, he the master [. . .] of the basin of water.[14]

Brasseur de Bourbourg regarded this as an account of a cataclysm that engulfed an island in the Atlantic in 9937 BC, whose survivors then colonised America and Egypt, and once he was on a roll there was no stopping him: *Monuments anciens du Mexique (Palenque, et autres ruines de l'ancienne civilisation du Mexique)* was published in 1866, featuring illustrations by Jean-Frédéric Waldeck.[15] These were based on first-hand observation of the ruins at Palenque, but although they are of a high quality, the style in which they were rendered invites spurious comparisons between Mayan art and architecture and that of classical Greece and Rome, which duly fuelled further speculations about New-World-Old-World-Atlantis interactions. In his publication *Quatre Lettres sur le Méxique* of 1868,[16] Brasseur de Bourbourg drew parallels between the society of Atlantis as described by Critias and the culture of the ancient Maya. He then proceeded to put together a history of Atlantis based on his readings of Mayan mythology, in which he perceived many correspondences with material from Egypt, and reached the predictable conclusion that Mayan and Egyptian mythology shared a common place of origin: Atlantis.

One other piece of speculation in Abbé Brasseur de Bourbourg's work has planted itself very firmly in the consciousness of Atlantis seekers, even though it makes the island even more remote from

Plato's original dialogues. Two of the Mayan glyphs in de Landa's 1566 'decipherment' of the Troano Codex seemed to the Abbé to have a tangential resemblance to the letters 'M' and 'U'. So he assembled them, and concluded that he'd discovered the island's name: Mu. Very few of Brasseur de Bourbourg's contemporaries took his ideas with anything other than a large dose of salt, but in due course 'alternative archaeology' would (and does) make much of Mu.[17]

One person to be inspired by Brasseur de Bourbourg was a fascinating amateur archaeologist named Augustus Le Plongeon (1826–1908), who also had a great interest in the Maya. He visited Yucatán in 1873, and is respected for the many excellent photographs that he took of the ruins there. In addition to the ruins, he also explored the possibility of links between them, Egypt and Atlantis. 'Upgrading' Brasseur de Bourbourg's translations from the Maya texts, he found a different narrative: one night, about 8,000 years before the Troano Codex was written, an incredibly violent volcanic event caused the Land of Mu suddenly to disappear, taking 64 million people with it. In addition to this, Le Plongeon also 'discovered' the tale of Princess Moo. In this story, Yucatán was an Atlantean/'Muvian' colony, and after Moo's spouse was murdered, the hapless princess was forced to flee from there to Mu itself. Unfortunately for Moo, Mu was no longer anywhere to be found, so she sought refuge in Egypt, which was also another Muvian colony. There she built the Sphinx of Giza to honour her late husband, and the Egyptians were in such awe of her that she became their goddess Isis, according to Le Plongeon. Bizarre as this sounds, and unsupported by any credible archaeological evidence as it is, the idea has stuck, and Le Plongeon can ultimately take the credit for any number of Atlantean/Muvian ideas that still persist.

Le Plongeon had the very aggressive attitude towards mainstream scholarship that characterises a great deal of current

233

'alternative' archaeological writing, be this officially published, self-published or posted on the internet: 'so-called learned men of our own days are the first to oppose new ideas and the bearers of these' is a typical accusation, but one without justification: the learned historians and archaeologists of today are generally the first to *embrace* new ideas – that is how and why their subjects have made such extraordinary progress and delivered so many wonderful new insights over the years – but they also want to scrutinise and test new ideas as rigorously as possible, in order to ascertain their value. However, they do oppose new ideas and their bearers if they are demonstrably false. On the other hand, Le Plongeon seldom opposed, scrutinised or tested any new idea for any reason, and he would have been very much at ease had he lived to see the year 2016, when Oxford Dictionaries declared that the adjective 'post-truth' was its international word of the year: it is defined as 'relating to or denoting circumstances in which objective facts are less influential in shaping public opinion than appeals to emotion and personal belief'.[18]

Among Le Plongeon's new ideas, in which objective facts were less influential than appeals to emotion and personal belief, were: an Erich von Däniken-esque suggestion that various zigzag lines on a Mayan carving depicted telegraph wires ('alternative' archaeologists love to project their own cutting-edge technology onto the ancients, although they seldom think beyond it – the Atlanteans were never said to have anything remotely resembling the internet, for instance); the suggestion that the writing on the wall at Belshazzar's Feast in Chapter 5 of the *Book of Daniel* (MENE, MENE, TEKEL, PARSIN = 'God has numbered the days of your reign and brought it to an end [twice]; You have been weighed on the scales and found wanting; Your kingdom is divided and given to the Medes and Persians') was actually Mayan; that Jesus didn't cry out 'My God, My God, why have You forsaken me'[19] in Aramaic, but 'Now, Now, sinking, black ink over nose' [sic] in Mayan; that the pre-Columbian Chacmool statues – depicting human figures reclining with their knees raised, the body sitting up, resting on their elbows, and with the head usually turned sideways through ninety degrees – were really very accurate maps of the east coast of the Americas from Newfoundland to Cape Horn; that the symbols of Freemasonry went back to the Maya, and that this ancient knowledge had also been transmitted to ancient Egypt via Atlantis. Typically, his writings got pretty short shrift in serious scholarly circles and were easily disproven, but what mattered in the world of Atlantis thinking was not that his ideas were misguided, but that they were out there (in all senses of the phrase).

TWENTY THOUSAND LEAGUES UNDER THE SEA

Up until the latter part of the nineteenth century, most discussions about Atlantis, regardless of where they ended up, involved people educated in the Greek and Roman classics, whose knowledge of Atlantis would primarily have come from Plato at first hand. But that situation was to change in the 1870s with the release of one of the most celebrated and influential of all the Atlantis-related publications. This was the revolutionary science-fiction novel *Twenty Thousand Leagues Under the Sea* by Jules Verne (1828–1905), whose deluxe version included 111 iconic illustrations that brought an especial vibrancy to both the text and the sunken world that it described.[20] The narrator of the story is Pierre Aronnax, Professor in the Museum of Paris; the person who acts as guide in the visit to Atlantis is Captain Nemo, whose name clearly references Homer's *Odyssey*, where, in his encounter with the Cyclops in the course of his maritime adventures, Odysseus cunningly gives his name as 'No-man', which translates into Latin as *Nemo*.

Captain Nemo proposes a 'curious excursion' to Monsieur Aronnax, who accepts. So they put on their diving gear and head out from their vessel, the *Nautilus*, into the deep:

The rosy light which guided us increased and lit up the horizon. The presence of this fire under water puzzled me in the highest degree. Was I going towards a natural phenomenon as yet unknown to the *savants* of the earth? Or even (for this thought crossed my brain) had the hand of man aught to do with this conflagration? Had he fanned this flame? Was I to meet in these depths companions and friends of Captain Nemo whom he was going to visit, and who, like him, led this strange existence? Should I find down there a whole colony of exiles who, weary of the miseries of this earth, had sought and found independence in the deep ocean? All these foolish and unreasonable ideas pursued me. And in this condition of mind, over-excited by the succession of wonders continually passing before my eyes, I should not have been surprised to meet at the bottom of the sea one of those submarine towns of which Captain Nemo dreamed.

[They proceed, heading towards a mountain summit where the light was coming from. Nemo confidently leads the way.] We had now arrived on the first platform, where other surprises awaited me. Before us lay some picturesque ruins, which betrayed the hand of man and not that of the Creator. There were vast heaps of stone, amongst which might be traced the vague and shadowy forms of castles and temples, clothed with a world of blossoming zoophytes, and over which, instead of ivy, sea-weed and fucus threw a thick vegetable mantle. But what was this portion of the globe which had been swallowed by cataclysms? Who had placed those rocks and stones like cromlechs of prehistoric times? Where was I? Whither had Captain Nemo's fancy hurried me?

I would fain have asked him; not being able to, I stopped him – I seized his arm. But, shaking his head, and pointing to the highest point of the mountain, he seemed to say:

'Come, come along; come higher!'

[Aronnax follows Nemo to the top, surveys the view, and realises that the mountain was a volcano.]

There indeed under my eyes, ruined, destroyed, lay a town – its roofs open to the sky, its temples fallen, its arches dislocated, its columns lying on the ground, from which one would still recognise the massive character of Tuscan architecture. Further on, some remains of a gigantic aqueduct; here the high base of an Acropolis, with the floating outline of a Parthenon; there traces of a quay, as if an ancient port had formerly abutted on the borders of the ocean, and disappeared with its merchant vessels and its war-galleys. Farther on again, long lines of sunken walls and broad, deserted streets – perfect Pompeii escaped beneath the waters. Such was the sight that Captain Nemo brought before my eyes!

Where was I? Where was I? I must know at any cost. I tried to speak, but Captain Nemo stopped me by a gesture, and, picking up a piece of chalk-stone, advanced to a rock of black basalt, and traced the one word:

ATLANTIS

What a light shot through my mind! Atlantis! the Atlantis of Plato, that continent denied by Origen and Humboldt, who placed its disappearance amongst the legendary tales. I had it there now before my eyes, bearing upon it the unexceptionable testimony of its catastrophe. The region thus engulfed was beyond Europe, Asia, and Lybia, beyond the columns of Hercules, where those powerful people, the

Atlantides, lived, against whom the first wars of ancient Greeks were waged.

Thus, led by the strangest destiny, I was treading under foot the mountains of this continent, touching with my hand those ruins a thousand generations old and contemporary with the geological epochs. I was walking on the very spot where the contemporaries of the first man had walked.

Twenty Thousand Leagues Under the Sea was an enormous success; Verne and Atlantis became household names; the Atlantis story really captured the imagination of writers and their readers as it never had done before; Jules Verne had 'brought the idea of Atlantis into the emerging popular culture of the industrial and urban West and its accompanying cultic milieu of esoteric beliefs about history and science'.[21]

IGNATIUS DONNELLY: THE SUPREME ATLANTIST

Jules Verne's Atlantis was a fictional Utopia (the word means 'Noplace' in Greek), but Thomas-Henri Martin's point 7, that 'we had best stop looking for Atlantis', went completely unheeded, and in that context the 'cultic milieu of esoteric beliefs about history and science' owes an enormous debt of gratitude to a fascinating individual by the name of Ignatius Donnelly (1831–1901). He is the towering figure of Atlantis speculation, and once he had left his mark, nothing Atlantis-related would ever be the same again.

Donnelly was the son of an Irish immigrant, born in Philadelphia in 1831. He went on to Minnesota to follow a topsy-turvy career in both business and politics, which took him to the United States House of Representatives from 1863 to 1869.[22] He made the most of his access to the Library of Congress and became, depending on one's perspective, 'perhaps the most erudite man ever to sit in the House of Representatives',[23] or someone 'with an extremely active mind, but possessing also that haste to form judgments and that lack of critical sense in testing them, which are often the result of self-education conducted by immense and unsystematic reading'.[24] He supported equal opportunities for African- and Native Americans, defected to the Democrats, returned to the Republicans, left high-level politics, flirted unsuccessfully with farming, and finally turned to writing. In the 1880s he published, among others, four significant works:

1. *Atlantis: The Antediluvian World*:[25] unquestionably his most influential and commercially successful book;
2. *Ragnarok: The Age of Fire and Gravel*:[26] a recycling of Gian Rinaldo Carli's ideas, but also influenced by Jules Verne's *Off on a Comet* (1877), suggesting that the Pleistocene Ice Age occurred after the earth had a catastrophic near-miss with a comet;[27]
3. *The Great Cryptogram: Francis Bacon's Cipher in the So-called Shakespeare plays*:[28] a catastrophically unsuccessful attempt to argue that Shakespeare's plays were actually written by Sir Francis Bacon;
4. *Caesar's Column: A Story of the Twentieth Century*:[29] a novel in which oppressed workers bring down the United States in 1998, written under the pseudonym of Edmund Boisgilbert.

The heady mix of Verne's *Twenty Thousand Leagues Under the Sea* and Donnelly's *Atlantis: The Antediluvian World* really gripped the public imagination, somewhat ironically at a time when scientific and archaeological discoveries were telling heavily against the likelihood of Plato's Atlantis having existed in a concrete way. But like many of his followers, Donnelly was undeterred by doubt and scepticism:

> The fact that the story of Atlantis was for thousands of years regarded as a fable proves nothing. There is an unbelief which grows out of ignorance, as well as a scepticism which is born of intelligence. The people nearest to the past are not always those who are best informed concerning the past.[30]

To give him his due, Donnelly deployed some of the best scientific and historical scholarship that was available in his day, although he missed or ignored other aspects of it.

Right at the start of the book Donnelly sets out his 'several distinct and novel propositions':

1. That there once existed in the Atlantic Ocean, opposite the mouth of the Mediterranean Sea, a large island, which was the remnant of an Atlantic continent, and known to the ancient world as Atlantis.
2. That the description of this island given by Plato is not, as has been long supposed, fable, but veritable history.
3. That Atlantis was the region where man first rose from a state of barbarism to civilization.
4. That it became, in the course of ages, a populous and mighty nation, from whose overflowings the shores of the Gulf of Mexico, the Mississippi River, the Amazon, the Pacific coast of South America, the Mediterranean, the west coast of Europe and Africa, the Baltic, the Black Sea, and the Caspian were populated by civilized nations.
5. That it was the true Antediluvian world; the Garden of Eden; the Gardens of the Hesperides; the Elysian Fields; the Gardens of Alcinous; the Mesomphalos; the

Olympos; the Asgard of the traditions of the ancient nations; representing a universal memory of a great land, where early mankind dwelt for ages in peace and happiness.

6. That the gods and goddesses of the ancient Greeks, the Phoenicians, the Hindoos, and the Scandinavians were simply the kings, queens, and heroes of Atlantis; and the acts attributed to them in mythology are a confused recollection of real historical events.

7. That the mythology of Egypt and Peru represented the original religion of Atlantis, which was sun-worship.

8. That the oldest colony formed by the Atlanteans was probably in Egypt, whose civilization was a reproduction of that of the Atlantic island.

9. That the implements of the 'Bronze Age' of Europe were derived from Atlantis. The Atlanteans were also the first manufacturers of iron.

10. That the Phoenician alphabet, parent of all the European alphabets, was derived from an Atlantis alphabet, which was also conveyed from Atlantis to the Mayas of Central America.

11. That Atlantis was the original seat of the Aryan or Indo-European family of nations, as well as of the Semitic peoples, and possibly also of the Turanian races.

12. That Atlantis perished in a terrible convulsion of nature, in which the whole island sunk into the ocean, with nearly all its inhabitants.

13. That a few persons escaped in ships and on rafts, and carried to the nations east and west the tidings of the appalling catastrophe, which has survived to our own time in the Flood and Deluge legends of the different nations of the old and new worlds.[31]

In the rest of the book Donnelly delivers a staggering amount of material in favour of the existence of Atlantis. Although his raw material and the way it is deployed do not stand up to forensic scrutiny, his work has a distinctly legalistic flavour to it,[32] as he traverses pretty well the entire globe, trying his hand at archaeology, art history, biology, botany, ethnology, geography, geology, mythology, philology, religion and more along the way. But if the scope of the subject matter is bewildering, so is some of the analysis. Sprague de Camp wrote:

> Since Donnelly's formidable learning is likely to stun the average reader into taking his statements at face value, a close look at his book is needed to show how careless, tendentious, and generally worthless it is.[33]

Many of Donnelly's conclusions are spurious, many of his arguments are circular, and many of his assumptions are wildly overoptimistic, and he falls victim to the type of approach lamented by the great Egyptian archaeologist Flinders Petrie:

> It is useless to state the real truth of the matter, as it has no effect on those who are subject to this type of hallucination. They can be but left with the flat earth believers and other people to whom a theory is dearer than a fact.[34]

It is easy enough to exemplify Donnelly's modus operandi.[35] For instance:

1. He compares the Old World with the New, and asserts:

If we find on both sides of the Atlantic precisely the same arts, sciences, religious beliefs, habits, customs, and traditions, it

is absurd to say that the peoples of the two continents arrived
separately, by precisely the same ends.[36]

This type of statement is commonly found in much pro-Atlantis
thinking and has found its way into a plethora of memes doing the
rounds on the internet, but, although the rhetoric is seductive, the
reasoning is badly flawed and depends on very glib and lazy hyperdiffusionist analysis. The habits, customs, arts, sciences, religious
beliefs and traditions of the Old and New Worlds are nothing like
'precisely the same'. For instance, the Europeans had wheeled vehi-
cles and draught animals at a time when the New World did not.
Furthermore, it is entirely possible for things or customs that appear
on both sides of the Atlantic to have separate origins. The classic
example is the so-called similarity between the Mesoamerican pyramids and the Egyptian ones, which Donnelly and others cling to
extremely tenaciously. This is extremely superficial: leaving aside
the enormous time difference, the Mesoamerican pyramids were
generally built of earth and then faced with stone, and they are typically stepped and topped by a platform or temple structure, like the
Pyramid of the Magician at Uxmal, dating from c. AD 560 (the Great
Pyramid was built by Khufu, who ascended the throne around 2551
BC). The only thing they have in common is that they're wider at the
bottom than they are at the top – their origins, construction, purpose,
use and chronology are entirely unconnected. They were independent creations and they only appear similar if you don't look for
differences.

2. He plays similarly fast and loose with the evidence when
   he analyses the Indian mounds of North America, whose
   builders, he says, were part of 'the Atlantean American
   Empire'.[37] He thinks that the mounds supposedly provide
   significant evidence for a connection:

> The chief characteristic of the Mound Builders was that from which they derived their name – the creation of great structures of earth or stone, not unlike the pyramids of Mexico and Egypt.

It is by no means a given that the mounds are the 'chief characteristic' of their builders, and any connection with either Mexico or Egypt is entirely out of the question – again, the mounds are utterly unlike the pyramids of Mexico, let alone Egypt, and they come from a different period. Donnelly has simply started with an answer rather than a problem or a question, looked around for the evidence to prove it, chosen the material that fits his answer, ignored or rejected any other inconvenient evidence, and arrived at the 'conclusions' from which he started.

3. He performs similar contortions with language – it takes an extraordinary leap of imagination, plus a gross violation of the laws of comparative linguistics, to show 'that the very word "Olumpos" is a transformation from "Atlantis" '.[38] In fairness to Donnelly, the cutting-edge German scholarship of the day in this field, as typified by the work of Friedrich Max Müller, was not readily available to him, but by not being aware of significant new ideas and new areas of study that would in fact undermine his Atlantis theory, he became unwittingly guilty of goropism in its purest form.

It should be acknowledged that Donnelly had no access to the types of technology and information that twenty-first-century archaeologists do, particularly in relation to establishing secure chronologies, and he had no way of anticipating the finds and insights that would enhance our areas of understanding. His approach was certainly unorthodox, but elements of it were reasonable enough by late nineteenth-century standards, and archaeological exploration (as opposed to treasure-hunting) was still in its infancy: Heinrich Schliemann's six controversial excavations at Troy took place between 1870 and 1890, for instance. Donnelly's ideas were possible, if not plausible, given the state of contemporary knowledge, and he acquired many admirers, including the British Prime Minister William Gladstone, who corresponded with him.[39]

Donnelly was not alone in postulating the existence of all sorts of 'lost continents and extinct geographies'.[40] Explorations of the floor of the Atlantic Ocean were thought possibly to reveal the remains of a submerged continent, specifically in the existence of the mid-Atlantic ridge, which runs from Iceland down to the South Atlantic, but later research conclusively disproved that conclusion: although von Humboldt had put forward ideas on continental drift, Alfred L. Wegener's definitive exposition of the theory, which itself was not entirely well-received when he first posited it, had not yet been formulated. Current knowledge categorically rules out the possibility of a massive sunken island on the floor of the Atlantic: the mid-Atlantic ridge is, in geological terms, relatively recent, and is moving *upwards* from the ocean floor as the North American and South American tectonic plates gradually move apart from the Eurasian and African ones, allowing material from the earth's mantle to rise up into the rift at the centre;[41] it is not the remnants of an island that has sunk, and there is certainly no credible geological evidence indicating that any significant landmass has sunk in the Atlantic in the last 9,600 years. Neither does the presence of tachylyte, a black volcanic glass formed by the chilling of basaltic magma,[42] which has been found on the ocean bed off the Azores, imply the existence of a sunken island in the area. It used to be thought that tachylyte could only be formed in the open air, which prompted speculation that the area where it is found must once have been above water but had then sunk. Some Atlantological writers quite like this idea, but it is rejected by geologists because tachylyte can in fact be formed under water. In short, geologists have categorically ruled out any possibility that the mid-Atlantic ridge is the remnant of a sunken continent.

Meanwhile, as *Atlantis: The Antediluvian World* was flying off the shelves of bookshops, Ernst Haeckel and Melchior Neumayer were formulating a theory about a land bridge connecting South Africa and India. This was named Lemuria by the English zoologist Philip Sclater, and in due course it would metamorphose into a Pacific version of Atlantis, becoming very attractive to pseudohistorians and occultists, either as Lemuria or just as Mu.[43] The entire concept of 'Atlantis' was moving further and further away from its Platonic origins.

Ignatius Donnelly was optimistic about his theories:

> Who shall say that one hundred years from now the great museums of the world may not be adorned with gems, statues, arms, and implements from Atlantis, while the libraries of the world shall contain translations of its inscriptions, throwing new light upon all the past history of the human race and all the great problems which now perplex the thinkers of our day?[44]

It is now 135 years later, and we are still waiting.

Donnelly also had enemies who gave him unkind nicknames like 'the wild Jackass of the Prairie', 'Ignominious Donnelly', 'the prince of crackpots' and 'Ignis Fatuus' (= 'foolish/idiotic fire' in Latin), and, within a generation, advances in scholarship had shattered practically all his arguments in favour of a historical Atlantis, but in a sense that was irrelevant: he had taken ownership of it away from Plato and had laid the foundations for a modern mythology.

Atlantis could now become the place of the origin of human civilisation; the source of legends of an earthly paradise; the inspiration for the gods of the ancients; and the event behind flood myths across the world. In the wake of these ideas came 'Atlantism' and 'Atlantology', whose exponents frequently interpolate Donnelly's ideas into their own. Donnelly is unquestionably the most influential writer on Atlantis since Plato.

CHAPTER 13

The Occult, Pseudoarchaeology and the Nazis

....

Contemporary scholarship holds differing and nuanced views about the historical or fictional nature of Plato's Atlantis, or at least the degree of that history or fiction,[1] but while academic conferences, books and articles in peer-reviewed journals still acknowledge, scrutinise and discuss Donnelly's ideas and their legacy, others have taken the discussion, quite literally, to another world, throwing the supernatural, super-scientific knowledge and/or space aliens into the mix. Others again have used Atlantis-related speculation to further far more sinister ideologies.

MADAME BLAVATSKY: THE FOURTH ROOT RACE

One very colourful character who took the ideas of Donnelly and Le Plongeon and turned them into something truly extraordinary (in all senses of the word) was Helena Petrovna Blavatsky (1831–91), or HPB as she liked to style herself, or Madame Blavatsky as she is generally called. She (it is striking and illuminating to observe how few women engage in speculation about Atlantis) was not content with connecting the Atlanteans with the likes of the Goths, Druids, Swedes, Israelites, Mayans, Egyptians or others, or seeking to locate their island in the Mediterranean, the Caucasus, Sweden, Mexico, the British Isles, the Caribbean, Spitsbergen or elsewhere: she took

Atlantis to another plane entirely.

We know Madame Blavatsky through her own very quirky accounts, which raise serious questions about her reliability and credibility. Whether Ignatius Donnelly influenced HPB, or vice versa, or neither, is very hard to ascertain, but we do know that she developed a very strong and influential interest in Atlantis. Madame Blavatsky claimed she met the Tibetan Master Morya at the London Exhibition in 1851, after which she went out to Tibet and studied for seven years with the Masters or Adepts, of which Master Morya was one. She then established a séance business in Cairo that collapsed following accusations of fraud, after which she moved via Paris to New York where, from 1875 onwards, she was involved in forming the Theosophical Society, and she published a guide to Theosophy entitled *Isis Unveiled, A Master-Key to the Mysteries of Ancient and Modern Science and Theology* in 1877.[2] There are four references to Atlantis in the book, which all concern the reality of Atlantis as it appears in Plato.

Having become a naturalised citizen of the United States, Madame Blavatsky relocated to India, where allegations of dodgy practices led Richard Hodgson of the Society for Psychical Research to investigate her in 1884. He reported that her 'precipitated letters', and the existence of the Masters, were a massive fraud: 'she has achieved a title to permanent remembrance as one of the most accomplished, ingenious, and interesting impostors of history'.[3] Obviously her supporters have dismissed Hodgson's report ever since, but in order to escape the glare of negative publicity, she moved on to Germany in 1885, where she produced *The Secret Doctrine, The Synthesis of Science, Religion, and Philosophy*.[4] This contains an extraordinary account of the evolution of the universe and mankind, and also presents us with an occult Atlantis. None of her ideas were backed up by any credible form of research, but this wasn't strictly necessary, given that she claimed to have acquired the information in trances where the Masters or Mahatmas of Tibet (there is no evidence for their existence) gave her information and let her read the *Book of Dzyan*, composed in Atlantis using the lost language of Senzar. Needless to say, no scholar of ancient languages has ever come across any reference whatsoever to the *Book of Dzyan* or the Senzar language, but Blavatsky's ideas have been enormously influential among occult and spiritualist groups.[5]

HPB's new Atlantis takes us a very long way from Plato's. In *The Secret Doctrine*, she asserts that there are/will be seven eras in world history that are associated with seven 'Root Races', each of which (apart from the first two) is divided into seven sub-races. The First Root Race came from the moon and inhabited the 'Imperishable Sacred Land';[6] the sexless Second Root Race lived on the arctic continent of Hyperborea and had 'boneless' bodies;[7] Hyperborea sank into the ocean, to be replaced by Lemuria rising in the Pacific; the reddish-coloured apelike hermaphrodite Lemurians, who reproduced by laying eggs, and had four arms and an eye in the back of their heads, were the Third Root Race, and developed proper bodies about 18 million years ago; but then the Lemurians discovered sex, thereby incurring the wrath of the Theosophical gods, and Lemuria sank back into the Pacific. Madame Blavatsky's Atlantis arose about 850,000 years ago and became the home of the more human-looking Fourth Root Race.[8] Interestingly, in the light of various attempts to 'correct' Plato's dates by dividing them by ten, HPB thought he must have meant not 9,000 but 900,000 years ago.

One of the most influential aspects of Blavatsky's Atlantis is that its inhabitants had the type of extraordinarily advanced scientific knowledge that has become a standard feature of Atlantological books, both fictional and those purporting to be non-fiction. Her Atlanteans were bigger, more intelligent and generally better than present-day humans. They invented aeroplanes and electricity, and disseminated their civilisation to other parts of the world, including, inevitably, Egypt and Mexico, where the Egyptian and Mesoamerican pyramids, not to mention various Druid temples, are the remains of their culture. But then, just as in Plato, Atlantis was smitten by earthquakes and sank beneath the waves roughly 11,000 years ago.[9] The Fifth Root Race and its first sub-race, the human beings known as the Aryans, then arose in Central Asia; the Sixth and Seventh Root Races have not yet come to be; and new continents like 'Nuatlantis' will emerge in the South Atlantic in the future.

After Madame Blavatsky died in 1891, various other Theosophists, notably William Scott-Elliot (1849–1919), fleshed out the details of her prehistory of the world, adding more detail about the earlier Root Races, Lemuria and Atlantis.[10] Like HPB, Scott-Elliot had access to 'astral clairvoyance' in the shape of direct mental communication with the Mahatmas and their Senzar books. In his version, new races emerged on Atlantis following the demise of Lemuria, starting with the black-skinned 'Rmoahal', then the 'copper coloured' Tlavatli, then the eight-foot tall Toltecs whose technology included 'airships', then the First Turanians and the Original Semites, who in turn produced the sub-races of the Akkadians and Mongolians. Some of these Akkadians migrated to Britain 100,000 years ago and built Stonehenge to make a rather moral point straight out of Plato's *Critias*:

> The rude simplicity of Stonehenge was intended as a protest against the extravagant ornament and over-decoration of the existing temples in Atlantis, where the debased worship of their own images was being carried on by the inhabitants.[11]

Like their Platonic parallels, Scott-Elliot's Atlanteans deserved their fate, although in their case they were punished for getting involved in sorcery.[12] Their Atlantis split into separate islands called

Daitya and Ruta, with the latter surviving slightly longer than its twin under the name of Poseidonis, until it disappeared as well.

EDGAR CAYCE: THE 'SLEEPING PROPHET'

One other of the legion of occult practitioners with an interest in Atlantis was Edgar Cayce (1877–1945), aka the 'sleeping prophet', who acquired celebrity for dispensing quite accurate and efficacious medical advice from his trances. But he also seemed to have knowledge that it should have been impossible for him to possess. Cayce was a Christian, but he also believed in reincarnation, which allowed him to gain access to the former lives of his 'patients', and pass details of this on to them. For his part, he said, Cayce had been a Persian king, a Greek medic from Troy and, inevitably, an Atlantean. 'And some of you, if Edgar Cayce saw it clear, may have had lifetimes and perhaps some heavy karma associated with Atlantis'.[13]

Like Madame Blavatsky, Cayce said he had access to the Akashic Records, stored in the fifth element or Akasha, which contained information about everything that had happened since the universe began.[14] Cayce's trances, he said, allowed his spirit to consult these Akashic Records, be this about the past or the future. Seven hundred of the people that he did life-readings for had, apparently, once lived on Atlantis,[15] and they gave him enough information to re-create the island's history. This started, millions of years ago, with spirits who would inhabit physical bodies from time to time until, in due course, the spirits became trapped in this corporeal existence. This shows clear parallels with the passage about the transmigration of souls in Virgil's *Aeneid*, where the ghost of Anchises tells his son Aeneas about the way in which our bodies taint our souls:

First, you must know that the heavens, the earth, the watery
plains

Of the sea, the moon's bright globe, the sun and the stars
are all
Sustained by a spirit within; for immanent Mind, flowing
Through all its parts and leavening its mass, makes the
universe work.
This union produced mankind, the beasts, the birds of the
air,
And the strange creatures that live under the sea's smooth
face.
The life-force of those seeds is fire, their source celestial,
But they are deadened and dimmed by the sinful bodies
they live in.[16]

This situation pertained until circa 10.5 million years BP, when evolution changed some of these spirits into human beings, who duly created the first civilisation on Atlantis.

Cayce's Atlantis had some astonishingly advanced technology, much of it driven by energy derived from the power of crystals. This Atlantean crystal-power facilitated air travel, lasers, something akin to atomic energy, sophisticated communication devices (although they didn't have the internet) and photography.[17] But like Plato's Atlanteans, Cayce's also had moral and ethical issues to deal with, because their bodies tainted their souls, rather like in Virgil:

Yes, not even when the last flicker of life has left us,
Does evil, or the ills that flesh is heir to, quite
Relinquish our souls; it must be that many a taint grows
deeply,
Mysteriously grained in their being from long contact with
the body.
Therefore the dead are disciplined in purgatory, and pay

The penalty of old evil [. . .] until, in the fullness of time, the
  ages
Have purged that ingrown stain, and nothing is left but
  pure
Ethereal sentience and the spirit's essential flame.
All these souls, when they have finished their thousand-year
  cycle
God sends for, and they come in crowds to the river of
  Lethe,
So that, you see, with memory washed out, they may revisit
The earth above and begin to wish to be born again.[18]

The degeneration on Cayce's Atlantis saw a split in the population: the Children of the Law of One adhered to all the right spiritual
values, and the Sons of Belial, who, rather like Plato's Atlanteans,
were greedy, materialistic and inharmonious. Not only that, the
Sons of Belial had sex with weird creatures and generated hybrid
monsters, which in tandem with some rather dinosauresque beings,
threatened mankind's existence. So in 50,722 BC the Atlanteans
deployed the shock and awe of their super-weaponry to annihilate
the monsters, but the collateral damage involved volcanic eruptions,
which caused the continents of Atlantis and Lemuria to break up,
parts of them to disappear beneath the sea, the earth's axis to shift,
and the North and South Poles to alter their locations. Some
Atlanteans did survive, however, and their memories came through
to posterity in descriptions of the Garden of Eden or Paradise (albeit
without the Atlantosauruses). If elements of this look decidedly
Platonic, believers in Cayce's ideas could argue that this was because
the story had somehow found its way into Plato's consciousness,
rather than that Plato's story had found its way into Cayce's.

But that was not the end. There was a First Atlantean Renaissance
between 50,000 and 28,000 BC, in which they possessed some even

more advanced scientific developments akin to radio, television, radar and anti-gravity, plus some other quite mystifying technologies (but still no internet), not to mention highly attuned psychic capabilities. Predictably, the Children of the Law of One exploited this knowledge for beneficial purposes, while the Sons of Belial did the opposite. In particular, they clashed over the treatment of the sub-human 'Things': the Sons of Belial wanted to use the Things as slaves; the Children of the Law of One thought they should be granted full humanity. This is classic Platonic moral and spiritual decay all over again, even though, according to his supporters, Cayce had never read Plato, or Ignatius Donnelly for that matter.

Around 28,000 BC, Cayce's world suffered cataclysms which he equated with Noah's flood, and Atlantis fragmented into a number of smaller islands, although it isn't clear whether the abuse of Atlantean technology was the cause of this. Again, some Atlanteans relocated, particularly to the Americas, and Cayce's Association for Research and Enlightenment rather likes the idea that DNA analysis could prove a mass diaspora from Mu during the First Atlantean Renaissance. This is not an opinion that is widely shared among geneticists.[19]

However, Cayce tells us, despite the biblical flood event, Atlantis survived and a Second Atlantean Renaissance took place between 28,000 to 10,000 BC. But unfortunately the Atlanteans never seemed to learn: the Children of the Law of One and the Sons of Belial remained in conflict, and although the Atlanteans' technological know-how continued to advance, the Sons of Belial used the power-crystals or 'firestones' in immoral ways, with the inevitable seismogenic consequences. What was left of Atlantis sank into the Atlantic Ocean, leaving only the highest mountaintops visible above the waves.

These events didn't quite put an end to Cayce's Atlantis, however. He asserted that, prior to the destruction at the end of the Second

Atlantean Renaissance, a number of crucial documents pertaining to the history of humanity (perplexingly, in the light of the Atlanteans' technological prowess, including stone tablets) had been hidden in three Halls of Record. These are predictably located in the Yucatán and Egypt (under the Sphinx's paw), but also 'under the slime of ages of sea water' near the Bahamian island of Bimini. Because Cayce could see into the future, he predicted that part of Atlantis would surface near to Bimini in 1968 or 1969. Sadly, it didn't, although Atlantologists often trumpet the discovery in September 1968 of the so-called Bimini Road as confirming Cayce's prophetic date. The Bimini Road is made up of straight rows of what seem to be regular limestone blocks, largely buried in the sand. This feature is to be found in some shallow waters, and it runs more or less parallel to the island's shoreline for, it is said, some 600 metres. Quite close by there is another row of stones that turns back on itself to form a 'j' shape. For the Cayceans, this is an Atlantean road; for geologists and archaeologists it is naturally and commonly occurring Pleistocene Beach Rock,[20] following the shoreline as it was when the sea level was lower at the end of the last Ice Age. Carbon-14 dating of the shells in the limestone blocks comes out at *c.* 200 BC, although in 2011 Cayce's Association for Research and Enlightenment claimed to have a rock from an underwater 'foundation wall' near Bimini C14-dated to 20,000 BC. However, there is no archaeological 'context' or provenance for this, and neither are there any man-made artefacts – potsherds, tools, etc. – that relate to the blocks, other than a few bits of modern marine debris and discarded ships' ballast.

So believers in Atlantis claim the stones are ruins from the lost island while geologists and archaeologists consider them to be natural. Supporters of Cayce also claim that the discovery of the Bimini Road is proof of his prophetic abilities, although we might note that Cayce also predicted that Jesus Christ would return in 1998, along with another series of titanic earthquakes that again would change the face of the earth. Meanwhile, the search for Cayce's Halls of Record continues . . .

LEWIS SPENCE: CRO-MAGNON ATLANTIS

By the early decades of the twentieth century, Atlantis could be found anywhere, everywhere, and across an astonishing range of potential chronologies, largely in the musings of 'well-meaning enthusiasts who usually have a theory to develop'.[21] Into this milieu walked a journalist by the name of Lewis Spence, the one-time editor of the *Atlantis Quarterly*, whose 1924 publication, *The Problem of Atlantis*, was once described as 'about the best pro-Atlantis work published to date'.[22] This is not to say that it wasn't replete with misconceptions about chronology, geology, archaeology and ethnography, but it certainly added to the Atlantis narrative, as did his *Atlantis in America* and *History of Atlantis*,[23] among other works.

Spence believed Plato's story to the letter, including that Atlantis had been destroyed in around 9640 BC,[24] but he was also aware of the problems concerning this incredibly early date for a technologically advanced culture. So he posited the existence of a landmass in the North Atlantic that lasted until the end of the Miocene period (23 to 5.3 million years BP), when it split in two, creating the islands of Atlantis and Antillia. Its original inhabitants, said Spence, were the Cro-Magnons (the human beings of the Upper Palaeolithic era – *c.* 40,000 to *c.*10,000 BP – who scientists now call 'Anatomically Modern Human' (AMH) or 'Early Modern Human' (EMH),[25] who, he says, were

the first of those immigrant waves which surged over Europe at a period when the continent of Atlantis was experiencing cataclysm after cataclysm.[26]

Spence changes his Cro-Magnons from the Stone-Age cave-dwellers that they really were, into domesticated, horse-riding, village people who 'had their cave-temples and their trades, their rulers and social grades'.[27] They were a 'remarkable', 'highly developed race', 'animated with a compelling sense of truth', good-looking and intelligent:

> The average height of Cro-Magnon man was 6 feet 1½ inches, he had relatively short arms, a sign of high racial development, the brain-case being extra-ordinarily large in capacity.[28]

They had also, Spence believed, left Atlantis and populated the world, North America included. But then the Cro-Magnon-Atlanteans were conquered by the Azilians under the leadership of Poseidon, which led to the cultural degeneration described in Plato's dialogues.

The 'creation' of Antillia (even though the name Antillia goes back to fifteenth-century navigators' maps), which according to Spence was destroyed after Atlantis, allowed the Cro-Magnon Atlantis survivors to 'island-hop' to the New World. However, the links that Spence finds between Atlantis/Antillia and the Old and New Worlds are based on the same type of superficial false etymological comparisons favoured by Ignatius Donnelly. With wayward abandon he assimilates the Aztec Aztlan with Atlantis (overlooking some staggering chronological discrepancies – the Aztecs thought they had left Aztlan in AD 1168); equates Cleito with the Toltec goddess Coatlicue, and Atlas with the first part of the name of Coatlicue's son Uitzilopochtli; and he introduces a hideously distorted comparatist methodology in support of his theory, as he shoehorns Plato's Atlantis into American mythology:

The Peruvian god arrived, as Poseidon had done, in a hilly country. But the people reviled him, and he sent a great flood upon them, so that their village was destroyed. [In Plato Poseidon came to an island; the Atlanteans worshipped him, and did not revile him; there was no flood in that sense.] He met a beautiful maiden, Choque Suso, who was weeping bitterly. [Spence equates her with Cleito, although he argues for Cleito's similarity with Coatlicue elsewhere, on the grounds that the two names are quite similar.] He enquired the cause of her grief, and she informed him that the maize crop was dying for lack of water. He assured her that he would revive the maize if she would bestow her affections on him. [None of these motifs occur in Plato.] When she consented to his suit he irrigated the land by canals. Eventually he turned his wife into a statue. [Poseidon did not turn Cleito into a statue.][29]

This theorising appeals to Spence very much, but when he triumphantly concludes, 'Is it possible for [these] circumstances to be more positively paralleled?' the only possible response is, 'Yes'.

This is a very typical piece of Atlantological pseudoscientific speculation, against which the most pertinent geological objection is that there is no proof of Antillia's existence – it is simply a figment of Spence's imagination. To a large extent, the shortcomings of Spence's work come from his flawed methodology. Early in his *History of Atlantis* he says:

It must be manifest how great a part inspiration has played in the disentangling of archaeological problems during the last century.[30]

Then, after mentioning the decipherment of Egyptian hiero-glyphics and the Mesopotamian cuneiform writings, and referring to Schliemann's discovery of Troy, he continues:

Inspirational methods, indeed, will be found to be those of the Archaeology of the Future. The Tape-Measure School, dull and full of the credulity of incredulity, is doomed.[31]

Leaving aside the staggering amount of knowledge that 'The Tape-Measure School' has in fact contributed to our knowledge of the past, it is very interesting to observe the anti-intellectual attitude that underlies Spence's comments. This stance is frequently adopted in certain pro-Atlantis circles to the point where those with true expertise are often dismissed amidst a torrent of verbiage, and long-since disproved ideas are rehashed or presented as new when in fact they go back as far as the fifteenth century. It is also frequently maintained that the fact that archaeologists and others reject these theories means that (a) they know nothing, (b) that they know every-thing, but are keeping it hidden for some nefarious reason, and (c) often both at the same time. The Atlantologists are very happy to present a preposterous picture of highly sophisticated city life in the tenth millennium BC, when the reality is one of Palaeolithic hunter-gatherers who had yet to develop significant villages, let alone towns, city-states like Athens, Ideal States like palaeo-Athens or decadent barbaric empires like that of Plato's Atlantis. There is a deep irony in the search for Atlantis that Plato, who stands at the centre of our intellectual tradition, has become the victim of an anti-intellectual approach.

Lewis Spence was subjected to a good deal of criticism in profes-sional journals in his day, but his enduring appeal in certain quar-ters is nicely characterised by a review of *The Problem of Atlantis* in the *Geographical Journal*:

Mr. Spence is an industrious writer, and, even if he fails to convince, has done service in marshalling the evidence and has produced an entertaining volume which is well worth reading.[32]

NAZI ATLANTIS: THOSE WHO CAN MAKE YOU BELIEVE ABSURDITIES CAN MAKE YOU COMMIT ATROCITIES

For many of its practitioners and consumers, what is currently called pseudoarchaeology can be great fun – harmless, entertaining, thought-provoking and, like Lewis Spence, well worth reading. But it can also have a very dark side. Mainstream archaeology is often harnessed or subverted to serve political purposes, and the same can go for pseudoarchaeology, which, although it still persists with pernicious outcomes in a number of areas in the twenty-first century, really hit home hardest in connection with Nazi ideology.

It is rightly said that what makes pseudoarchaeology is not *who* does it, but *how*.[33] We have continually seen that it operates with deeply flawed approaches towards evidence about the past, and the way that 'evidence' is deployed; it 'transforms fantastic coincidences into a grand synthesis that once and for all solves the mystery';[34] it persuades/deceives its readers by using highly rhetorical techniques and by exploiting their social assumptions; it is highly selective about what scholarship, if any, it cites; it sidesteps, or dismisses out of hand, criticism and/or contradictory evidence; the chronology of its archaeological evidence is often highly suspect; it recycles outdated and/or discredited material to the exclusion of current research; its observations of archaeological materials are often superficial and/or unrepeatable; it plays fast and loose with context and provenance, and a great deal of 'evidence' appears once and then simply gets lost; it uses randomly selected photographs and/or maps to support theories that they have nothing to do with; it rejects the constraints of proper evidence, making it highly susceptible to social, political and/or personal biases,[35] not to mention financial motives – pseudoarchaeology sells in a way that conventional archaeology does not;[36] its popularity and commercial success come about precisely *because* it is pseudoscientific – it loves unfalsifiable theories (ones not founded on evidence and reason, but which assert that they are true despite the fact that they can't possibly be contradicted by observation or experiment), which allow their inventors to abandon the realm of rational discourse – a hypothesis is not correct just because it can't be proved to be wrong;[37] it cites popular appeal as evidence for correctness; and it turns its rejection by real experts in the field to its own advantage by treating this as a conspiracy to suppress new or controversial ideas.[38]

The alternatives to 'alternative archaeology' are by no means perfect, since 'normal' archaeology is an evolving and ever-changing discipline where old theories are challenged in the light of new finds, techniques and evidence. Yet even here there are discernible trends in certain areas of more mainstream academia that embrace the early twenty-first-century notion of 'alternative facts', and try to muddy the waters between history and fiction, regarding them as alternate forms of narrative, with neither of them being more or less trustworthy than the other. What matters in this way of thinking is not the weight of the evidence or the quality of the argument, but whether the ideas are psychologically and culturally useful. In other words, the material is judged by political criteria, not on the usual principles for getting at the truth.

However, the failure to challenge pseudoscience can have appalling consequences, which in particular stem from the hyperdiffusionist aspects of Atlantis speculation. Hyperdiffusionism takes the idea of the influence of one culture on another to an extreme level, and usually regards one society as the originator of all major cultural developments, which are then diffused to so-called primitive societies who could not possibly have arrived at those developments independently. These ideas owe nothing to Plato, but started to emerge as the Conquistadors sought to 'explain' the rich cultures of the New World ('how could these savages have built pyramids if they didn't get the ideas from Egypt/Atlantis?'), and became embedded in the writings of Donnelly, Spence and others.

The potential power of this type of approach, when put to nefarious ends, is well captured by George Orwell in his novel *Nineteen Eighty-Four*. In Part 1, Chapter 1, we encounter the slogans of the Party, inscribed in enormous letters on the white pyramid of the Ministry of Truth:

WAR IS PEACE

FREEDOM IS SLAVERY

IGNORANCE IS STRENGTH

The third one is especially pertinent here: Big Brother can manipulate both the past and the future by exploiting the ignorance of the people, suppressing their independence, terrorising them through propaganda, and ultimately making them accept whatever he decrees, no matter how ludicrous or contradictory the basis for that is. The Records Department of the Ministry of Truth devotes considerable time to rewriting the history books to suit the Party's ideology:

> By 2050 – earlier probably – all real knowledge of Oldspeak [i.e. standard English] will have disappeared. The whole literature of the past will have been destroyed. Chaucer, Shakespeare, Milton, Byron – they'll exist only in Newspeak versions, not merely changed into something different, but actually changed into something contradictory of what they used to be.[39]

And in real life, this type of approach, particularly as applied to hyperdiffusionism, entered the Atlantis story, as Donnelly, Spence and Blavatsky's ideas underwent a radical change of ethos in twenti-eth-century Germany.

Helena Blavatsky's thoughts on Atlantis can, and do, generate benign New Age fantasies, but her ideas about the Root Races could be hijacked to serve much more sinister ends, particularly as it was the Aryans who were the most developed of these. The overtones that 'Aryan' now carries, conjuring up rather chilling images of the Nazis in the 1930s and early 1940s, were not always there: the word derives from Sanskrit *arya* (= noble), and was used in the nineteenth century as a synonym for what we now call 'Indo-European', a desig-nation that applies to peoples from India to northern Europe whose languages have common origins. But because by this time pseudo-scientists had habitually situated Atlantis in northern Europe, it is perhaps not surprising that Nazi ideology was happy to embrace the idea that the Atlanteans generated the Aryan race.

In 1922 Karl Georg Zschaetzsch published *Atlantis, the Original Homeland of the Aryans, with one Map*.[40] The map in question shows Atlantis in the mid-Atlantic slightly larger than Iceland and on the same latitude as Spain and Morocco. Zschaetzsch then makes a Rudbeck-esque mash-up of Plato, Jordanes (a sixth-century AD Roman writer whose *Getica* is an invaluable source for the history of the Goths) and the medieval Icelandic *Eddas*, and argues that when Jordanes writes about the Goths being reputed to have come forth long ago from the island of Scandza 'as from a laboratory of races or a womb of nations (*officina gentium aut* [. . .] *vagina nationum*)',[41] he is really referring to Atlantis, the true Gothic homeland. In Zschaetzsch's theory there were vestiges of Atlantis among the Franks, Saxons and Incas, and mythical figures as diverse as Heracles, Indra, Thor and Inti-Kapak all hailed from Atlantis. In short, the key idea of the book was this:

Without Aryan principles, no State can exist.[42]

Probably the best-known German Atlantis-novel was Edmund Kiss' *The Last Queen of Atlantis*.[43] Combining ancient mysticism and alternative archaeology with hyperdiffusionism and Nazi dogma, Kiss locates the Atlanteans on the mythical northerly island of Thule, mentioned and discussed in ancient writers such as Pytheas, Polybius, Strabo, Pliny the Elder, Seneca and Virgil, who coined the term *Ultima Thule*,[44] 'Farthest Thule'. All humanity stemmed from there:

> The inhabitants of Northern Atlantis were led by their leader Baldur Wieborg, a native of the mythical Thule who migrated all across the world.[45]

Kiss became a member of the SS but escaped condemnation at the post-war Nuremberg Trials on the grounds that he was only an archaeologist. But, reinforcing the point that pseudoarchaeology is a matter of how rather than who, of practice rather than its practitioners, we find other archaeologists working to validate Nazism.

Three years after *The Last Queen of Atlantis*, another author, Albert Herrmann (1886–1945), the Professor of Historical Geography at the University of Berlin, put out *Our Ancestors and Atlantis: The maritime empire of the men of the North, from Scandinavia to North Africa*.[46] He dismisses Zschaetzsch's 'perilous leap into the Atlantic Ocean' and says that he will keep it real. The quest for that reality took Herrmann to southern Tunisia, where traces of ancient irrigation works in a village called Rhelissia generated another claim to have found Atlantis. If Herrmann was right, Plato was wrong, and the Professor argued that:

1. Like Herodotus, Plato had misinterpreted 'Atlantic' as the sea, when it was really Lake Tritonis;
2. Atlantis' demise was in the fourteenth or thirteenth century BC, not the ninety-sixth;
3. The conversation between the Greek Solon and the Egyptian priest got distorted in translation, particularly in relation to Egyptian measurements which came out as thirty times too large. So Herrmann divided all Plato's measurements by thirty, which allowed the plain of Plato's Atlantis to fit his chosen Tunisian locality.

We have constantly seen that the gratuitous and selective manipulation of Plato's dates and dimensions are a characteristic of Atlantological speculation, as is the relocation of the island, and Herrmann now needed to do this in order to take his theory to the next level. So he said that his Tunisian Atlantis was not the mother island: it was merely a colony, and (predictably) the mother culture was from Friesland (now in the Netherlands), and therefore Germanic. So now his German ancestors were not the barbarians they were once thought to be: it was the introduction of Christianity that was responsible for that misconception, he argued, but his Atlantean inquiries had now rehabilitated his Ur-Germans into a glittering non-barbarian culture that predated the Mycenaean Greek civilisation, never mind Christianity.

Albert Herrmann achieves this to his own satisfaction by exploiting the *Oera Linda Book*, aka *The Chronicle of Ura-Linda*, aka *The Nordic Bible*, aka *Himmler's Bible*. This is a manuscript found in 1867, which purports to cover historical, mythological and religious matters between 2194 BC and AD 803. By as early as 1879, it was more or less universally recognised to be a fake, although it still crops up in Atlantis-speculation from time to time. But Herrmann didn't care whether it was a dodgy document or not: the archaeological remains of his ancient Atlanto-Germanic empire could be found as far afield as Karnak in Egypt and Stonehenge in England, and the ancestry of the people who created these 'megaliths', as he called them, went back to three mother-figures: Frya (or Freya), who came from Germanic legend; Lyda who was black; and Finda who was brown. The Empire disappeared in 1680 BC, he said, but the peoples of the north lived on to appear in Homer's *Iliad* and *Odyssey*:[47] the fact that Poseidon helped to build Troy's walls confirms its Atlantean heritage; Scherie was obviously in Tunisia;[48] there was a temple of the sea-deity Poseidon on Phaeacia and Frya's father Njord was particularly associated with the sea, and seafaring; QED, Homer was all about Germans.

The Führer himself wasn't particularly interested in Atlantis,[49] but his head of the Schutzstaffel, Heinrich Himmler, was a champion of both archaeological and pseudoarchaeological research. But this was not research for research's sake: the eighteenth-century Atlantis-in-the-north theories of Rudbeck and Bailly,[50] allied to the notions that it was a super-advanced civilisation and Cayce's assertions concerning the Atlanteans' astoundingly advanced technology,[51] tallied with Himmler's belief that the Aryans were in fact ancient Germans, and that they had acquired sophisticated scientific knowledge. So archaeologists were instructed to ascertain whether Atlantis really was the origin of Aryan supremacy.[52] Turning the Aryans into Atlanteans took just a few simple steps:

1. the Atlanteans were extremely advanced;
2. the Atlanteans had modern technology before anyone else;
3. Atlantis was in northern Europe;
4. the historical roots of the twentieth-century Germans were also in northern Europe;

5. therefore the Germans must be descended from the Atlanteans (be this figuratively or literally).

With this spurious connection duly made,[53] a dedicated institute called the *Ahnenerbe* (Institute of Ancestral Heritage) was established in 1935 to research and disseminate scientific evidence for Germany's wondrous history. But the fact that Germany's history in the 1930s and 1940s is anything but wondrous owes a certain amount to the kind of manipulation of the truth that pseudoscientific Atlantis speculation perpetrates. In her important study, Hannah Arendt famously wrote,

The ideal subject of totalitarian rule is not the convinced Nazi or the dedicated Communist, but people for whom the distinction between fact and fiction (i.e. the reality of experience) and the distinction between true and false (i.e. the standards of thought), no longer exist.[54]

In fact, the dangers of this type of thinking have been recognised at least since the time of Voltaire, who made a similar point in his own eloquent way:

Once your faith, sir, persuades you to believe what your intelligence declares to be absurd, beware lest you likewise sacrifice your reason in the conduct of your life. In days gone by, there were people who said to us: 'You believe in incomprehensible, contradictory and impossible things because we have commanded you to; now then, commit unjust acts because we likewise order you to do so.' Nothing could be more convincing. Certainly any one who has the power to make you believe absurdities has the power to make you commit injustices. If you do not use the intelligence with

which God endowed your mind to resist believing impossi-
bilities, you will not be able to use the sense of injustice
which God planted in your heart to resist a command to do
evil. Once a single faculty of your soul has been tyrannized,
all the other faculties will submit to the same fate. This has
been the cause of all the religious crimes that have flooded
the earth.[55]

Or to quote the common paraphrase: 'Those who can make you
believe absurdities can make you commit atrocities'. Pseudoscience
can be extremely dangerous.

CHAPTER 14

Post Second World War Atlantis: Catastrophism, Etc.

....

WORLD ICE THEORY (*WELTEISLEHRE*)

One major influence on Edmund Kiss' *The Last Queen of Atlantis* was another pseudoscientific approach that very much appealed to the Nazis: World Ice Theory (*Welteislehre* in German, WEL for short). This was the brainchild of the Austrian engineer Hanns Hörbiger, and was almost totally devoid of science and maths – 'Calculation can only lead you astray', boasted Hörbiger, in a typically pseudoscientific anti-expert jibe – which made it diametrically opposed to Einstein's science-and-maths heavy 'Jewish' Theory of Relativity.

Hörbiger said that he had long known the moon and the planets to be made of ice, after which he moved on to assert that space is full of water vapour. In this moist environment, small stars cool down to become ice-stars, then gravitate towards bigger stars where they remain for millions of years until they finally turn into steam, and explode. Matter blasted into space by these explosions then coagulates to form planets, which gradually decelerate in their orbits around the sun and get pulled towards it, although the smaller ice-stars are drawn into the gravitational fields of the outer planets. Smaller planets sometimes get 'captured' as moons by larger ones, in a process that generates floods and earthquakes until they settle down into stable orbits, at least until they finally decelerate and fall down onto their host planets. As they fall, their gravitational attraction drags water up into the equatorial regions, which are flooded, while the oceans recede from the polar regions, at least until the falling planets disintegrate and lose their gravitational pull, at which point the oceans rush back to the poles.

Those who believe WEL think that it explains every single catastrophe/flood-myth of every single culture. Atlantis inevitably comes into the equation because, rather like the Greeks described by Solon's Egyptian priest, mankind doesn't remember the first (at least) five of these events, although they do recollect the fall of the moon in the Cenozoic era (65.5 million years ago to the present), which supposedly inundated all the tropics except parts of Peru and Ethiopia around 250,000 BP. Atlantis met its end, Hörbiger will have us believe, when the ex-planet Luna was captured and became our current moon. This is also said to underlie Ezekiel 26.3–5, where God says

> I am against you, Tyre, and I will bring many nations against you, like the sea casting up its waves. They will destroy the walls of Tyre and pull down her towers; I will scrape away her rubble and make her a bare rock. Out in the sea she will become a place to spread fishnets, for I have spoken, declares the Sovereign LORD.

For Hanns Hörbiger, Tyre = Atlantis here, and so does Babylon in Revelation 17–18.

Hörbiger became a huge celebrity with millions of followers. His theories were manifestly untenable, but his fans didn't care, and neither did he. 'Out with astronomical orthodoxy! Give us Hörbiger!' became the cry of his supporters, and he was bullish in his own defence: 'Either you believe in me and learn, or you must be treated as an enemy.' And if anyone disagreed with him he simply shouted:

Instead of trusting me you trust equations! How long will you need to learn that mathematics is valueless and deceptive?

It was pseudoscience at its absolute worst. Plato, who believed that the ability to tell the difference between one, two and three, in other words, to count and calculate, is what leads the mind towards truth, and that philosophers should learn these skills in order to escape from this transient world to reality,[1] would have turned in his grave.

IMMANUEL VELIKOVSKY: WORLDS IN COLLISION

Hanns Hörbiger may have had some wild ideas, but there was a sense in which he and others tapped into 'some sort of cosmic collision Zeitgeist':[2]

An even madder theory of periodical catastrophes was brought out more recently by Immanuel Velikovsky [1895– 1997], a Russo-Israeli physician and amateur cosmogonist whose publishers stirred up an extraordinary hoopla in 1950 to sell his book.[3]

The book in question was *Worlds in Collision* (1950),[4] which was followed by *Ages in Chaos* (1952)[5] and *Earth in Upheaval* (1955),[6] which expanded Velikovsky's ideas on the basis of astronomy, history and geology respectively. The ideas were by no means original. They went back to the writings of William Whiston (1667– 1752), whose *A New Theory of the Earth, From its Original, to the Consummation of All Things*[7] had attributed Noah's flood to a close encounter with a comet, to Gian Rinaldo Carli's comet, to Ignatius Donnelly and to Karl Georg Zschaetzsch. Velikovsky also conceded that his ideas originated before he'd done any research to verify them,[8] which did little to endear him to the wider scholarly community, who felt the process should work the opposite way around. But Velikovsky was undoubtedly one of the twentieth century's most influential pseudohistorical and pseudoscientific exponents, and his books were underpinned by copious research, clear ideas and an encyclopaedic knowledge of world mythology, and they were presented in an appropriate scholarly vocabulary. His claims were audacious, controversial, easy to refute[9] and extremely popular.

The main tenet of *Worlds in Collision* is that the planet Venus actually emerged from Jupiter as a comet, which had a very near miss with earth in *c.* 1500 BC. This caused earthquakes, enormous tsunamis, volcanic eruptions and hurricanes across the globe, in which the 'onrushing dust sweeping in from interplanetary space' generated the biblical Ten Plagues of Egypt and the parting of the Red Sea. When the comet Venus' tail passed the earth, it caused the precipitation of hydrocarbons which created deposits of oil, manna from Heaven, and the pillar of smoke and the pillar of fire that guided Moses and his people through the desert. Essentially it was good for the Children of Israel and catastrophic for everyone else.

Then, fifty-two years later, Velikovsky claimed, comet Venus returned, again bringing earthquakes, storms, tidal waves and volcanism, which devastated vegetable, animal and human life, and was behind the story of Jericho's walls coming tumbling down. This time, though, Venus got so close that the earth temporarily stopped rotating, and the angle of the earth's axis could have shifted:

> The swift shifting of the atmosphere under the impact of the gaseous parts of the comet, the draft of air attracted by the body of the comet, and the rush of the atmosphere resulting from the inertia when the earth stopped rotating or shifted

its poles, all contributed to produce hurricanes of enormous velocity and force and of world-wide dimensions.[10]

Velikovsky thought this helped Joshua to defeat the five kings of the Amorites at the battle of Gibeon:

As they fled before Israel on the road down from Beth Horon to Azekah, the LORD hurled large hailstones down on them, and more of them died from the hail than were killed by the swords of the Israelites.

On the day the LORD gave the Amorites over to Israel, Joshua said to the LORD in the presence of Israel:

'Sun, stand still over Gibeon,
    and you, moon, over the Valley of Aijalon.'
So the sun stood still,
    and the moon stopped,
    till the nation avenged itself on its enemies,
as it is written in the Book of Jashar.

The sun stopped in the middle of the sky and delayed going down about a full day. There has never been a day like it before or since, a day when the LORD listened to a human being. Surely the LORD was fighting for Israel![11]

Needless to say, Velikovsky placed the downfall of Atlantis at this period, even though it posed a severe chronological problem by being far too early to coincide with the biblical events. But Velikovsky's solution was simple:

There is one zero too many here. [He says that the cause of this mistake is that] numbers that we hear in childhood often grow in our memory, as do dimensions. When revisiting our childhood home, we are surprised at the smallness of the rooms – we had remembered them as much larger.[12]

Problem solved.

Velikovsky's supporting evidence was nothing if not eclectic. He quotes the Troano Codex in Brasseur de Bourbourg's bizarre translation,[13] the Psalms and the Popul Vuh (the K'iche' Mayan Book of Creation, which is a favourite Atlantological text, now in the Newberry Library in Chicago), which contains a vivid account of a flood:

Again there comes [. . .] a humiliation, destruction, and demolition. The manikins, woodcarvings [the K'iche' Maya believed that men were carved from wood, women from reeds] were killed when the heart of the sky devised a flood for them [. . .] There came a rain of resin from the sky [. . .] They were pounded down to the bones and tendons, smashed and pulverized even to their bones [. . .] The earth was blackened because of this; the black rainstorm began, rain all day and rain all night [. . .] their faces were crushed by things of wood and stone.[14]

And Atlantis is deployed via the passage in Plato's *Timaeus* 22c–d where the Egyptian priest references the Phaethon myth:

Phaethon, the son of Helios the Sun god, harnessed his father's chariot, but wasn't able to drive it along his father's course, incinerated things that were on the earth and was himself destroyed by a thunderbolt – this story is told in a way that gives it the appearance of a myth, but the truth is that there is a deviation of the bodies moving in the heavens around the earth, and a destruction, which recurs after long periods of time, of the things on the earth in a massive conflagration.

To Velikovsky's satisfaction Plato had validated his theory of comet-caused catastrophe.

That was not the end of Velikovsky's cosmic upheaval, however. The Venus-comet's destructive tendencies were terminated when 'the planet Mars saved the terrestrial globe from a major catastrophe by colliding with Venus', even though this in turn knocked Mars off its orbit, and made it come alarmingly close to the earth in the eighth and seventh centuries BC, thereby lengthening the earth's orbit from 360 to 365 days. Velikovsky accounts for the absence of these very significant events from the historical tradition by telling us that the human race suffered 'a collective amnesia':

The memory of the cataclysms was erased, not because of a lack of written traditions, but because some characteristic processes that later caused entire nations, together with literate men, to read into these traditions allegories or metaphors where actually cosmic disturbances were clearly described.[15]

For Velikovsky, one of those allegories can be found in Homer's *Iliad*, which he reads as a conflict between Ares (= planet Mars) and Athene (= comet Venus, despite the fact that Venus is the Roman Aphrodite, not Athena).

At this point Velikovsky's dates do not fit the accepted Bronze Age chronologies; they are roughly 500 years adrift. Had he been correct, a great deal of ancient history would have to be revised or rewritten. This would not necessarily have been a problem: professional archaeologists and ancient historians are quite comfortable (in a way that non-specialists often aren't) living in the subjunctive world (described on p. 49), and with the idea that chronologies of ancient history are often tentative, controversial, and subject to revision in the light of new finds and new approaches – but Velikovsky's ideas were seldom taken seriously, not because it would entail extra work for archaeologists and historians who would have to rewrite their life's work, but because his evidence was fatally flawed, even leaving aside the new scientific techniques of dating (C-14, dendrochronology, analysing the layers in the arctic ice-cores) that were being developed during his lifetime. In short, his proposed chronology could not be reconciled with the secure archaeological data: his ideas were not so much inconvenient and subversive, as just plain wrong.

Yet it wasn't just archaeological evidence that Velikovsky rejected. He also spurned the theories of continental drift and plate tectonics that were just starting to gain traction. Continental drift happens very slowly and takes millions of years – Europe and Africa drift apart from America at the same rate as human fingernails grow: the process endorses 'uniformitarianism', the unexciting idea of incremental change that is endorsed by establishment science, making it anathema to Velikovsky's sexier 'catastrophism', where the natural is shaped by sudden, violent events. Research over the last sixty years or so has failed to produce any evidence to confirm Velikovsky's hypotheses; on the contrary, it has discovered a great deal that undermines them, even if 'neo-catastrophism' is now an entirely valid approach in the earth sciences and astronomy. Neo-catastrophism favours the idea of 'punctuated equilibrium': geological and biological change proceeds very gradually in the natural world, but very occasionally a significant event causes intense and rapid developments, such as the apparent extinction of the dinosaurs at around 65 million years BP.[16] But as for comet-Venus devastating the earth around 1500 BC and Mars doing the same about 700 BC . . . no credible evidence whatsoever.

It was pertinently said by Leroy Ellenberger, Professor of Astronomy at the University of Western Ontario, that

> The less one knows about science, the more plausible Velikovsky's scenario appears [. . .] Conversely, the more knowledgeable the reader, the easier it is to see that Velikovsky's entire physical scenario is untenable. But unless a critic explains why something is wrong, the rejection is more ex cathedra than a credible refutation.[17]

Interestingly, in this respect, scholarly efforts to debunk Velikovsky didn't always succeed, partly because he was badly treated by some of his opponents. Attempts to hinder the publication of his work generated sympathy for him, even among people who didn't agree with him, and the controversy made people feel that the experts ought to prove Velikovsky wrong, rather than that he ought to furnish credible proof for his wild ideas. As far back as the eighteenth century, the great philosopher David Hume had advised that you should always think it more likely that you've been deceived than that the laws of nature should be suspended, writing that 'no testimony is sufficient to establish a miracle, unless the testimony be of such a kind, that its falsehood would be more miraculous than the fact which it endeavours to establish',[18] later condensed by Marcello Truzzi into 'Extraordinary claims require extraordinary proof',[19] and popularised by Bertrand Russell's celestial teapot[20] and the so-called Sagan rule:

> Positive claims require positive evidence and extraordinary claims require extraordinary evidence.[21]

Yet Velikovsky was adept at sidestepping these requirements – his claims were vague and slippery, and he effectively deployed the rhetorical tactic favoured by pseudohistorians, pseudoscientists and trial lawyers of muddying the waters between what is possible and what is probable, while at the same time exploiting a trend towards anti-intellectualism that allowed him to make his opponents look like the arrogant bullies that some of them were. In the world of pseudoarchaeology, insinuating that there is an Establishment conspiracy to conceal the evidence for humanity's enormous antiquity never goes amiss, even if it is never made clear why the Establishment would want to do this, especially when the evidence is already out there.

EARTH/CRUSTAL DISPLACEMENT THEORY

Immanuel Velikovsky had put catastrophism very firmly on the metaphorical map, and one person who followed on from him, using a genuine 'mysterious ancient' sixteenth-century map, was Charles H. Hapgood (1904–82), a geography teacher at Keene State College, New Hampshire. His ideas didn't emanate from nowhere: in *Smithsonian Reports*, 1923, A. E. Eddington had suggested that the sliding of the earth's crust caused gradual pole shifts;[22] in 1948, Hugh Auchincloss Brown had broached the idea that the weight of polar ice made the earth unbalanced and disrupted its rotation;[23] and in *Scientific Monthly*, 1952, Karl Pauly had hypothesised that crustal sliding made the poles shift, causing the Ice Age.[24] But in 1958 Hapgood was to take these ideas to a completely new level.

Hapgood's *The Earth's Shifting Crust: A Key to Some Basic Problems of Earth Science* [25] suggested that the earth's hard crust slides around its semi-fluid core, which has allowed the poles regularly to shift position throughout its history:

The crust is very thin [. . .] made of comparatively rigid, crystalline rock [. . .] Immediately under the crust is a layer that is thought to be extremely weak, because it is, presumably, too hot to crystallize. Moreover, it is thought that pressure at that depth renders the rock extremely plastic [. . .] The rock at that depth is supposed to have high viscosity; that is, it is fluid but very stiff, as tar may be [. . .] If a gentle push is exerted horizontally on the earth's crust, to shove it in a given direction, and if the push is maintained steadily for a long time, it is highly probable that the crust will be displaced over this plastic and viscous lower layer. The crust, in this case, will move as a single unit, the whole crust at the same time.[26]

He surmised that there are periods of movement lasting approximately 5,000 years, after which the poles enjoy eras of stability lasting between 10,000 and 30,000 years. This, says Hapgood, is what causes the cycles of the Ice Ages: the temperate zones areas drift into the polar regions and vice versa:

Let us visualize briefly the consequences of a displacement of the whole crustal shell of the earth. First, there will be the changes in latitude. Places on the earth's surface will change their distances from the equator. Some will be shifted nearer the equator, and others farther away. Points on opposite sides of the earth will move in opposite directions. For example, if New York should be moved 2,000 miles south, the Indian Ocean, diametrically opposite, would have to be shifted 2,000 miles north.[27]

The glaciers advance and recede in synch with these rhythms, and the crustal shifts happen when there is so much polar ice that the planet's weight distribution becomes lopsided, causing the crust to rotate until it settles down in a new location. Hapgood managed to pique the curiosity of Albert Einstein, and the great man wrote the foreword to his book:

> I frequently receive communications from people who wish to consult me concerning their unpublished ideas. It goes without saying that these ideas are very seldom possessed of scientific validity. The very first communication, however, that I received from Mr. Hapgood electrified me. His idea is original, of great simplicity, and – if it continues to prove itself – of great importance to everything that is related to the history of the earth's surface.[28]

Einstein's circumspect, 'if it continues to prove itself' was often overlooked in the discussions that followed.

Hapgood's pole shifts, entailing the physical relocation of the poles, should not be confused with the pole shifts related to changes in the polarity of the earth's magnetic field, which are regular occurrences in geological terms. But would there be any dramatic effects from any of the hundreds of these past magnetic polarity reversals? The answer, from the geologic and fossil records we have, seems to be 'no':

> Sediment cores taken from deep ocean floors can tell scientists about magnetic polarity shifts, providing a direct link between magnetic field activity and the fossil record. The Earth's magnetic field determines the magnetization of lava as it is laid down on the ocean floor on either side of the Mid-Atlantic Rift where the North American and European continental plates are spreading apart. As the lava solidifies, it creates a record of the orientation of past magnetic fields much like a tape recorder records sound. The last time that Earth's poles flipped in a major reversal was about 780,000

years ago, in what scientists call the Brunhes-Matuyama reversal. The fossil record shows no drastic changes in plant or animal life. Deep ocean sediment cores from this period also indicate no changes in glacial activity, based on the amount of oxygen isotopes in the cores. This is also proof that a polarity reversal would not affect the rotation axis of Earth, as the planet's rotation axis tilt has a significant effect on climate and glaciation and any change would be evident in the glacial record.[29]

In 1966, before he finally distanced himself from his pole-shifts theory in the face of the increasing knowledge of continental drift and plate tectonics, which was exposing the weaknesses of his ideas,[30] Charles Hapgood took Atlantean speculation into some intriguing new territory by publishing *Maps of the Ancient Sea Kings: Evidence of Advanced Civilization in the Ice Age.*[31] This focused on a map produced in 1513 by the Turkish admiral Piri Re'is ('Captain Piri') under Sultan Suleiman I 'the Magnificent', who later had him executed. Now in the Topkapı Sarayı Müsesi in Istanbul, this an exquisite piece of Ottoman cartography, even if its geographical accuracy sometimes falls short of its artistic excellence.[32] The surviving part of it shows the east coast of South America and part of Africa, and Piri Re'is claimed that he used twenty different maps to make his, including one drawn by 'a Genoese infidel [whose] name was Columbo'.

Hapgood was drawn to the Piri Re'is map by a radio programme broadcast on 26 August 1956 which featured Arlington H. Mallery (1877–1968), who worked as an engineer with the US Navy Hydrographic Office, and had a strong amateur interest in archaeology and the history of cartography. Mallery suggested that the coastline at the bottom of the map accurately represented the coastline of Queen Maud Land (Antarctica), but without the ice, and therefore

Piri Re'is must have drawn his map using information from some very ancient maps indeed. This was perfect for the Atlantologists, and Hapgood set to work to test Mallery's hypothesis.

The most intriguing aspect of the Piri Re'is map, from the Atlantological perspective, is that its southernmost section depicts a large continent on the bottom of the world, but roughly 300 years before European travellers first glimpsed mainland Antarctica. There should be nothing too odd about this – Europeans since the time of Aristotle had assumed that the laws of balance and symmetry required it to be there to counterbalance the weight of the lands of the north – but Hapgood believed that the Piri Re'is map showed the coastline of an ice-free Antarctica, whose shape roughly approximated to maps of sub-glacial Antarctica that were being plotted in the 1950s. But given that Antarctica hadn't been visited by European explorers until William Smith sighted Livingston Island on 19 February 1819, this was extraordinary. Prior to that, nobody knew what Antarctica looked like with the ice, let alone without it.

Hapgood's solution was this: an advanced Ice Age civilisation going back anywhere from 10,000 to 6000 BC, but possessing scientific and technological knowledge equivalent to that of Enlightenment Europe (roughly the eighteenth century). These people sailed all around the world, including to Antarctica before it froze over in a Hapgoodesque pole shift. However, the Ancient Sea Kings of his book title possessed maps that were transmitted to Greeks, Carthaginians, Romans, Byzantines, Crusaders and Ottoman Turks like Piri Re'is, who used them to plot his chart with Antarctica on it.

Once it is subjected to even the most cursory scrutiny, however, Hapgood's notion that the Piri Re'is map depicts the coastline of Antarctica melts into nothingness.[33] Hapgood had simply misunderstood the nature of sixteenth-century cartography, where, as we have seen with Abraham Ortelius,[34] speculative or imaginary features are interpolated to compensate for concrete geographical knowledge. Hapgood supported his speculations with other depictions of *Terra Australis*, the Southern Land, on sixteenth- and seventeenth-century maps, but missed the crucial point that people had believed in a great southern continent since ancient times, not because they knew it was there, but because the world needed a counterweight to the territory in the northern hemisphere. So the lands which cartographers added to the southern oceans and the Antarctic from the beginning of the sixteenth century onwards were purely speculative.[35]

One such cartographer was the Frenchman Oronce Finé, aka Finaeus, whose heart-shaped map of 1531, possibly influenced by Johannes Schöner's lost globe of 1523, included an Antarctic land that Hapgood and others claim looks very similar to Antarctica without ice. But Finaeus' theoretical Antarctic landmass is roughly nine times bigger than the real one, and Hapgood had to rotate it by twenty degrees of longitude, move the South Pole a thousand miles, and ignore the existence of the 900-mile Palmer Peninsula in order to make the comparison work. It is also noteworthy that although Finaeus' depiction of *Terra Australis* has a superficial resemblance to the real Antarctica, those of his contemporaries are very different.[36] Gerardus Mercator's maps, also from the sixteenth century, similarly feature a *Terra Australis*, but they don't really help the *Terra Australis* cause, since they also include a landmass at the North Pole where there isn't any land.

A final point to settle the Atlantis-in-Antarctica debate might have been the studies of ice cores from Antarctica, which show that it has in fact been covered by ice for at least 100,000 years. These clearly do nothing to endorse the idea of an advanced Ice Age civilisation exploring an ice-free Antarctica around 10,000 BC,[37] but the Antarctic Atlantists are nothing if not tenacious. It might also reasonably be objected that Charles H. Hapgood's ideas seem a very long way removed from Plato, but in their 1995 publication *When the Sky Fell: In Search of Atlantis*, Rand and Rose Flem-Ath took hold of Hapgood's ideas and reintegrated them into the great philosopher's.[38] Their book opens with this statement by their fellow pro-Atlantean Colin Wilson, with whom Rand Flem-Ath subsequently co-authored *The Atlantis Blueprint*:[39]

> The thesis of this book is so simple and yet so startling that it will almost certainly earn Rand and Rose Flem-Ath a permanent place in the history of the earth sciences. It can be summarized in seven words: Antarctica is the lost continent of Atlantis.[40]

The Flem-Aths' readings of, and correspondence with, Hapgood led them to a very literal reading of Plato's Atlantis dialogues, with one enormous exception: his Atlantis was a real place, but it was entirely unconnected with either the Atlantic Ocean or Pillars of Hercules (which should not be taken literally): a supposed misunderstanding of what the Greeks meant by 'Atlantic Ocean' and 'Pillars of Hercules' has restricted the search for Atlantis to either the North Atlantic Ocean or the Mediterranean Sea. But this Atlantis was in the 'real ocean', the 'World Ocean', of oceanographers.[41]

As we saw with Olof Rudbeck,[42] relocating the Pillars of Heracles to suit your theory is a common enough tactic to enable you similarly to relocate Plato's Atlantis. The authors also use the Piri Re'is map and the Hadji Ahmed map of 1559.[43] The latter is claimed to show an accurate projection of North America, drawn by the Arabs (Hadji Ahmed was from Tunis) from information they got from Atlanteans, who didn't enjoy living there because they disliked the cold. Hadji Ahmed's map also portrays an enormous Antarctic continent, which extends up beyond Madagascar in the east, and beyond South America, almost into the Tropic of Capricorn in the west. Also included in the discussion is Athanasius Kircher's map featuring Atlantis,[44] which is compared with a map of sub-glacial Antarctica 'according to recent seismic surveys', so that we can 'immediately see that the Egyptian map [which is what Kircher's has metamorphosed into during the discussion] of Atlantis represents in size, shape, scale, and position, an ice-free Antarctica'.[45]

The leap of faith required to accept the alleged similarities in the various maps is a large one, but having made it, and leaning heavily on Hapgood's *The Earth's Shifting Crust* and *Maps of the Ancient Sea Kings*, the Flem-Aths inform us that crustal shift displaced Atlantis into the Antarctic where it froze over 'roughly 11,600 years ago (9600 BC)' – a date selected to accord with Plato's *Timaeus* 23e (when Athens is *founded*, not destroyed), if not with *Critias* 108e (which puts the war with Atlantis at *c.* 9429 BC). And Atlantis is still down there:

> We could use only the most sophisticated, least intrusive, instruments to peer beneath the ice. If evidence of a civilization is found, a surgical probe could be made. We would hold our breath as we waited to glimpse the ancient city locked in ice.
>
> The quest would be reborn.
> Our past and future would meet.
> Science and myth might merge.[46]

The Flem-Ath approach is essentially to read Plato's Atlantis story as unvarnished truth, in a context where rapid crustal shift causes not just Plato's cataclysm but also world-wide climate change, all of which filters down to posterity through myth-telling:

> One thing that seems certain is that a tremendous amount of things were happening around 9600 BC [. . .] Melting ice

caps. Mass extinctions in North and South America. Suddenly, virtually simultaneously, agriculture appears on several continents but with different crops. I believe a single idea, mobile crust, solves these problems on a global scale.[47]

The Flem-Aths are known outside Atlantean circles for their use of long-outdated and discredited material, but this does not really deter them or their readership. They make the suggestion that Kircher got his information from an ancient Egyptian map that was stolen by the Romans. In a conversation with Rand Flem-Ath, Mark Adams explored the possibilities:

I was trying to keep an open mind. I asked where the Egyptians would have gotten the maps.

'I think the survivors of Atlantis are those that got the boats,' Flem-Ath told me. 'On boats you have two things that are portable: astronomy and maps.'

He had a point. 'Is there any way you could ever prove this?' I asked.

'Well, the easiest thing would be if a large part of ice fell off Antarctica and there were human structures underneath.'[48]

Adams grows increasingly sceptical and irritated:

'Rand, all of this stuff you're telling me is considered beyond the fringe. It's been discredited.'

'Well, maybe, but that's not a very important part of my theory [. . .] I'm better off bypassing scientists and reaching for a general audience, maybe two or three generations down the road.'[49]

In the same years that the Flem-Aths' *When the Sky Fell* was published, Graham Hancock's multi-million bestseller *Fingerprints of the Gods* started flying off the shelves.[50] In this, Hancock presents several familiar suggestions: an advanced civilisation existed *c.* 15,000 to 10,000 BC; it possessed scientific and technological expertise equal to, or better than, that of the twenty-first century; a sudden crustal shift moved the arctic into the tropics (and vice versa); the concomitant global cataclysm all but wiped out the super-civilisation; the survivors salvaged some vestiges of their amazing society's knowledge; this is embedded in the catastrophe myths of cultures across the globe; and Antarctica was where the lost super-civilisation based itself.[51]

In 2015, Hancock unleashed his 'long, strange and exceedingly convoluted'[52] *Magicians of the Gods*.[53] However, in his own words this is

a completely new book filled from front to back with completely new evidence, completely new travels to the world's most mysterious archaeological sites, and completely new insights, based on the latest scientific evidence, into the global cataclysm that wiped an advanced civilization from the earth and made us a species with amnesia, forced to begin again like children with no memory of what went before.[54]

Rather neatly, Hancock seems to be casting himself as the Egyptian priest in Plato's *Timaeus* 22b, who said, 'Oh Solon, Solon, you Greeks are always children', and told him the Atlantis tale in the first instance.

The ideas of *Magicians of the Gods* are not entirely 'completely new'. To paraphrase Hancock's summary, evidence revealed in the book shows 'beyond reasonable doubt' that near the end of the last

Ice Age, 12,800 years ago, a giant comet entered the solar system and broke into multiple fragments, some of which struck the earth's northern ice caps, liquidising millions of square kilometres of ice and destabilising the earth's crust, and thereby causing the global Deluge that is remembered in myths all around the world. Then there was a second series of impacts, equally devastating, causing further cataclysmic flooding, which occurred 11,600 years ago (i.e. our old friend 9600 BC), 'the exact date that Plato gives for the destruction and submergence of Atlantis'.[55] Hancock laments the fact that mainstream thinkers 'dismiss Plato's "outlandish" story' of this mythical water world 'by any and every possible means',[56] although in this instance he might have been better advised to choose 9429 BC, the date of the Atlanto-Athenian war in *Critias* 108e for his destruction horizon, rather than 9600 BC, which is when Plato's Archaeo-Athens was founded.

So much, so familiar. The usual theories, which invite the usual objections. But there is more: the survivors, 'Magicians of the Gods', travelled the world in their great ships doing all in their power to keep the spark of civilisation burning, and settled in all the favourite pseudoarchaeological sites, taking with them the memory of a time when mankind had fallen out of harmony with the universe and paid a heavy price. And, finally, a warning to the future: 'the comet that wrought such destruction between 12,800 and 11,600 years [ago? A word missing on the website?] may not be done with us yet [. . .] an astronomical message encoded at Gobekli Tepe, and in the Sphinx and the pyramids of Egypt, warns that the "Great Return" will occur in our time'.[57]

Interviewed about the book, Hancock seems to want to have his cake and eat it: on the one hand, he reads Plato's tale euhemeristically – it is a literal account of real events, not an allegory – and on the other hand he reads Plato's tale allegorically:

We have fallen out of harmony with the universe [...] In mythological terms, we tick all the boxes for the next lost civilisation [...] Plato says it very clearly about the citizens of Atlantis: there was a time when they loved a pure and good life but they became arrogant and cruel and no longer bore their prosperity with moderation. I think we sound a lot like that.[58]

Hancock certainly gets the message that Plato, as ever, is not just a great thinker, but 'good to think with'.

ERICH VON DÄNIKEN: WAS GOD AN ASTRONAUT, AND WAS ATLANTIS AT TROY?

A book on Atlantis would seem incomplete without some reference to Erich von Däniken, who is probably still the most famous advocate for ancient-alien-astronauts-visiting-the-earth-thousands-of-years-ago-in-spaceships-bringing-civilisation-to-mankind-mating-with-primitive-humans-and-producing-you-and-me school of thought. His first book *Chariots of the Gods? Unsolved Mysteries of the Past* (1968)[59] and the 1970 documentary film *Chariots of the Gods*, directed by Harald Reinl (as Dr Harald Reinl), which grossed over $25 million, owed part of their incredible commercial success not only to the burgeoning interest in UFOs that had begun in 1947 with the supposed sighting of flying saucers near Mount Rainer, Washington, and the alleged crash of an alien spaceship near Roswell, New Mexico, but also to the fact that von Däniken's work presented a glossy veneer of scientific and historical credibility. In fact, *Chariots of the Gods?* was based primarily on pseudoscientific and pseudohistorical 'evidence', at least when it was not simply bogus. As Ronald H. Fritze puts it, 'von Däniken is at best not a careful scholar and at worst, as many regard him, a cynical charlatan'.[60] Von Däniken is particularly adept at initially broaching an idea as speculative and then treating it as a proven fact, and his techniques are highly effective: he has struck a very deep chord in many people.

Chariots of the Gods? again uses the Piri Re'is map, claiming that it is an 'absolutely accurate' azimuthal projection[61] centred on Cairo, so accurate that it could only have been based on an aerial photograph taken from a spaceship flying over the city. In fact, the straight parallels of latitude on the Piri Re'is map show that the map is not azimuthal (the equator would in that case be curved), but a cylindrical projection[62] with appropriately equally spaced parallels of latitude. Despite von Däniken's assertions, the Piri Re'is map and the alien photographs barely match up with reality at all – everything is in the wrong place and more than 3,200 km of South American coastline have gone missing, along with the Strait of Magellan. Presumably von Däniken's analogue aliens didn't have access to high quality digital photography, and furthermore, in his 1998 book *Odyssey of the Gods: The Alien History of Ancient Greece*, von Däniken himself writes, 'it is obvious that Piri Reis had problems with Cuba',[63] which is undoubtedly a bit of a mess on the map. But von Däniken has both questions and an answer for this:

> What did the original ancient map – which might well have come from the library at Alexandria [a classic unfalsifiable theory, given the destruction of the Library] – have in the place of Cuba? How does someone like Piri Reis come to make such a mess of the Caribbean island of Cuba, yet get the coastline of Antarctica so exact? Something else, probably a large island, must no doubt have been on the unknown original. Could it have been Atlantis?[64]

At this point, he surprises us by claiming not to have the answer, at least until he deftly deploys the ancient rhetorical technique of paralepsis, apophasis or praeteritio (drawing attention to something by saying that you won't mention it), to suggest that he might:

> A few indications, though, can give us pause for thought. Columbus named his newly-discovered land 'Hispaniola', but the native Indians called it 'Quisqueya' or 'Mother of Lands'. Was this a reference to ancient tradition? In the Greek version of the Atlantis legend, Plato calls it 'Polis Atlantis' or 'City of Atlas'.[65]

In fact, Plato *never* explicitly calls it *polis Atlantis* – it is *nēsos Atlantis*, the island of Atlas – although the idea of it as an 'ancient mother-city' does occur in Plato's text.[66] But these are mere details to von Däniken, who indulges in some more goropist spurious etymology linking Atlas with the Mayan Aztlan, and concluding:

> Although I don't want to go searching for Atlantis, I wouldn't mind betting that it lay somewhere in the Caribbean region.[67]

Yet in spite of this, he is adamant that 'one thing which is quite certain from a geological perspective. Atlantis cannot have "gone under", in the sense of simply sinking under the waves'.[68] In that he was probably right.

However, in spite of the fact that von Däniken protests that he doesn't want to go on searching for Atlantis, he devotes two out of the six chapters of *Odyssey of the Gods* to 'Atlantis – the millennia-old whodunit' and 'Help for Plato'. He also devotes a great deal of effort to debunking the geoarchaeologist Eberhard Zangger's suggestion that Atlantis could be Homer's Troy: 'a bit rich, one would have thought, to assume he had solved the riddle of Atlantis'.[69]

Zangger's theory is that Plato's Atlantis story is actually the tale of the Trojan War.[70] His hypothesis is constructed on two main premises:

1. The Atlantis story told by the Egyptian priest was really a confused version of the Trojan War (or in fact, of *a* Trojan War), but it had been so drastically altered in transmission that Solon didn't recognise it for what it was; it was then handed down across the generations to Plato.
2. The archaeology of Troy meshes beautifully with Plato's description of the Atlantean capital city.

Zangger is less interested in the question of 'did Atlantis exist?' than in 'how could Plato's account of the past differ from reality?'[71] Sticking closely to Plato's text, he speculates whether Plato's Athenian Ideal State, which is assaulted by Atlantis, might contain echoes of the Mycenaean civilisation of Bronze Age Greece, and whether we are looking at a conflict between Greece and a foreign enemy (even though the Greeks are the invaders in Homer). In relation to the destruction of Plato's Ideal Athens, Zangger draws on his own fieldwork at the important Mycenaean fortress of Tiryns, where he argues that a flash flood triggered by an earthquake may have been a significant factor in that settlement's decline. This, Zangger feels, is part of a wider series of natural upheavals that shook Aegean civilisation in about 1200 BC, which approximates to the conventional dates that are given for the Trojan War.[72] So Plato's Athenians were not defending themselves from an island superpower from the west when they were destroyed, but attacking a mainland one in the east, namely Troy, which mythology says was captured by the Mycenaean King Agamemnon after a ten-year siege.

It is relatively easy to find superficial similarities between Atlantis and almost any Bronze Age society, and Zangger adduces numerous arguments for parallels between Plato's Atlantis and the Troy of myth and archaeology. In an article in 1993, he catalogued many commonalities between Plato's Atlantis and the way Troy might have looked in the late Bronze Age.[73] The main citadel of Troy is relatively small, but he argues that it was just part of a much bigger city that featured impressive engineering projects in the shape of artificial harbours and canals. Recent excavations at Troy have certainly raised the possibility that Troy could have been a vibrant trading post and a significant power in the eastern Mediterranean during the Late Bronze Age. But although Troy's location overlooking a plain near the sea and the existence of hot and cold springs in Homer's description may resonate slightly with Plato's description, there are also irreconcilable differences: the mound of Hisarlik where the Troy site is located bears little resemblance to Plato's Atlantic island, and although earthquake damage may be detected at certain levels, none of the cities in Homer was swallowed beneath the waves. It is a long way from 'an outpost vassal state of the Hittite empire'[74] to the east of Greece, to a decadent imperial power to the west.

Zangger also encounters the usual Atlantean problem that if you relocate Plato's massive island from the Atlantic – where geologists categorically assure us that it could never have existed – then you have fundamentally to alter dimensions, directions and dates to make everything fit. As Sprague de Camp eloquently put it:

> The problem is this: You cannot change all the details of Plato's story and still claim to have Plato's story. That is like saying the legendary King Arthur is 'really' Queen Cleopatra. All you have to do is to change Cleopatra's sex, nationality, period, temperament, moral character, and other details and the resemblance becomes obvious.[75]

Zangger flounders in the shoal-waters of Plato's statement that the Atlantic Ocean became non-navigable where Atlantis sank, trying to argue that in reality the Greeks temporarily lost the knowledge of how to navigate the narrow straits between the Aegean and the Black Sea. He is also unable to argue that Troy was destroyed by floods because the archaeological and geological evidence contradicts him. This leaves the sinking of Atlantis beneath the waves as a monstrous anomaly, although it should be said that, to his credit, Zangger concludes his book with a series of eight arguments *against* his own theory – an extraordinary thing for a scholar investigating Atlantis to do.

CHAPTER 15

Minoan Atlantis: Crete and Santorini

....

Eberhart Zangger was not the only scholar to locate Atlantis in the Greek Bronze Age rather than in Plato's Stone Age. But whereas he had looked eastwards from Greece to Troy, others were to look southwards, to the islands of Crete and Santorini (Thera) in the Aegean Sea.

CRETAN MYTHOLOGY

As Odysseus says in Homer's *Odyssey*:

> Out in the wine-dark sea there lies a land called Crete, a rich and lovely land, washed by the waves on every side, densely peopled and boasting ninety cities [. . .] One of the ninety towns is a great city called Knossos, and there, for nine years, King Minos ruled.[1]

Knossos is about 5 km from the sea in the middle of Crete's northern coast, and Atlantis hunters are sometimes attracted to it because of the mythical tradition that makes King Minos the first to establish rule over the sea, the abundance of bull imagery in the stories, Crete's connections with Athens and the involvement of Poseidon.[2]

In myth, Minos sought to establish sole rule over Crete, but ran into opposition. He tried to substantiate his claim to be divinely supported by praying to Poseidon that a bull should appear from the sea, vowing to sacrifice it when it did. The sea god duly sent him a magnificent white bull, and Minos secured the kingship, but he couldn't bring himself to slaughter the fabulous beast. Poseidon's angry response was to turn the animal feral, and to instil an erotic passion for it in Minos' wife, Pasiphae ('All-Shining').

Pasiphae required an accomplice to fulfil her monstrous desires, and she found one in Daedalus, who exercised his artistic and technological ingenuity on her behalf by constructing a highly authentic hollow wooden cow on wheels, covering it in genuine cowhide, and pasturing it with the bull. Pasiphae climbed inside, the bull took Daedalus' construction for the real thing, and the inevitable happened. The fruit of this union was the Minotaur (*Minotauros* = Bull of Minos), a hybrid creature with a bull's head on a human body. Horrified, Minos shut the Minotaur up in the Labyrinth, a complex underground structure purpose-built by Daedalus.

Minos also had a son called Androgeus, who was a brilliant athlete. However, Androgeus' outstanding performances at a festival in Athens were his undoing: some sources say he was murdered by jealous competitors; others that the Athenian King Aegeus had him assassinated because he feared he might usurp his throne; others again that Aegeus sent him to deal with the Bull of Marathon – the same beast that had mated with Pasiphae – which destroyed him. Minos sought revenge, and, being the dominant naval power in the region, he took the offensive with his fleet.[3] The conflict dragged on indecisively until the Athenians became afflicted by plague and famine. An oracle instructed them to grant Minos whatever satisfaction he might choose, and the Cretan ruler ordered them to pay a tax of seven youths and seven maidens as food for the Minotaur, to be delivered annually or at nine-year intervals.

Aegeus and his wife Aethra had a son who became Athens' greatest hero: Theseus. However, it was also said that Poseidon was his father, having had sex with Aethra on the same night as Aegeus. When the third selection of youths and maidens departed for Crete, Theseus was among them, either as a volunteer, chosen by lot or handpicked by Minos himself. But whatever the method of his selection, Theseus intended to terminate both the Minotaur and the tribute. On the journey Minos assaulted the maiden Eriboea. When Theseus intervened, Minos prayed to Zeus to signal that the deity was Minos' father (which would essentially allow Minos to behave however he liked), and a lightning flash confirmed the issue. Minos then challenged Theseus to verify that he was the son of Poseidon. The poet Bacchylides (c. 520–450 BC) wrote about how Minos tossed a golden ring into the sea, and Theseus retrieved it, along with a crimson cloak and a garland 'dark with roses besides', gifts from Poseidon's wife Amphitrite:

> The crowd of young
> Athenians had trembled when
> the hero leapt into the sea, and from
> their lily-lustrous eyes they shed
> tears, expecting compulsion's heavy grip.
> Dolphins, meanwhile, those salt-dwellers,
> quickly carried the great Theseus to the home of his
> father, the god of horses; and he came
> to the sea god's hall. [. . .]
> He [. . .] saw the dear wife of his father
> there in the lovely house, august
> ox-eyed Amphitrite,
> who clothed him in a mantle of sea-purple
> and set upon his thick-curled locks
> a plaited garland without flaws,
> which earlier, at her marriage,
> deceitful Aphrodite had given her, dark with roses.[4]

On arrival in Crete, Theseus attracted the amorous interest of Minos' daughter Ariadne, who proposed to help him, on condition that he took her back to Athens and made her his wife. Theseus agreed, and Ariadne persuaded the Labyrinth-designer Daedalus to reveal how to find the exit. And at his suggestion she gave Theseus a ball of thread. He was to attach one end to the lintel of the door on entering the Labyrinth, and then unwind the thread as he penetrated into the heart of the structure, until he found the Minotaur.[5] Theseus did as he was told and found the Minotaur in the bowels of the Labyrinth. They fought to the death. Theseus won, and the thread enabled him to find his way out again. He assembled his compatriots, and set sail with Ariadne on board his vessel.

Plato would have been brought up on these stories, and Minos' external seaborne aggression towards Athens could be read as sharing something in common with that of the Atlanteans, even though it comes from a very different place, and has very different motives and outcomes. If there is an Atlantis connection here, it is conspicuous by its complete absence from any of the Greek mythical and historical traditions pertaining to Crete.

KNOSSOS AND THE MINOANS

In 1878, a Cretan antiquarian, coincidentally named Minos, Minos Kalokairinos, discovered the remains of some large storage jars at Knossos, and initiated an international race to find the ancient city and turn the myth into reality. The victor in that race was Arthur Evans, Keeper of the Ashmolean Museum in Oxford, who purchased the site, secured the agreement of the Greek authorities, and commenced his excavations on 23 March 1900. He unearthed the remains of a flourishing civilisation that had created some stupendous art and architecture, which suggested that their wealth and quality of life were on a par with their contemporaries in Pharaonic

Egypt.[6] He called this culture 'Minoan', even though we don't know how the people referred to themselves, although it is likely that *Keftiu* (Egyptian), *Kaptaru* (Akkadian) and *Caphtor* (Hebrew) could all refer to them.

The centrepiece of the Minoan civilisation is the extensive, multi-storeyed complex at Knossos. Displaying very high-quality construction techniques, and containing archives, storage facilities and sophisticated drainage, it was established in the region of 1900 BC. Evans believed that 'the Palace traditionally built for Minos by his great craftsman Daedalus has proved to be no baseless fabric of the imagination',[7] and so he called it 'the Palace of Minos', even though there is nothing to prove that it was a king's palace, let alone that of Minos.

Minoan-style frescoes found at Tel Kabri in Israel and Tel el-Dab'a in Egypt indicate vigorous overseas trade; women, working a highly distinctive bare-breasted, flouncy-skirted look, are notice-ably prominent in Minoan art; and evidence for bulls can be found everywhere. One fine fresco now in the Heraklion Archaeological Museum shows a white-skinned figure, whose hair is knotted at the nape of the neck, wearing a variegated kilt with a codpiece, calf-length boots and lots of jewellery, grabbing at a mighty onrushing bull; in the centre, a person with burnt-sienna coloured skin, a quite plain yellow kilt and no jewellery, performs a back-flip over the bull's back, which would bring the figure to earth facing away from the beast; behind the bull, facing it, with outstretched hands, stands a second white figure who resembles the first. Many questions remain about the meaning and significance of this scene, but there are enough representations in other media to indicate that this type of activity did take place, and the horns of some excavated bull skulls have been sawn down, presumably for 'health and safety' reasons. The north entrance of the Palace of Minos was adorned with a large Bull fresco, and Plato's description of bull-hunting with sticks and lassoes at *Critias* 119d–e[8] often reminds people of scenes on the beautiful gold Vapheio cups, which were made *c.* 1500–1450 BC.

Ultimately, however, the flowering of Minoan Crete came to an end amidst widespread destruction by fire in *c.* 1425 BC (by the 'conventional' chronology), and the archaeological evidence tells us that, after this, new people arrived on Crete. They were the Mycenaeans.

ATLANTIS ON CRETE

On Friday, 19 February 1909, an anonymous letter published in *The Times*, which was in fact written by the archaeologist K. T. Frost, floated the idea that the end of Minoan culture in the mid-to-late fifteenth century BC[9] lay behind the story of Atlantis:

> The Minoan civilization was essentially Mediterranean, and is most sharply distinguished from any that arose in Egypt or the East. In some respects also it is strikingly modern. The many-storeyed palaces, some of the pottery, even the dresses of the ladies seem to belong to the modern rather than the ancient world. At the same time the number of Minoan sites and their extraordinary richness far exceed anything that Crete could be expected to produce, and must be due in part to that sea power which the ancient legends attributed to Minos.
>
> Thus, when the Minoan power was at its greatest, its rulers must have seemed to the other nations to be mighty indeed, and their prestige must have been increased by the mystery of the lands over which they ruled (which seemed to Syrians and Egyptians to be the far West), and by their mastery over that element which the ancient world always held in awe. Strange stories, too, must have floated round the

Levant of vast bewildering palaces, of sports and dances, and above all of the bullfight. The Minoan realm, therefore, was a vast and ancient power which was united by the same sea which divided it from other nations, so that it seemed to be a separate continent with a genius of its own.

Suddenly a swift and terrible destruction blotted out the Cretan power. Confident in their long supremacy at sea, the Minoans had left their cities unfortified, and the neglect of their land defences proved their ruin. The evidence is conclusive that some shock broke the sea power of Knossos when it was still full of vigour, still growing and developing; that a raid sacked the capital and desolated the island, and that thereafter the whole Minoan civilization decayed and finally vanished.

A new order of things arose [. . .] It is true that Minoan influence lingered on in the art of the Aegean, but except for the legends of Minos, the very memory of the Minoans perished. As a political and commercial force, therefore, Knossos and its allied cities were swept away just when they seemed strongest and safest. It was as if the whole kingdom had sunk in the sea, as if the tale of Atlantis were true.

The parallel is not fortuitous. If the account of Atlantis is compared with the history of Crete and her relationship with Greece and Egypt, it seems almost certain that here we have an echo of the Minoans.[10]

The reply on behalf of *The Times* concluded:

The correspondences noted by our Correspondent between the story of Atlantis and the revelations of Knossos may very well engage the serious attention of scholars and archaeologists.

The Times was right. In the late 1930s, a Greek archaeologist called Spyridon Marinatos was also struck by the similarities between Minoan culture, the reasons for whose demise still remain somewhat unclear, and Plato's Atlantis.

The idea is not entirely unappealing. It generally distances itself from pseudoarchaeology, and champions of the 'Minoan Crete = Atlantis' equation are drawn to perceived cultural, architectural and sanitary similarities;[11] the prominence of bulls in Cretan myth and Minoan art invites comparisons with the bull hunts of the Atlantean Kings;[12] Crete, like Atlantis, is an island with impressive mountains and large plains; and Crete's location in the 'inland' Mediterranean mirrors Atlantis in the Atlantic, contained within the 'opposite continent'.[13] So could the connection be, as J. V. Luce suggested,[14] the result of a bizarre process of 'Chinese Whispers' from Atlantis to Egypt to Solon to Plato? Could it be that the Egyptian priest spoke of the Keftiu, prompting a mystified Solon to ask where these people lived, and to be told that it was in the far west (at least from the Egyptian perspective), as a result of which he located Crete-Atlantis outside the Pillars of Heracles? Could it be that Solon identified the island with Ogygia, the island of Atlas' daughter Calypso, and so called it 'the Island of Atlas'? Could it be that the tale was developed over the years, but without losing 'the hard core of the legend [. . .] the tradition of a great and civilized island empire [. . .] which came to an end as the result of a natural catastrophe'?[15] Those who answer 'yes' to these questions can certainly be drawn towards the idea that Plato's Atlantis was Minoan Crete.

There are, as Christopher Gill, points out,[16] some fundamental problems with these theories, which depend on some highly subjective judgement calls. To many observers, the Minoan 'palace' at Knossos bears no conceivable resemblance to Atlantis city, and the two islands are unalike in crucial ways:

1. Plato's Atlantis is called Atlantis, not Crete.
2. Atlantis is located in the Atlantic Ocean, Crete is not.
3. Atlantis' culture predates the Minoans by millennia.
4. Atlantis is massively bigger than Crete.
5. Knossos is on the north of Crete, but Atlantis-city is on the south.
6. Plato's measurements of Atlantisville need to remain roughly same to fit Knossos, but be divided by ten to make the plain of Atlantis fit the plain of Messara on Crete.
7. The political arrangements of Atlantis are fundamentally different from the Cretan ones that we know from the Linear B tablets.[17]
8. The bull motif is not remarkable: bull sacrifice was by no means unique to Crete, where the striking activity was not bull hunting but bull jumping, which Plato's Atlanteans do not do.
9. The idea that Plato's account is based on some kind of record of Minoan civilisation, whose power and extent were not generally known in Plato's day outside vague echoes in the mythology of Minos, and which only Plato had access to, is hard to accept.
10. There are also considerable obstacles to accepting that Plato (or Solon) could have received detailed information about Crete from the Egyptians, whose records contain very little indeed about the Keftiu, and absolutely nothing that hints of Keftiu-Atlanteans being a hostile maritime power.
11. There is nothing in the surviving Egyptian records of the type that could give Solon/Critias/Plato detailed information about Cretan topography, architecture and sanitation, or to make measurements accurate to the nearest 200 m.

12. The fourth-century BC Athenians knew a certain amount about Minoan culture, and certainly more than the Egyptians, via their key myth of Theseus and the Minotaur – it is implausible to suggest that Solon/Critias/Plato could have heard an account of Minoan civilisation from the Egyptians, but not recognised it for what it was.[18]

13. The wonders of Cretan technology as invented by Daedalus are already embedded in Athenian thinking well before Plato, and Minos is presented as a maritime imperialist: the Greeks have no need to import ideas like this from Egypt.

Overall, the parallels between Plato's Atlantis and Minoan Crete are small, weak and superficial, while some of the differences are enormous.

ATLANTIS ON SANTORINI

In the late 1960s, Spyridon Marinatos' excavations at the site of Akrotiri on the Cycladic island of Santorini (Thera) produced some stunning results. He had unearthed a significant and clearly thriving harbour settlement, with a culture that was visually very much like that of Minoan Crete, which had been buried in an enormous volcanic event. Crete is only about 100 km to the south of Santorini, and the eruption itself could well have been more ferocious than the devastating Krakatau eruption of 1883, which could be heard 3,000 km away and which claimed 35,000 lives in the tsunamis. The world has not witnessed cataclysm on that scale since.

The excavations at Akrotiri show us that its inhabitants were in the process of rebuilding their property, damaged by a very powerful earthquake which had fairly recently hit the island, when the eruption began with four explosive steam blasts, which between them left an ash deposit 10–15 cm thick. This possibly prompted a mass exodus from the island – no bodies have yet been discovered in the archaeological remains, and there is a dearth of precious or easily portable material left behind. However, the harbour area has not yet been excavated: many casualties of the eruption of Mount Vesuvius in AD 79 were found at a similar location in excavations at Herculaneum in the 1980s. It is possible that the main eruption took place some weeks later, generating an eruption column some 30–40 km high in less than twenty-four hours. This deposited around 6 m of debris, which buried and preserved much of the settlement at Akrotiri, filling the lower storeys of the buildings, but leaving the uncovered areas exposed to the incredibly violent events that were to come.

What goes up must come down and, as the eruption column collapsed, it created a 'base surge', where clouds of hot gas expanded outwards horizontally at very high velocity. This destroyed all the protruding parts of the buildings and made dune-like deposits of pumice between 8 and 12 m deep. Four enormous explosions then generated pyroclastic flows – fast-moving currents of hot gas and rock – which laid down deposits up to 55 m deep in places. Finally, further massive, gas-rich and much more fluid pyroclastic flows deposited ash, pumice and small lithics to a depth of 40–50m. The general consensus (always subject to challenge) is that the entire event lasted just three or four days, emitting 30–40 km^3 of material.[19]

That much is widely agreed. Yet the major issues surrounding both the date and effects of the eruption are much more controversial. At first, Marinatos made the eruption coeval with the first wave of destructions on Crete in *c.* 1450 BC, but subsequent studies of pottery forced him to revise this theory in favour of making the eruption of Santorini and the destruction on Crete two discrete events separated by one or two generations. However, a revised date of 1500 BC for the eruption was still close enough for cause and effect to apply, and by the 1970s his theory was widely accepted.[20]

Marinatos was also struck by the Minoan-looking artefacts and wall paintings that he found in the town, which showed a very high level of culture and prosperity, and posited that the eruption not only destroyed the Minoan civilisation, but was also the origin of the Atlantis myth.[21] Santorini's caldera is four times wider than that of Krakatau, and a lot deeper, so it was a reasonable surmise that earthquakes, airborne debris, fire, tsunamis and temporary climate change resulting in months of darkness might have terminated an entire civilisation, and that news of it could have reached Egypt and been documented:

> I think we may safely preclude the fable. Plato's imagination could not possibly have conjured up an account so unique and unusual to classical literature – it was only later that this form of writing appears, such as Lucian employs in his *True History* [*Alēthes Historia*] – nor does the account follow this form [. . .]
>
> The myth of Atlantis may be considered as historical tradition which, in the manner typical of the distortion of such events, grew from the fusion of various disparate episodes. The destruction of Thera [. . .] and the simultaneous disappearance of the Cretans from the trade with Egypt, gave rise to a myth of an island, beyond all measure powerful and rich, being submerged.[22]

Marinatos explains the transference of the island to the Atlantic Ocean by the circumnavigation of Africa by Phoenician sailors, and goes on to suggest that invasions by central Mediterranean peoples were added to the myth as invaders from Atlantis. Their repulse by the Mycenaeans, in conjunction with the bravery of Ionian Greek mercenary soldiers in the service of the kings of Saïs, then account for the conquering Athenian army. He then concludes that

> the core of these events, embodied in a single historical myth, is the eruption of Thera and the year is about 1500 BC.[23]

However, if Atlantis was a memory of Minoan Crete and the Late Bronze Age eruption at Santorini, we are still left with the awkward fact that Plato's Atlantis dialogues are the only ancient sources that appear to link the demise of the Minoans with the volcano. And we also need to explain how and why Plato knew so much about Minoan civilisation, and the way it collapsed, when no other Greek writer did.

Furthermore, another major problem with plugging these events into Plato's Atlantis myth is the dates. Marinatos' 1500 BC does not correlate too well with Plato's 9600 BC (to choose the favourite Atlantological date). However, Marinatos 'solved' this problem by using the same coup that Eudoxus of Cnidus, Diodorus Siculus, Plutarch, Francisco Cervantes de Salazar, Olof Rudbeck, and others had already used: Plato's numbers have become distorted in transition by a factor of ten; what Solon interpreted as 9,000 was really 900, so Solon's *c.* 600 BC + 900 = 1500 BC:

> The most recent elements of the myth descend to about 600 BC. Nine hundred years have thus been covered which the Saite priest projected into the tenfold abyss of the past. It thus reached, together with so much else that was impossible, the impossible chronology of nine thousand years before Solon's era.[24]

As ever, there are very valid objections to this neat solution: if it is applied to the dimensions of Plato's city we get something ludicrously small, rather along the lines of the Stonehenge scene in the film *This Is Spinal Tap*, where the set designer builds a replica of the monument 18 inches high instead of 18 feet.

Furthermore, as the Platonic scholar Luc Brisson has rightly pointed out, the literal interpretation of mythological time is not a valid thing to do.[25]

> The temporal context in which these events are situated can only be the past. For 'to remember' (*mimnēiskesthai*) is 'to be mindful'[26] of events which unfolded 'in the past' (*palai*),[27] or of 'past things' (*palaia*),[28] or of 'ancient things' (*archaia*).[29]

As we have seen in discussing Herodotus' *historia*,[30] the past that history talks about is not the same as the past that applies to myth. Greek mythical events have happened so long ago that whoever relates them cannot possibly prove their validity: they didn't witness them, and they can't cite anyone else who did either. Plato never uses *mythos* when talking about the Persian and Peloponnesian Wars, but he does use *mythos* or *mythos*-compounds when he references the Cyclops, and the founding and fall of Troy.[31] And again, as Brisson says, the fact that a myth brings to mind events from a past that is recorded by tradition, not by eyewitness testimony, creates two significant consequences that separate myth from what we call history:

1. absence of any precise dating;
2. ignorance about what really happened.

Myth cannot say exactly when the events that it mentions took place. Solon's exchanges with the Egyptian priest are a good example of this. Solon really flounders when he tries to organise the chronology of Phoroneus, Niobe, Deucalion and Pyrrha: 'by recording the years since the events of which he was speaking, he tried to work out their dates'.[32] This draws the very judgemental response, 'Oh Solon, Solon, you Greeks are always children: Greek old men don't exist', after which the priest launches into his account of Athens versus Atlantis war, pretending that he's speaking about the Athens of 9,000 years ago, 1,000 years older than Saïs, whose account has 'all been written down since ancient times and has been kept safe in the temples'.[33]

'Precise dating is as essential to history as measure is to physics.'[34] But mythical time is unspecific: Plato constantly uses *pote*, 'once', and *ēn pote*, 'once upon a time', and even where numbers do enter mythical narratives, they don't function in the same way as they do in historical contexts:

> These numbers (they are for the most part typical recurring numbers which indicate all kinds of measures) are generally fortuitous and cannot be used as a basis for calculating operations or for proving that events are contemporary. They only indicate a general order of size, and simply symbolize a long duration. Here, there is practically no interest in chronology, whether relative or absolute.[35]

In essence, the Egyptian priest is telling Solon, 'I can give precise dates; you can't', and therefore, 'My account is true history; yours is just a myth.' And in any case, time exacerbates our lack of knowledge about mythical events, especially when our knowledge of them comes from an oral tradition or poetry. Whereas a historian must respect the reality of the affairs he recounts, 'the poet may decide for himself what actually constitutes reality',[36] and quite pertinently for the development of the Atlantis story, Plato knows that our hazy grasp of the ancient past allows the myth teller to manipulate it in a variety of different ways. Socrates said that in mythical tales, because we are ignorant of the truth about antiquity, we make what is false look like what is true, and make it useful.[37] This is exactly what the Egyptian priest is doing.

One obvious problem with linking the demise of Minoan Crete and the Santorini eruption with Atlantis is that Plato's island is not destroyed by a volcano: it sinks beneath the sea along with Athens. So if an ancient report of Santorini and Crete had filtered down to him, it is strange that he fails to mention such an important part of it. It is also curious that Herodotus' visit to Saïs between Solon's visit and Plato's telling of the story elicited absolutely no information about Cretan catastrophes or Atlantean inundations. Herodotus also informs us that Cadmus, son of Agenor, founded a Phoenician colony on Santorini, but doesn't take the opportunity to link the island to either Atlantis or Crete.[38] Nor does any other Greek writer before Plato. The scholarly Apollonius of Rhodes, librarian at Alexandria in Egypt after Plato's death, tells us about the creation of Santorini by the Argonaut Euphemus: as Jason and the Argonauts go westwards towards their near-miss with Heracles near to Lake Tritonis and the Garden of the Hesperides, the god Triton gave Euphemus a clod of earth as a gift, before conducting the *Argo* back into the Mediterranean. In the final stages of the Argonauts' voyage, Euphemus dropped his clod of earth into the sea just north of Crete, and it became the island of Calliste (Thera/Santorini).[39] But Apollonius has nothing to say about its destruction. We might note in passing that a number of later pseudoscientific theories postulate that various ancient documents pertaining to Atlantis in one way or another, such as the Piri Re'is map, were transmitted to posterity via the Library of Alexandria. If those documents were present in Apollonius' day, it seems bizarre that he would miss a trick and not exploit the information: his work is incredibly scholarly, and there was nothing that the poets of his day liked more than abstruse mythological allusions. But there is nothing: not from Apollonius; not from his great rival Callimachus, whose *Pinakes* was a learned catalogue of the holdings of the Library, categorised under the headings of rhetoric, law, epic, tragedy, comedy, lyric poetry, history, medicine, mathematics, natural science and miscellanies; not from their near contemporary Lycophron, whose *Alexandra* consists of a prophecy uttered by Cassandra and concerns the later fortunes of Troy and of the Greek and Trojan heroes, including an enormous number of references to obscure names and uncommon myths; not from anyone else.

In terms of the dates of the Late Bronze Age eruption, a major challenge to the linkage with Crete/Atlantis emerged in the 1980s from Carbon-14 dating techniques. These suggested that the Santorini eruption could have taken place around 1628–1606 BC, which moves us way too far from the end of Minoan civilisation to link it to the volcano. This dating seems to be backed up by dendrochronology, which shows that massive volcanic events can create 'frost events' on the earth's surface, which manifest themselves in narrow annual growth rings in trees. Bristle-cone pines in the United States show precisely such characteristics between 1628 and 1626 BC, but no evidence of frost damage from the 1500s or 1400s BC; and Irish bog oaks also exhibit narrow rings in 1628 BC, as do trees that grew in England and Germany. Santorini could be the cause of this. Interestingly, dendrochronological data from Asia Minor records a highly unusual 'growth event' which matches the 1628 BC data from America and Europe, and it has been mooted that this must be due to unusually cool and wet weather in an area that was normally warm and dry, again caused by the eruption of Santorini.

A volcanic eruption can also emit vast amounts of sulphur dioxide into the atmosphere, which eventually falls back to earth as acid rain and becomes incorporated into the annual layers of ice in the polar icecaps. Danish scientists working in Greenland have suggested that the Santorini eruption took place in around 1645 BC, with an error margin of $\pm$ twenty years (i.e. 1665 to 1625 BC), which would dovetail with the dendrochronological evidence for a major volcanic eruption affecting the global climate around 1628 BC.[40] Furthermore, in 2002, while exploring the upper caldera cliffs near Athinios harbour, Tom Pfeiffer found the branch of an olive tree that had been buried and preserved in an upright position by the pumice of the eruption.[41] Analysis of this has provided a dating of 1613 BC, $\pm$ thirteen calendar years,[42] and although, as always, there is discussion about the precision of the dating, recent work encompassing textual analysis, archaeology and science supports this 'high', radiocarbon-based, chronology for the eruption to be in the later seventeenth century BC.[43]

The Late Bronze Age eruption at Santorini certainly impacted upon the eastern Mediterranean: air-fall debris from the volcano is found in an arc reaching from Turkey to Cos, Rhodes, eastern Crete and Egypt. This caused damage to buildings in places, and also disruption to farming, but the ash falls on Crete only amount to around 1 to 5 cm, and although there is considerable academic discussion concerning the size of the tsunamis that probably hit the northern coast, they seem to have been no higher than 8 m, so it is unlikely that agriculture was devastated by the ash or that ports and fleets were wiped out by the waves. The 'palace' of Knossos is too far inland to have been inundated, and the one at Phaestus is on the opposite side of the island. This doesn't necessarily tell against the Atlantis connection – Plato could have made the link even if there wasn't one – but it does diminish his motivation for doing so. As Christopher Gill points out, it seems that the cart is being put before the horse: 'it was the fact that Plato seemed to provide unique documentary support for the theory of volcanic destruction of Crete that made his story suddenly seem so important to archaeologists.'[44]

So, overall, current research has led to the conclusion that the Bronze Age eruption happened in the seventeenth century BC, and that it did not precipitate the demise of Minoan Crete – the two events are simply too far apart in time (around 175 years). Indeed, if those dates are correct, the greatest flowering of Minoan culture comes *after* the eruption. The theory, of course, is not unchallenged, since recent finds of pumice at Tel el-Dab'a in Egypt in contexts dating to around 1540 BC have been shown to be from Santorini, but the final analysis does not change: we cannot make a definitive link between the Late Bronze Age eruption, the destruction of Minoan Crete and the destruction of Atlantis.

So, if the Thera eruption did not destroy the Minoan civilisation, what did? From around 1450 BC, the architecture in the Cretan countryside started to place greater emphasis on security and storage; was this the result of internal tensions? The destruction on Crete appears to be much more comprehensive than would be needed to facilitate a political take-over: earthquake, insurrection, civil war, socioeconomic collapse or some combination of these seems more likely. Certainly, and all of a sudden, Minoan exports went into decline, and in Egypt, as we enter the Late Minoan II pottery phase, the tomb paintings of Amenemhab, Kenemun and Anen, which purport to portray Keftiu, actually show figures that are not authentic Minoans. The Keftiu on the tomb of Useramon, dating from 1451 BC, have their codpieces painted over with Mycenaean-looking kilts in the tomb of Rekhmire a generation later, perhaps indicating a new style of clothing on Crete. Something has gone wrong, but it is neither volcanic nor Atlantic, and the beneficiaries were the Mycenaeans, who proceeded to exercise their own period of hegemony on the island.

So was Atlantis the island of Santorini itself? The modern tourist industry certainly makes great play of the fact that it might be, and the possibility has attracted the interest of a number of serious scholars. Allied to the cataclysmic volcanic event, there is the manifestly high level of culture at Akrotiri, where the pro-Santorini lobby point to the use of variegated blackish and reddish stones in some of the buildings as echoes of *Critias* 116a–b, and the geography of the island itself. (See Figs. 5 and 7a.) The current vaguely circular, if very fragmentary, arrangements of the Santorini complex of islands (Thera, Therasia, Aspronisi, Palaea Kameni and Nea Kameni) have sometimes been said, largely on the basis of aerial photographs, to have been an influence on Plato's Atlantisville (although it looks far more Atlantean from maps or aerial photographs than it does in real life). Volcanological research has now enabled us to reconstruct the topography of the island in the period immediately preceding the Late Bronze Age eruption to some extent. The analysis of air-fall debris (tephra) embedded in cliffs, which are such a distinctive feature of the island's topography, shows that these cliffs must already have been in existence before the eruption:

> distribution of these deposits implies that there was a circular, 6-km-diameter depression located [in the south of the island] before the Minoan eruption . . . The presence of phreatomagmatic tuffs [i.e. fine rocks created when water meets hot lava] implies that this depression was flooded then, as it is now.[45]

Various proposals have been put forward to reconstruct the shape of the island prior to the eruption (see Fig. 7),[46] and while these can have an Atlantis-like look about them to those who want to see it, in the form of (possibly) a central island with almost a surrounding ring of land, it is still a very long way from the city which Critias describes, with its central island, two ring islands and three circular waterways, even before one arrives at the surrounding

Fig. 7:

SANTORINI IN THE 21st CENTURY
AND IN THE LATE BRONZE AGE

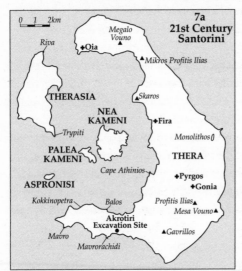

7a
21st Century
Santorini

7b

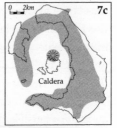

7c

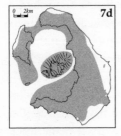

7d

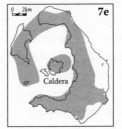

7e

7f

Key:

+ Modern town
▲ Mountain
● Archaeological site
········· Shoreline of current island group
▓ Proposed extent of Late Bronze Age island

walled city, the plain, the mountains and the hinterland. The current formation of the island complex, which is rather seductive to Atlantis theorising, is also somewhat misleading, since Palaea Kameni (see Fig. 7a) emerged in the first century AD in an eruption described by the Roman historian Dio Cassius:

> This year [AD 47] a small islet, hitherto unknown, made an appearance close to the island of Thera.[47]

Furthermore, the prominent central island of Nea Kameni, now roughly twice the diameter of Atlantis' palace-island, is an even more recent feature of the landscape, having emerged during eruptions which took place from 1701 to 1711 (see Fig. 7a). Had Plato himself visited the island (we have no reason to think that he did), or had anyone described the view to him, they would not have seen the same vista that we see.

The Crete/Santorini = Atlantis concept is certainly one of saner and more plausible theories, and it probably has more, although by no means unanimous, support than any of the other literal readings of Plato. It does have the advantage (or perhaps disadvantage if you are a pseudohistorian) over other proposed locations that you can go and walk through the ruins at Knossos and Akrotiri, admire the artworks of a culture with finely tuned aesthetic sensibilities in the Heraklion and Thera Archaeological Museums, and stand on the rim of the caldera at Santorini in a kind of 'box seat in the theatre of creation', where you can muse over the evidence as you survey the water-filled crater that was once part of the island complex, and evaluate the evidence over a bottle of Atlantis wine from beneath the Atlantis Hotel in Fira. But overall, as Christopher Gill indicates, if the Minoan/Santorini connection doesn't hold up, 'there is no other scholarly defence of the view that Plato's story is, in a straightforward sense, a factual account of a historical event or culture'.[48] Whether Santorini represents any real source of inspiration for Plato's tale, and if so how it was transmitted to him (or Solon) alone, and in what form, only the great philosopher himself can say. And it is notable that he is very quiet on the subject.

CHAPTER 16

Plato's Atlantis: Where, What and Why?

....

The Atlantis passages from Plato's *Timaeus* and *Critias* that have been translated in this book take up just over thirty pages of Greek print in the Oxford Classical Text edition. Yet their influence and interest are out of all proportion to their brevity. They have captured the imagination of readers from all around the world in the most vivid way imaginable. And they have done this for hundreds of years. The whole notion of an ancient, yet extraordinarily advanced, civilisation living on an enormous and beautiful island that is suddenly engulfed by the waters of the Atlantic Ocean is powerful, exciting and mysterious. Many thinkers have speculated over the meaning of the story; many have sought to appropriate it for their own political, religious or cultural ends; and many have tried to find traces of the island in pretty well every corner of the globe – indeed, many continue to do all of these. But questions still remain to be resolved: why did nobody tell the tale before Plato did? Where do we stand on the spectrum of regarding Plato's Atlantis as 100 per cent true to 100 per cent made up? Was he inspired by genuine events and/or places, and if so what were they? What was Plato's reason for telling the story?

Plato is enigmatic in this regard, and much of the fascination stems from the variety of ways in which his work can be interpreted, many of which have been explored in the preceding chapters. Was it, as his student Aristotle thought, a literary creation for philosophical ends, or was it 'pure history' (although, as we have seen, the concept of '*historia*' in ancient Greece represents something very different from the idea of 'history' in the twenty-first century)? Should we take it factually? Metaphysically? Allegorically? Plato's ancient readers were as divided on this as his modern ones are: 'no one in the ancient world really had any evidence about the status of Plato's story, or about his motives for telling it, which is not available to us'.[1] So one of the great attractions, or dangers, in the story of Atlantis is that it allows its readers, be they harmless hippies or Heinrich Himmler, to interpret it in whatever ways they wish.

'UTTERLY EXTRAORDINARY, BUT TOTALLY TRUE' ATLANTIS?

Was Plato's Atlantis real? In a sense, it was, at least in as much as it is an amalgamation of a variety of places and events that Plato would have been aware of from his own upbringing, reading and life experiences. Some of these were real and some were mythical.

We saw in Chapter 1 that the Greek mythical tradition gave him Calypso's paradise island of Ogygia, which often had Atlantic connections. He also had the model of the Phaeacians' far-distant homeland of Scherie, with its temple of Poseidon, the glittering palace of Alcinous, luxuriant vegetation and twin springs. Plato would also have been aware of Homer's neat ruse of having Poseidon turn the Phaeacian ship that took Odysseus back to Ithaca into stone, and essentially writing the Phaeacians out of Greek geography, in a similar tactic to the way he makes the same god help to obliterate the Achaean wall which Homer invented at Troy: the story itself neatly destroys the evidence for its own existence. Plato could also journey in his imagination beyond the Pillars of Heracles to the sea-girt Red Land of Erytheia in the far west, or beyond the sunset to Hesperia, or beyond the North Wind to the land of the blessed Hyperboreans, into whose main river Phaethon crashed after his disastrous attempt to drive the chariot of the Sun.

On the other hand, Plato also had the Athens of his own time in mind, as we can see from the fact that his account of Athens' greatest achievement emanates from her greatest statesman, Solon, at a festival of her greatest goddess, Athena. Critias deliberately references the first sentences of both Herodotus and Thucydides, whose work dealt with major conflicts from Athens' past. The Atlantis story might be 'fake history', but it is still highly relevant to Athens' 'true history', and in Chapters 2 and 3 we looked at the great range of material that Plato could have assimilated from the historical traditions of Athens, and from his own observations: Solon, with his links to Plato's own family, publishing his laws on *kyrbeis*, like the Atlantean kings do on their *oreikhalkon* pillar; Cleisthenes' division of the Athenians into ten tribes with ten generals; the significant natural disasters caused by earthquakes and flooding at Orobiae, an island called Atalante, and a city called Helice which had a famous temple of Poseidon; Herodotus' descriptions of Babylon, with its astonishing walls, temples, canals and general fecundity, and Ecbatana, with its central palace surrounded by multiple circular walls with their multi-coloured battlements with overlays of precious metal; Darius I making a seaborne invasion that was repulsed by the underdog Athenian hoplites; and Xerxes' *hybris*, engineering projects and unsuccessful attempt to overwhelm Athens with his vast barbarian army. When Plato's proto-Athens repulses the imperialist Atlanteans, his readers would see the connection with the real-life Persian invasions by Darius I and Xerxes: antediluvian Athens = sixth- and fifth-century BC Athens.

Historical Athens became a byword for resistance to alien invasion, but on the other hand it also made a significant change from land-power to sea-power and embarked on the journey of unsuccessful and unpopular maritime imperialism that we see in Thucydides: there is chaotic hubbub in the Piraeus, plague and moral degeneration in Athens, catastrophic defeat for the Athenian naval assault on Sicily (whose geography Plato knew at first hand from his visits to Syracuse, and which has a vaguely Atlantean flavour), political failures seen close-up through the involvement of Plato's own family, and a shattering defeat in the Peloponnesian War.

The antediluvian/sixth- and fifth-century BC Athens is not the fourth-century BC Athens where Plato wrote the *Timaeus* and *Critias*. Far from it: archaeo-Athens has no harbour, navy, market-place or elaborate temples; it is a land-power with a large military ruling class, not a sea-power; and it has a lot of land. Atlantis, on the other hand, is like the Athens of Plato's own lifetime: its great material wealth, like that of mid-fifth century BC Athens, is acquired through maritime trade and naval power, and it expands from simple isola-tion to become a lavishly decorated, noisy, chaotic commercial centre. A fourth-century BC Athenian would easily get the analogy: this is Athens' history between the Persian and Peloponnesian wars as told by Thucydides. Furthermore, in Thucydides' account of the Sicilian expedition, the Sicilian general Hermocrates, who is both one of Plato's characters in the Atlantis story and a key real-life player in Athens' defeat, makes a pertinent accusation:

> in the struggle against the Persians, the Athenians did not fight for the liberty of the Greeks [. . .] but to make their countrymen serve them instead of the Persian King.[2]

Plato has effectively rewritten history to create a very un-Athe-nian antediluvian Ideal Athens and a very mid-fifth/fourth-century Athenian-looking Atlantis. The Atlanto-Athenian War is part Persian Wars, with Greekness confronting barbarism, but also part Peloponnesian War, with the Spartan land-power elephant confront-ing the Athenian naval-power whale and emerging victorious, largely because Athens brought on its own downfall by invading

Sicily. It can be no accident that Hermocrates was one of the inter-locutors in the dialogues.[3]

So if we really want to find a historical basis for the Atlantis story, this is it. Atlantis is not a geological feature that was plunged into the depths of the Atlantic Ocean in the tenth millennium BC. It is Athens in the mid-fifth century BC. So, in an incredible twist of irony, the modern-day pseudohistorians of Atlantis are engaged in the search for an imaginary island created by a pseudohistorian.

SEARCH CRITERIA

Atlantis can be found in all these inspirational places, but the inten-sity of the search for Plato's 'real' Atlantis (or indeed for many other people's Atlantis) shows no sign of abating. In 2005, the International Conference on 'The Atlantis Hypothesis: Searching for a Lost Land' drew up a list of twenty-four criteria to help focus the search for Plato's Atlantis (as opposed to any lost civilisation anywhere on earth). All seekers of the lost land were encouraged to use them:[4]

1. Atlantis was located on an island.
2. The Metropolis of Atlantis had a distinct geomorphology composed of alternating concentric rings of land and water.
3. On a low hill about 50 *stadia* (10 km) inland within the capital city itself, an inner citadel was erected to protect the original home of Cleito and Poseidon.
4. Atlantis had hot- and cold-water springs, with mineral deposits.
5. Atlantis had red, white and black rocks.
6. Atlantis was located outside the Pillars of Hercules.
7. Atlantis was larger than Libya and Asia combined.
8. Atlantis sheltered a wealthy population with literate, building, mining, metallurgical and navigational skills.

9. The main region of Atlantis lay on a coastal plain, measuring 2,000 x 3,000 *stadia*, surrounded by mountains which rose precipitously high above sea level.

10. The coastal plain of Atlantis faced south and was sheltered from the northern winds.

11. The Atlantes had created a checkerboard pattern of canals for irrigation.

12. Atlantis had mineral resources and a rich spectrum of wild and domesticated flora and fauna, including elephants.

13. Atlantis had a high population density, enough to support a large army composed of 1.2 million men, 10,000 chariots and 1,200 ships.

14. Within the Strait of Gibraltar, Atlantis controlled Libya up to the borders of Egypt and Europe as far as Tyrrhenia (i.e. Italy).

15. The religion of Atlantis involved the sacrifice of bulls.

16. The kings of Atlantis assembled alternately every fifth and sixth year to consult on matters of mutual interest and it is during those assemblies that they sacrificed bulls.

17. The Metropolis of Atlantis was destroyed by a devastating physical destruction of unprecedented proportions.

18. Earthquakes and floods of extraordinary violence were the precursors of Atlantis' destruction.

19. The Metropolis of Atlantis was swallowed by the sea and vanished under the water, following the occurrence of earthquakes and floods.

20. At the time of its destruction, Atlantis was at war with Athens.

21. Atlantis should have been reachable from Athens by sea.

22. After the destruction of Atlantis, the passage of ships was blocked by shallows due to mud just below the surface, the remains of the sunken island.

23. The Metropolis of Atlantis was destroyed 9,000 years before the sixth century BC.

24. No physically or geologically impossible processes were involved in the formation and destruction of the Metropolis of Atlantis, but could not have been respon- sible for the destruction of a landmass the size of a conti- nent. Also, no physically or geologically impossible processes were involved in the formation of hot-water springs and in the formation of red, white and black rocks.

Following the conference, however, the Atlantis researcher Thorwald C. Franke felt that he couldn't find answers to some very basic problems of Atlantis research in these twenty-four criteria, so along with Ulrich Hofmann, Ulf Richter, Christian M. Schoppe and Siegfried G. Schoppe he put together the Atlantis Research Charter, published online in 2006.[5] Demanding openness for research, they are for a scientific approach, and against pseudoscience, dogmatism and abuse. They are in favour of rationality, objectivity, verifiable documentation, clarity, up-to-dateness, expert research and an evolv- ing process of knowledge acquisition. They reject the taking of Plato's Atlantis dialogues literally word for word, and in particular they consider Plato's datings and the imagination of Atlantis as the eighth continent in the Atlantic Ocean as scientifically long-since disproved. They further dismiss the notion that a possible existence of Plato's Atlantis could not be understood within the framework of established historiography and would require complete rewriting of history: they have no time for extraterrestrial influence, flying saucers, nuclear weapons, energy crystals, crustal shift, hollow earth and world ice theories. They also regret 'the prevailing ignorance and disorientation regarding ancient times and texts',[6] as well as the recurrent repetition of long-since disproved errors, and the mystification and mythification of Plato's Atlantis which has developed over thousands of years regarding the original. Finally, they are implacably opposed to the combination of Atlantis research with sensationalism and greed for money, claims on Plato's Atlantis by religions and mysticism ('Atlantis does not fit into the category of metaphysical enthusiasm like New Age and parapsychology'),[7] approaches that are based on excessive enthusiasm and biased love for local history, and to the abuse of Plato's Atlantis for political and ideological purposes, be it nationalism, socialism or racism.

Aspects of the twenty-four criteria can be found in the vast number of claims to have located Atlantis, but by no means all Atlantis-seekers are signed up to the Atlantis Research Charter, and this book makes no pretence of having been able to cover all the authors or all their theories. Tony O'Connell's useful resource, the *Atlantipedia* website,[8] gives an indication of the enormity of the task, listing ninety-eight different theories that were produced between 2000 and 2011 alone, covering pretty well every corner of the globe: Alaska; Albania; Algeria; America; Andalusia; Antarctica; Argentina; Australia; the Azores; the Bahamas; Bolivia; the Caribbean; Cuba; the Cyclades; Cyprus, Dholavira in India; the Dominican Republic; Egypt; Europe (north-west or south-west); Faro; Florida; Gibraltar; Greenland; the Indus Culture; Ireland; Israel/Sinai; Iberia; the Josephine Seamount between Madeira and Portugal; Mount Kilimanjaro; Libya; Malta; Meroë on the Nile; Mexico; Morocco; the Pannonian Plain centred on Hungary; Persia; Pharos in the Nile Delta; Sardinia; Sherbro Island off the coast of Sierra Leone; Sicily; Soqotra in the Arabian Sea; the Sundaland region of south-eastern Asia; Thera; the Tropics; Troy; Tunisia; Yucatán; not to mention the Atlantic Ocean, the Sea of Azov, and the Mediterranean, Adriatic, Black, North, and South China Seas.[9]

Not all of these theories can be correct, but they could all be wrong. A very common, yet seductive, approach is simply to assume that Greek myths are historical facts, make partial and one-dimensional selections from the material, distort the details where necessary, and arrive at the desired pre-conceived conclusion. Looking for Atlantis resembles trying to find Hogwarts in J. K. Rowling's Harry Potter novels on the basis of its veneer of reality: it is a coeducational, secondary boarding school for pupils aged eleven to eighteen, and exhibits the characteristic features of the British public school house system; you can get to it by train from King's Cross railway station; it stands on the shore of a loch called the Black Lake somewhere in Scotland (near Dufftown in Moray in the film *Harry Potter and the Prisoner of Azkaban*); and it boasts extensive grounds with sloping lawns, flowerbeds, vegetable patches, a large forest, several greenhouses, various outbuildings, a Quidditch pitch and an owlery. Unlike the super-civilised Atlantises on the Edgar Cayce model, Hogwarts lacks computers, radar and electricity, although it does have radios, because these are powered by magic, not by electricity. Muggles cannot see the school: various charms and spells mean that we see only ruins and warnings of danger. Could someone reading J. K. Rowling 2,500 years from now, and discovering that many of the details of Hogwarts were founded in late twentieth/early twenty-first-century reality, justifiably assert that Hogwarts was therefore not a fictional place, go looking for it, and claim to have discovered it on the banks of a Scottish loch? No. There is no need to do this. It is all about the story.

MYTHICAL ATLANTIS

The reason for the initial telling of the Atlantis tale is that Socrates wanted to see how the citizens of the Ideal State would display their excellence when they were put under extreme stress, particularly in wartime. Critias delivers everything that Socrates asked for, but his account belongs in the realms of the subjunctive and the optative:

his truth belongs in the way these citizens *would* behave, not in how they actually did. In the *Republic* 382d Plato explicitly states that we are ignorant of the truth about antiquity. This means that ancient tales (*mythologiai*) are necessarily false.[10] But they are also edifying, and Plato can use this story from the mists of time because his readers know hardly anything about ancient history, which means they can suspend their disbelief. It is true that Critias uses historiographical methods to back up what he says, but this only makes his account *seem* more historical, whereas it is really deceptive. Plato's purposes demand that he presents a plausible fiction (*pseudos*), so he lures the Muse of History into the crime of making the Atlantis story appear more truth-like than it actually was.

Socrates says that the fact that Atlantis is 'true history [*logos*] and not an invented myth [*mythos*] is massively important',[11] but we should not be misled by this. Socrates is being ironic, and there are strong indications that Plato wants us to treat what Critias says as though it were a normal traditional tale (*mythos*). As Luc Brisson pointed out,[12] the setting of the story is in the *mythical* past, when gods and 'godlike' men or heroes walked the earth.[13] By making Critias say that Solon would have been as famous as Homer and Hesiod if only he had finished his poem,[14] Plato is aligning him with the key transmitters of Greek mythical knowledge, many of the timescales, themes and locations of which find their way into Critias' narrative: the fecundity of the earth and the lifestyle of the people of Atlantis and palaeo-Athens, are reminiscent of Hesiod's Golden Race of mortal men who lived in the time of Cronus[15] and of Homer's Phaeacians; we have seen how Atlas and Atlantis can bring to mind the myth of the Garden of the Hesperides and its Golden Apples, situated 'beyond the Ocean';[16] Atlas belongs to the liminal areas of the world, too, usually in the far west, but sometimes beneath the sea or under the earth.[17] So 'Atlas' (and hence 'Atlantis' = 'of Atlas') = faraway, watery, subterranean and fabulous. He is also one of the

Titans, and although he himself does not take part in it, his siblings wage a violent war against Zeus, known as the Titanomachy:

> The boundless sea roared terribly around,
> The great earth rumbled, and broad heaven groaned,
> shaken; and tall Olympos was disturbed
> down to its roots, when the immortals charged.
> The heavy quaking from their footsteps reached
> Down to dark Tartarus, and piercing sounds
> Of awful battle, and their mighty shafts.
> They hurled their wounding missiles, and the voice
> Of both sides, shouting, reached the starry sky.[18]

Clearly there is no need for Plato to derive many of his Atlantis motifs from Egyptian sources: the Atlantean War is Titanic in the full Greek mythological sense.

ALLEGORICAL ATLANTIS

Plato's Atlantis myth might be a lie, but it is a 'noble lie', replete with deep philosophical and political truths. In the frenzied search for the lost island, the seekers' focus on its potential whereabouts leads them to miss the crucial point that Atlantis is not the star of the show: archaeo-Athens is. The ideal archaeo-Athenians are governed by a group of 20,000 Guardians who are focused entirely on their role as warriors, live apart from the rest of the population with no private property, have no internal elite group, regard everything they have as communal, receive nothing from the other citizens apart from their basic sustenance, and control a cohesive and stable state. These Athenians are invincible. Despite fighting against over-whelming odds, they repulse their Atlantean assailants who are led by ten rulers with no checks and balances on their power, whose possession of individual wealth leads to disunity, moral 'drunken-ness', political degeneration, military defeat and, finally, the inunda-tion of their entire island. The message is crystal clear. To the Greek way of thinking, Atlantis is sick, both morally and physically.

When Timaeus speaks about physical health later in the *Timaeus*,[19] he says that this depends on each element of the body – fire, air, water and earth – staying inside its proper boundaries, but in the moral universe maritime Atlantis (= water) transgresses its boundaries by impinging on land-based Athens (= earth). Furthermore, one cause of the Atlanteans' moral disease is the desire for luxury,[20] which drives their imperialism. The Greek medical term for one element encroaching on the territory of another is *pleonexia* (= 'greed'), but in the *Republic* Socrates also says that *pleonexia* causes wars.[21] The warmongering Atlanteans are sick; the just, moderate Athenians are healthy. That is why Athens triumphs over Atlantis. Socrates never gets the opportunity to comment on what must have been exactly the type of story he was hoping for, because the *Critias* breaks off in mid-sentence, but he would undoubtedly have expressed approval for what can be plausibly regarded as an allegorical fable.[22] Overall, the message of the Atlantis dialogues might be taken as a timeless one about the pernicious effects of wealth on the ruling class, or as an early precursor of Sir John Dalberg-Acton's 'power tends to corrupt, and absolute power corrupts absolutely'.[23]

A WONDERFUL STORY

Yet, with all the search for hidden places and hidden meanings, there is something else which often gets overlooked in the Atlantis story, and which surely lies behind much of its enduring appeal and influence. It is a fabulous, fantastic story (in all the possible mean-ings of those words), a wonderfully engaging, imaginative and origi-nal piece of what we might call 'creative fiction'. And the Atlantis tale is not unique in the way its author deploys mythological material. For instance, in the *Gorgias*, Socrates tells a story about the Isles of the Blessed and Tartarus, introduced like this:

> Give ear then [. . .] to a very fine story, which will seem fiction to you but is fact to me; what I am going to tell you I tell you as the truth.[24]

In the *Republic*, Socrates comments:

> We begin by telling children stories. These are, in general, fiction, though they contain some truth.[25]

He then talks about how to make the fiction as like the truth as possible, in order to make the lie or untruth useful. Socrates also poses this question in the *Protagoras*:

> Now shall I, as an old man speaking to his juniors, put my explanation in the form of a story or give it a reasoned argument? [And he answers his own question:] I think it will be pleasanter to tell you a story.[26]

And, perhaps most significantly in the light of the professed Egyptian origins of the whole Atlantis story, the eponymous character in the *Phaedrus* listens to Socrates speak about the 'ancient' tradition concerning the story of Theuth and Ammon, and then exclaims,

> Socrates, how easily you make up stories, from Egypt or from anywhere else you like![27]

This is easy to get away with, since, as Herodotus said, 'the Greeks know nothing at all about Egyptian character and custom'.[28]

It is the sheer seductive brilliance of Plato's story-telling that contributes to its plausibility. As we read his text it is easy to imagine the glittering lifestyle of the decadent, doomed Atlanteans, over-indulging in the luxuries of their vast, gorgeous island which provides them with all that they could wish for. We are probably right to seek deeper motives for the Atlantis myth. Far too much is never enough for an Atlantean; they want even more, and they bring about their own destruction in search of it, providing a dire warning not only to the Athenians of Plato's time, but to us too. Yet there is also a great deal in the *Timaeus* and *Critias* that is purely narrative, descriptive and un-symbolic, and we should never forget the simple fact that this is a really great story, beautifully told.

As we have seen throughout our explorations of the reception of Plato's Atlantis story, there is a very widespread drive to believe in it, which sits comfortably with the early twenty-first-century post-truth penchant for conspiracy theories, fake news and alternative facts. It is an attitude that is exquisitely captured by T. S. Eliot in his *Four Quartets*: in 'Burnt Norton' he suggests that 'human kind/Cannot bear too much reality'; and in 'The Dry Salvages' he describes the process:

> To communicate with Mars, converse with spirits
> To report the behaviour of the sea monster.
> Describe the horoscope, haruspicate or scry,
> Observe disease in signatures, evoke
> Biography from the wrinkles of the palm
> And tragedy from fingers; release omens
> By sortilege, or tea leaves, riddle the inevitable
> With playing cards, fiddle with pentagrams, barbituric
>   acids, or dissect
> The recurrent images into pre-conscious terrors

To explore the womb, or tomb, or dreams; all these are
    usual
Pastimes and drugs, and features of the press.
And always will be, some of them especially
When there is distress of nations and perplexity
Whether on the shores of Asia, or in the Edgware Road.
Man's curiosity searches past and future
And clings to that dimension.[29]

Too many difficulties get in the way of accepting Plato's story at face value: the chronology of putting a developed civilisation in the Mesolithic period; the geological impossibility of there being a sunken continent beneath the Atlantic; the total absence of any finds from the ancient world carrying the name Atlantis; and the fact that there is no mention anywhere of Atlantis in any ancient text prior to Plato's – not even in Herodotus or Solon. Put bluntly, there is no source of the Atlantis story other than Plato. Atlantis is just a tale from Egypt, 'the most brilliant and enduring of all hoaxes'.[30]

As Plato himself makes Socrates say in the *Republic*, when we don't know the truth about the past we can invent a lie as close to it as possible, blurring the boundaries between what is false and what is real, in order to make it useful.[31] And that is what Plato is doing in the *Timaeus* and *Critias*: there is no need to seek his Atlantis in Antarctica, Bolivia, Cuba, Dholavira, Egypt, Florida, Greenland or anywhere else, because its location is not the 'mystery' that enters the titles and subtitles of so many Atlantean publications. It certainly existed, but it existed in Plato's imagination. And so it should have done. Myths are good to think with.

The Flood Myths of Deucalion, Noah, Gilgamesh, Atrahasis and Hathor

....

In the Greek tradition, Apollodorus says that Prometheus had a son called Deucalion who married Pyrrha, the daughter of Epimetheus and Pandora. In this version, rather than letting the bronze race men destroy themselves, as they do in Hesiod, Zeus decides to eradicate them by means of a deluge. Deucalion takes his father's advice, builds a chest, stocks it with provisions, and embarks in it with Pyrrha. Zeus' torrential rain floods most of Greece and overwhelms everywhere outside the Isthmus of Corinth and the Peloponnese, destroying everyone except the few who fled to the mountains. Deucalion floated in his chest for nine days and nights, and when the rain finally abated he made landfall on Mount Parnassos. He sacrificed to Zeus, who sent Hermes to grant him whatever he wished. Deucalion chose to make humans, which he and Pyrrha did by taking stones and tossing them over their heads: his stones became men; hers became women.

This is both similar to, and very different from, the account of Noah's flood in Genesis: God 'saw that the wickedness of man was great in the earth, and that every imagination of the thoughts of his heart was only evil continually'; but Noah (aged 600) 'found grace in the eyes of the LORD', and on His instructions, he built an ark measuring 300 x 50 x 60 cubits and, along with his sons Shem, Ham and Japheth, his wife and the three wives of his sons, went into the ark, accompanied by 'every beast after his kind, and all the cattle after their kind, and every creeping thing that creepeth upon the earth after his kind, and every fowl after his kind, every bird of every sort [. . .] two and two of all flesh, wherein is the breath of life'; 'the flood was forty days upon the earth'; all the mountains were covered, and 'all that was in the dry land, died'; 'the waters prevailed upon the earth an hundred and fifty days' after which the waters abated, 'And the ark rested in the seventh month, on the seventeenth day of the month, upon the mountains of Ararat', after which the waters decreased continually until the dove that Noah kept sending out came back with an olive leaf in her mouth; seven days later, when the dove did not return, Noah stepped onto dry land and disembarked his family and the animals; Noah offered burnt offerings on the altar; the LORD promised never to 'smite any more every thing living, as I have done', blessed Noah and his sons, told them, 'Be fruitful, and multiply, and replenish the earth', and reaffirmed that 'the waters shall no more become a flood to destroy all flesh'; Noah lived for a further 350 years.

In the *Epic of Gilgamesh*, tablet XI, composed *c.* 1100 BC, a survivor of the Great Flood called Ut-napishtim tells Gilgamesh about it: from the city of Shuruppak on the Euphrates, the Great Gods decided to inflict the Flood; Ea, the Prince, repeated their talk to the reed house: 'Reed house, reed house! Wall, wall! O [Ut-napishtim], tear down the house and build a boat! Abandon wealth and seek living beings! Spurn possessions and keep alive living beings! Make [the seed of] all living beings go up into the boat'; the boat's length had to correspond to its width, and its roof was to be like the firmament in the primordial waters, and ultimately it was a cube with sides of 120 cubits, with six decks dividing it into seven levels; the inside of it, says Ut-napishtim, was divided into nine compartments; the boat was finished by sunset; the launching was very difficult; Ut-napishtim said, 'whatever silver I had I loaded on it, whatever gold I had I loaded on it. All the living beings that I had I loaded on it, I had all my kith and kin go up into the boat, all the beasts and animals of the field and the craftsmen I had go up'; after the sun god Shamas sent a shower of loaves of bread and a rain of wheat, the weather deteriorated and Ut-napishtim went into the boat and sealed the entry; the storm god Adad rumbled, preceded by Sack and Suppression as heralds, Erragal the god of destruction pulled out the mooring poles, the war god Ninurta made the dikes overflow, the gods set the land ablaze with torches, light turned to darkness, Adad broke the land into pieces like a pot, the South Wind blew, and 'then the Flood came, overwhelming the people like an attack'; even the gods were frightened by the flood, and retreated to heaven where they cowered like dogs and humbly sat weeping; when the seventh day arrived, the whirlwind fell still and the flood stopped; Ut-napishtim saw that all the human beings had turned to clay; his boat lodged firm on Mount Nimush; when a seventh day arrived, Ut-napishtim released a dove and then a swallow, both of which returned, followed by a raven which did not; he sacrificed; Enlil was enraged that anyone had survived the annihilation, but the other deities were more compassionate; Enlil softened his attitude and he blessed Ut-napishtim and his wife, saying, 'Previously Ut-napishtim was a human being. But now let Ut-napishtim and his wife become like us, the gods!'; and finally the gods settled Ut-napishtim and his wife at the Mouth of the Rivers.

The *Epic of Gilgamesh* tale sometimes quotes almost word-for-word from the account of the Great Flood at the end of the Mesopotamian *Epic of Atrahasis*, whose text comes down to us in two versions written by Assyrian scribes (one in the Assyrian, one in the Babylonian dialect), and another written during the reign of King Ammi-saduqa of Babylonia (1647–1626 BC). In this version, men are making so much noise that the gods decide to eradicate them with a flood. However, their plan is revealed to Atrahasis by

the god Enki, who tells him, 'Wall, listen to me! Reed wall, pay attention to all my words! Flee the house, build a boat, forsake possessions, and save life'; this boat must 'be equal' (the text is uncertain,
but presumably in its dimensions), with a roof like the firmament in
the primordial waters; Enki says he will shower down a windfall of
birds and a spate of fishes, and then primes a water clock and tells it
of the coming of the seven-day deluge; Atrahasis builds his boat and
brings various animals on board, as well as his family; the storm god
Adad begins to roar; the boat is released from its moorings; Anzu
rends the sky with his talons; there is a fragmentary reference to 'the
land and broke its clamour like a pot [sic]'; the flood comes forth
upon the peoples like a battle; people cannot see one another in the
dense darkness; the deluge bellows like a bull and the wind resounds
like a screaming eagle; and the gist of the highly fragmentary text
that follows seems to be that the gods become hungry because there
are no surviving farmers and no sacrifices taking place, and when
they find out that Atrahasis has survived, they decide that the noise
will remain within limits, invent childbirth and infant mortality, and
establish celibate priestesses and high priestesses in order to cut
down childbirth.

In Egypt, we encounter a rather different tradition. The 'equivalent' flood myth has significant differences to the ones above,
perhaps unsurprisingly, given that the flooding of the Nile is of great
benefit to the country. The tale starts with Ra, the sun god, fearing
that the mortals were going to overthrow him. So he dispatched the
goddess Hathor, who was his eye, to punish the human race. She,
however, was over-zealous in carrying out the task, which was to
chastise, not annihilate, and her frenzy of killing threatened the
total destruction of mankind: so many were slaughtered that their
blood flowed into the Nile river and the ocean, causing a flood. Ra
put a stop to this by ordering the creation of a lake of beer, dyed red
to look like blood, and brewed from the sleep-inducing mandrake

root. When Hathor looked down upon the flooded land of Egypt, rather like the Greek Narcissus, she saw herself reflected in the beer, bent down to kiss her own lovely image, and started to drink. She ended up so drunk and sleepy that she was incapable of finishing her orgy of destruction, which in turn allowed the survivors to resume their normal existence. In essence, in the Egyptian tradition, a benign flood *rescues* the human race.

Further Reading

......

WEB

Typing 'Atlantis' into a web browser will bring up over 93 million results. These websites are a good starting point for any explorations:

'Atlantipedia': http://atlantipedia.ie/samples
'Atlantis-Scout': https://www.atlantis-scout.de
'Bad Archaeology': http://www.badarchaeology.com/lost-civilisations/lost-continents/atlantis–2
Oxford University's 'Plato's Atlantis' course website: http://open.conted.ox.ac.uk/series/platos-atlantis

BOOKS

Adams, M., *Meet Me in Atlantis: My Obsessive Quest to Find the Sunken City* (New York: Dutton, 2015).
de Acosta, J., *The Naturall and Morall Historie of the East and West Indies*, translated by Edward Grimston (London: Sims, 1604).
Alican, N. P., *Rethinking Plato: A Cartesian Quest for the Real Plato* (Leiden: Brill, 2012).
Allen, J. M., *Atlantis and the Persian Empire* (Cambridge: J. M. Allen, 2012).
Annas, J., 'The Atlantis Story: The *Republic* and the *Timaeus*', in M. McPherran (ed.), *Plato's Republic: A Critical Guide* (New York: Cambridge University Press, 2011).
Antonopoulos, J., 'The tsunami of 426BC in the Maliakos Gulf, Eastern Greece', *Natural Hazards*, no. 5 (1992), pp. 83–93.
Archer-Hind, R. D. (ed. and trans.), *The Timaeus of Plato* (London: Macmillan & Co., 1888; reprinted, Salem, NH: Ayers Co. Publishers, 1988).
Ashe, G., *Atlantis: Lost Lands, Ancient Wisdom* (London: Thames & Hudson, 2012).

Babcock, W. H., 'Atlantis and Antillia', *Geographical Review*, no. 3 (1917), pp. 392–5.

Babcock, W. H., *Legendary Islands in the Atlantic: A Study in Medieval Geography* (New York: American Geographical Society, 1922).

Baer, F.-C., *Essai historique et critique sur les Atlantiques dans lequel on se propose de faire voire la conformité qu'il y a entre de ce peuple et celle des Hébreux* (Paris, 1762).

Bailly, J.-S., *Histoire de l'astronomie ancienne depuis son origine jusqu'à l'établissement de l'école d'Alexandrie* (Paris: Debure, 1775).

Bailly, J.-S., *Histoire de l'astronomie moderne depuis la fondation de l'école d'Alexandrie, jusqu'à l'époque de M.D.CC.XXX* (Paris: Debure, 1779).

Bailly, J.-S., *Lettres sur l'Atlantide de Platon et sur l'ancienne histoire de l'Asie* (London and Paris: Debure, 1779).

Bellamy, H., *The Atlantis Myth* (New York: Faber & Faber, 1948).

Benite, Z. B.-D., *The Ten Lost Tribes* (Oxford: Oxford University Press, 2009).

Bernal, M., *Black Athena: The Afroasiatic Roots of Classical Civilization. Vol. I: The Fabrication of Ancient Greece* (New Brunswick, NJ: Rutgers University Press, 1987).

Bernal, M., *Black Athena: The Afroasiatic Roots of Classical Civilization. Vol. II: The Archaeological and Documentary Evidence* (New Brunswick, NJ: Rutgers University Press, 1991).

Blavatsky, H. P., *The Secret Doctrine, The Synthesis of Science, Religion, and Philosophy* (Pasadena, CA: Theosophical University Press, 1888).

Brandwood, L., *The Chronology of Plato's Dialogues* (Cambridge: Cambridge University Press, 1990).

Bremmer, J. (ed.), *Interpretations of Greek Mythology* (London and New York: Routledge, 1988).

Brisson, L., *How Philosophers Saved Myths: Allegorical Interpretation and Classical Mythology* (Chicago and London: University of Chicago Press, 2004).

Brisson, L., *Plato the Myth Maker* (Chicago: University of Chicago Press, 1998).

Broadie, S., *Nature and Divinity in Plato's Timaeus* (Cambridge: Cambridge University Press, 2012).

Brooks, D., *Atlantis Pyramids Floods*, third edition, lulu.com (2016).

Buccini, S., *The Americas in Italian Literature and Culture, 1700–1825* (University Park, PA: Penn State University Press, 1996).

Burnet, J. (ed.), *Platonis Opera*, vol. IV (Oxford: Clarendon Press, 1902).

Bury, R. G. (ed. and trans.), *Plato: Timaeus, Critias, Cleitophon, Menexenus, Epistles* (Cambridge, MA: Loeb Classical Library, 1960).

Byrne, S., *Ficino in Spain* (Toronto, Buffalo and London: University of Toronto Press, 2015).

Calvo, T. and L. Brisson (eds), *Interpreting the Timaeus and Critias* (Sankt Augustin: Akademia Verlag, 1997).

de Camp, L. S., *Lost Continents: The Atlantis Theme in History, Science and Literature* (New York: Gnome Press, 1954).

Castleden, R., *Atlantis Destroyed* (London: Routledge, 1998).

Cayce, H. L. (ed.), *Edgar Cayce on Atlantis* (New York: Warner, 1968).

Cline, E., *1177 BC: The Year Civilization Collapsed* (Princeton, NJ: Princeton University Press, 2014).

Cole, J., 'Cult archaeology and unscientific method and theory', *Advances in Archaeological Method and Theory*, no. 3 (1980), pp. 1–33.

Cornford, F. M., *Plato's Cosmology* (London: Routledge & Kegan Paul, 1937; reprinted, Indianapolis, IN: Hackett Publishing Co., 1997).

Cranston, S., *HPB: the extraordinary life and influence of Helena Blavatsky, founder of the modern Theosophical movement* (New York: Putnam, 1993).

Davies, J. K., *Athenian Propertied Families 600–300 BC* (Oxford: Oxford University Press, 1971).

Delisle de Sales, J-.B-.C., *Histoire nouvelle de tous les peuples du monde, ou Histoire des Hommes* (Paris, 1779).

Diehl, E. (ed.), *Procli Diadochi In Platonis Timaeum commentaria* (Bibliotheca scriptorum Graecorum et Romanorum Teubneriana) (Leipzig: Teubner, 1903–6).

Dillon, J. M. (ed. and trans.), *Iamblichi Chalcidensis in Platonis dialogos commentariorum fragmenta* (Leiden: Brill, 1973).

Donnelly, I., *Atlantis: The Antediluvian World* (New York: Harper and Brothers, 1882).

Donnelly, I., *The Great Cryptogram: Francis Bacon's Cipher in the So-called Shakespeare Plays* (New York & London: Peale, 1888).

Donnelly, I., *Ragnarok: The Age of Fire and Gravel* (New York: Appleton, 1883).

Dubay, E., *The Atlantean Conspiracy (Final Edition)*, lulu.com (2013).

Euremius, J., *Atlantica Orientalis sive Atlantis* (Berlin, Stralsund and Leipzig: Langium, 1764).

Fagan, G. G. (ed.), *Archaeological Fantasies: How Pseudoarchaeology Misrepresents the Past and Misleads the Public* (London and New York: Routledge, 2006).

Feder, K. L., *Frauds, Myths and Mysteries: Science and Pseudoscience in Archaeology* (New York: McGraw-Hill College, 2005).

Feder, K. L. 'Irrationality and popular archaeology', *American Antiquity*, no. 49 (1984), pp. 525–41.

Festugière, A.-J. (trans.), *Commentaire sur le Timée*, 5 vols, Bibliothèque des textes philosophiques (Paris: Vrin, 1966–8).

Fjagesund, P., *The Dream of the North: A Cultural History to 1920* (Amsterdam and New York: Rodopi, 2014).

Flem-Ath, R. and R., *Atlantis Beneath the Ice: The Fate of the Lost Continent* (Rochester, VT: Bear & Company, 2012).

Flem-Ath, R. and R., *When the Sky Fell: In Search of Atlantis* (London: Weidenfeld & Nicolson, 1995).

Flem-Ath, R. and C. Wilson, *The Atlantis Blueprint: Unlocking the Ancient Mysteries of a Long-Lost Civilization* (London: Little, Brown, 2000).

Forsyth, P. Y., *Atlantis: The Making of Myth* (Montreal: McGill-Queen's University Press, 1980).

Forsyth, P. Y., *Thera in the Bronze Age* (New York: Lang, 1999).

Fracastoro, G., *Syphilis sive morbus Gallicus*, trans. M. S. Claiborne, in *Hieronymus Fracastor's Syphilis, from the original Latin; a translation in prose of Fracastor's immortal poem* (St Louis: The Philmar Company, 1911).

Franke, T. C., *Aristotle and Atlantis: What Did the Philosopher Really Think About Plato's Island Empire?* (Norderstedt: Books on Demand, 2012).

Freund, R., *Digging Through History: Archaeology and Religion from Atlantis to the Holocaust* (Latham, MD: Rowman & Littlefield, 2012).

Friedrich, W. L., *Fire in the Sea: The Santorini Volcano: Natural History and the Legend of Atlantis* (Cambridge: Cambridge University Press, 2000).

Fritze, R. H., *Invented Knowledge: False History, Fake Science and Pseudo-Religions* (London: Reaktion Books, 2009).

Ganopoulos, A. G. and E. Bacon, *Atlantis: The Truth Behind the Legend* (Indianapolis, IN: Bobbs-Merrill, 1969).

Gill, C., 'The genre of the Atlantis story', *Classical Philology*, no. 72 (1977), pp. 287–304.

Gill, C., 'The origin of the Atlantis myth', *Trivium*, no. 11 (1976), pp. 1–11.

Gill, C., 'Plato's Atlantis story and the birth of fiction', *Philosophy and Literature*, no. 3 (1979), pp. 64–78.

Gill, C., *Plato: The Atlantis Story* (Bristol: Bristol Classical Press, 1980).

Godwin, J., *Atlantis and the Cycles of Time: Prophecies, Traditions, and Occult Revelations* (Rochester, VT: Inner Traditions, 2011).

Gordon, C. H., *Before Columbus: Links Between the Old World and Ancient America* (New York: Crown, 1971).

Greer, J. M., *Atlantis: Ancient Legacy, Hidden Prophecy* (Woodbury: Llewellyn Publications, 2007).

Guidoboni, E., A. Comastri and G. Traina, *Catalogue of ancient earthquakes in the Mediterranean area up to the 10th century* (Bologna: SGA Storia Geofisica Ambiente, 1994).

Hale, C., *Himmler's Crusade: The Nazi expedition to find the origins of the Aryan Race* (New Jersey: Wiley, 2003).

Hancock, G., *Fingerprints of the Gods: A Quest for the Beginning and the End* (London: Heinemann, 1995).

Hancock, G., *Magicians of the Gods: The Forgotten Wisdom of Earth's Lost Civilization* (New York: Thomas Dunne Books/St Martin's Press, 2015).

Hapgood, C. H., *Maps of the Ancient Sea Kings: Evidence of Advanced Civilization in the Ice Age* (Philadelphia, PA: Chilton, 1966).

Hapgood, C. H. and J. H. Campbell, *The Earth's Shifting Crust: A Key to Some Basic Problems of Earth Science* (New York: Pantheon, 1958).

Hardy, D. A. (ed.), *Thera and the Aegean World III: Earth Sciences* (London: The Thera Foundation, 1990).

Haughton, B., *Hidden History: Lost Civilizations, Secret Knowledge, and Ancient Mysteries* (Franklin Lakes, NJ: New Page Books, 2007).

Holley, M., 'Blake's Atlantis', *Colby Quarterly*, no. 30 (1994), pp. 109–18.

Johansen, T. K., *Plato's Natural Philosophy: A Study of the Timaeus-Critias* (Cambridge: Cambridge University Press, 2004).

Jordan, P., *The Atlantis Syndrome* (Stroud: Sutton, 2001).

Kennedy, J. B., *The Musical Structure of Plato's Dialogues* (Durham: Acumen, 2011).

Kennedy, J. B., 'Plato's forms, Pythagorean mathematics, and stichometry', *Apeiron*, vol. 43, no. 1 (2010), pp. 1–32.

Kershaw, S. P., *A Brief Guide to Classical Civilization* (London: Robinson, 2010).

Kershaw, S. P., *A Brief Guide to the Greek Myths* (London: Robinson, 2007).

King, D., *Finding Atlantis: A True Story of Genius, Madness, and an Extraordinary Quest for a Lost World* (New York: Harmony Books, 2005).

Kircher, A., *Mundus subterraneus, in XII libros digestus: qvo divinum subterrestris mundi opificium, mira ergasteriorum naturae in eo distributio, verbo [pantamorphon] Protei regnum, universae denique naturae majestas & divitiae summa rerum varietate exponuntur, abditorum effectuum causae acri indagine inquistae demonstrantur, cognitae per artis & naturae conjugium ad humanae vitae necessarium usum vario experimentorum apparata, necnon novo modo & ratione applicantur. Ad Alexandrum VII. pont. opt. max.* (Amsterdam: Joannem Janssonium à Waesberge & filios, 1678).

Ledger, G. R., *Re-counting Plato: A Computer Analysis of Plato's Style* (Oxford: Clarendon Press, 1989).

Lee, D. (trans.), *Timaeus and Critias* (London: Penguin Books; 1972; revised by T. K. Johansen, 2008)

Lefkowitz, M., *Not Out of Africa: How Afrocentrism Became an Excuse to Teach Myth as History* (New York: New Republic and Basic Books, 1997).

Luce, J. V., *The End of Atlantis: New Light on an Old Legend* (New Aspects of Antiquity series) (London: Thames & Hudson, 1969).

Luce, J. V., 'The sources and literary form of Plato's Atlantis narrative', in E. S. Ramage (ed.), *Atlantis: Fact or Fiction?* (Bloomington, IN, and London: Indiana University Press, 1978).

Magee, J., *On Plato's Timaeus – Calcidius, Edited and translated by John Magee* (Cambridge, MA, and London: Harvard University Press, 2016).

Marinatos, S., *Some Words About the Legend of Atlantis* (Athens: Archaeological Deltion – No. 12 – of the General Direction of Antiquities and Restoration, second edition, 1971).

Martin, T. H., *Etudes sur le Timée de Platon* (Paris: Ladrange, 1841).

Mavor, J., *Voyage to Atlantis* (New York: Putnam, 1969).

McClain, E., *The Pythagorean Plato* (Stony Brook, NY: Nicolas Hays, 1987).

Misfud, A. et al., *Malta: Echoes of Plato's Island* (Msida: The Prehistorical Society of Malta, 2001).

Muck, O., *The Secret of Atlantis* (London: Collins, 1978).

Nails, D., *The People of Plato: A Prosopography of Plato and Other Socratics* (Indianapolis, IN: Hackett, 2002).

Nielsen, F. A. J., *The Tragedy in History: Herodotus and the Deuteronomistic History* (Sheffield: Sheffield Academic Press, 1997).

Novotny, F., *The Posthumous Life of Plato* (The Hague: Martinus Nijhoff, 1977).

Oesterle, A., 'The office of ancestral inheritance and folklore scholarship', in J. R. Dow and H. Lixfeld (eds), *The Nazification of an academic discipline: Folklore in the Third Reich* (Bloomington and Indianapolis, IN: Indiana University Press, 1994), pp. 189–246.

Palmer, T., *Perilous Planet Earth: Catastrophes and Catastrophism through the Ages* (Cambridge: Cambridge University Press, 2003).

Papamarinopoulos, S. P. (ed.), *Proceedings of the International Conference on 'The Atlantis Hypothesis: Searching for a Lost Land' (ATLANTIS 2005) 11–13 July 2005, Milos Island, Greece* (Athens: Heliotropos Publications, 2007).

Papamarinopoulos, S. P. (ed.), *Proceedings of the 2nd International Conference on 'The Atlantis Hypothesis: Searching for a Lost Land' (ATLANTIS 2008) 10–11 November, Athens, Greece* (Athens: Heliotropos Publications, 2010).

Papazachos, B. C. and C. B. Papazachou, *The Earthquakes of Greece* (Thessaloniki: Ziti, 1997).

Papazachos, B. C., C. Papaioannou, C. B. Papazachos and A. A. Savvaidis, *Atlas of isoseismals maps for strong earthquakes in Greece and surrounding area* (Thessaloniki: Publ. Geoph. Lab. Univ., 1997).

Parfitt, T., *The Lost Tribes of Israel: The History of a Myth* (London: Weidenfeld & Nicolson, 2002).

Pelikan, J., *What has Athens to do with Jerusalem? Timaeus and Genesis in Counterpoint* (Ann Arbor, MI: The University of Michigan Press, 1997).

Popkin, R. H., *Isaac la Peyrère (1596–1676): His Life, Work and Influence* (Leiden: Brill, 1987).

Pringle, H., *The Master Plan: Himmler's Scholars and the Holocaust* (London: Fourth Estate, 2006).

Proclus, *In Timaeum*, E. Diehl (ed.) (Leipzig: Teubner, 1903).

Ramage, E. S. (ed.), *Atlantis: Fact or Fiction?* (Bloomington, IN, and London: Indiana University Press, 1978).

Ramaswamy, S., *The Lost Land of Lemuria; Fabulous Geographies, Catastrophic Histories* (Berkeley, CA: University of California Press, 2004).

Ridge, M., *Ignatius Donnelly: Portrait of a Politician* (Chicago: University of Chicago Press, 1962).

Rosenmeyer, T. G., 'Plato's Atlantis Myth: "Timaeus" or "Critias"?', *Phoenix*, vol. 10, no. 4 (1956), pp. 163–72.

Runia, D. T., *Philo of Alexandria and The Timaeus of Plato* (Leiden: Brill, 1986).

Sagan, C., *The Demon-Haunted World: Science as a Candle in the Dark* (New York: Ballantine, 1996).

Sayre, G. M., 'Prehistoric diasporas: Colonial theories of the origins of Native American peoples', in P. Beidler, G. Taylor (eds), *Writing Race Across the Atlantic World: Medieval to Modern* (New York and Basingstoke: Palgrave Macmillan, 2005), pp. 51–76.

Scott-Elliot, W., *The Story of Atlantis & The Lost Lemuria* (London: Theosophical Publishing House, 1925).

Simkin, T. and R. S. Fiske, *Krakatau, 1883, the Volcanic Eruption and Its Effects* (Washington, DC: Smithsonian Institution Scholarly Press, 1983).

Soloviev, S. L. et al., *Tsunamis in the Mediterranean Sea 2000 BC–2000 AD* (Dordrecht, Boston and London: Kulwer Academic Publishers, 2000).

Spanuth, J., *Atlantis of the North* (New York: Van Nostrand Reinhold, 1980).

Spence, L., *Atlantis in America* (London: Benn, 1925).

Spence, L., *The History of Atlantis* (London: Rider, 1927).

Spence, L., *The Problem of Atlantis* (London: Rider, 1924).

Stein, W., *Atlantis Opposing Views* (San Diego, CA: Greenhaven, 1989).

Stiebing, W. R., *Ancient Astronauts, Cosmic Collisions, and Other Popular Theories about Man's Past* (Buffalo, NY: Prometheus, 1984).

Swan, J., *Speculum mundi: Or A glasse representing the face of the world shewing both that it did begin, and must also end: the manner how, and time when, being largely examined. Whereunto is joyned an hexameron, or a serious discourse of the causes, continuance, and qualities of things in nature; occasioned as matter pertinent to the work done in the six dayes of the worlds creation* (Cambridge: University of Cambridge, 1635).

Sweeney, E. J., *Atlantis: The Evidence of Science* (New York: Algora Publishing, 2010).

Tarrant, H., *Proclus: Commentary on Plato's Timaeus, Vol. 1, Book 1: Proclus on the Socratic State and Atlantis* (Cambridge: Cambridge University Press, 2007).

Taylor, A. E., *A Commentary on Plato's Timaeus* (Oxford: Clarendon Press, 1928; reprinted, New York: Garland, 1967).

Taylor, T. (trans.), *Proclus: Proclus' Commentary on the Timaeus of Plato* (The Thomas Taylor series 15–16) (Frome: Prometheus Trust, 1998).

Tsakmakis, A. and M. Tamiolaki (eds), *Thucydides Between History and Literature* (Berlin and Boston: Walter de Gruyter, 2013).

Velikovsky, I., *Worlds in Collision* (Garden City, NY: Doubleday, 1950).

Velikovsky, I., *Ages in Chaos* (Garden City, NY: Doubleday, 1952).

Velikovsky, I., *Earth in Upheaval* (Garden City, NY: Doubleday, 1955).

Vidal-Naquet, P., 'Athens and Atlantis: structure and meaning of a Platonic myth', in R. L. Gordon (ed.), *Myth, Religion and Society: Structuralist Essays by M. Detienne, L. Gernet, J.-P. Vernant and P. Vidal-Naquet* (Cambridge: Cambridge University Press/Paris: Éditions de la Maison des Sciences de l'Homme, 1981), pp. 201–14.

Vidal-Naquet, P., 'Atlantis and the nations', trans. J. Lloyd, *Critical Inquiry*, no. 18 (1992), pp. 300–26.

Vidal-Naquet, P., *The Atlantis Story: A Short History of Plato's Myth*, trans. J. Lloyd (Exeter: University of Exeter Press, 2007).

Von Däniken, E., *Erinnerungen an die Zukunft: Ungelöste Rätsel der Vergangenheit* (Düsseldorf: Econ, 1968).

Von Däniken, E., *Odyssey of the Gods: The Alien History of Ancient Greece* (London: Vega 1998).

Vougioukalakis, G. E., *The Minoan Eruption of the Thera Volcano and the Aegean World* (Athens: Society for the Promotion of Studies on Prehistoric Thera, 2006).

Warburton, D. A. (ed.), *Time's up! Dating the Minoan eruption of Santorini* (Athens: Danish Institute at Athens, 2009).

Waterfield, R. (trans.), *Timaeus and Critias (with introduction and notes by A. Gregory)*, (Oxford: Oxford University Press, 2008).

Wauchope, R., *Lost Tribes and Sunken Continents. Myth and Method in the Study of American Indians* (Chicago: Chicago University Press, 1962).

White, J., *Pole Shift: Predictions and Prophecies of the Ultimate Disaster* (New York: Doubleday, 1980).

Winchester, S., *Krakatoa: The Day the World Exploded* (London: Penguin, 2004).

Zangger, E., *The Flood from Heaven: Deciphering the Atlantis Legend* (New York: Morrow, 1992).

Zhirov, N., *Atlantis: Atlantology – Basic Problems* (Honolulu: University Press of the Pacific, 2001).

Notes

....

1 Whether Critias the Elder or Critias the Younger is the one who tells the Atlantis story is still a matter of dispute, although, in the light of recent research, it seems more likely to have been Critias the Elder. See D. Nails, 'Critias III' and 'Critias IV' in *The People of Plato: A Prosopography of Plato and Other Socratics* (Indianapolis: Hackett, 2002).

2 'Antediluvian' is derived from the Latin words *ante* ('before') and *diluvium* ('deluge'). Properly this refers to Noah's flood in the Bible, but it can also refer to things of great antiquity in general. However, since the ancient Athens of Plato's story was destroyed in the same flood that overwhelmed Atlantis, it will often be referred to as 'antediluvian Athens' to distinguish it from the historical Athens of Classical Geeece.

3 The *Homeric Hymns* in question are 11 *Athena*, 28 *Athena*, 20 *Hephaestus*, 22 *Poseidon*, and 23 *Zeus*.

4 The Roman orator Cicero (*On the Laws* 1.5) is the first writer we know of to give him this title. Less charitable critics also called him 'The Father of Lies'.

5 See Homer, *Iliad* 23.71–6, *Odyssey* 10.488–540, 11 *passim*, 24.1–204; Lucian, *Dialogues of the Dead*; Virgil, *Aeneid* 6.

6 Homer, *Odyssey* 5.64 ff., trans. A. T. Murray, *Homer: The Odyssey with an English Translation* (Cambridge, MA: Harvard University Press; London: William Heinemann, 1919).

7 Strabo, 1.18, trans. H. L. Jones, *Strabo: Geography, Volume I: Books 1–2* (Cambridge, MA: Harvard University Press, 1917).

8 1 *stadion* (i.e. the length of a Greek athletics track) was 600 Greek feet. This varied from place to place, but one *stadion* approximates to 200 m. The plural of *stadion* is *stadia*.

9 Plutarch, *Concerning the Face which Appears in the Orb of the Moon* 26, trans. C. W. King, *Plutarch's Morals: Theosophical Essays* (London: Bell and Sons, 1910).

10 Homer, *Odyssey* 6.262 ff., trans. Murray, op. cit.

11 Homer, *Odyssey* 7.82 ff., trans. Murray, op. cit.

12 Plato, *Republic* 600e.

13 There are in-depth discussions of Homer's poetry and its effects in the *Republic* and the *Ion*. See, for example, C. L. Griswold, 'Plato on Rhetoric and Poetry', in E. N. Zalta (ed.), *The Stanford Encyclopedia of Philosophy* (Fall 2016 edition), https://plato.stanford.edu/archives/fall2016/entries/plato-rhetoric [accessed 26 December 2016].

14 Thucydides 1.25.4, trans. R. Crawley, *Thucydides: The Peloponnesian War* (London: J. M. Dent; New York: E. P. Dutton, 1910).

15 Quoted by Strabo, 7.3.6.

16 See P. Jones, *Homer's Odyssey: A Commentary* (Bristol: Bristol Classical Press, 1998), p. 80.
17 Callimachus of Cyrene (*fl.* about 250 BC) was indeed a scholar: he was librarian at Alexandria and wrote some 800 works in both prose and verse.
18 See Strabo, 7.3.6.
19 Homer, *Iliad* 21.194 ff., trans. S. Butler, *The Iliad of Homer, Rendered into English Prose for the use of those who cannot read the original* (London, New York and Bombay: Longmans, Green and Co., 1898).
20 The Pillars of Heracles will become another point of speculation in various Atlantis theories. See pp. 194, 285.
21 Hesiod, *Theogony* 294.
22 Stesichorus, trans. J. March, in *The Cassell Dictionary of Classical Mythology* (London: Cassell, 2001), s.v. 'Geryon'.
23 See p. 173.
24 Herodotus 4.8.1, trans. A. D. Godley, *Herodotus: Histories* (Cambridge, MA: Harvard University Press, 1922).
25 Apollodorus 2.106–9.
26 Now called the Guadalquivir. It flows into the Atlantic just north of Cadiz.
27 Also known as Gades, modern Cadiz, which is on the coast just north-west of Gibraltar.
28 This is a reference to silver that was mined in the region.
29 Stesichorus, fragment S7.
30 Strabo, *Geography* 3.2.11, trans. H. J. Jones, *Strabo: Geography* (Cambridge, MA: Harvard University Press, 1923).
31 Ibid., 3.5.4.
32 That is, the sea between Egypt and Arabia that is now still called the Red Sea.
33 Pliny, *Natural History* 4.36, trans. J. Bostock, *Pliny the Elder: The Natural History* (London: Taylor and Francis, 1855).
34 Strabo 7.3.6, trans. Jones, op. cit.
35 Plato, *Critias* 114b.
36 Or from the Latin *vitulus* = 'calf'.
37 Strabo, *Geography* 3.2.13, trans. Jones, op. cit.
38 *Isthmian* 4.52–5.
39 Herodotus 2.45, trans. A. de Sélincourt, *Herodotus, the Histories* (Harmondsworth: Penguin, rev. edn, 1972).
40 Apollodorus 2.5.11.
41 Apollonius Rhodius, *Argonautica* 4.1138–49.
42 Aeschylus, *Libation Bearers* 372 ff., trans. H. Weir Smyth, *Aeschylus, with an English translation by Herbert Weir Smyth, PhD in two volumes. 2. Libation Bearers* (Cambridge, MA: Harvard University Press, 1926).
43 See Strabo 7.3.6 and cf. 7.3.1.
44 Strabo 7.3.1.
45 Herodotus, 4.36, trans. Godley, op. cit.
46 Herodotus' description of world geography is at 4.36 ff.
47 Ovid, *Metamorphoses* 2.47 ff.
48 See S. Kershaw, *A Brief Guide to the Greek Myths* (London: Robinson, 2007), p. 263 f.
49 *Timaeus* 22c.
50 See the discussions of the theories of Carli, Donnelly, Zschaetzsch, Velikovsky and Hancock below. See also, for example, R. Dalton, 'Archaeology Blast in the

Past', *Nature*, no. CDXLVII (2007), pp. 256–7; E. Spedicato, 'The Deucalion catastroph [*sic*] 1: the passage of the Red Sea by Moses and the Phaethon explosion, in S. P. Papamarinopoulos (ed.), *Proceedings of the International Conference on 'The Atlantis Hypothesis: Searching for a Lost Land' (ATLANTIS 2005)* (Santorini: Heliotropos, 2007), pp. 113–29; 'The Deucalion catastrophe 2: The Phaethon explosion and some of its effects outside Egypt', in Papamarinopoulos, op. cit. (2007), pp. 131–43; 'The Deucalion catastrophe 3: chronological and geographical questions', in Papamarinopoulos, op. cit. (2007), pp. 145–61; S. P. Papamarinopoulos, 'Phaethon or Phaethousa. A shining comet in the 12th century BC?', in Papamarinopoulos, op. cit. (2007), pp. 163–77; A. Galanopoulos and E. Bacon, *The Legend of Phaethon Under the Light of Science* (Santorini: Grafikes Technes Papoulias et al., 1971), pp. 396 ff (in Greek).

51 Caesar, *Gallic War* 5.12–13, trans. A. and P. Wiseman, in K. Chisholm and J. Ferguson, *Rome: The Augustan Age* (Oxford: Oxford University Press, 1981).

52 Strabo 2.3.6 is a particularly important passage. See p. 113.

53 That is, 4,300 or 4,400 *stadia*.

54 Strabo 4.5.1–2, trans. J. C. Mann and R. G. Penmann (eds), *LACT Literary Sources for Roman Britain* (London: LACT Publications, 1978).

55 Pomponius Mela 3.6.49, trans. Mann and Penmann, op. cit.

56 Tacitus, *Agricola* R11, trans. M. Hutton, *Tacitus: Agricola, Germania, Dialogus* (London: Heinemann; Cambridge, MA: Harvard University Press, 1970).

57 Tacitus, *Agricola*, trans. Hutton, op. cit.

58 Horace, *Odes* 1.35.29–30.

59 Horace, *Odes* 4.14.47–8.

CHAPTER 2

1 Plato, *Timaeus* 20e.

2 A *tyrannos* was not necessarily 'tyrannical': he simply overthrew the incumbent rulers. See S. P. Kershaw, *A Brief Guide to Classical Civilization* (London: Robinson, 2010), pp. 82 ff.

3 Aristotle, *Politics* 1274a15.

4 See, for example, N. Robertson, 'Solon's Axones and Kyrbeis, and the Sixth-Century Background (Figs 1–2)', *Historia: Zeitschrift Für Alte Geschichte*, vol. 35, no. 2 (1986), pp. 147–76.

5 Plutarch, *Solon* 25.4, cf. Aristotle, *Constitution of Athens* 11.

6 Aristotle, *Constitution of Athens* 11; Plutarch, *Solon* 26.

7 Plutarch, *Solon* 26.1.

8 Plato mentions the kinship of Critias, his maternal uncle, with Solon in the dialogue *Charmides* 155a.

9 Plato's *Critias*, where he gives his description of Atlantis, breaks off in mid-sentence. See p. 107.

10 Plutarch, *Solon* 31.3–32.2, trans. B. Perrin, *Plutarch's Lives with an English Translation* (Cambridge, MA: Harvard University Press; London: Heinemann, 1914); Solon, fragment 18 (Bergk); fragment 26 (Bergk).

11 Plutarch, *Solon* 27.1, trans. Perrin, op. cit.

12 Herodotus 1.29–33.

13 Plutarch, *Solon* 29.4.

14 'Solon's mother, according to Heracleides Ponticus, was a cousin of the mother of Peisistratus', Plutarch, *Solon* 1.2. Plutarch also hints that they might have been lovers.

15 See, for example, B. M. Lavelle, *Fame, Money and Power: The Rise of Peisistratos and 'Democratic' Tyranny at Athens* (Ann Arbor, MI: University of Michigan Press, 2005); Kershaw, op. cit. (2010), p. 86.
16 Plutarch, *Solon* 32.3.
17 Herodotus 1.64.3.
18 Aristotle, *Constitution of Athens* 16.2, trans. P. J. Rhodes, *Aristotle: The Athenian Constitution* (Harmondsworth: Penguin, 1984).
19 Ibid., 17.3.
20 See Kershaw, op. cit. (2010), p. 86 f.
21 See Herodotus 5.66–80; Aristotle, *Constitution of Athens* 20–2; Kershaw, op. cit. (2010), p. 87 f.
22 Thucydides 1.23.1. He is pretty sceptical about the size of the Greek expedition to Troy: it might have been far more noteworthy than any that came before it, but its facts and fame have been greatly exaggerated by the poets: 'Indeed, as to the events of the period just preceding [the Peloponnesian War] and those of a still earlier date, it was impossible to get clear information on account of lapse of time; but from evidence which, on pushing my inquiries to the furthest point, I find that I can trust, I think that they were not really great either as regards the wars then waged or in other particulars' (1.1.2–3, trans. C. F. Smith, *Thucydides: History of the Peloponnesian War, Volume I: Books 1–2.* (Cambridge, MA: Harvard University Press, 1919)).
23 Herodotus 2.154. Neither did he speak Persian, although again he refers to interpreters at the Persian court, where there were also Greek officials: 3.38, 3.140.
24 Herodotus 2.28.1. See F. A. J. Nielsen, *The Tragedy in History: Herodotus and the Deuteronomistic History* (Sheffield: Sheffield Academic Press, 1997), pp. 36 ff.
25 Herodotus 2.143; cf. Plato, *Timaeus* 21e ff.
26 Herodotus 2.58.1, trans. Godley, op. cit.
27 Thucydides 1.22.4, trans. Smith, op. cit (1919).
28 Lucian, *Herodotus* 1–2.
29 A. B. Lloyd, *Herodotus, Book II. Études préliminaires aux religions orientales dans l'Empire romain 43* (Leiden: Brill, 1993), p. 4.
30 Nielsen, op. cit, p. 42; cf. O. K. Armayor, 'Did Herodotus Ever Go to Egypt?', *JARCE* 15 (1978), pp. 59–73.
31 D. Fehling, *Herodotos and His 'Sources': Citation, Invention, and Narrative Art*, Arca Classical and Medieval Texts, Papers and Monographs 21, translated from the German by J. G. Howie (Liverpool: Cairns, 1989), pp. 4–6. See also E. Baragwanath and M. de Bakker, 'Herodotus', *Oxford Bibliographies Online Research Guide* (Oxford: Oxford University Press, 2010), p. 19.
32 See, for example, J. Romm, *Herodotus* (New Haven, CT: Yale University Press, 1998), p. 6.
33 See p. 371, n.100.
34 The Babylonian 'royal cubit' (which slightly longer than the Egyptian royal cubit) is actually calculated at from 53.2 (or 53.3) to 52.5 cm. 1 cubit = approx. 50 cm, so 25 m.
35 Herodotus 1.178, trans. Godley, op. cit.
36 Antipater of Sidon lived around 100 BC; Antipatros of Thessalonica was a contemporary of L. Calpurnius Piso Frugi, who lived between 48 BC and AD 32. The two are frequently confused.
37 *Greek Anthology* 9.58, trans. W. R. Paton, *The Greek Anthology* (London: Heinemann, 1915).

38 This works out as slightly less than ten times the volume of the Great Pyramid at Giza (conventionally calculated at 2,583,283 m³), and slightly less than twice the height of Nelson's Column (51.6 m).

39 Herodotus, 1.179.3–193.4, trans. G. Rawlinson, *The History of Herodotus, vol. 1* (New York: Appleton, 1885).

40 The legendary first king of the Medes. The Medes were subsequently conquered by Cyrus the Great of Persia in the sixth century BC. See, for example, J. Lendering, 'Medes', http://www.livius.org/articles/people/medes/ [accessed 28 December 2016].

41 Herodotus, 1.98.2–99.1, trans. Rawlinson, op. cit.

42 British Museum 35382. See http://www.britishmuseum.org/research/collection_online/collection_object_details.aspx?objectId=327273&partId=1 [accessed 28 December 2016]. For a translation see http://www.livius.org/cg-cm/chronicles/abc7/abc7_nabonidus1.html [accessed 28 December 2016].

43 Xenophon, *Anabasis* 3.5.15.

44 See Plato, *Critias* 115c ff.

45 See Kershaw, op. cit. (2010), pp. 89–92.

46 Plutarch, *Themistocles* 19. Plato's Atlanteans would share similar ambitions.

47 Herodotus 7.144.2.

48 See p. 321f.

49 See Herodotus 7.59–88.

50 Herodotus 7.186.2.

51 See Plato, *Critias* 119a–b, where the capital city alone can field 1.4 million fighters.

52 *Megalophrosynēs* in Greek.

53 Herodotus, 7.22–4, trans. Godley, op. cit.

54 See, http://www.world-archaeology.com/features/xerxes-canal.htm [accessed 21 December 2016].

55 Herodotus 7.34–5, trans. Godley, op. cit.

56 Aeschylus, *The Persians* 408 ff., trans. P. Vellacott, in *Aeschylus: Prometheus Bound, The Suppliants, Seven Against Thebes, The Persians* (Harmondsworth: Penguin, 1973).

57 It may be that no such agreement ever existed – scholarly debate revolves around the possibility of a notorious 'missing' entry for 449/448 BC on the inscription which records the money dedicated to Athena from 454/453 to 440/439 BC – but, if it did, it stipulated that the Aegean Sea was to belong to the Delian League, while Egypt and Cyprus were to belong to Persia, with the Asia Minor seaboard as a sort of 'demilitarised zone'.

58 Thucydides, 1.76, trans. R. Warner, *Thucydides: History of the Peloponnesian War* (Harmondsworth: Penguin, 1972).

59 Plato, *Phaedo* 98b.

60 Aristotle, *Politics* 1267b22–8a14.

61 See, for example, A. Burns, 'Hippodamus and the Planned City', *Historia: Zeitschrift Für Alte Geschichte*, vol. 25, no. 4 (1976), pp. 414–28; D. W. J. Gill, 'Hippodamus and the Piraeus', *Historia: Zeitschrift Für Alte Geschichte*, vol. 55, no. 1 (2006), pp. 1–15.

62 See Plato, *Critias* 115c ff.; 117e.

63 Thucydides, 1.23, trans. Warner, op. cit.

64 P. Vidal-Naquet, *The Atlantis Story: A Short History of Plato's Myth*, trans. J. Lloyd (Exeter: University of Exeter Press, 2007), p. 94.

65 Thucydides 2.70.1.

66 Thucydides 2.79.1–7.

67 Plato, *Symposium* 220d-e.

68 According to Thucydides 2.48.1.

69 Thucydides 2.47 ff.

70 See, for example, R. J. Littman, 'The plague of Athens: epidemiology and paleo-pathology', *Mount Sinai Journal of Medicine*, vol. 76, no. 5 (2009), pp. 456–67; G. D. Scarrow, 'The Athenian Plague. A possible diagnosis', *Ancient History Bulletin*, no. 11 (1988), pp. 4–8; A. D. Langmuir et al., 'The Thucydides Syndrome', *New England Journal of Medicine* (1985), pp. 1027–30.

71 Thucydides 2.36.1, trans. Smith, op. cit. (1919).

72 Ibid., 2.35 ff.

73 Ibid., 2.52.3 ff.

74 Plato, *Timaeus* 19b–c.

75 Thucydides 2.52.2, trans. Smith, op. cit. (1919).

CHAPTER 3

1 Diogenes Laertius, *Lives of Eminent Philosophers* 3.4, trans. R. D. Hicks, *Diogenes Laertius. Lives of Eminent Philosophers, Volume I: Books 1–5* (Cambridge, MA: Harvard University Press, 1925). The historian Neanthes of Cyzicus was honoured at Delphi in 287 BC. The decree still survives: *Fouilles de Delphes* 1.429 = *FGrHist* 84 T 2.

2 See N. P. Alican, *Rethinking Plato: A Cartesian Quest for the Real Plato* (Leiden: Brill, 2012), p. 13.

3 Diogenes Laertius' dates are also tricky to establish: he mentions Sextus Empiricus, so they must be after c.AD 200, and Stephanus of Byzantium and Sopater of Apamea (c. AD 500) quote him. He is usually assumed to have flourished in the first half of the third century, around the time of the Roman Emperor Alexander Severus (AD 222–35).

4 He was the librarian at Alexandria in the first century BC.

5 Diogenes Laertius, *Lives of Eminent Philosophers* 3.2.

6 Plato was present at Socrates' trial (Plato, *Apology* 34a; 38b) but absent at his execution (Plato, *Phaedo* 59b).

7 Diogenes Laertius, *Lives of Eminent Philosophers* 3.6.

8 Hermippus of Smyrna, a third-century BC Greek grammarian who lived in Alexandria.

9 Diogenes Laertius, *Lives of Eminent Philosophers* 3.2. R. D. Hicks' translation, 'in his eighty-first year', is misleading.

10 A second-century AD philosopher noted for his eloquence, learning and sexual ambiguity.

11 Theopompus of Chios, 378 or 377–c.320 BC, was a Greek historian whose lost but much quoted *Philippica* dealt with the reign of Philip II of Macedon. For his relevance to the Atlantis story see p. 108.

12 Diogenes Laertius, *Lives of Eminent Philosophers* 3.40, trans. Hicks, op. cit.

13 Olympiodorus, *Anonymous Prolegomena* 6.1–7.

14 Diogenes Laertius, *Lives of Eminent Philosophers* 3.3, trans. Hicks, op. cit.

15 Eusebius' *Chronicle* puts Plato's birth year in the fourth year of the 88th Olympiad, when Stratocles was archon; the *Alexandrian Chronicle* mentions the 89th Olympiad, in the archonship of Isarchus; according to the *Suda*, Plato was born in the 88th Olympiad and lived eighty-two years.

16 See, for example, D. Nails, 'Ariston/Perictione', op. cit., (2002); D. Nails, 'The Life of Plato of Athens', in H. Benson (ed.), *A Companion to Plato* (Oxford: Blackwell, 2006). Nails favours dates of 424/423 to 348/347 BC.

17 Diogenes Laertius, *Lives of Eminent Philosophers* 3.3, trans. Hicks, op. cit. Aegina is regarded as Plato's place of birth by the *Suda*.

18 John Burnet gives Glaucon as Plato's grandfather: see J. Burnet, *Greek Philosophy* (1914), p. 351; cf. *Charmides* 154b. Diogenes Laertius, *Lives of Eminent Philosophers* 3.4 gives Aristocles as Plato's grandfather – see passage quoted above. The family tree at Fig. 2 is the nearest we can get to an accurate picture based on current evidence – see Nails, 'Plato', op. cit. (2002).

19 Thrasylus of Mendes, aka Thrasyllus of Alexandria (d. AD 36), was a grammarian and astrologer who edited Plato's writings.

20 Diogenes Laertius, *Lives of Eminent Philosophers* 3.1, trans. Hicks, op. cit.

21 Diogenes Laertius, *Lives of Eminent Philosophers* 3.1–2. Needless to say, there is a number of variants on this genealogy.

22 See W. K. C. Guthrie, *A History of Greek Philosophy, Volume 4: Plato: The Man and His Dialogues: Earlier Period* (Cambridge: Cambridge University Press, 1975), p. 10 n. 4.

23 Diogenes Laertius, *Lives of Eminent Philosophers* 3.4.

24 In Plato's *Charmides* we are told that Pyrilampes was Charmides' uncle, and Charmides was Plato's mother's brother. His mother's remarriage to her nearest male relative was normal Athenian practice in Plato's day.

25 See Plato, *Parmenides* 126a–b.

26 Xenophon, *Hellenica* 2.3–4.

27 Thucydides 3.89, trans. C. F. Smith, in *Thucydides. History of the Peloponnesian War, Volume II: Books 3–4* (Cambridge, MA: Harvard University Press, 1920).

28 Strabo 1.3.20; Diodorus 12.58.

29 See, for example, J. Antonopoulos, 'The tsunami of 426 BC in the Maliakos Gulf, Eastern Greece', *Natural Hazards*, no. 5 (1992), pp. 83–93; E. Guidoboni, A. Comastri and G. Traina, *Catalogue of Ancient Earthquakes in the Mediterranean Area up to the 10th century* (Bologna: SGA Storia Geofisica Ambiente, 1994); G. A. Papadopoulos, 'Tsunamis in the East Mediterranean: A catalogue for the area of Greece and adjacent seas', *Proc. IOC-IUGG Internatl. Workshop Tsunami Risk Assessment Beyond 2000: Theory, Practice and Plans, June 14–16, Moscow, 2000* (2001), pp. 34–43; I. Papaioannou, G. A. Papadopoulos and S. Pavlides, 'The earthquake of 426 BC, in N. Evoikos, *Gulf Revisited: Amalgamation of Two Different Strong Earthquake Events?'*, *Bulletin of the Geological Society of Greece*, no. 36 (2004), www.geo.auth.gr/ege2004/articles/SE15_172.pdf [accessed 30 December 2016].

30 Plato, *Laches* 181b; *Symposium* 221a.

31 Explored in Plato's *Phaedrus* (418–416 BC) and *Symposium* (416 BC).

32 Thucydides 5.101, trans. Warner, op. cit.

33 Xenophon, *Hellenica* 1.7.16–33.

34 However, there are good arguments in favour of his grandfather, Critias the Elder, having this honour. See Nails, op. cit (2002), s.v. 'Critias III' and 'Critias IV'.

35 Plato, *Phaedo* 118a.

36 Diogenes Laertius, *Lives of Eminent Philosophers* 3.6.

37 Ibid., trans. Hicks, op. cit.

38 Cicero, *De Re Publica* 1.10.16, *De Finibus* 5.29.87. Cyrene is only mentioned by Apuleius, Diogenes Laertius and Olympiodorus.

39 *Index Academicorum* (P. Herc. 1021 and 164), ed. S. Mekler, p. 6, col. 10. See also
T. Dorandi, *Filodemo. Storia dei filosofi. Platone e l'Academia* (P. Herc. 1021 and
164) (Naples: Bibliopolis, 1991); W. Burkert, *Platon in Nahaufnahme: Ein Buch aus
Herculaneum* (Stuttgart and Leipzig: Teubner, 1993).

40 Plutarch, *Solon* 2.3.

41 See, for example, *Phaedrus* 274c–5b; *Philebus* 19b. See also J. Kerschensteiner,
Platon und der Orient (Stuttgart: Kohlhammer, 1945), pp. 46 ff.

42 There is a fictional letter (Epistle 28 in the Letters of the Socratic School in R.
Hercher (ed.), *Epistolographi Graeci* [Paris: Didot, 1871]) supposedly written by
Phaedrus to Plato, who is staying in Saïs pondering 'about Everything' (*peri tou
sympantos*), wanting information about the pyramids and weird Egyptian animals,
but this proves nothing.

43 Strabo 17.1.29. He was apparently shown the *diatribai* ('hang-outs') of Plato and
his pupil Eudoxus of Cnidus.

44 Plato, *Seventh Letter*, 324a.

45 See Cicero, *De Finibus* 5.29.87, *De Re Publica* 1.10.16, *Tusculan Disputations*
1.17.39.

46 This translates the Greek *bios eudaimōn* in Plato's *Seventh Letter*, 326b.

47 Diodorus 15.7; Plutarch, *Dion* 5; Diogenes Laertius, *Lives of Eminent Philosophers*
3.19–21.

48 See Diogenes Laertius, *Lives of Eminent Philosophers* 3.7.

49 Plato, *Seventh Letter*, 326a.

50 See Isocrates, *Panegyric* 115–22.

51 See, for example, J. Cargill, *The Second Athenian League: Empire or Free Alliance?*
(Berkeley, CA: University of California Press, 1981).

52 IG II243, trans. G. W. Botsford, *A Source Book of Ancient History* (London:
Macmillan, 1934).

53 Homer, *Iliad* 20.403.

54 That is, in 373 BC.

55 Strabo 8.7.2; cf. 1.3.18; and see also http://www.helikeproject.gr/, http://
www.helike.org/, http://www.bbc.co.uk/science/horizon/2001/helike.shtml,
http://www.ancient-origins.net/ancient-places-europe/uncovering-lost-city-
helike-002510, http://www.oceanus.upatras.gr/?q=node/134 [accessed 30
December 2016].

56 Plato, *Seventh Letter* 328b-c.

57 Plato, *Seventh Letter* 329c; *Third Letter* 316c–d.

58 Plato, *Seventh Letter* 329c–30b.

59 Plato, *Seventh Letter* 338a; Plutarch, *Dion* 17.

60 Plato, *Third Letter* 316e–17a; *Seventh Letter* 338a–b.

61 Plato, *Third Letter* 317a–b; *Seventh Letter* 338b–c.

62 Plato, *Third Letter* 317a; *Seventh Letter* 338c.

63 Plato, *Seventh Letter* 339a–b.

64 Ibid., 350a–b.

65 Diogenes Laertius, *Lives of Eminent Philosophers* 3.30, trans. Hicks, op. cit. = *Anth.
Pal.* 7.99.

66 Diogenes Laertius, *Lives of Eminent Philosophers* 3.41.

CHAPTER 4

1 T. K. Johansen, *Plato's Natural Philosophy: A Study of the Timaeus-Critias* (Cambridge: Cambridge University Press, 2004), p. 1.

2 Plato, *Timaeus* 90d, trans. W. R. M. Lamb, *Plato in Twelve Volumes, Vol. 9* (Cambridge, MA: Harvard University Press; London: Heinemann, 1925).

3 *Timaeus* 29b–d. For a good discussion of the distinction between *eikōs logos* and *eikōs muthos* see Johansen, op. cit., pp. 62–4.

4 *Timaeus* 29c7–8.

5 *Timaeus* 29c3.

6 *Timaeus* 29b6.

7 *Timaeus* cf. 68b6–8.

8 *Timaeus* cf. 54b1–2, 55d4–6.

9 *Timaeus* 29d1.

10 *Timaeus* 53d4–7, trans. Lamb, op. cit. See discussion by Johansen, op. cit., pp. 55–6.

11 http://www.enotes.com/topics/timaeus, [accessed 10 November 2016].

12 See Nails, op. cit. (2002), p. 107.

13 Plato, *Critias* 120d ff.

14 Athena: *Timaeus* 21a, 26e; Bendis: *Republic* 327a, 354a.

15 T. Wyatt, 'Constraints on the search for Atlantis', in Papamarinopoulos, op. cit. (2007), p.65.

16 In most of the Socratic dialogues, Socrates is either the main or a central figure. But in the *Timaeus* he plays quite a minor role. The *Timaeus* is less of a dialogue – although there is a degree of conversation – than a virtuoso performance of ideas about the Universe by Timaeus.

17 We don't know who the fourth guest might have been (suggestions include Plato himself, or Pericles) or why Plato included a missing person in the group. Proclus, *In Timaeum* 14.4–26.20 discusses the numbers and their possible significance: 'One should also bear in mind that the dialogue is Pythagorean, and one should make one's interpretative comments in a manner appropriate to them' (*In Timaeum* 15.24). But the question of the relationship between Plato and Pythagoreanism is a vexed one. Like Socrates, Pythagoras (*c.*570 to *c.*490 BC) wrote nothing, but unlike with Socrates there are no detailed contemporary accounts of his thought (see, for example, C. Huffman, 'Pythagoras', in Edward N. Zalta (ed.), *The Stanford Encyclopedia of Philosophy* (Summer 2014 edition), https://plato.stanford.edu/archives/sum2014/entries/pythagoras/ [accessed 17 December 2016]). However, there have been numerous ingenious attempts to link the Atlantis material to Pythagorean ideas. In *The Pythagorean Plato* (Stony Brook, NY: Nicolas Hays, 1987, p. 77), E. McClain suggests that the *Republic, Timaeus, Critias, Statesman* and *Laws* embodied a systematic treatise on harmonics, and that the Atlantis story is 'a sophisticated entertainment for Pythagoreans only [. . .] For the musically innocent, it is and must remain a purely Platonic fairy tale, incomprehensively loaded with absolutely meaningless numerical detail.'

Others, such as John Bremer ('Some Arithmetical Patterns in Plato's *Republic*', *Hermathena*, no. 169 [2000], pp. 69–97), have sought meaning in numbers by counting lines and/or syllables and exploring the proportions contained in them, or indeed in the time taken to read them (although it is unclear just how accurate any estimate of ancient Greek reading speeds might be). In his article 'Plato, Pythagoras, and Stichometry' (*Stichting Pythagoras: Pythagoras Foundation Newsletter*, no. 15 [December 2010], http://instituteofphi-losophy.org/plato/plato-pythagoras-and-stichometry-2/ [accessed 17 December 16]) John Bremer recounts how Bremer (he talks about himself in the third person) 'laboriously counted the syllables in the *Republic*', asserts that the *Republic* takes twelve hours to recount (twelve becomes a very significant number in this type of analysis, rather than the Pythagorean ten), and that it was 'possible to identify accurately patterns and symmetries in the *Republic*, all based on the arith-metical counting of syllables'. These 'revealed patterns were [. . .] an essential, perhaps the essential, part of the dialogue', and could also be applied to the *Timaeus* and *Critias*. The upshot of all this was that 'the number of syllables [counting from 'the total number of years that has gone by since the war that took place between the people living outside the Pillars of Heracles and all those within them, was 9,000' (*Critias* 118e)] to the end of the *Critias* is 9000' (quoted in M. Adams, *Meet Me in Atlantis: My Obsessive Quest to Find the Sunken City* [New York: Dutton, 2015], p. 273). He is aware that the transmission of the manuscripts of Plato is a long and precarious process, involving the hand-copying, correcting and annotating of the text throughout quite an extensive 'family tree' of manu-scripts that goes back hundreds of years (see G. Jonkers, *The Textual Tradition of Plato's Timaeus and Critias* [Leiden and Boston: Brill, 2017]): any editor or transla-tor is constantly faced with difficult choices about what the Greek text should be (e.g., *karta* or *kata* at *Timaeus* 25d, or the choice between *epinoōn* ('intending' in our translation), *noōn* or *epinoun* at *Critias* 113a, which have four, two and three syllables respectively). But Bremer is undeterred, and although he also shies away from the issue of whether or not the *Critias* is unfinished, he says, 'I don't feel very upset if it turns out that there are 9017 syllables. With all of my numbers, if it's within 1 percent, it's probably intentional' (Adams, op. cit., p. 273). But precision is everything here: if the mathematics work exactly, the method works perfectly; if they don't, it conspicuously fails the test.

Bremmer, however, takes exception to the 'pure hype – or rather impure hype' – that a 'science historian' (J. B. Kennedy) has 'cracked "The Plato Code" [in his article 'Plato's forms, Pythagorean mathematics, and stichometry', *Apeiron*, vol. 43, no. 1 (2010), pp. 1–32, and developed further in *The Musical Structure of Plato's Dialogues* (Durham: Acumen, 2011)] – the long disputed secret messages hidden in the great philosopher's writing'. There is, Bremmer argues, 'no "hidden code" except in the sense that anyone who reads anything needs to know how to read'. Kennedy's thesis, based on 'stichometry' (counting the lines in the text), is essentially that 'the stichometric structure of the dialogues is a musical scale' (op. cit. [2010], p. 16). This scale, he argues, contains a harmonic sequence of twelve notes, and if you divide the dialogues into equal 'musical' sections, you will find symbolically significant allegorical passage at the end of each section. So the musical structure unlocks the hidden meaning of the dialogues. But acceptance of the theory depends on it being granted a good measure of leeway: Kennedy observes that his overall line counts come out to round multiples of 12, but only 'with about one to two percent accuracy' (op. cit. [2010], p. 9 f.). As with Bremer's syllables, a 1 to 2 per cent margin of error simply allows for too much subjectivity, and for the significant notes to be located at the theorist's whim, which invali-dates the method. In essence, Plato's *Timaeus–Critias* is not a 'code' to be 'deci-phered'. See J. Z. McKay and A. Rehding, 'The structure of Plato's dialogues and Greek music theory: A response to J. B. Kennedy', *Apeiron*, vol. 44, no. 4 (2011), pp. 359–75. For a less academic discussion of Pythagorean ideas in relation to Atlantis, see Adams, op. cit., pp. 170–80, 259–74.

18 The description of the previous day's intellectual conversation as a 'feast' means that it is an appropriate activity for a festival.

19 The word translated as 'constitution' here is *politeia*: it has a range of meanings which also encompass 'state' and 'politics' (also used in this translation). There is a discussion on the topic of the constitution in Plato's *Republic*, some of whose political ideas, especially from books 2–5, are briefly recapitulated in the *Timaeus*. Some commentators imagine the conversation of the *Republic*, which involves Socrates, Thrasymachus, Glaucon and Adeimantus, as taking place two days ago, with Socrates relating the details of it to Timaeus, Critias, Hermocrates and the unnamed fourth person 'yesterday'. So they date the dramatic setting of *Timaeus* two days after that of the *Republic*. In reality, several years separate the two works, and Plato's thought has moved on in some important respects.

20 See *Republic* 369e ff., 374e ff.

21 Cf. *Republic* 375b ff.

22 Cf. *Republic* 376d ff.

23 Cf. *Republic* 416d ff.

24 Cf. *Republic* 451c ff.

25 The Greek word *sunarmosteon* ('must be harmonised') refers to the correct blend of spirited and philosophic elements, which exist in women as in men (*Republic* 456a). Essentially Plato thinks that women who are of the same character as the male Guardians should be educated alongside them, and that the female Guardians should have their natures adapted/harmonised so that they start to resemble the male Guardians. Plato often thinks of education as a kind of 'harmonisation' of a person's character (e.g. *Republic* 412a, 443d–e).

26 Cf. *Republic* 457 ff., 461d.

27 Cf. *Republic* 458 ff., where the breeding of the Guardians is organised on eugenic principles. The best Guardians mate with one another at special festivals in order to produce the best children, and the relationships are made to seem random by the use of (rigged) lotteries to assign sexual partners to one another.

28 Cf. *Republic* 415b–c., 423c, 459d ff.

29 Socrates is referring to the instructions he supposedly gave on the day before. In the *Republic* (472d ff., 592a–b) he compared the Ideal State to an artist's pattern, which people can use as a standard; here, he is more interested in *action:* he wants to see the painting move, and he wants to explore the practical ramifications of his theories. So he invites the other three to draw a picture of his Ideal State *in actual existence.* This makes it clear that the Atlantis story is only 'real history' in a 'special Platonic sense: it is a story which is fabricated about the past in order to reflect a general truth about how ideal citizens would fare in war. The story thereby provides a practical example of how virtue, understood along the lines of the *Republic*, would prevail in this world even in the most adverse of conditions.' (Johansen, op. cit., p. 24). Socrates wants to see the successful 'learning outcomes' of his education system brought to fruition, with the citizens putting their rearing and education into practice, and in this context the question of the historicity or fictionality of the account becomes irrelevant: it makes no difference from Socrates' point of view whether Critias' account is fiction rather than history, provided that it shows the citizens in motion in a way that accords with their education in the *Republic*. The relationship between history and fiction in the *Republic* is a complex one, but there Socrates makes a point that is crucial

for any interpretation of the Atlantis tale, namely that stories about the ancient past should be taken as *useful inventions*:

> Also in the fables (*en mythologiais*) of which we were just now speaking, owing to our ignorance of the truth about antiquity, we liken the false [or 'falsehood' – *pseudos* in Greek] to the true as far as we may and so make it edifying (*Republic* 382d1–3, trans. P. Shorey, *Plato: Plato in Twelve Volumes, Vols 5 & 6* [Cambridge, MA: Harvard University Press/London: Heinemann, 1969]).

Essentially Socrates thinks there are good and bad 'lies' or stories (*pseudē*), and although we try to make tales about the past as close to the truth as possible, we still construct them without any historical knowledge. This in turn means that the truth to which we equate the tales cannot be historical: it is another type of truth, and the purpose of telling tales about what the gods did in the past is to illustrate this truth (i.e. how the gods would behave, given that they are good, *Republic* 379b). Crucially it is not to report any historical knowledge about particular divine acts – we have no knowledge of that whatsoever.

30 Socrates wants an encomium/eulogy of the city (*tēn polin egkōmiasthai*, 19d2). This affects how we should read the story. Pseudo-Aristotle's *Rhetorica ad Alexandrum* 35 says that the demonstration and magnification of great deeds are an essential part of an encomium, which would normally conclude with a catalogue of notable deeds. So, by praising the great deeds of its citizens, the *Timaeus*, *Critias* and *Hermocrates* would be concluding the encomium of the Ideal State that Socrates started in the *Republic*. Indeed, when Critias comes to tell his story, his 'history' is specifically constructed for this occasion: his ideal citizens will be identified specifically with Athenians (not, say, Spartans, Cretans, Thebans or anyone else), and his speech will become an encomium of Athens, an idealised version of history filtered through the lens of Athenian ideology (see N. Loreaux, *The Invention of Athens: The Funeral Oration in the Classical City*, trans. Alans Sheridan [Cambridge, MA: Harvard University Press, 1986], pp. 296–304), but one designed to 'appropriate the Athenians' forebears in the service of a new set of philosophical ideals' (Johansen, op. cit., pp. 38–9).

31 Despite the fact that the *Timaeus* and *Critias* will be full of imagination and politics, Socrates doesn't seem to think of himself as an imaginative writer or as a politician in the conventional sense. He had never been a man of action or taken part in politics and his self-proclaimed ignorance is legendary. It is typical of him to suggest that this task is beyond him.

32 For poetry as an 'imitative' art, see *Republic* 392d, 579e ff.

33 'Works of art' might also be translated 'deeds' (the Greek word *ergois* could mean either here), but nevertheless the remark seems to reflect Plato's interest in using the story as an exercise in imaginative narrative (See C. Gill, *Plato: The Atlantis Story* (Bristol: Bristol Classical Press, 1980), p. 37.

34 Around the middle of the fifth century BC, educational practice at Athens was shaken to the core by the arrival of people known as Sophists. The Greek word *sophistēs* originally meant simply 'wise man', but gradually it acquired the sense from which we get our words 'sophistical' and 'sophistry'. Our evidence about the Sophists comes primarily from hostile sources, who regarded them as verbal tricksters who charged outrageous fees for turning their pupils into immoral know-it-alls, but their teaching really developed in response both to the practical

demands of democratic life and to a new atmosphere of inquiry and scepticism in Greece. Many Sophists had their own special subjects, like mathematics and astronomy, but they were primarily tutors of rhetoric. However, some of them also claimed to be able to teach *aretē* (often translated 'virtue', but also covering 'goodness', 'excellence' and 'social effectiveness'), as Protagoras did when Socrates quizzed him about his curriculum:

> 'Do I follow you?' said I. 'I take you to be describing the art of politics, and promising to make men good citizens.' 'That,' said he, 'is exactly what I profess to do.' (Plato, *Protagoras* 319a, trans. W. K. C. Guthrie, *Plato: Protagoras and Meno* (Harmondsworth: Penguin, 1956).

However, Xenophon (*On Hunting* 13.1) felt that while they professed to direct the young towards virtue, they actually did the exact opposite, and Socrates told Protagoras, 'I do not believe that *aretē* can be taught' (Plato, *Protagoras* 320c). What worried Socrates most was the thought of the Sophists' students exploiting their new-found skills regardless of what was right and good. See, for example, Kershaw, op. cit. (2010), p. 129f.; J. V. Muir, 'Religion and the new education: the challenge of the Sophists', in P. E. Easterling and J. V. Muir (eds), *Greek Religion and Society* (Cambridge: Cambridge University Press, 1985), pp. 191–218.

35 We don't know who Timaeus is: the likelihood is that he is fictional. The other two probably are real people. Hermocrates was a Syracusan general who was instrumental in defeating the Athenian Sicilian expedition in 415–413 BC (see p. 58), although he was subsequently exiled by the radical democracy at Syracuse, and died in 408 BC while attempting to seize Syracuse with the aid of supporters inside the city, who included Dionysius I. Critias III the Younger was a poet and an intellectual – ironically sometimes regarded as one of the Sophists – who belonged to the same family as Plato, but he also led the Thirty Tyrants installed by the Spartans to replace the democracy after they defeated Athens in the Peloponnesian War in 404 BC. If he is the speaker (and not Critias II the Elder), it seems as if both men are chosen to fit Plato's own anti-democratic views on Athenian history.

36 The constitution of Epizephyrian Locris in the south of Italy was attributed to Zaleucus in the mid-seventh century BC (Aristotle, *Politics* 1274a22). In Plato's *Laws* (638b), the Athenian says that the Locrians supposedly have the best laws of any state in the West, so if Timaeus *is* a made-up character, this would explain why Plato chose to make him come from Locris.

37 This is the only time that Hermocrates speaks in the *Timaeus*. His tone of voice is very assertive.

38 The Greek word *logos* = 'account/story'. Plato is here using it in the accusative case, which changes its ending to *logon*. For the nuances of the word *logos* see Chapters 4, 6 and 15.

39 This time Plato uses *logos* in the genitive case, so its morphology changes to *logou*.

40 Much has been made of this statement. However, when Socrates follows up by asking Critias whether he tells his tale as being simply a story or as something that had been genuinely performed by this city (21a), Critias is evasive: he just says that he'll narrate an old story that he heard from an old man. In fact, Critias makes twenty-two assertions that the Atlantis story is true (fifteen in *Timaeus*; seven in *Critias*). See A. N. Kontaratos, 'Atlantis: Fact or fiction?' in

Paramarinopoulos, op. cit. (2007), pp. 79–81. The gentleman doth protest too much, methinks.

The reason he pretends it is true is that if you present made-up stories as history, people will be more likely to believe them, and people are more likely to believe a story about the past than they are about the present. This is, of course, very much the case with Atlantis, and the reason Plato does this is because there are good lies and bad lies:

> 'How, then,' said [Socrates], 'might we contrive one of those opportune false-hoods [*pseudōn*] of which we were just now speaking, so as by one noble lie to persuade if possible the rulers themselves, but failing that the rest of the city?' 'What kind of lie do you mean?' said [Glaucon]. 'Nothing unprecedented,' said [Socrates], 'but a sort of Phoenician tale, something that has happened before now in many parts of the world, as the poets aver and have induced men to believe, but that has not happened and perhaps would not be likely to happen in our day and demanding no little persuasion to make it believable.' (*Republic* 414b8–c7, trans. Shorey, op. cit. [with alterations – 'lie' for 'fiction']).

So a 'noble lie' – literally false, but conveying deep and permanent truths about humanity – is not necessarily a bad thing.

41 If the speaker is Critias II the Elder (more likely), 'my grandfather' is Critias I; if the speaker is Critias III the Younger, 'my grandfather' is Critias II the Elder. See Figs 2 and 3. The reasons Plato chooses Solon as the 'source' for the story are to give it the kind of credibility conferred by a famous Athenian statesman noted for his political knowledge and wisdom, and one who wrote poetry on moral and political themes (see p. 27). If Critias III the Younger is the speaker, he has omitted two generations of his own family tree and identified himself with his own grandfather Critias II the Elder. This could be a mistake – Plato's story is riddled with problematical inconsistencies (see n. 67) – or it may be deliberate: he knew his own family perfectly well, but just wanted Critias to be closer to Solon, and therefore to the source of the 'ancient story'. Certainly, the various details are all designed to make it *seem* like the story was handed down from the distant past, and to link Critias directly to that past. See J. K. Davies, *Athenian Propertied Families 600–300 BC* (Oxford: Clarendon Press, 1971), pp. 325–6.

42 The idea that the story was transmitted orally will be directly contradicted in *Critias* 113b, where it is said to have been written down.

43 Plato's work frequently contains the idea of the periodic destruction of mankind. See, for example, *Statesman* 270c–d, *Laws* 677a ff., *Timaeus* 21d, 22c, 25d, *Critias* 109d, 111a ff.

44 This would be entirely normal practice: the Panathenaia festival held in Athens in honour of Athena would feature speeches in honour of Athens' great achievements, like winning the Battle of Marathon, and also hymns to Athena.

45 This is problematical if Critias III the Younger is the speaker: his ninety-year-old grandfather Critias II the Elder was born in c.530 BC and Solon died in c.558 BC, so they couldn't have met personally: see A. Giovannini, 'Peut-on démythier l'Atlantide?', *Museum Helveticum*, vol. 42 (1985), p. 152.

46 The Apatouria Festival was celebrated in honour of Dionysus. On its third day, called the 'Children's Day' (*Kouteōtis* in Greek), young children were enrolled in their 'brotherhoods' (*phratriai*). It is possible that Plato name checks this festival

because *Apatouria* has resonances of deception (*apatē* in Greek). Certainly, by having his tale told by a very old man to gullible ten-year olds, Plato puts a heavy question mark over how believable it is.

47 Note that in fact they were nothing of the sort if Critias III the Younger is the speaker: Solon's poems were written in the early sixth century BC, so they were hardly a 'novelty' in the lifetime of this Critias' grandfather (born *c.*530 BC), and they were positively archaic in Critias' day (born *c.* 460 BC): see Davies, op. cit., pp. 325–6.

48 This is a fair comment: Solon was a wealthy man who did not have to pander to a patron, and his poetry expressed his political views very forcibly.

49 Homer, composer of the *Iliad* and *Odyssey*, was the universally acknowledged number-one poet of the Greek world; Hesiod wrote important and respected works on, among other things, the origins of the Greek gods. In *Republic* 599a, Plato says that anyone who knew how to make both an original and a copy would focus much more on the original: or 'those who can, do, those who can't, write poetry' (Johansen, op. cit., p. 34). So, the fact that Solon didn't write his poem implies that he must have had useful knowledge, and the demand for that knowledge prevented him writing poetry. For his contemporaries, Solon was far too important to be allowed to write poetry, no matter how sensational the theme: addressing the 'class struggles and other evils' was much more pressing. See p. 27f.

50 The Greek implies that Solon *hears* it 'as true' and *tells* it 'as true'.

51 Amasis II aka Ahmose II was a 26th-Dynasty king who reigned at Saïs, then the royal capital, from 570 to 526 BC. He was well disposed to Greeks: see Herodotus 2.162 ff., where he is depicted as a shrewd and opportunistic pharaoh who both promoted and strictly regulated Greek trade with Egypt. He was on good terms with Polycrates, the Greek tyrant of Samos, and also made donations toward rebuilding the temple at Delphi. Just six months after his death, Egypt was invaded by Cambyses II, the Achaemenid King of Persia. Egypt was under Persian control during Plato's lifetime, and remained so until it was 'liberated' by Alexander the Great in 332 BC.

52 The divine founding of cities is a significant motif in Plato's narrative: see *Timaeus* 23d–e, 24c–d, *Critias* 109, 111a6 ff. Traditionally Athens was founded by Cecrops, a son of the earth with a human body with a serpent's tail, who settled the dispute between Athena and Poseidon over the possession of Athens in Athena's favour. See Kershaw, op. cit. (2007), pp. 258 ff. Some Greek sources (Diodorus 1.29; Schol. ad Arist. Plut. 773) say that Cecrops immigrated into Greece with a group of colonists from Saïs, and Herodotus identified Athena with the Egyptian goddess Neïth, who is the patron of the temple at Saïs where the Atlantis story is said to have come from. It is also sometimes suggested that the Athena versus Poseidon conflict is comparable to that between Neïth and Seth in Egyptian mythology. M. Bernal, *Black Athena: The Afroasiatic Roots of Classical Civilization. Vol. II: The Archaeological and Documentary Evidence* (New York: Rutgers University Press, 1991), makes a highly contentious claim for the Egyptian Neïth as sounding At(h)anait, and links it to the Greek Athēnē/Athānā, and possibly the Linear B *A-ta-na*. Prior to the decipherment of Linear B, Sir Arthur Evans made a similar connection, asserting that 'the Minoan 8-shaped shield is itself the outcome of that which formed part of the emblem of the Egypto-Libyan Delta goddess Neith. A Minoan goddess holding this shield seen at Mycenae seems to have been the pre-historic forerunner of Athena' (*Nature*, vol. CXII [1923], p.

660). Neïth is known as a creator of canals, which will feature prominently in Critias' account of Atlantis, and it has been suggested that the Atlantean canals could be echoes of the goddess Neïth. See Wyatt, op. cit., p. 66. Cf. Herodotus 2.28, who mentions a 'recorder of the sacred treasures of Athena in the Egyptian city of Saïs'. Plutarch, however identified Neïth with Isis.

53 Herodotus 1.30 mentions Solon's visit to Amasis, and the activities that Solon supposedly undertakes in Plato's account (studying the past using Egyptian records that predate the Greek traditions quite considerably) look very much like what Herodotus was doing (2.44 ff., 2.53 ff., 2.100, etc.). As C. Gill, op. cit., pp. xvii, xx–xxi and 40, n. 21e7, observes, this is part of Plato's pastiche of history.

54 Like the Old Testament, the Babylonian *Epic of Gilgamesh*, the Mesopotamian *Epic of Atrahasis*, and the mythology of cultures as far afield as North America, Greek mythology has a myth of a Great Flood. See Appendix, p. 334.

55 Plato again stresses that the type of story being related here is that which a very old man tells to kids. It is also clear why he makes Solon learn his ancient history from the Egyptians: Herodotus says that the Egyptians have existed since the human race came into being (2.15.3), and that those Egyptians who live in the cultivated part of the country are the most learned people of all when it comes to preserving the memory/history of the past, and that none of the people that he questioned was so skilled in history (2.77.1). Critias will claim that the Athenians are the oldest nation on earth, but he will also assert that unlike the Athenians, whose literate population was entirely eradicated at the same time as Atlantis, the Egyptians are the only ones whose *culture* has been unbroken from the beginning, making them technically the oldest literate nation in the world (*Timaeus* 22e–3b). Athens has greater antiquity and cultural achievements; Egypt has longer uninterrupted civilisation.

56 A great deal of pseudoscientific commentary on Atlantis, particularly on the internet, makes great play of the sophistication and antiquity of Egypt. But Plato is not so pro-Egyptian. In the *Laws*, the Athenian Stranger undoubtedly admires the fact that the Egyptians have rules that forbid artistic and musical innovations (656d–7a), but he is also keen to stress that you would 'still find other things that are bad in Egypt' (657a). In fact, he specifically says that various educational subjects such as economics, politics, the crafts and especially arithmetic are a good thing,

> provided that you can remove illiberality [*aneleutheria*] and love of money [*philokhrēmatia*] [. . .] from the souls of those who are to acquire them adequately and to profit by them; otherwise you will find that you have unwittingly produced the so-called 'knavery' [*panourgia*] instead of wisdom [*sophia*]. Examples of this we can see today in the effect produced on the Egyptians and Phoenicians and many other nations by the illiberal character of their possessions and their other institutions. (*Laws* 747b–c, trans. R. G. Bury, *Plato: Plato in Twelve Volumes, Vols 10 & 11* (Cambridge, MA: Harvard University Press/London: Heinemann, 1967 and 1968, with adjustments).

He then suggests that one reason for this negative outcome of the Egyptians' education is the effect of their environment on their character (747d–e), thereby directly contradicting the inference made at *Timaeus* 22d–e that Egypt's

NOTES

environment is the reason why we *should* trust their historical information. In the *Republic* 436a we are also told about 'the love of money which [. . .] is not least likely to be found in Phoenicians and the population of Egypt'. The Greeks regarded the Egyptians as traders, and therefore greedy and duplicitous, on the model of the 'cunning traders from Phoenicia' (Homer, *Odyssey* 15.15) and the Phoenician whom Odysseus describes as 'well versed in guile, a greedy knave, who had already wrought much evil among men' (Homer, *Odyssey* 14.288–9). Stereotypical cheating, lying Egyptians can be found in Aeschylus, *fragment* 373, where they 'devise contrivances', Aristophanes, *Thesmophoriazousae* 921–2, where the third woman says of Euripides 'You seem to me to be a cunning rascal too; you are in collusion with this man, and it wasn't for nothing that you kept babbling about Egypt' (*ēigyptiazet*', on which the ancient commentator says, 'the Egyptians are rascally knaves'), and Cratinus, fragment 378 (Kock) which explains the verb *aigyptiazein* as 'to act in a rascally manner and deal perversely'. Essentially, to 'be/speak like an Egyptian' is to be sly and crafty. Plato acknowledges that the Egyptian education system is praiseworthy, but he feels that its learning outcomes are to make the Egyptians deviously clever rather than virtuously wise: they love money more than the truth, which means that we should expect a story related by an Egyptian to be full of deceit. By providing us with an Egyptian source for the Atlantis story, Plato places an enormous question mark over the veracity of the tale.

57 See pp. 118 and 144. Cf. Kershaw, op. cit. (2007), pp. 263 ff.
58 Plato uses the distinction between myth (*mythou* in the Greek) and truth (*alēthes*) here to emphasise that there is a difference between the myth of Phaethon (i.e. the story itself) and the truth that is contained within it (i.e. the explanation of how the celestial bodies move). We should be wary of imposing modern ideas of 'fiction' onto Plato's texts: as Johansen (op. cit., p. 29) rightly points out, for Plato stories are fictional in the important sense that they are created or fabricated, and that which characterises the *mythos* is that it has been created *without any regard for particular facts of history*. Plato's *mythoi* are 'factual' in as much as they represent *general truths* about the nature of the gods and good men, and Socrates would certainly regard those truths as far more significant than any particular historical facts, but the manner in which the details of *mythoi* are fabricated in the image of general truths shows just how unimportant Socrates thinks historical facts are in comparison to philosophical truths.
59 The passage is rather like Plato's *Statesman* 258e ff., where Greek myths are also explained by a periodic 'deviation' (*parallaxis* in Greek) of cosmic movement. But in the *Statesman* the 'explanation' is also mythical in character, whereas this passage is closer to *Laws* 677, where Plato examines periodic natural calamities and their impact on the continuity of civilisation in a more realistic way. Theories of cataclysmic events, and hence the destruction of Atlantis, caused by comets have had currency at least since the time of Comte Gian Rinaldo Carli in the eighteenth century. See pp. 199ff.
60 The meaning of this is not entirely clear. The Nile is 'set free', either by the melting of the snow that constitutes its source, or by the opening of dams and sluices in the Egyptian irrigation system. In the light of the emphasis on irrigation systems in Atlantis as a source of water in hot weather (see *Critias* 118e), the latter may be what Plato has in mind. The water 'rises from below' because it comes from the Nile but, controlled by the irrigation system, it does not devastate the land (like heavy rains do) and disrupt Egyptian civilisation. Interestingly, Egyptian

mythology lacks destructive flood myths – the Nile floods are benign and benefi-cial. See Appendix, p. 334ff.

61 Cf. Plato, *Laws* 677b.

62 The Greek word *legetai* here doesn't mean 'are said to be': the Egyptian traditions *are* the oldest because, although mankind isn't totally annihilated anywhere, the illiterate survivors of the catastrophes don't keep any records.

63 'Stories' translates *mythōn* here: in other words, the genealogies that Solon had reported to the priests at Saïs were *oral traditions* in contrast to the *written records* that were preserved in their temples.

64 This is explicitly contradicted at *Critias* 112a, which suggests that the Greeks clearly remember three.

65 The context suggests that this is presumably the flood that destroyed Athens and Atlantis, rather than Deucalion's more recent flood.

66 Critias' *claim* to historicity is forceful. Solon wants to hear everything 'in detail' (*di' akribeias*), and the priests oblige: he gets the outline now, and a promise of the specific details of everything (*to akribes*) later (*Timaeus* 23e). But, as Thucydides says, that *akribeia* ('detail'/'accuracy') is impossible in ancient history:

> Now the state of affairs in early times [*ta palaia*] I have found to have been such as I have described, although it is difficult in such matters to credit any and every piece of testimony. For men accept from one another hearsay reports [*tas akoas*] of former events, neglecting to test them just the same [as if they took place in some distant land], even though these events belong to the history of their own country (Thucydides 1.20.1, trans. Smith, op. cit. [1919].

The fourth-century BC historian Ephorus agrees:

> On contemporary events we regard as most believable those who give the most detailed account [*akribestata*]. On events in the distant past [*tōn palaiōn*], however, we consider such an account wholly implausible on the grounds that it is unlikely that all actions and most speeches would be remembered over so long a period of time (Ephorus, fragment 9 [Jacoby], trans. T. P. Weisman).

Neither, even if we ignore the general Greek views about the Egyptians' untrustworthiness, does it help to claim that Critias' 9,000-year-old story is 'accu-rate/detailed' because it comes from the Egyptians. Even if we assume that they started recording their history the moment their country was established, 8,000 years ago (*Timaeus* 23e; see note 67), that still leaves 1,000 years in which they have to rely on hearsay (*akoē*; *Timaeus* 23a).

67 This is a crucial detail. Palaeo-Athens is therefore established in around 9600 BC, while the Egyptian civilisation dates from 8600 BC: Egypt might be incredibly old in Greek eyes, but Plato's primaeval Athens is a millennium older. Plato is vague and inconsistent with his dates, though: in the *Laws* the Athenian Stranger insists that the Egyptian records are *literally* 10,000 years old and in the *Critias* 108e we will be told the war that destroyed Athens and Atlantis happened 9,000 years ago, rather than the foundation of Athens by Athena. *Critias* 111a will also put the destruction at 9,000 years before the dialogue (i.e. *c.*9429 BC).

NOTES

DATE ANOMALIES

TIMAEUS	CRITIAS	LAWS
23e: The Egyptian priest, talking in *c.* 600 BC, says 'our' civilisation is recorded as being 8,000 years old (*c.* 8600 BC); 'your' fellow-citizens lived 9,000 years ago (*c.* 9600 BC). He also dates the start of Egyptian civilisation to 8600 BC.	108e: The dramatic setting of the *Critias* is *c.* 429 BC. The war that destroyed Athens and Atlantis happened 9,000 years ago (i.e. 9429 BC), not the foundation of Athens.	656e–7a: Egyptian culture is 10,000 years old at least (+ date of writing, *c.*348 BC = 10,348 BC]: 'You will find that the things depicted there 10,000 years ago (I mean what I say, not loosely but literally 10,000) are no better or worse than the productions of today.'
	111a: Critias says that many great floods have occurred during the 9,000 years since Athens was inundated at the same time as Atlantis, i.e. *c.*9429 BC.	

Plato is a philosopher, not a historian: he is playing fast and loose with the Egyptians' perceived antiquity, and with the reliability of Critias' account. What matters to him is the ideas, not the accuracy of dates, and over-concentration on dating the destruction of Atlantis has led many to miss the philosophical thrust of Plato's tale.

68 That is, from the elements earth and fire (Hephaestus is the blacksmith god): at *Timaeus* 31b we are told that without fire nothing could become visible, or tangible without some solidity, or solid without earth, so in the beginning the deity constructed the All out of fire and earth. This passage also references the myth of Erichthonius, whose name also carries earth connections (Greek *khthon* = 'earth'). The most common tale of his birth is that Athena visited Hephaestus' forge to have some weapons made, but Hephaestus had been spurned by his wife Aphrodite and was overwhelmed with lust for the virgin goddess. Despite his lameness, he got close to her and attempted to have intercourse, but she refused to submit, and his premature ejaculation landed on her thigh. Disgusted, she wiped his semen off with some wool, which she then threw away. The moment it touched the ground, the ever-fertile Gaea (Earth) produced Erichthonius, and gave him to Athena (Homer, *Iliad* 2.547; Euripides, *Ion*).

69 The 'writings' are never produced, and quite how the Egyptians are supposed to have gathered detailed information about the exploits and laws of Athens which predate their own records by 1,000 years is never made clear. Placing the foundation of Athens at *c.* 9600 BC would put it towards the end of the Palaeolithic era (the 'Stone Age'), which is traditionally held to end around 10,000 years ago, coinciding with the end of the Ice Age (the Pleistocene) and the onset of the Holocene climatic period. At that stage, humans lived on a non-productive economy (scavenging, hunting, gathering), and based most of their technology on

stone tool-making; there were no settlements remotely resembling fourth-century BC Athens, let alone the Atlantis that Plato will describe in the *Critias*. There is a number of pseudoscientific theories that assert otherwise, which do have their adherents.

70 Making comparisons between the institutions of Greece and Egypt in this way is a standard cliché that goes back to Herodotus.

71 In the *Busiris* by Plato's contemporary Isocrates (written between the *Republic* and the *Timaeus* and also based on Herodotus 2.164–8), the author tells the 'the false tale of Heracles and Busiris' (11.30–40) in which Busiris, the son of Poseidon and grandson of the river-god Nilus (the Nile), is a particularly nasty king of Egypt who is credited with founding the Egyptian civilisation, complete with an ideal constitution, caste system included, that parodies Plato's *Republic*. See N. Livingstone, *A Commentary on Isocrates' Busiris* (Leiden: Brill, 2001).

72 The similarities in weaponry have nothing extraordinary about them at all: both the Egyptians and the Greeks used shields and spears, as did practically every other ancient fighting force.

73 Herodotus (2.83, 2.84) says that the Egyptians regulate the practice of divination and medicine, but the idea that the order and regularity of the heavens can provide a model for the organisation of human life is distinctively Platonic – see *Timaeus* 90; *Laws* Book 10 and Book 12, 966c ff. – and this explains why there is such a stress placed on 'divine' organisation of a society like this.

74 It is a standard ancient idea (see, for example, Hippocrates, *Airs, Waters, Places*; Euripides, *Medea* 825 ff.; Aristotle, *Politics* 7.7) that a 'well-balanced' climate produces 'well-balanced' people. The Greeks (naturally) felt that their climate was the world's best and most well-balanced.

75 That is, the ones described in Egypt above.

76 This was manifestly not the case. No surviving material from Egypt shows any interest in recording or admiring the history or achievements of ancient Athens.

77 *Hybris* in Greek can indicate both an attitude of extreme arrogance and also the violent physical behaviour that goes with it. It was the word for GBH.

78 Presumably Critias regards the Atlantic as navigable because Atlantis and the various other islands allowed the ancient seafarers to find suitable harbours in which to moor their vessels. There is considerable vagueness in the Atlantis dialogues about precisely when seafaring began: imperialist Atlantis has an enormous fleet, but when Poseidon first established the settlement there were no ships and no seafaring. See *Critias* 113e, and cf. Thucydides 1.4, where Minos of Crete, who is clearly later in his mythical date than Atlantis, is said to be the first to have developed a navy.

79 The Greek word *nēson* (the accusative form of *nēsos*) must mean 'island' here, not 'peninsula/promontory' as some theories about Atlantis want it to. *Nēsos* is used repeatedly in the lines that follow, and it must have the same meaning each time. The word can be applied to promontories, but that is not its default meaning and the speaker is talking unequivocally about islands: it would make no sense whatsoever to make each occurrence of 'island' in the translation read 'promontory'. Where Plato does want to indicate that a piece of land is a peninsula/promontory, he does so very clearly, as at *Critias* 111a.

80 The 'Pillars of Heracles' (*Hērakleous stēlas* here) were established by Heracles on his way to fetch the Cattle of Geryon. They stood opposite each other at the boundaries of Europe and Libya, and defined what is now known as the Strait of Gibraltar (see. p. 11). Certain Atlantis-theorists would like to move them to various

other locations in order to make them fit their speculations, but as its context makes explicitly and unequivocally clear, the Greek text here provides no grounds for doing so: Plato has just located the Atlantis island in the Atlantic Ocean. As C. G. Doumas puts it, 'with such a detailed and precise description it is astonishing that there are still people who force themselves to place Atlantis not only in various parts of the world beyond the Atlantic ocean, not only in continental regions disregarding its clear description as an island, but also inside the Mediterranean, the Aegean Sea in particular' ('The search for Atlantis: The Utopia of a Utopia', in Papamarinopoulos, op. cit. [2007], p. 2).

81 The Greek word translated 'bigger' here is *meizōn*, and Critias uses the same word in the same context at *Critias* 108e. Various Atlantis theories propose that there was an error in the transcription of Solon's notes, which actually read *meson* ('between'), allowing the island to be located 'between Libya and Asia' (see, for example, P. B. S. Andrews, 'Larger than Africa and Asia?', *Greece and Rome*, no. 14 [1967], pp. 76–9). But these fail to read the rest of the Greek accurately, since if this reading is proposed, the crucial word *hama* (here translated as 'put together') would make no sense whatsoever: 'The island was between Libya and Asia put together': pure nonsense. In seeking to move Atlantis, proponents of this idea fail to recognise that Plato *had* to place Atlantis in the Ocean outside the Pillars of Heracles because it was deliberately made far too big to fit into the Mediterranean. See J. V. Luce, *The End of Atlantis* (London: Paladin, 1972), p. 32.

82 In Greek, 'Libya' means the whole of Africa.

83 Plato alters the traditional Greek worldview in two respects here. He suggests that the 'real' sea (i.e. the sea that is of real size and geographical significance) is not the Mediterranean, to which Greek navigation was confined (and which he describes as a mere 'harbour') but the Atlantic Ocean. And he suggests that the world is bounded not by the Ocean (a belief going back to Homer) but by an all-embracing continent. The *Etymologicum Magnum* connects *ēpeiros* ('continent') with *apeiros* ('boundless'): it is land not bounded by sea like an island is. The outer continent is 'unbounded' because it forms a completely unbroken ring (compare Fig. 1 with Fig. 4). Why Plato suggests this is not clear, but his ideas don't appear to owe anything to any genuine information from sailors. The first alteration is part of Plato's expansion of the normal horizons of space and time in his story; the second suggestion reflects his preference for land over sea. Plato's use of 'genuine' and 'true' is part of his own pseudoscientific vocabulary in the story.

84 That is, the Mediterranean region.

85 Tyrrhenia, or Etruria/Tuscany, stands for Italy here.

86 This sentence is practically identical to the one Plato uses to eulogise Athenian courage at the Battle of Arginusae – 'the excellence and strength of our State was conspicuous' (*Menexenus* 243b–c) – which tells heavily against the words being those of Solon's Egyptian source. It is also noticeable that the entire passage strikingly resembles Herodotus' praise of Athens' leadership role in the Persian Wars: 'To say that the Athenians were the saviours of Greece is to hit the truth. It was the Athenians who held the balance; whichever side they joined was sure to prevail. Choosing that Greece should preserve her freedom, the Athenians roused to battle the other Greek states which had not yet gone over to the Persians and, after the gods, were responsible for driving the king off' (Herodotus, 7.139.5, trans. Godley, op. cit.).

87 Plato uses a different word for Pillars here – *stēlai* have become *horoi* – 'boundary markers'.

88 This is a crucial detail that is frequently overlooked in Atlantis discussions: the word *hōsautōs* ('in the same way') makes it explicit that Plato's Athens is destroyed by the same cataclysm that inundates Atlantis.

89 Cf. *Critias* 112a: Critias' flood-myth knowledge is hazy and contradictory. There is an important and explicit contrast between the relative fates of the two cities: Athens, the land-power, is swallowed by the earth (*kata gēs*); Atlantis, the sea-power, is swallowed by the sea (*kata tēs thalattēs*).

90 The interpretation of these words is problematical because our manuscripts have variant readings: some read *karta brakheos* (= 'extremely shallow'), others have *kata brakheos* (= 'at a little depth'/'just below the surface'). The latter is the one that I have used here. See F. M. Cornford, *Plato's Cosmology* (London: Routledge & Kegan Paul; reprinted, Indianapolis: Hackett Publishing Co., 1997), pp. 366–7. In the *Theaetetus* (147a–c) Plato's discussion of the different ways of defining mud (*pēlos*) shows that he usually uses *pēlos* for water-infused solids that are slippery and can be moulded, like you do when making pottery, earthenware and bricks, so he is not talking about very soft mud here. Proclus feels that Plato's description is more suited to 'surface-reefs', i.e. submerged rocks with water over them (*In Timaeum* 188.17–24. See p. 153). As C. Gill observes, although Plato's statement has some basis in the actual continental shelf off Gibraltar, essentially it is 'one of the ways in which he (rather arbitrarily) blocks off the various areas that he has created, and destroys the people he has created' (op cit., p. 45).

91 Plato implicitly emphasises the tenuous way in which the story has been transmitted (see Fig. 3).

92 He will, though, contradict himself on this at *Critias* 107e. See p. 87 and n. 4.

93 At *Timaeus* 20c.

94 Once again there is great stress placed on the fact that Critias relies heavily on his memory, and that the tale is the kind of story that very old men tell to children.

95 The Greek word *thēsomen* ('transfer') could equally well be rendered 'suppose': Plato plays on its double meaning.

96 Critias makes a clear contrast between myth (*hōs en mythōi* = 'as in a myth') and the truth (*t'alēthes*) here, although it is interesting that he characterises the Ideal State that Socrates talked of yesterday as myth, and the Athens-Atlantis tale, which apparently depends on written testimony, as truth. Socrates later comments (*Timaeus* 26e), doubtless ironically, that it is absolutely crucial that the Atlantis story is an *alēthinon* ('true') *logon* and not a *plasthenta* ('invented') *mython*.

97 The Greek word *hōs*, 'as', is a crucial word here: see n. 102 below.

98 *Alēthinon logon*, not *plasthenta mython*. It is important to realise (a) that Plato is *pretending* that his account is historical, and (b) why he is doing this. In the *Republic*, he says that that the reason why people make up stories but then present them as history is so that people can be induced to believe in the possibility of events in the past that they would probably not believe in the present. When Socrates wants to get the citizens of the Ideal State to accept his three-tiered social order, he suggests that they are told 'one noble lie' (see p. 361, n. 40). This takes the form of his '*mythos* of the three metals', and after he has told it, he asks Glaucon, 'Can you think of any scheme so that they will believe this story [*mythos*]?', and Glaucon replies, 'No, not they themselves but their sons and then thereafter the rest of the generations.' In other words, people are more gullible about unlikely things if they are set in the past than if they are set in the here-and-now. So, Plato's Atlantis story is set in the past to make its hearers believe things that they would absolutely disbelieve if they were set in the present. It is also

crucial that the setting of the Atlantis story is one about which the hearers know practically nothing. Plato places it in the past, but he could equally have placed it in the future or in the present but in somewhere far off (cf. *Republic* 6.499c–d. See Johansen, op. cit, pp. 44 ff.). This all has the flavour of 'once upon a time in a galaxy far, far away', and in a sense the Atlantis tale plays on its listeners' ignorance of the ancient past and their relative ignorance of foreign places like Egypt to make Plato's fiction seem plausible. His method has proved to be spectacularly successful right up to the twenty-first century, with a number of contemporary Atlantis-related publications doing precisely what he wanted them to do.

99 The words that Socrates uses when he describes Critias' story as 'true history and not an invented myth' actually imply criticism of that myth/history distinction. The word *pammega* (*pan* = 'all'; *mega* = 'big'), translated 'massively' here, doesn't occur in the work of any other known Greek author, and Plato often uses *pan*-compounds to express disapproval through rhetorical exaggeration (see R. S. W. Hawtry, '*Pan*-compounds in Plato', *Classical Quarterly*, no. 33 [1983], pp. 56–65); the word *pou* (translated 'I suppose' here) introduces a further indication of scepticism, of 'doubt thrown in as an afterthought' (J. D. Denniston, *Greek Particles* [Oxford: Oxford University Press, 1959], p. 493): it indicates that the speaker is being uncertain.

100 Despite the fact that Socrates is being polite and positive in his response here, it is obvious that his words are dripping with irony. He also studiously avoids any reference to the implications of taking the story from highly unreliable Egyptian sources (see Johansen, op. cit, pp. 45–6), and when he mentions Good Luck (*agathēi tykhēi*), he implies that it's rather too good to be true that the Atlantis story has emerged at this incredibly convenient juncture: after all, 'how and where shall we find other stories, if we reject these?' It could be that Socrates regards it as a *plastheis mythos* ('a fabricated story'), but he could also be attacking the distinction between *plastheis muthos* and *alēthinos logos* in relation to the Atlantis tale, suggesting that the marvellous actions of his Ideal Citizens are, in a way, both *plastheis muthos* and also *alēthinos logos*. So, the Atlantis story might not be *literally* or *historically* true, but it does still express a *general* truth: it is an 'opportune falsehood', a 'noble lie', as opposed to any old lie (see *Republic* 414b–c, quoted on p. 362, n. 40); it *illustrates* a truth, in this case about how Ideal Citizens behave in action, which is what Socrates said he wanted at *Timaeus* 19e.

101 By this he means the Guardian class in the Ideal State (see *Timaeus* 18a), who Socrates wanted to have depicted in an account of a great achievement (see *Timaeus* 19b ff.).

102 *Hōs* again. The translation 'virtual court' also renders *hōs* (literally 'as before jurors'). The use of the Greek word *hōs* is very significant. It carries associations of *as if*, both here and at 26c–d above. Both passages make the transfer of Socrates' ideal citizens to the real world depend on 'speech acts' (e.g. 'we shall posit': see Johansen, op. cit., p. 37), and at 27b these speech acts are those of the law courts. Like Athenian jurors, we can grant citizenship to the Ideal Citizens on the basis of the spoken report of the old writings and the account of the law of Solon, which granted citizen rights to the lowest of Athens' economic classes and to exiles (cf. Aristotle, *Politics* 1273b34 ff.). So in essence we can make Socrates' Ideal Citizens into Athenian citizens by simply saying so, granting them that status by a kind of judicial process. By referring to Solon's law, Critias may be implying that new citizens are being created. As Johansen argues (op. cit., p. 38), the passage 'is carefully composed to allow for a reading that takes Critias' history

as constructed in the act of telling it'. In other words, Critias is improvising, creating history on the hoof, rather than relating a true story. This is crucial for the
interpretation of the Atlantis story, and when Plato uses these words he is making
his fiction explicit. When Critias says that he will take the Guardian class of
Socrates' Ideal State and treat them 'as if they were' the Athenian citizens of
Solon's story, he is effectively telling us that the story will be an imaginative exploration of the political theme of the *Republic*. But because Plato doesn't make
Critias explicitly state that Solon's' story is itself an invention, he can maintain the
superficial illusion that the story is basically a true one. In the Greek, this sentence
is difficult and convoluted, which itself could indicate that Plato knows just how
difficult and convoluted is the project with which he is getting involved (see C.
Gill, op cit., p. 47, n. 27b3–6).
103 *Hōs.*

CHAPTER 5

1 Plato, *Timaeus* 107a–b, trans. Bury, op. cit.
2 'Imitations' renders the Greek word *mimēsin*. Plato can be deeply disapproving of
'imitation' because it strays from truth and reality, but he is prepared to tolerate it
(as he does here) if it talks about 'brave, temperate men, pious, free, and all such
things' (*Republic* 395c). Narrative content of this type isn't dangerous, even if it is
fiction, so long as it can educate people in a positive way. It could be a 'noble lie'
(*Republic* 414b–c), or a 'useful lie' (*Republic* 382d quoted on p. 360, n. 29).
Essentially, it makes no difference to Plato whether the Atlantis story is true or
not, so long as it is useful. See T. Parisaki, 'The story of Atlantis and platonic
mimesis', in Papamarinopoulos, op. cit. (2010), pp. 35–46; Johansen, op. cit., p.
34 f.
3 Plato, *Timaeus* 107b–d, trans. Bury, op. cit.
4 This conspicuously contradicts *Timaeus* 26a, where Critias said that he didn't
want to speak on the spur of the moment because he didn't trust his own
memory. So it seems that, despite what he says there, his story *is* specially
concocted for this occasion. As Johansen points out (op. cit., p. 42), Critias'
elaborate demonstration of his sources and their authority is designed to *suggest*
that he is using a critical historical method to reconstruct a set of historical
events, but Plato is not a historian, and his 'history' often contains spectacular
anachronisms: in the *Menexenus*, Socrates, who died in 399 BC, talks about the
Corinthian War, fought between 396 and 386 BC, and in the *Symposium* Socrates
also outlines the history of Athens down to the King's Peace of 386 BC which
brought that war to a close (see, for example, K. Dover [ed.], *Plato Symposium*
[Cambridge: Cambridge University Press, 1980], p. 10). Plato's readership
would obviously know this, so in fact these 'historical' references make it clear
that the dialogues are *not* historical documents, and actually emphasise the
pretence to historicity (see C. J. Rowe, 'On Plato, Homer and archaeology', *Arion*,
no. 6 [1998], pp. 134–44; 'Myth, history and dialectic in Plato's *Republic* and
Timaeus-Critias', in R. G. A. Buxton [ed.], *From Myth to Reason? Studies in the
Development of Greek Thought* [Oxford: Oxford University Press, 1999], pp.
263–78).
5 Plato, *Critias* 107e, trans. Bury, op. cit.
6 We have an instant chronological anomaly here: see p. 366, n. 67.

NOTES

7 Right at the start of the story Plato is emphasising an explicit contrast between the *polis* (city-state) of Athens and the *basileis* (kings) of Atlantis. The two sides are diametrically opposed in political terms.

8 *Nēson* (= 'island') again: see *Timaeus* 24e and p. 368, n. 79. As there, to translate this as 'promontory' would violate the original Greek. When Plato means 'promontory' he says so unambiguously – see *Critias* 111a.

9 The Greek word he uses here is *meizō*. See *Timaeus* 24e and n. 81.

10 Cf. *Timaeus* 25d and n. 90.

11 The statement is absolutely crucial, and all too often lost in the great quest for Atlantis. What matters most in Plato's account is Athens, not Atlantis. As Pierre Vidal-Naquet puts it, 'the historian who wishes to understand the myth of Atlantis [. . .] must not sunder the two cities which Plato has linked so closely together' ('Athens and Atlantis: structure and meaning of a Platonic myth', in R. L. Gordon [ed.], *Myth, Religion and Society: Structuralist essays by M. Detienne, L. Gernet, J.-P. Vernant and P. Vidal-Naquet* [Cambridge: Cambridge University Press/Paris: Éditions de la Maison des Sciences de l'Homme, 1981], p.202; see also O. Broneer, 'Plato's description of early Athens and the origin of Metageitnia', *Hesperia*, Supplement 8 [Commemorative studies in honour of T. L. Shear] [1949], pp. 47–59). The description of Athens that follows bears a very strong resemblance to Plato's 'Ideal State' as outlined in the *Republic*, albeit with some crucial modifications: Plato is continually refining his vision of what the Ideal State should look like.

12 Critias is essentially rewriting Greek mythology here. His statement is at odds with, for example, *Menexenus* 237c, where Socrates says the fact that the gods *did* contend for control of Athens is proof that she is god-beloved. In actuality, the myth of the strife between Poseidon and Athena for possession of Athens and Attica, where he struck the Acropolis with his trident and created a salt-water spring, and she created the first olive tree (thereby winning the contest and prompting him to flood the plain of Attica), was a very well-known one, famously depicted on the west pediment of the Parthenon and commemorated by a trident-mark and an olive tree in the precinct of the Erekhtheion (see Kershaw, op. cit. [2007], pp. 260–3; Kershaw, op. cit. [2010], pp. 213–15). In the Athens of Plato's day, Athena and Poseidon were both worshipped in the Erekhtheion, but Poseidon, god of the sea and of earthquakes, has no place whatsoever in the religious observances of palaeo-Athens: he is the prime deity of Atlantis, which is a sea-power, and so has nothing to do with antediluvian Athens, which is depicted as a land-power, stemming from the seed of Hephaestus and Gaea. See *Timaeus* 23e and n. 68. See also L. Brisson, 'De la philosophie politique à l'épopée: le Critias de Platon', *Revue de Metaphysique et de Morale*, no. 75 (1970), pp. 412 ff.; P. Vidal-Naquet, op. cit. (1981), pp. 206–8; and Wyatt, op cit., p. 65f., who suggests that the squabbles between the two deities 'appear to cast a quite different and rather local light on the geographical problems posed by *Atlantis*', and to postulate that this represents 'a conflict between two cults, perhaps between pastoralists (*disorder* is one of Poseidon's attributes) and cultivators. It is not perhaps coincidence that one of Solon's achievements as a legislator was to resolve political and economic strife between social classes in Attica.'

13 The *Homeric Hymn 12 to Hephaestus* also links Athena and Hephaestus: 'With Athena of the glittering eyes Hephaestus taught men on earth wondrous crafts' (20.2–3).

14 That is, the Athenian heroes Cecrops, Erechtheus, Erichthonius and Erysichthon, mentioned at *Critias* 110a. For their various mythologies, see Kershaw, op. cit. (2007), pp. 259 ff.

15 At *Timaeus* 22d–3c.

16 The notion that societies have to fulfil their basic needs before they can indulge in the luxury of intellectual activity is common enough – see, for example, Aristotle, *Metaphysics* 981b19 ff. At *Timaeus* 22a ff., it was the Athenian Solon who was doing the 'myth-telling' and the Egyptians who were 'investigating the past', and Solon's story will be used to back up this idea that investigation into the past is something that takes a long time to evolve: here the relatively recently civilised Athenians can only remember the names of their rulers, whereas in Egypt, where knowledge is 'grey-haired with age', the priests not only have their names, but also records of their achievements, including, of course, the Athens v. Atlantis conflict (cf. *Timaeus* 22b ff.).

17 This selection of Athenian heroes is significant. Throughout the narrative that follows, Athens will be very closely associated with the land, and the four mythical kings name-checked here reinforce that link: Erechtheus and Erichthonius were regarded as autochthonous (born from the land), and Erichthonius and Erysichthon's names have the word *chthon* (land) embedded in them. Cf. A. Rivaud, *Timée-Critias, vol. X* (Paris: Budé, 1969), pp. 234 ff.; Brisson, op. cit. (1970), pp. 409 ff.; Vidal-Naquet, op. cit (1981), p. 207 f.

18 The awkwardness of the translation reflects the awkwardness of Critias' Greek here.

19 This statue of the warrior-goddess Athena, who was represented on the Acropolis in Plato's lifetime by two colossal statues, the chryselephantine (gold and ivory) Athena Parthenos in the Parthenon, and the bronze Athena Promakhos ('Athena Who Fights for Us') by Pheidias, serves to reinforce the idea of women's equality in antediluvian Athens. Cf. *Timaeus* 18c and the discussions at *Republic* 453 ff.

20 Cf. *Timaeus* 17d ff.; 24a–b. The idea of a settled Ancient Greece, or more properly 'Hellas', is somewhat at odds with Thucydides' account (1.2.) of ancient cultures: the land was not called Hellas until after Deucalion's flood; it was not settled with fixed habitations; migration was the norm; each tribe readily left its own land whenever they were forced out by more numerous people; there was no mercantile traffic; all interactions were overshadowed by fear; farming was at bare subsistence level; there was no surplus wealth; no one planted orchards because invaders might despoil them at any moment; the settlements had no walls; the people thought that they could get the sustenance for their daily needs by regularly changing their abodes; and neither cities nor their resources were strong. Thucydides' early Athens, however, was at least free from internal quarrels because of the thinness of its soil, so it was always inhabited by the same people, and as a result it became a focal point for influential refugees from other parts of Hellas, until population pressure forced it to establish colonies; but unlike Plato's ideal Athenians, Thucydides' were 'among the very first to lay aside their arms and, adopting an easier mode of life, to change to more luxurious ways' (1.6.3).

21 Cf. *Republic* 376c ff.; *Timaeus*. 17d ff.

22 Antediluvian Athens controls considerably more territory than fourth-century BC Athens.

23 Notice the stress on the land – the real Athens of the fifth and fourth centuries BC was a sea-power, but the fictitious ancient Athens is closely associated with the land: its strength is its army, not its navy. Plato studiously avoids any

reference to maritime life, and although the promontory of palaeo-Attica is surrounded by the sea, it has no harbours. It is 'the antithesis of the real city of the fifth and fourth centuries – in a word, an anti-Athens'. Vidal-Naquet, op. cit. (1981), p. 208.

24 As C. Gill, op. cit., p. 56 f., n. 1112 ff. rightly points out, Plato's theory about soil erosion is consistent with his theory of periodic natural catastrophes (cf. *Critias* 109d, *Timaeus* 22c ff., *Laws* 677), and his concern with providing proof for his theories ('proof', 110e; 'credible', 111a; 'proves', 111d) is a sign of his growing interest in the techniques of prehistorical enquiry. But although he claims to discover such phenomena by empirical research, they are also determined by the requirements of his politico-philosophical fable (cf. *Critias* 110e).

25 The Greek word used for 'promontory' here is *akra*. This conclusively tells against Atlantean interpretations that want *hē Atlantis nēsos* to mean 'the Atlantis promontory' rather than 'the Atlantis island'.

26 That is, 9,000 years since the same cataclysm that destroyed Atlantis. Cf. *Critias* 108e and *Timaeus* 23e.

27 He is doubtless thinking of the typical small rocky Greek islands, like those of the Cyclades, where the vegetation is very sparse.

28 The text is corrupt at this point, and some words seem to have dropped out, placing major doubts over the stichometric interpretations of the Atlantis dialogues. See I. Burnett, *Platonis Opera: tomus IV tetralogiam VIII continens* (Oxford: Oxford University Press, 1902), n. 1115. But the overall sense is clear enough.

29 These are very much 'Ideal State' farmers, highly motivated to do a job to which they are naturally suited, and with a strong sense of honour. Cf. *Republic* 401c–d.

30 Another indication of the perfection of palaeo-Athens. The picture of a place with abundant crops and water supplies is very much a stereotype of the ideal past. Cf. the description of Alcinous' palace in Homer's *Odyssey* 84 ff. (quoted on p. 8f) and Hesiod's Golden Race of men, who 'had all good things; for the fruitful earth unforced bare them fruit abundantly and without stint. They dwelt in ease and peace upon their lands with many good things, rich in flocks and loved by the blessed gods', *Works and Days* 116 ff., trans. H. G. Evelyn-White, *Hesiod, The Homeric Hymns and Homerica with an English Translation* (Cambridge, MA: Harvard University Press; London: Heinemann, 1914).

31 Cf. *Timaeus* 24c and n. 74. Antediluvian Athens is heavily idealised here.

32 There is a certain amount of vagueness here: at *Timaeus* 25d, it is implied that this particular flood was the one that terminated the conflict between Athens and Atlantis. Also, at *Timaeus* 23b, Deucalion's flood is said to be the only one that the Greeks know about. Cf. also *Timaeus* 22a, and see the Appendix, p. 334ff.

33 The Eridanus (not the same as the river of Hyperborea) ran on the north side of Athens, the Ilissus on the south. The Pnyx is west of the Acropolis; Lycabettus is a prominent hill to the north-east. Plato's super-Acropolis is roughly the same size as the whole ancient city, vastly bigger than the rock that he would have seen on a daily basis. It has to be like this partly because it will have to accommodate 20,000 warriors (*Critias* 112d).

34 Members of the warrior class have a lifestyle that is highly unified, and they are strictly separated from all the other classes. Plato rams this home with the phrase *auto kath' hauto*, translated 'alone by themselves' here.

35 'Alone', 'one' and 'single' are crucial aspects of this: Athenian simplicity (= good) contrasts with Atlantean complexity (= bad).

36 Another key detail: this rejection of precious metals is deliberately set against Atlantis, where lavish wealth generates political instability: see *Critias* 115c ff., 121a ff. Cf. *Timaeus* 18b; *Republic* 416d, 'In the first place, none [of the Guardians] must possess any private property save the indispensable. Secondly, none must have any habitation or treasure-house which is not open for all to enter at will. Their food [should be] in such quantities as are needful for athletes of war sober and brave . . .', trans. Shorey, op. cit.

37 Again, notice the emphasis on palaeo-Athenian simplicity and changelessness. It is 'the political manifestation of the Same', Vidal-Naquet, op. cit. (1981), p. 208.

38 Just one is enough, with a temperature perfect for both summer and winter, unlike the waters of Atlantis.

39 Plato's contemporaries would regard this as weird: it is nothing like the classical 'city-state'. The proto-Athenians are not organised on a tribal basis like their fourth-century BC counterparts, who were divided into ten tribes: unity is everything in the Ideal State, and it will be noticeable that Atlantis, which embodies much that Plato disapproves of in the Athens of his day, has ten kings, ten regions and so on (see, for example, *Critias* 113e).

40 This consenting (*hekontōn*) acceptance of the land-based Athenians' primordial leadership deliberately contrasts with that of the fifth-century BC maritime Athenians in the Peloponnesian War, who were accused of imposing a tyranny over unwilling (*akontas*) subjects: see Thucydides 3.37.2 and cf. *Timaeus* 25c.

41 Again, note the emphasis on lack of change.

42 Cf. *Timaeus* 21a ff.

43 This is a normal process. For example, a large East Greek *situla* (pottery jar) found in the Nile Delta (British Museum, BM 1888.0208.1) shows the 'translation' of an Egyptian myth into Greek: the overthrowing of Seth by Horus has been converted into a conflict between Typhon and Apollo. The usual Greek tradition makes Zeus fight Typhon, but because the Greeks equated Horus with Apollo, we have a change of mythical personnel in the illustration. See F. Goddio and A. Masson-Berghoff, *Sunken Cities: Egypt's Lost Worlds* (London: Thames & Hudson, 2016), p. 214.

44 This mention of a manuscript comes completely out of the blue, and flatly contradicts Critias' previous comments about the oral transmission of the tale: at *Timaeus* 26b–c, he had been awake during the night trying to remember the story; he felt the need to invoke Mnemosyne (Memory) at *Critias* 108d; and he was worrying about his memory at *Critias* 112e. In *Lost Atlantis* (London: Cobden Sanderson, 1937, p. 61f), James Bramwell puts it quite neatly:

> The fake in Plato's case should be apparent from the fact that the 'papers of Solon,' which are represented as family heirlooms, have never been heard of by anybody outside the family. Also, there is a suspicious contradiction in his account of the transmission of the Solon story. In *Critias* Critias says: 'His actual papers were once in my father's hands, and are in my own to this day.' But elsewhere he tells his audience that he has been reflecting all night to try and remember the story he heard in his youth [. . .] Now why, if he had the MS., did he have to rely on his memory?

> Possessing a written document would certainly explain how an old man like Critias, who doubts his own memory, might accurately recall quite a lot of prehistoric barbarian names that were transliterated into Greek, but the inconsistency

NOTES

'indicates that Plato does not take the historical status of his account very seriously' (C. Gill, op. cit., p. 59, n. 113b2.). The probability that a person as important as Solon, one of the Seven Sages of Greece, gave Critias' family an unfinished manuscript of a work of earth-shattering importance, which was then left neglected for several generations, is minimal. See A. Giovannini, 'Peut-on démythier l'Atlantide?', *Museum Helveticum*, vol. 42 (1985), p. 152.

45 *Timaeus* 109b.

46 More properly, 'the island of Atlas' (*tēn nēson . . . tēn Atlantida*).

47 That is, in the middle of the coastal strip, not in the centre of the island, which was utterly enormous.

48 Fifty *stadia*.

49 Like the Athenians, the original Atlanteans are autochthonous, in as much as Cleito's father Euenor is earth-born, and she will bear a son called Autochthon, but their divine genetic links to the earth will be diluted by interbreeding with mortals, with disastrous consequences.

50 Their names carry associations of power and magnificence: Euenor = Good/ Brave Man; Cleito = Splendid/Famous; Leucippe = White Horse (horses were associated with Poseidon, and will be with Atlantis). The genealogy that Plato has created here doesn't occur anywhere else in Greek mythology.

51 Poseidon's lust (*epithumian*) is set against the love of wisdom (*philosphiai*) that motivates Athena when she founds Athens (cf. *Critias* 109c).

52 The rather vague Greek phrase translated 'from the middle of the island' could have one of several meanings: 1. 'from the mid-point of the coastal strip'; 2. 'from the middle of the "island" that Poseidon has just created around the hill'; or, least likely geographically but the most natural way to take it, 3. 'from the exact centre of the entire island'. The highly distinctive circular layout of the features surrounding Cleito's residence have become crucial to the quest to locate Plato's island, but Plato might not be thinking of a real place at all: in the *Timaeus* 33b, for instance, the Demiurge made the world 'into a round, in the shape of a sphere, equidistant in all directions from the centre to its extremities'. But even if Plato is referencing the *Timaeus*, he doesn't necessarily want us to see Poseidon and the Atlanteans' complicated engineering projects in a positive light: the proto-Athenians show unity and stability and make their urban design conform organically to their natural environment (see *Critias* 111e ff.); Poseidon and the kings of Atlantis will make their highly artificial, varied and complex structures dominate the natural environment (see, for example, *Critias* 118c and 119a ff.), only to see the whole 'edifice' sink under the weight of their greed (*Critias* 120e ff.).

53 Plato generally sees the influence of the sea as a bad thing: at *Laws* 705a, quoting the poet Alcman, he calls it 'a right briny and bitter neighbour', and while he admits that there is 'sweetness in its proximity for the uses of daily life', he hates the fact that 'by filling the markets of the city with foreign merchandise and retail trading, and breeding in men's souls knavish and tricky ways [cf. his attitude to the Egyptians], it renders the city faithless and loveless, not to itself only, but to the rest of the world as well', tr. Bury, op. cit. So it is understandable that he will make Poseidon insulate Cleito from the sea, and that no good will come of it when the Atlanteans ultimately join the 'ancient mother-city' to it (*Critias* 115c ff.). Also, by making Poseidon anti-sea, Plato is departing from the mainstream Greek mythological tradition. Cf. the *Homeric Hymn 12 to Poseidon*:

I begin to sing about Poseidon, the great god, mover of the earth and fruitless sea, god of the deep who is also lord of Helicon and wide Aegae. A two-fold office the gods allotted you, O Shaker of the Earth, to be a tamer of horses and a saviour of ships! Hail, Poseidon, Holder of the Earth, dark-haired lord! O blessed one, be kindly in heart and help those who voyage in ships! (Trans. Evelyn-White, op. cit.)

We might also note the absence of any reference to Atlantis in this hymn.

54 In contrast to palaeo-Athens, which had one spring that provided perfect water all the year round: where Athens is simple, Atlantis is complex.

55 The number ten plays a significant role in Atlantis. As the sum of the first four primary numbers (1, 2, 3, 4) it corresponds to the *tetractys*, the mystical arrangement of points in rows of 1, 2, 3 and 4 elements so as to form a triangle, which is significant in both Pythagoreanism and in Plato (see, for example, E. Moore, 'Middle Platonism', http://www.iep.utm.edu/midplato [accessed 12 December 2016]). Atlantis has some Pythagorean features, but others which are not (for instance, the 5 x 2 = 10 arrangements being outlined here). But if Plato is thinking of real-life examples, he is most likely referencing the units of ten that were deeply embedded in the fifth- and fourth-century BC Athenian democratic system (ten tribes, ten generals, ten Prytanneis, etc.; see p. 31). In any case, the overarching political structure of Atlantis looks like that of the quintessentially barbarian Persian Empire, where powerful Satraps governed their own regions, but under the overall command of the Great King (cf. *Critias* 115c–17a).

56 Atlantis is a monarchy; it is not an Ideal State.

57 He therefore has a Greek and a barbarian name. Eumelus means 'Rich in Sheep'. Gadeira corresponds to modern-day Cadiz, the locality of which has sometimes been popular with Atlantis-seekers.

58 'Well-built'; 'Well-fitted on Both Sides'.

59 'Of Good Blood'.

60 'Memory Man'.

61 'The One Sprung from the Soil He Inhabits'.

62 'Driver of Horses'.

63 'Advisor'.

64 'Parched'; (possibly) 'Dark-skinned'.

65 'Magnificent'.

66 *Nesōn*: again, context dictates that this must be 'islands' not 'promontories', and Atlantis is a *nēsos*.

67 *Timaeus* 25a–b.

68 This is completely at odds with the procedures of Plato's Ideal State.

69 Atlantis' staggering wealth, particularly in gold and silver, is in total contrast with the Ideal State at *Timaeus* 18b and palaeo-Athens at *Critias* 112c.

70 Critias makes no mention of imported goods in antediluvian Athens; the Atlanteans import things even though they have no need to: they have enough, but they want more.

71 For example, tin and lead, which melt at relatively low temperatures.

72 It sparkles (*Critias* 116 c), but otherwise it is difficult to identify because it is a mythical substance. Cf. Hesiod, *The Shield* 122, where Heracles wears 'leg greaves of shining mountain-bronze', and the *Homeric Hymn 6 to Aphrodite* 9, where Aphrodite wears earrings made from it.

73 The first mention of elephants in Greek literature occurs in Herodotus 4.191 (although ivory was known a long time before that). Aristotle has quite a lot about elephants in his *Historia Animalium*, but Plato is the only other Greek writer to mention them before him.

74 Again, the implication is that *we* are moderate, but the Atlanteans are gluttonous.

75 The idyllic fertility of Atlantis is strikingly similar to that of Ogygia and Phaeacia in Homer's *Odyssey* (see pp. 6–9), and it is also worth comparing Hesiod, *Works and Days* 116 ff (quoted on p. 375, n. 30). But Plato believes that the natural environment has a big effect on moral character, and Atlantis is too rich for its own good: it can support massive voracious beasts; it encourages large-scale eating for eating's sake; and the Atlanteans will use a variety of stones to adorn their buildings, unlike the Athenians, whose life embodies simplicity and moderation (*Critias* 112c).

76 The Atlanteans don't know when to stop. The description that Critias gives here draws on Herodotus' descriptions of Ecbatana (quoted on p. 36), Babylon (quoted on p. 34), the Athos canal built by Xerxes (see p. 40), and the Great King's bridging of the Hellespont (see p. 41). The last two make an explicit connection between large-scale engineering and *hybris* and barbarity. But as well as making the Atlanteans produce overtly 'barbarian' projects, Critias is also alluding to construction works in Athens such as the walls and harbours, including Hippodamus of Miletus' grid-pattern town-plan and harbour works at Piraeus. Plato regards this type of thing as morally dubious, and his Athenian readership would be expected to notice the parallels and take heed.

77 This is impressive, but the Atlanteans' pretentious and competitive display of luxury again stands against the simplicity and stability of the antediluvian Athenians, who leave their residences unchanged.

78 In Greek, this is 3 *plethra* x 100 feet x 50 *stadia*, which is clearly an enormous project, especially as we are told at *Critias* 118a that 'the entire country was said to be extremely high and to rise precipitously above the level of the sea': the side walls of the canal must have been extraordinarily high, and the problems of reconciling this with what would happen when the canal reached the city are never thought through. The Atlantis canal would have been longer than the Corinth Canal (6.3 km long, 8 m deep, maximum 25 m wide), and considerably wider and deeper than most of the Panama Canal (lock chambers 12.56 m deep and 33.53 m wide), and still deeper than the recently upgraded Suez Canal (24 m deep, 205/225 m wide). Herodotus (7.22–4, quoted on p. 40) was at pains to emphasise the difficulties encountered by Xerxes' workers in constructing the Mount Athos canal, which was only 2.4 km long and just wide enough to take two triremes abreast. The construction of the Atlantis canal now terminates the isolation of Cleito's island by opening the city to the sea, creating another phase in the developing disunity of Atlantean society.

79 The big picture is clear here, but the details are a mess. The bridges and underground passages of Plato's central island make a road that joins it to the Ocean. But the bridge across the outer ring just leads straight into the canal, and it is not apparent how the bridge is supported on the external side (see Fig 5). And as we shall see, the canal is three times as wide as the bridge (*Critias* 116a, 115d). Plato is a philosopher, not a civil engineer.

80 Three *stadia*.

81 Two *stadia*.

82 One *stadion*.

83 Five *stadia*.

84 The 1, 2, 3 proportions might be influenced by Pythagorean thinking.

85 *Plethriaian*, i.e. 1 *plethron* (33.3 m).

86 This is tricky to imagine accurately, but on each ring the wall stops on either side of the bridges, the gates are on the bridges, and the towers are at each side, either on or right by the bridges (the Greek is ambiguous).

87 The discovery of white, black and red stone (which occurs at Akrotiri on Santorini, but also in numerous other volcanic contexts) has become a significant diagnostic feature for many who want to locate the 'real' Atlantis. See p. 315. However, it is the variegated nature of the building work that matters here: it is not 'simple' but 'patterned' (*poikilos*), which is not a good thing. See n. 89.

88 The precise location of these dockyards is not specified.

89 *Poikila* ('patterned'): this is another key word, one that Plato frequently uses to characterise both democracy (which like Atlantis is also pleasure-filled – *hēdeia*) and tyranny, neither of which he approves of (see, e.g. *Republic* 557c–d, 558c, 561c, 568d). Plato does not like diversity – at *Timaeus* 81e–2b he also links *poikilos* with bodily diseases – so to see this quality manifested in Atlantean material culture indicates his disapproval (cf. 118b). The stonework and design here sound a lot like Herodotus' description of Ecbatana: see p. 36.

90 Again, this is fabulously gorgeous and impressive, but from Plato's point of view it is also morally dubious and un-primordial Athenian: palaeo-Athens has neither gold nor silver (*Critias* 112c).

91 One *stadion* x three *plethora*.

92 A crucial comment, which reinforces the non-Greekness of the Atlanteans.

93 The temple's design is typically Greek, and Plato's readers might well have been reminded of the Parthenon on the Athenian Acropolis. But it is about three times as big as the Parthenon (which was roughly 70 m x 31 m), which would entail 'proportionate' columns around 30 m high, and this, plus its over-the-top decoration, makes it 'barbaric': the temple at Babylon used large amounts of gold (Herodotus 1.183). The decoration of the walls and roof also harks back to Alcinous' palace in Homer's *Odyssey*, which was decorated with precious metals (Homer, *Odyssey* 7.84, and cf. *Critias* 117a). Also, the Phaeacian royal house traced its descent back to Poseidon (see Homer, *Odyssey* 7.56 ff., and cf. *Critias* 113d).

94 In the mainstream Greek mythological tradition, there were fifty Nereids (see Hesiod, *Theogony* 240 ff.; Pindar, *Isthmian* 5.6): even minor sea-deities come in vastly increased quantities on Atlantis.

95 Plato may have some real-life examples in mind here: possibly the Athena Parthenos; possibly the famous Statue of Zeus at Olympia, which was said to have almost touched the ceiling with his head (Strabo 8.3.53); or possibly the highly praised 'Sea Thiasos' group by Plato's contemporary, the celebrity sculptor Scopas, which depicted Poseidon with Thetis and Achilles accompanied by Nereids riding on dolphins, hippocamps ('sea-horses') and other sea-creatures (Pliny, *Natural History* 36.26). Poseidon's symbol of the hippocamp also appeared on the bronze statue of the god in Helice (Strabo, 8.1.2), leading D. Katsonopoulou to suggest that 'Helike was for Plato a unique source of inspiration which furnished his imagination with real data to clothe his fascinating story of Atlantis' ('Helike and mythical Atlantis: An illuminating comparison', in Papamarimopoulos, op. cit. [2007], p. 335).

96 Cf. *Critias* 113e, 112c–d. See also Homer, *Iliad* 22.147 ff., where there are two springs at Troy, one that flows with warm water, and one that flows as cold as hail or snow or ice, even in summer.

97 The palaeo-Athenians only have winter mess-rooms (*Critias* 112c).

98 Again, note the extraordinary diversity of the Atlantean arrangements: even animals live in luxury on Atlantis.

99 Plato's Atlantean plumbing systems have led to speculation about links to Minoan Crete and/or Akrotiri on Santorini, which also had impressive water facilities. But a much more obvious parallel comes from the royal gardens of the palace on Phaeacia in Homer's *Odyssey* 7.114 ff (see p. 8f). Plato places considerable emphasis on water supplies in *Laws* 761a ff.

100 The Greek uses 'many' four times here, ramming home the contrast with Athens: Atlantis has 'many' of everything; Athens has just one temple, one garden, one set of living quarters.

101 That is, the larger of the rings of land (cf. 113d). 'Island(s)', once again, translates *nēsōn* and *nēsōi* here – they are clearly not promontories. Every use of 'island' in the rest of the translation renders a grammatical form of *nēsos*.

102 Again, this is extraordinary. The Greek word translated '200 m' here is *stadion*, i.e. the *length* of a normal stadium. Supersize Atlantis has a stadium that is as wide as everybody else's is long. The god Poseidon is also very closely associated with horses.

103 The Athenians particularly associated bodyguards with tyrants, and the Greek word used here (literally, 'spear-carriers') is the specific term for the bodyguard of a tyrant (cf. *Republic* 567d, 575b). The physical arrangements of Atlantis city show us very clearly that it is a military joint-dictatorship, not an Ideal State.

104 At what point ships and seafaring were developed in order for Atlantis to have a massive fleet of state-of-the-art warships is not made clear. We were told that back in Cleito's day there were no ships, and people didn't know how to sail (see *Critias* 113e). The trireme was the standard Greek warship of Plato's time, and Thucydides (1.13.2–5) says that was introduced to Greece by the Corinthians in the late eighth century BC, but although Diodorus Siculus (14.42.3) takes this to mean that the trireme was invented in Corinth, it may be that the earliest examples were developed by the Phoenicians. The attribution of seafaring to the incredibly ancient Atlanteans directly contradicts Thucydides' statement (1.4) that Minos of Crete was the most ancient of the people that the Greeks know of to have built a navy.

105 Critias is imagining walking down the main road, away from the citadel, over the three bridges, and then down the side of the canal to the sea. The circuit wall is about 20 km in diameter.

106 This is a Platonic nightmare, but again he is thinking of fourth-century BC Athens. The description would make an Athenian picture the living conditions around the Athenian fortification walls, and the activity down at the port of Piraeus. For Plato, the construction of the Piraeus and the Long Walls were linked to the deterioration of the moral character of the Athenians, who 'with no consideration for discretion and justice [. . .] crammed the city with harbours and dockyards and fortifications and tribute and similar idiotic things' (Plato, *Gorgias* 519a), thereby promoting material greed of the type shown by the Atlanteans.

107 That is, first to Solon by the Egyptian priests, and subsequently to Critias himself.

108 Critias does not claim to be 100 per cent accurate – 'more or less' (*skhedon* in Greek) indicates vagueness, and he admits that he's speaking from memory (*apomnēmoneusai*). The manuscript mentioned at *Critias* 113b seems to have been forgotten about, too.

109 In many of the quests to locate the 'real Atlantis', the ensuing aspects of Critias' description are frequently overlooked, ignored or cherry-picked: their focus tends to stay on the city itself rather than its hinterland, whereas the wider area of the island is just as important to Plato's vision.

110 This creates enormous unresolved problems for the construction of the Atlantis canal, given that Atlantis city must clearly be located at a considerable height above sea level.

111 That is, 3,000 x 2,000 *stadia*. The plain of Atlantis alone occupies an area almost ten times greater than the entire island of Sicily, which is the largest island in the Mediterranean (240,000 km² for Atlantis; 25,706 km² for Sicily).

112 A key detail: any potential 'real Atlantis' location ought to be south-facing.

113 *Poikilēn* again: the diversity of Atlantis' natural environment is once more emphasised, with all the negative associations which this holds for Plato. See *Critias* 116a–b, and nn. 87 and 89.

114 Again, the Atlanteans are meddling with their natural environment, seeking to dominate it, unlike their proto-Athenian counterparts who live in harmony with it. In discussion of post-Deucalion society in the *Laws* (677a ff.), there is a phase in which humans colonise the plains, which they do under a constitution that 'mixes all types of political system and all their modifications, and shows similar variety and change in the states themselves' (*Laws* 681d). This is close to the description of democracy at *Republic* 557d ff., and therefore, from Plato's perspective, not a good thing. There is also an echo of Atlantis in *Laws* 628b, where the Athenian Stranger (quoting Homer's *Iliad* 20.216 ff. in the process) says that Troy was founded on a low hill that had many rivers flowing down from Mount Ida above, after the people moved from the highlands down to a large and noble plain.

115 A crucial comment: the Greek particle *ge* (= 'at any rate'/'at least') is used in a very telling way here: its implication is 'whether it's true or not', hence the translation. Even Critias has his doubts about the story.

116 One *plethron* deep; one *stadion* wide.

117 Length 3,000 *stadia* x breadth 2,000 (*Critias* 118a) = 10,000 *stadia* around the entire perimeter, i.e. 2,000 km. Roughly 13.3 billion m³ of rock/soil would need to be excavated to make this grand canal, which encloses almost 250,000 km². It would be rather like building the Suez Canal ten times over, or the Corinth Canal more than 10,000 times. It is highly unlikely that Plato approves of this, awesome though it is, because it again brings to mind the barbarity, excess and *hybris* of Xerxes' engineering projects (see Herodotus 7.22–4; 7.33–6 ff. quoted on p. 40, and nn. 52 and 54).

118 Through the canal running through the city.

119 One hundred Greek feet.

120 One hundred *stadia*.

121 The system involves two sets of canals: 1. running north–south, with the canals discharging into the ditch on the seaward side; 2. a set of transverse east–west channels that joins the north–south canals at right-angles. Plato doesn't tell us how far apart they are, but 20 km is a reasonable assumption in the light of the land divisions that determine Atlantis' military arrangements (see *Critias* 119a).

122 In palaeo-Athens the irrigation is entirely natural, and comes from Zeus. Again, there are reminiscences of Calypso's island and Alcinous' palace in Homer's *Odyssey* (5.64 ff., 7.82 ff.). See pp. 6–9.

123 It looks like Critias is thinking of the land divisions created by the criss-cross pattern of the canals, 600 units in all, probably squares of 20 x 20 km, subdivided

into 100 allotments of 2 x 2 km (10 x 10 *stadia*), giving a total of 60,000 allotments, which are used for the military organisation.

124 In Homeric warfare, the charioteer drove the combatant into battle, where he dismounted to fight. (The Greek is a little obscure at this point.)

125 Ever since antiquity, commentators have pored over the possible meaning of the numbers in the account (and of pretty well every other number that Plato cites). There is a stress, very explicit in the Greek, on alternating odds and evens: the plain is 2,000 x 3,000 *stadia*; we have a pair of horses with three soldiers; two hoplites, slingers and archers, three stone-throwers and javelin-men, four sailors; the Atlantean kings meet alternately in the fifth and sixth year, giving an equal share to odds and evens (see 119d), and so on. But whatever esoteric meanings might be extracted from this, one crucial point is that the arrangements are needlessly complicated. The whole catalogue reminds us of Herodotus' list of Xerxes' mighty and barbaric forces (Herodotus, 7.59–88, see p. 39), and the Atlantean military is clearly to be thought of as a mixture of Greek and barbarian – some Greek armies deployed slingers, but stone-throwers and the strange riders-who-dismount are very un-Greek; chariots have Homeric precedents, but were not used by Greek armies in Plato's day, although the Persians did use them; and the numbers of fighters are beyond astonishing: 10,000 chariots; 60,000 'dismounters' backed up by 120,000 grooms; 120,000 hoplites; 120,000 archers; 120,000 slingers; 180,000 stone-throwers; 180,000 javelin-men; and 240,000 sailors for 1,200 ships – 1.4 million fighters in total, and that was just for the royal city. They are backed up by the men of the nine other cities and the 'infinite' numbers from the mountains and elsewhere.

126 The Atlantean constitution is 'mixed', a combination of monarchy and oligarchy/aristocracy. In its earliest phases, it works along the lines of successful mixed constitutions like those Plato describes in the *Statesman*, *Timaeus*, *Philebus* and *Laws*, but ultimately it will not be able to maintain its unity, and disaster will follow.

127 Almost every mention of a number in Plato has provoked speculation from antiquity up until the present. Aristotle (*Metaphysics* 986a22–6) tells us that the Pythagoreans 'recognised ten principles, which they list in two parallel columns:

Limited	Unlimited
Equal	Unequal
Unity	Plurality
Right	Left
Male	Female
Still	Moved
Straight line	Curve
Light	Dark
Good	Bad
Square	Oblong.'

Those on the left are good, those on the right are bad, and it is noticeable that several, although not all, of the right-hand-column qualities might be applied to Atlantis. In his book *Plato's Mathematical Imagination* (Bloomington: Indiana University Press, 1957, pp. 17–59), R. S. Brumbaugh also noted the prominence of the numbers six and five on Plato's Atlantis: five pairs of twins; five enclosures; the centre of the island measures five *stadia* across; there is a 6:5 relationship between the total area of the rings of water and that of the rings of earth; Poseidon's statue shows him driving six horses; the central plain measures 6 million *stadia*[2] and is rectangular, rather than square, putting it on the 'bad' side of the Pythagorean 'table of opposites'; the number six and/or multiples of six are intrinsic to Atlantis' military organisation; and so on. Plato makes it explicit that the opposition between five and six is between odd and even, hence in Pythagorean terms between equal and unequal, and so between good and evil. Plato's Atlantis is the template for a bad society.

128 The bull was Poseidon's special animal. The capture of bulls in a way that resembles the process described by Critias is depicted on the Creto-Mycenaean gold Vapheio Cups found in a tholos tomb in Laconia, which are now in the National Archaeological Museum in Athens (1758, 1759). Dating from the first half of fifteenth century BC, cup 1758 shows a man tying a rope around a bull's leg while it mates with a cow in the company of three grazing bulls, while cup 1759 depicts a bull trapped in a net and another one attacking its hunters.

129 There is a great deal of discussion about this ritual, and what, if anything, might have influenced Plato here, but Critias' account has much in common with Herodotus' description (2.142–54) of how Psammeticus came to be sole-ruler of Egypt. Following the reign of the king/priest-of-Hephaestus called Sethus, the Egyptians, despite having been made free, found that they could never live without a king, so they divided Egypt into twelve districts and set up twelve kings who intermarried, and agreed not to depose one another. Their rituals involved libations and solemn drinking, and in order to preserve the memory of their names they constructed a labyrinth, whose labour and cost far outdid anything the Greeks had ever constructed, and which surpassed even the Pyramids. Herodotus says that it had twelve roofed courts, but that he wasn't allowed inside because the Egyptian caretakers said that was where the burial vaults of the kings who first built the labyrinth were, as well as those of the sacred crocodiles. Herodotus adds that the artificial lake Moeris, on which the labyrinth stood, along with various pyramids and colossal statues, was even more impressive. In the end, the sacred agreement between the twelve kings fell apart, and, in accordance with an oracle, Psammetichus ousted the other eleven and made himself master of all Egypt. Plato would certainly have been aware of this part of Herodotus' writings, and C. Gill, op. cit., p. 69, n. 119d7 ff., suggests that the latter part of Herodotus's story may have been the way that Plato intended to continue the unfinished narrative of the *Critias*. The people of Pylos also sacrifice bulls to Poseidon in Homer's *Odyssey* 3.6. See also Brisson, op. cit. (1970), pp. 432–5.

130 The very dark blue colour (*kyaneos*) is suitable for descendants of the sea-god Poseidon: *kyaneos* is also used to describe the deep sea (Euripides, *I.T.* l.7. Cf. Aristotle, *Problemata* 932a31; Xenarchus 1.7; Theophrastus, *de Sensu* 7.7).

131 *Hōs logos* – again, even Critias places a very big question mark over the whole story.

132 The moral point of the Atlantis story is being rammed home here. This is not a historical tale about a wondrous island, it's a terrifying warning about the dangers of confusing material prosperity with happiness and moral goodness. Scratch the glossy surface of the Atlanteans and you see their true degenerate nature: this is how Plato's readers are expected to respond. This whole image of the political and moral degeneration of Atlantis is also very similar to the account that he'll give in the *Laws* (694a–b, 695b, 697c–8a) of the decline of Persia after the reigns of Cyrus and Darius I, which led directly to Xerxes' invasion of Greece (*Laws* 698b

NOTES

ff.), and was unquestionably one of the genuine historical models for the Atlantis tale. Furthermore, 'greed and a lawless sense of power' (*pleonexias adikou kai dynameōs*) are key terms in the Greek vocabulary of imperialism, and other crucial examples of imperialism leading to catastrophe are Athens' Sicilian expedition and Athens' experience with her rebellious allies at around the time that Plato wrote the Atlantis story. Atlantis' disastrous belligerence mirrors that of both Persia *and* historical Athens.

133 Punishment in order to 'harmonise' is a very Platonic idea. See, for example, *Protagoras* 324a–c, *Republic* 443d–e, *Timaeus* 106b. Because the narrative ends abruptly, we never get the opportunity to discover whether there is any possibility of redemption for the Atlanteans.

134 See, for example, T. G. Rosenmeyer, 'Plato's Atlantis myth: "Timaeus" or "Critias"?', *Phoenix*, vol. 10, no. 4 (1956), pp. 163–72.

CHAPTER 6

1 Dionysius of Halicarnassus, *Letter to Pompey*, 6, trans. S. Usher, in *Dionysius of Halicarnassus: Critical Essays, Volume II: On Literary Composition. Dinarchus. Letters to Ammaeus and Pompeius* (Cambridge, MA: Harvard University Press, 1985).

2 F 259 = FGrH 115, referenced by Athenaeus, *Deipnosophistai* 11.508c–d.

3 See E. Rohde, *Der griechische Roman und seine Vorläufer* (Leipzig: Breitkopf und Härtel, third edition, 1914), pp. 204–8.

4 Midas of Phrygia is he of the 'Midas touch'; Silenus is the leader of the satyrs and of Dionysus' followers.

5 Theopompus, F 75c = *FGrH* 115, quoted in Aelian, *Varia Historia* 3.18, trans. N. G. Wilson, in *Aelian: Historical Miscellany* (Cambridge, MA: Harvard University Press, 1997).

6 R. Graves, *The Greek Myths* (Harmondsworth: Penguin, 1955), s.v. 'Midas'.

7 Strabo 7.3.6.

8 Lysimachus (*c.*360–281 BC) came to rule Macedon after Alexander's death in 323 BC; Antigonus was one of Alexander's generals who tried to take over his empire but was killed at the Battle of Ipsus in 301 BC.

9 Aelian, *On the Characteristics of Animals* 15.2, trans. A. F. Schofield, in *Aelian. On Animals, Volume III: Books 12–17* (Cambridge, MA: Harvard University Press, 1959).

10 'Inventor of stories' translates the Greek *mythologos*.

11 Aelian, *Varia Historia* 3.18, trans. Wilson, op. cit.

12 Proclus, *In Timeum* 190.4–8, trans. H. Tarrant, *Proclus: Commentary on Plato's Timaeus, Vol. 1, Book 1: Proclus on the Socratic State and Atlantis* (Cambridge: Cambridge University Press, 2007).

13 Homer, *Odyssey* 13.125 ff.

14 Homer, *Iliad* 7.433, 441, 12.1 ff.

15 'Achaeans' is a common designation for the Greeks in Homer.

16 The most explicit reference to the truth or otherwise of the story in Plato is when Socrates says, 'the fact that it is true history and not an invented myth is massively important, I suppose', *Timaeus* 26e. See p. 371 and n. 99.

17 Strabo 2.3.6, trans. Jones, op. cit.

18 Poseidonius F49.297–303 Kidd.

19 *Timaeus* 25d, there translated 'disappeared'.

20 *Timaeus* 26e.

21 See Johansen, op. cit., pp. 45–6.

22 Strabo 13.1.36, trans. Jones, op. cit.

23 See, for example, W. Haase and M. Reinhold (eds), *The Classical Tradition and the Americas. Volume 1: European Images of the Americas and the Classical Tradition, Part 1* (Berlin and New York: De Gruyter, 1994), pp. 43 ff. For Columbus and Atlantis, see p. 162ff.

24 Again, it is clear that the Pillars of Heracles are at the Strait of Gibraltar, not anywhere else.

25 Aristotle, *De Caelo* II, 14, 289a, trans. J. L. Stocks, *De Caelo* (Oxford: Clarendon Press, 1922). Plato also taught that earth was spherical, although he doesn't offer any proof: Plato, *Phaedo* 108, 110b. Cf. *Timaeus* 33. See D. R. Dicks, *Early Greek Astronomy to Aristotle* (Ithaca: Cornell University Press, 1970).

26 *Critias* 114e–15a.

27 Aristotle, *Meteorologica* II, 354a22.

28 Plato, *Timaeus* 25d. They use the same word for mud – *pēlon* – here.

29 [Aristotle], *de Mirabilibus Auscultationibus* 836b30 ff., trans. W. S. Hett, in *Aristotle. Minor Works: On Colours. On Things Heard. Physiognomics. On Plants. On Marvellous Things Heard. Mechanical Problems. On Indivisible Lines. The Situations and Names of Winds. On Melissus, Xenophanes, Gorgias* (Cambridge, MA: Harvard University Press, 1936).

30 [Aristotle], *de Mirabilibus Auscultationibus* 844a25 ff., trans. Hett, op. cit.

31 The Greek word *metagrapsanta*, rendered 'translated' here, really = 'transferred to a different culture', and it does not imply that the Egyptian ideas were ever committed to writing.

32 The Greek *tosouton* here is ambiguous: to some translators it means 'so little', others 'so much', although it makes no difference to the argument here.

33 Proclus, *In Timaeum* 75.26–6.10, trans. Tarrant, op. cit., with minor amendments. The following discussions owe much to Tarrant's excellent analysis at pp. 61–70.

34 For Herodotus and *historia*, see p. 33.

35 See, for example, Cicero, *On Laws* 1.6–7 and *ad Fam* 5.12, where he writes to the historian Lucceius asking him to include a favourable account of his actions during Catiline's conspiracy: this is an exciting story, he says, so praise my actions more than you perhaps feel they deserve, and more than the truth justifies.

36 The moon features in a rather different light in Proclus' analysis of Atlantis. See p. 151.

37 Proclus, *In Timaeum* 109.9–17, trans. Tarrant, op. cit.

38 See p. 33.

39 For a full discussion of this issue, see Tarrant, op. cit., pp. 61–5.

40 The words used are *mythos* and *plasma* respectively (the latter related to the verb *plassō* = 'invent').

41 Proclus, *In Timaeum* 76.10–12, trans. Tarrant, op. cit.

42 Ibid., 76.15–16.

43 Ibid., 76.17–21. Heraclitus of Ephesus (*c.* 535–*c.* 475 BC) was a pre-Socratic Greek philosopher. The quotation is B53 DK.

44 Proclus, *In Timaeum* 182.2–3, trans. Tarrant, op. cit.

45 For instance, M. Bernal, *Black Athena: The Afroasiatic Roots of Classical Civilization. Vol. 1: The Fabrication of Ancient Greece* (New Brunswick, NJ: Rutgers University Press, 1987), p. 106–7.

NOTES

46 Aristophanes, *Assembly Women* 571–690. Cf. *Timaeus* 18c–e.

47 Plato, *Timaeus* 24a–b.

48 Plato, *Timaeus* 24b–c. See p. 368, n. 73.

49 Plato, *Timaeus* 17c–19a. In the *Laws* (656d–7a, 747a–c) Plato does mention rules that he approves of – banning artistic innovations, emphasising mathematical education – which could have had a bit of an Egyptian flavour.

50 See, for example, Aristophanes, *Clouds* 545–59.

51 M. Lefkowitz, *Not Out of Africa: How Afrocentrism Became an Excuse to Teach Myth as History* (New York: New Republic and Basic Books, 1997), p. 75. She points out that 'the 'Egyptian Mystery System'' from which the Greeks were supposed to have derived their philosophy and scientific learning is in fact based on an eighteenth-century European fiction'. See 'Lefkowitz on Bernal on Lefkowitz', *Bryn Mawr Classical Review* (19 April 1996), http://bmcr.brynmawr.edu/1996/96.04.19.html#NT6 [accessed 2 January 2017].

52 Homer, *Odyssey* 14.285 ff., 15.415; Plato, *Republic* 436a; *Laws* 657a5, 747b8–c8. See also *Timaeus* 22b.

53 M. M. Garvey, 'Who and what is a Negro?' (1932), as quoted by H. Brotz (ed.), *Negro Social and Political Thought, 1859–1920, representative texts* (New York: Basic Books, 1966), pp. 561–2.

54 Like most of the Africans living north of the Sahara, the ancient Egyptians were not black: see, for instance, F. M. Snowden, *Blacks in Antiquity* (Cambridge, MA: Harvard University Press, 1970); F. M. Snowden, *Before Color Prejudice* (Cambridge, MA: Harvard University Press, 1983); Lefkowitz, op. cit (1997).

55 For example, C. A. Diop, *Civilization or Barbarism: An Authentic Anthropology*, trans. Yaa-Langi Meema Ngemi (Brooklyn, NY: Lawrence Hill Books, 1991). Cf. Bernal, op. cit. (1987); Bernal, op. cit. (1991).

56 Diop, op. cit., p. 338.

57 Ibid., pp. 337–40.

58 Ibid., pp. 341–3.

59 Diodorus 1.96.1

60 Plato, *Timaeus* 47a–c.

61 See Lefkowitz, op. cit. (1997), p. 83 f.

62 Strabo 17.1.29. See p. 59f.

63 Diogenes Laertius, *Lives of Eminent Philosophers* 3.6. See p. 59f.

64 Clement of Alexandria, *Stromata* 1.15.69 = Eudoxus T 18 Lasserre.

65 Proclus, *In Timaeum* 76.4 ff., trans. Tarrant, op. cit.

66 Plato, *Timaeus* 24a–c.

67 Plato, *Timaeus* 17a–19b.

68 Tarrant, op. cit., p. 68.

69 Ibid.

70 Ibid., p. 69.

71 Proclus, *In Timaeum* 76.7–9.

72 Plato, *Timaeus* 23a.

73 Tarrant, op. cit., p. 69 f.

74 National Museum of Alexandria 285, SCA 277.

75 Ruled 379/378–361/360 BC.

76 British Museum JE34002, SR5/9013. See J. Yoyotte, 'An extraordinary pair of twins: The steles of the Pharaoh Nektanebo I,' in F. Goddio and M. Clauss (eds), *Egypt's Sunken Treasures* (Munich: Prestel, 2006), pp. 316–23; A. S. von Bomhard,

The Decree of Saïs: The Stele of Thonis-Heracleion and Naukratis, Underwater Archaeology in the Canopic Region in Egypt (Oxford: Oxford Centre for Maritime Archaeology Monograph 7, 2012).

CHAPTER 7

1 Strabo 2.3.6; Poseidonius F49.297–303 Kidd. For the full quotation and more discussion, see p. 113.

2 Ptolemy I ruled Egypt between 323 and 285 BC, but precise dating of the establishment of the library is fraught with difficulty. See, for example, L. Canfora, *The Vanished Library: A Wonder of the Ancient World* (Los Angeles: University of California Press, 1990); K. Staikos, *The Great Libraries: From Antiquity to the Renaissance* (New Castle, DE: Oak Knoll Press, 2000).

3 Manetho's dates are uncertain, although he can be associated with the first three Ptolemies; Hecataeus of Abdera was in Egypt in the reign of Ptolemy I.

4 For example, G. G. M. James, *The Stolen Legacy* (New York: Philosophical Library, 1954). See Lefkowitz, op. cit (1997), pp. 2–5, 134–54.

5 Our sources indicate damage to the Library in 48 BC, AD 272, 391, 415 and 639. See, for example, H. Philips, 'The Great *Library* of Alexandria?', *Library Philosophy and Practice* (2010), http://unllib.unl.edu/LPP/phillips.htm [accessed 4 January 2017].

6 Proclus, *In Timaeum* 177.10–20.

7 Proclus, *In Timaeum* 181.14–15.

8 See p. 118.

9 Horace, *Odes* 1.37.25 f., trans. J. Michie, in *The Odes of Horace* (Harmondsworth: Penguin, 1967).

10 Diodorus, 3.53.1–6, 56–61.

11 'Amazon' is commonly derived from *a* = 'without' and *mazos*, a form of *mastos* = 'breast', and so means 'without a breast'. However, popular etymologies like this always work the other way round: they *confirm* the values already ascribed to the bearer of a name; they do not *produce* those values. See J. Bremmer (ed.), *Interpretations of Greek Mythology* (London and New York: Routledge, 1988).

12 Diodorus, 3.53.4–5, trans. C. H. Oldfather, in *Diodorus Siculus. Library of History, Volume II: Books 2.35–4.58* (Cambridge, MA: Harvard University Press, 1935).

13 Ibid., 3.54.1.

14 Ibid., 3.55.3.

15 Ibid., 3.60.1–2. At 4.2.27 Diodorus says that Atlas 'discovered the spherical nature of the stars'; numerous ancient writers refer to Atlas as the discoverer of astronomy.

16 Ibid., 3.60.5.

17 Vidal-Naquet, op. cit. (2007), p. 39.

18 See S. Kershaw, *A Brief History of the Roman Empire* (London: Robinson, 2013), pp. 1–49.

19 Philo lived from *c.*20 BC to AD 40.

20 Philo, *On the Eternity of the World* 140, trans. F. H. Colson, *Philo. Every Good Man is Free. On the Contemplative Life. On the Eternity of the World. Against Flaccus. Apology for the Jews. On Providence* (Cambridge, MA: Harvard University Press, 1941). It is not known who he is quoting here.

21 Ibid., 141. Cf. Plato, *Timaeus* 24e and 25c–d.

22 For example, H. Diels, *Doxographi Graeci, The Opinions of Physicians*, fragment 12 (Berlin, 1879); W. W. Fortenbaugh et al., *Theophrastus of Eresus, Sources for His Life, Writings, Thoughts and Influence*, vol. I (Leiden, New York and Cologne: Brill, 1992), p. 351.

23 For example, J. V. Luce, 'The sources and literary form of Plato's Atlantis narrative', in E, S. Ramage (ed.), *Atlantis: Fact or Fiction?* (Bloomington and London: Indiana University Press, 1978), p. 51; P. Jordan, *The Atlantis Syndrome* (Stroud: Sutton Publishing, 2001), p. 43.

24 See D. T. Runia, *Philo of Alexandria and The* Timaeus *of Plato* (Leiden: Brill, 1986), p. 85.

25 Seneca, *Natural Questions* 6.24.6, 6.25.4, 6.26.3, 6.32.8, 7.5.3, 7.16.1.

26 Pliny, *Natural History* 2.90.

27 Ibid., 6.202.

28 Plutarch, *Moralia* 1093a, trans. B. Einarson and P. H. de Lacy, *Plutarch: Moralia, Volume XIV: That Epicurus Actually Makes a Pleasant Life Impossible. Reply to Colotes in Defence of the Other Philosophers. Is 'Live Unknown' a Wise Precept? On Music* (Cambridge, MA: Harvard University Press, 1967).

29 Plato, *Critias* 106a at Plutarch, *Moralia* 1017b; Plato, *Critias* 109b–c at Plutarch, *Moralia* 483d and 801d.

30 Plato, *Timaeus* 21c.

31 Plutarch, *Solon* 26.1.

32 Plutarch, *Solon* 31.3; Plato, *Timaeus* 21c.

33 Plutarch, *Solon* 32.1–2, trans. Perrin, op. cit. For the whole passage, see p. 28.

34 Tarrant, op. cit, p. 81.

35 Plutarch, *Solon* 31.3.

36 Plato, *Timaeus*, 26e. In fact, Socrates is probably not intending his words to be taken at face value in any case. See p. 371, n. 99.

37 Tertullian, *Apology* 40.2–4, trans. T. R. Glover, in *Tertullian, Minucius Felix. Apology. De Spectaculis. Minucius Felix: Octavius* (Cambridge, MA: Harvard University Press, 1931).

38 Tertullian, *De Pallio* 2.3, trans. V. Hunink, in *Tertullian, De Pallio, a Commentary* (Amsterdam: Gieben, 2005).

39 See J. Seznec, *The Survival of the Pagan Gods: The Mythological Tradition and its Place in Renaissance Humanism and Art* (Princeton, NJ: Princeton University Press, 1953); L. Brisson, *How Philosophers Saved Myths: Allegorical Interpretation and Classical Mythology* (Chicago and London: University of Chicago Press, 2004); Kershaw, op. cit. (2007), p. 448 f.

40 Clement of Alexandria, *Stromata* 5.9, trans., A. Roberts and J. Donaldson, *The Ante-Nicene Fathers: Translations of The Writings of the Fathers down to* AD *325: Vol. II, Fathers of the Second Century*, http://www.tertullian.org/fathers2/ANF-02/anf02-65.htm [accessed 5 January 2017].

41 Proclus, *In Timaeum* 76.10–12. See p. 119.

42 Proclus, *In Timaeum* 77.3–5, trans. Tarrant, op. cit.

43 See p. 140f.

44 Numenius fragments 30–2, E. des Places, *Numénius, Fragments* (Paris: Belles Lettres, 1973).

45 Numenius fragment 33.

46 Numenius fragment 35.

47 Numenius fragment 38.

48 There is in fact some scholarly disagreement as to whether there were two think-ers called Origen, one Christian, the other neo-Platonist, or only one.

49 Origen fragment 12 in K.-O. Weber, *Origenes der Neuplatoniker* (Munich: Beck, 1962).

50 Proclus, *In Timaeum* 83.25, trans. Tarrant, op. cit.

51 76.10.

52 At *Timaeus* 26e. See also p. 84, n. 98.

53 Proclus, *In Timaeum* 76.21–30, trans. Tarrant, op. cit.

54 Plato, *Critias* 113e.

55 See, for example, Plotinus, *Enneads* 3.4.5, 3.7.13, 4.2.2, 4.8.22, 6.8.19. See also J.-M. Charrue, *Plotin, Lecteur de Platon* (Paris: Les Belles Lettres, 1978).

56 See Kershaw, op. cit. (2013), pp. 278–83.

57 See Proclus, *In Timaeum* 83.25–8, quoted on p. 141.

58 This is a quotation from Plato's *Phaedrus* 229d, where Socrates is talking about attempts to explain myths allegorically.

59 Proclus, *In Timaeum* 129.9–23, trans. Tarrant, op. cit.

60 The west is where Atlantis is.

61 Proclus, *In Timaeum* 77.5–24, trans. Tarrant, op. cit.

62 Ibid., 129.23–8.

63 Proclus, *In Timaeum* 7.7–12; 159.25–7; 165.16–19; 171.17–21. Cf. Plato, *Timaeus* 24c, 24d, 23e.

64 Plato, *Timaeus* 20d. See p. 74 and n. 40.

65 Proclus, *In Timaeum* 76.17–21, quoted on p. 119.

66 Proclus, *In Timaeum* 77.24–8; Iamblichus, *In Timaeum* fragment 7, trans. Tarrant, op. cit.

67 Probably a reference to the Phaethon myth.

68 Arnobius, *Against the Pagans* 1.4, trans. H. Bryce and H. Campbell, *The Seven Books of Arnobius adversus gentes* (Edinburgh: Clark, 1871).

69 Ibid., 1.5.1.

70 Born AD late 320s or early 330s; died after AD 390/1.

71 From a Greek word = 'to boil up'.

72 Eleusis wasn't an island, and it wasn't swallowed by an earthquake: it was destroyed by an inundation. See Strabo 12.2.18; Pausanias 12.24.2.

73 'Moving sideways'.

74 Ammianus Marcellinus 17.13, trans. J. C. Rolfe, *Ammianus Marcellinus. History, Volume I: Books 14–19* (Cambridge, MA: Harvard University Press, 1950).

75 See Proclus, *In Timaeum* 77.24–8, quoted on p. 145.

76 Proclus, *In Timaeum* 204.17–29.

77 Proclus, *In Timaeum* 76.10–12, quoted on p. 119.

78 Proclus, *In Timaeum* 76.12–16, trans. Tarrant, op. cit.

79 See p. 113.

80 Proclus, *In Timaeum* 190.8–10.

81 Plato, *Timaeus* 24e–5a. See p. 80f.

82 Proclus, *In Timaeum* 177.10–11.

83 See pp. 20ff.

84 Proclus, *In Timaeum* 177.16–21. For Marcellus see p. 130.

85 Ibid., 177.22–7, trans. Tarrant, op. cit.

86 Plato, *Timaeus* 25a–b.

87 Plato, *Phaedo* 109a–b, trans. H. N. Fowler, *Plato: Euthyphro, Apology, Crito, Phaedo, Phaedrus* (Cambridge, MA: Harvard University Press, 1914).

88 This is a common tactic. See, for example, https://www.uwgb.edu/dutchs/
   PSEUDOSC/SelfApptdExp.htm [accessed 21 January 2017].
89 Presumably Marcellus, although the plural is odd.
90 Proclus, *In Timaeum* 180.25–81.20.
91 Ibid., 181.23–82.2.
92 This is the one that happened on 24 August 358. See p. 147f.
93 Aristotle, *Meteorologica* 2.8, 368a34–b13.
94 Proclus, *In Timaeum* 187.20–88.14, trans. Tarrant, op. cit.
95 See p. 62f. Proclus is probably using Aristotle *Meteorologica* 343b1–4, 368b6–13,
   Theophrastus *Phys. Dox.* p. 490, Diels, and Pausanias 7.24–5.
96 Tarrant, op. cit., p. 287, n. 793.
97 Proclus, *In Timaeum* 188.15–16.
98 Aristotle, *Meteorologica* 354a22–3, see p. 115. Cf. Plato, *Timaeus* 25d.
99 Proclus, *In Timaeum* 188.17–24, trans. Tarrant, op. cit.
100 See p. 383, n. 127.
101 Proclus, *In Timaeum* 175.4–6.6.
102 Proclus, *In Timaeum* 174.8–10.
103 Proclus, *In Timaeum* 172.10–14, trans. Tarrant, op. cit.
104 Plato, *Timaeus* 30a.
105 Cosmas Indicopleustes, *Christian Topography* 12.376, trans. J. W. McCrindle, in
   The Christian Topography of Cosmas, an Egyptian Monk (London: Hakluyt Society,
   1897).
106 Ibid., 12.380.

Chapter 8

1 From here on, all dates will be assumed to be AD (CE if you prefer), unless otherwise specified.
2 See J. Magee, *On Plato's Timaeus – Calcidius, Edited and translated by John Magee*
  (Cambridge, MA and London: Harvard University Press, 2016). Calcidius'
  commentary goes as far as *Timaeus* 53c.
3 Eighth or ninth century AD. See I. Short and B. Merrilees (eds), *The Anglo-Norman
  Voyage of Saint Brendan* (Manchester: Manchester University Press, 1979).
4 See A. G. MacPherson, 'Pre-Columbian discoveries and exploration of North
  America', in J. L. Allen (ed.), *North American Exploration* (Lincoln, NE: University
  of Nebraska Press, 1997); P. Ó Riain, *Feastdays of the Saints: A History of Irish
  Martyrologies*, Subsidia Hagiographica 86 (Brussels: Société des Bollandistes,
  2006); J. Brotton, *A History of the World in Twelve Maps* (London: Penguin, 2013),
  pp. 82–113; J. Brotton, *Great Maps* (London: Dorling Kindersley, 2015), pp. 56–65;
  E. Brooke-Hitching, *The Phantom Atlas: The Greatest Myths, Lies and Blunders on
  Maps* (London, New York, Sydney, Toronto and New Delhi: Simon & Schuster,
  2016), pp. 9, 93, 159.
5 Plutarch, *Sertorius* 8.
6 Isidore of Seville, *Etymologiae* 16.6.8.
7 Bodleian Library, MS Pococke 375, dated 1553/960 H. See Brotton, op. cit. (2013),
  pp. 54–81; Brotton, op. cit. (2015), pp. 46–9; Brooke-Hitching, op. cit., p. 122f.
8 See p. 14.
9 See A. Cortesão, *The Nautical Chart of 1424 and the Early Discovery and
  Cartographical Representation of America* (Coimbra and Minneapolis, MN:

University of Coimbra, 1954), p. 156; Brooke-Hitching, op. cit., p. 210 f.; Brotton, op. cit. (2015), pp. 68–71.

10 A. von Humboldt, *Examen critique de l'histoire de la géographie du nouveau conti-nent et des progrès de l'astronomie nautique aux quinzième et seizième siècles* (Paris: Gide, 1837), vol. II, p. 192; M. D'Avezac, *Les îles fantastiques de l'océan occidental au moyen âge: fragment inédit d'une histoire des îles de l'Afrique* (Paris: Fain & Thunot, 1845), p. 27. See also W. H. Babcock, 'Antillia and the Antilles', *Geographical Review*, vol. 9, no. 2 (1920), pp. 109–24.

11 See L. Spence, *The Problem of Atlantis* (London: Rider, 1924), p.87.

12 M. Ficino, *Opera Omnia*, 2 vols (Basel: Henrici Petri, 1576). See also R. Marcel, *Marsile Ficin, 1433–1499* (Paris: Belles Lettres, 1958), p. 630 f.; M. Ficino, *All Things Natural: Ficino on Plato's Timaeus*, trans. A. Farndell (London: Shepheard-Walwyn, 2010). See also S. Byrne, *Ficino in Spain* (Toronto, Buffalo and London: University of Toronto Press, 2015).

13 *Rem miram quidem, sed omnino veram*, Ficino, op. cit. (1576), vol. II, p. 1485. See also vol. I, p. 1439.

14 B. de las Casas, *Historia de las Indias*, ed. A. Saint-Lu, (Caracas: Ayacucho, 1986), vol. I, p. 50.

15 Ibid., vol. I, p. 51.

16 F. Cervantes de Salazar, *Apólogo de la ociosidad i del trabajo intitulado Labricio PortvndoI, compuesto por el protonotario Lvis Mexia, glossado I moralizado por Francisco Cervantes de Salazar* (1772), n.p., cited from http://www.cervantesvir-tual.com [accessed 8 January 2017].

17 P. de Sarmiento de Gamboa, *The History of the Incas. English translation of Pedro Sarmiento de Gamboa's 1572 Historia de los Incas*, trans. and ed. Brian S. Bauer and Vania Smith, introduction by Brian S. Bauer and Jean Jacque Decoster (Austin, TX: University of Texas Press, 2007). n.117.

18 See Byrne, op. cit., p. 77.

19 See p. 162.

20 See p. 160.

21 See, for example, W. H. Babcock, 'Atlantis and Antillia', *Geographical Review*, no. 3 (1917), pp. 392–5; W. H. Babcock, *Legendary Islands in the Atlantic: A Study in Medieval Geography* (New York: American Geographical Society, 1922).

22 Seneca, *Medea* 375–9, trans. J. G. Fitch, in *Seneca. Tragedies, Volume I: Hercules. Trojan Women. Phoenician Women. Medea. Phaedra* (Cambridge, MA: Harvard University Press, 2002).

23 A. von Humboldt, *Examen critique de l'histoire de la géographie du Nouveau Continent*, 5 vols (Paris: Gide, 1836–9), vol. I, p. 167, p. 30.

24 See B. Keen, *The Life of the Admiral Christopher Columbus by His Son Ferdinand* (New Brunswick: Rutgers University Press, 1959), pp. 28–34.

25 C. Lévi-Strauss, *A World on the Wane*, trans. J. Russell (London: Hutchinson, 1961), p. 78.

26 P. Martyr D'Anghiera, *De Orbo Novo*, trans. R. Eden., *The decades of the newe worlde or west India conteynyng the nauigations and conquestes of the Spanyardes with the particular description of the moste ryche and large landes and Ilands lately founde in the west Ocean perteynyng to the inheritaunce of the kinges of Spayne* (London: William Powell, 1555). For the letter, see G. Randles, 'Le nouveau monde, l'autre monde et la pluralité des mondes', *Congreso internacional de Historia dos Descombrimentos, Actas* (Lisbon: Comissão Executiva das Comemorações do V Centenário da Morte do Infante D. Henrique, 1961), vol. IV, pp. 347–82.

27 W. Shakespeare, *The Tempest*, Act V, Scene 1.

28 Virgil, *Aeneid* 1.1.

29 G. Fracastoro, *Syphilis sive morbus Gallicus* 3.261 ff., trans. M. S. Claiborne, in *Hieronymus Fracastor's Syphilis, from the original Latin; a translation in prose of Fracastor's immortal poem* (St Louis, MO: The Philmar Company, 1911).

30 See, for example, J. N. Bremmer, 'Myth as propaganda: Athens and Sparta', *Zeitschrift für papyrologie und epigraphik*, no. 117 (1997), pp. 9–17, http://www.academia.edu/9799160/Myth_as_Propaganda_Athens_and_Sparta [accessed 28 January 2017].

31 Pliny, *Natural History* 5.3, 5.30, 6.31, 6.36. See Á. F. Bolaños, 'The historian and the Hesperides: Fernández de Oviedo and the limitations of imitation', *Bulletin of Hispanic Studies*, no. 72 (1995), p. 273–88. The complete work was not published until 1851–5 by the Spanish Academy of History.

32 Quoted on p. 116.

33 Vidal-Naquet, op. cit. (2007), p. 57 f.

34 See the discussion on Diego de Landa on p. 170f. See also, for example, R. Wauchope, *Lost Tribes and Sunken Continents. Myth and Method in the Study of American Indians* (Chicago: Chicago University Press, 1962); T. Parfitt, *The Lost Tribes of Israel: The History of a Myth* (London: Weidenfeld & Nicolson, 2002); Z. B.-D. Benite, *The Ten Lost Tribes* (Oxford: Oxford University Press, 2009).

35 IV Esdras 13.40–7.

36 Parfitt, op. cit., p. 2.

37 See, for example, J. Manuschevich, *La Atlántida: el mito descifrado* (Santiago de Chile: Autoedición, 2002).

38 G. M. Sayre, 'Prehistoric diasporas: Colonial theories of the origins of Native American peoples', in P. Beidler and G. Taylor (eds), *Writing Race Across the Atlantic World: Medieval to Modern* (New York and Basingstoke: Palgrave Macmillan, 2005), p. 58.

39 It still surfaces from time to time. Ignatius Donnelly used it some 400 years later: see p. 238.

40 Quoted in I. Clendinnen, *Ambivalent Conquests: Maya and Spaniard in Yucatan, 1517–1570* (Cambridge: Cambridge University Press, second edition, 2003).

41 A. Tozzer, *Landa's Relación de las Cosas de Yucatan* (Cambridge, MA: Peabody Museum, 1941), vol. XVII, pp. 16–7.

42 See p. 231ff.

43 Digital version available at http://digital.bodleian.ox.ac.uk/inquire/Discover/Search/#/?p=c+5,t+%22Hertford%20Atlas%22,rsrs+0,rsps+10,fa+,so+0x%3Aso rt%5Easc,scids+,pid+f19aeaf9–5aba–4cee-be32–584663ff1ef1,vi+ [accessed 29 November 2016]. See also Brooke-Hitching, op. cit., pp. 130–3.

44 See p. 282ff.

45 See p. 282.

46 A. Ortelius, *Thesaurus Geographicus* , trans. S. Kershaw (Antwerp: Plantin, 1587).

47 See p. 12.

48 J. G. Becanus, *Opera Joan. Goropii Becani hactenus in lucem non edita, nempe Hermathena, Hieroglyphica, Vertumnus, Gallica, Francica, Hispanica* (Antwerp: Plantin, 1580), pp. 35, 62, 105–8.

49 J. de Acosta, *The Naturall and Morall Historie of the East and West Indies*, trans. Edward Grimston (London: V. Sims, 1604).

50 *Usuta*, the Quichua word for sandals.

51 Acosta, op. cit.

52 M. Montaigne, *Essays*, trans. M. A. Screech (London: Penguin, 1991), Book I, chapter XXXI.

53 Ibid.

54 Ibid., Book III, chapter VI. See also G. Gliozzi, *Adamo e il Nuovo Mondo: La nàscita dell' antropologia corne ideologia coloniale: dalle genealogie bibliche alle teorie razziali (1500–1700)* (Florence: La Nuovo Italia Ed., 1977), pp. 352–67.

55 J. Lipsius, *De Constantia* 1.16, trans. J. Stradling, in *Justus Lipsius: His First Book of Constancy (Latin 1584, Englished by John Stradling 1594)* (Exeter: University of Exeter Press, 2006).

56 Letter to Darwin, 24 July 1866, in F. Burkhardt et al. (eds), *The Correspondence of Charles Darwin* (Cambridge: Cambridge University Press, 2004), vol. 14, p. 253.

57 Letter to J. D. Hooker, 20 July 1866, in Burkhardt, op. cit., p. 257. Bunbury had noted that Madeira lacked many of the European plants that would have been expected had Madeira and Europe been connected at any time.

58 British Library Additional MS 59681.

59 Ibid., p. 13.

60 Ibid.

61 See T. Green, 'John Dee, King Arthur, and the conquest of the Arctic', *Heroic Age: A Journal of Early Medieval Northwestern Europe*, no. 15 (2012).

62 The Appalachian Mountains.

63 A fictional advanced civilisation of pre-Contact New England.

64 British Library Additional MS 59681, p. 14.

Chapter 9

1 F. Bacon, *New Atlantis. A Worke unfinished*, in *Sylva Sylvarum: Or a Naturall Historie*, ed. William Rawley (London: John Haviland for William Lee, 1627). The quotation is from J. Spedding, R. L. Ellis and D. D. Heath (eds), *The Works of Francis Bacon* (Boston: Houghton Mifflin, 190?), vol. V, p. 377.

2 Ibid., pp. 378–9.

3 Ibid., p. 379.

4 Ibid., p. 413.

5 Ibid.

6 See R. Lewis, 'Francis Bacon, allegory and the use of myth', *Review of English Studies*, vol. 61, no. 250 (2010), pp. 360–89.

7 J. Swan, *Speculum mundi* . . . (Cambridge: University of Cambridge, 1635).

8 Ibid.

9 Augustine, *City of God Against the Pagans* 12.10, 18.40.

10 N. Stenonis, *Opera Philosophica*, ed. U. Marr (Copenhagen: Vilhelm Tryde, 1910), p. 224.

11 I. La Peyrère, *Praeadamitae, sive Exercitatis super versibus duodecimo, decimotertio, & decimoquarto, capitis quinti Epistolae D. Pauli ad Romanos. quibus inducuntur primi homines ante Adamum conditi* (Amsterdam, 1655), pp. 176–80. See also R. H. Popkin, *Isaac la Peyrère (1596–1676): His Life, Work and Influence* (Leiden: Brill, 1987).

12 A. Kircher, *Mundus subterraneus, in XII libros digestus: qvo divinum subterrestris mundi opificium, mira ergasteriorum naturae in eo distributio, verbo [pantamorphon] Protei regnum, universae denique naturae majestas & divitiae summa rerum varietate exponuntur*, 2 vols (Amsterdam: Joannem Janssonium & Elizeum Weyerstraten,

NOTES

1665). See also P. Findlen (ed.), *Athanasius Kircher: The Last Man Who Knew Everything* (New York and London: Routledge, 2004); D. Stolzenberg, *Egyptian Oedipus: Athanasius Kircher and the Secrets of Antiquity* (Chicago and London: University of Chicago Press, 2013).

13 See Brooke-Hitching, op. cit., pp. 24–9.
14 See, for instance, Kershaw, op. cit. (2013), pp. 339–81.
15 See p. 173.
16 F. Cervantes de Salazar, *Crónica de la Nueva España* (Madrid: Magallón, c.1564). This remains a tactic used by some who would like to date the destruction to around that time, to make it fit with the Late Bronze Age eruption of the Thera volcano. See p. 308.
17 See Strabo 1.3.4, 1.3.5, quoted on p. 208. Relocating the Pillars of Heracles is similarly popular in some more recent Atlantis quests.
18 For a more recent theory of Odysseus in the Baltic, see F. Vinci, *The Baltic Origins of Homer's Epic Tales. The Iliad, the Odyssey and the Migration of Myth* (Rochester, VT: Inner Traditions, 2006). For the Argonauts' voyage in Greek mythology, see Kershaw, op. cit. (2007), pp. 92 ff.
19 See p. 368, n. 79.
20 Rudbeck explained away the discrepancies between the names by referring to Plato's *Critias* 113a–b, where Critias says that the names that Solon recorded had been translated from Atlantean to Egyptian to Greek.
21 http://www.uu.se/en/about-uu/history/rudbeck/ [accessed 8 August 2016]. See also P. Fjagesund, *The Dream of the North: A Cultural History to 1920* (Amsterdam and New York: Rodopi, 2014).

CHAPTER 10

1 J. Le Rond d'Alembert, 'Éléments de philosophie', in *Mélanges de Littératur, d'Histoire, et de Philosophie*, 6 vols (Amsterdam: Zacharie Chatelain & Fils, 1759), vol. IV, p. 3.
2 L. S. de Camp, *Lost Continents: The Atlantis Theme in History, Science and Literature* (New York: Gnome Press, 1954), p. 179.
3 J. Starobinski, 'Le mythe au XVIII siècle', *Critique*, no. 366 (1977), pp. 29–30.
4 P.-D. Huet, *Demonstratio Evangelica ad serenissimum Delphinum* (Paris: Stephanus Michallet, 1679), p. 149.
5 C. M. Olivier, *Dissertation sur le Critias de Platon* (1726), in N.-P. Desmollets, *Continuation des Mémoires de littérature et d'histoire de Mr. de Salengre* (Paris: Simart, 1730), p. 29f.
6 H. Scharbau, *Observationes sacrae quibus varia Sacri Codicis Utriusque foederis loca illustrantur, multaqve sanctioris et elegantioris doctrinae capita explicantur* (Lübeck: Schmid, 1731), pp. 381–415.
7 J. Euremius, *Atlantica Orientalis Eller Atlands Näs, Til des rätta Belägenhet beskrifwet för många år sedan* (Strengnäs: Sweden, 1751); Latin translation published as *Atlantica Orientalis sive Atlantis* (Berlin, Stralsund and Leipzig: Langium, 1764).
8 F.-C. Baer, *Essai historique et critique sur les Atlantiques dans lequel on se propose de faire voire la conformité qu'il y a entre de ce peuple et celle des Hébreux* (Paris: Lambert, 1762).
9 D. Diderot, in F. M. Grimm, *Correspondance inédite de Grimm et Diderot*, vol. XV (Paris: Fournier, 1829), pp. 160–72.

10 Vidal-Naquet, op. cit. (2007), p. 158, n. 7.

11 See F. Hartog, *The Mirror of Herodotus*, trans. Janet Lloyd, Berkeley (Los Angeles and London: University of California Press, 1988), pp. 301–3.

12 G. R. Carli, *Delle lettere Americane* (Paris: Buisson, 1788), vol. 1, letter 19, p. 7.

13 Ibid., vol. 2, letter 2, p. 20.

14 Ibid., second edition, vol. 2, letter 12, p. 212.

15 See R. Dalton, 'Archaeology blast in the past', *Nature*, no. CDXLVII (2007), pp. 256–7.

16 Carli, op. cit., vol. 2, letter 16, p. 212.

17 See, for example, E. J. Sweeney, *Atlantis: The Evidence of Science* (New York: Algora Publishing, 2010).

18 Carli, op. cit., vol. 2, letter 4, p. 62.

19 John Francis Gemelli Careri, *Voyage Around the World*, in A. and J. Churchill, *A Collection of Voyages and Travels*, 6 vols (London: Lintot and Osborn, third edition, 1745), Part 4, 5:514. Pyramids will feature in many other Atlantis theories: see pp. 243, 251 and 263.

20 Carli, op. cit., vol. 2, letter 45, p. 428.

21 Ibid., vol. 2, letter 10, pp. 150–1.

22 See S. Buccini, *The Americas in Italian Literature and Culture, 1700–1825* (University Park, PE: Penn State University Press, 1996).

23 See, for example, J.-S. Bailly, *Histoire de l'astronomie ancienne depuis son origine jusqu'à l'établissement de l'école d'Alexandrie* (Paris: Debure, 1775); *Histoire de l'astronomie moderne depuis la fondation de l'école d'Alexandrie, jusqu'à l'époque de M.D.CC.XXX* (Paris: Debure, 1779); *Traité de l'astronomie indienne et orientale* (Paris: Debure, 1787); *Lettres sur l'Origine des Sciences et sur celles des peuples de l'Asie* (London and Paris: Debure, 1779); *Lettres sur l'Atlantide de Platon et sur l'ancienne histoire de l'Asie* (London and Paris: Debure, 1779).

24 Bailly, op. cit. (1779), p. 103.

25 Ibid., p. 54.

26 Ibid., p. 83.

27 'Observations sur les deux deluges ou innondations d'Ogygès et de Deucalion', *Histoires et Mémoires de l'Académie des Inscriptions*, vol. 23 (1749–51), p. 132.

28 Vidal-Naquet, op. cit. (2007), p. 87.

29 E. Gibbon, *The History of the Decline and Fall of the Roman Empire* (London: Strahan and Cadell, 1776), vol. 1, p. 394, n.230.

30 J. B. D'Anville, *Géographie ancienne abrégée* (Paris: Merlin, 1768), vol. III, pp. 122–3.

31 Voltaire, *Essai sur les mœurs et l'esprit des nations* (1769), in *Oeuvres complètes de Voltaire* (Paris: Garnier, 1883), vol. XI, pp. 3–5.

32 Kircher, op. cit., vol. I, p. 82.

33 For example, J. B. M. Bory de Saint-Vincent, *Essai sur les îsles Fortunées et l'antique Atlantique* (Paris: Baudoin, 1803), pp 427–522.

34 J. P. de Tournefort, *Relation d'un Voyage au Levant* (Lyon: Anisson & Posuel, 1717), letter XV, p. 409.

35 Strabo, 1.3.5, trans. Jones, op. cit. By 'inflow' he means the current into the Atlantis from the Mediterranean.

36 N. A. Boulanger, *L'Antiquité dévoilée par les usages ou examen critique des principes opinions, cérémonies et institutions réligieuses et politiques des différents peuples de la térre*, 3 vols (Amsterdam: Rey, 1766).

37 For Fabre d'Olivet's contributions to Atlantis theorising, see pp. 209ff.

NOTES

38 A. Fabre d'Olivet, *Histoire philosophique du genre humain, ou L'homme considéré sous ses rapports religieux et politiques dans l'état social, à toutes les époques et chez les différents peuples de la terre, précédée d'une dissertation introductive sur les motifs et l'objet de cet ouvrage*, 2 vols (Paris: Brière, 1824), vol. I, p. 125.

39 N. A. Boulanger, *Recherches sur l'origine du despotisme oriental* (Geneva, 1761), section 6, pp. 60–1.

40 Ibid., Paris 1765 edition, p. 54.

41 Boulanger, op. cit. (1766), vol. II, pp. 325–404.

42 L. Poinsinet de Sivry, *Origines des premières sociétés, des peuples, des sciences, des arts, et des idioms anciens et modernes* (Amsterdam, 1769).

43 Vidal-Naquet, op. cit. (2007), p. 92.

44 G. Bartoli, *Discours par lequel Sa Majesté le roi de Suède a fait l'ouverture de la Diète, en suèdois, traduit en français et en vers italiens, avec un essai sur l'explication historique que Platon a donnée à son Atlantide et qu'on a pas considérée jusqu'a present . . .* (Stockholm, 1779), pp. 190–1.

45 The *philosophes* were the literary men, scientists and thinkers of eighteenth-century France who were dedicated to the advancement of science and secular thought, and the new tolerance and open-mindedness of the Enlightenment, and who shared a conviction about the supremacy and efficacy of human reason.

46 Bartoli, op. cit., pp. 190–1.

47 See, for example, *Critias* 121b, and p. 45ff.

48 Bartoli, op. cit., pp. 106–7.

49 Ibid., pp. 224–5.

50 T.-H. Martin, *Etudes sur le Timée de Platon* (Paris: Ladrange, 1841), vol. II, p. 280.

CHAPTER 11

1 See, for example, *Encyclopaedia Britannica*, s.v. 'Romanticism', https://www.britannica.com/art/Romanticism [accessed 13 January 2017].

2 J.-B.-C. Delisle de Sales, *Histoire nouvelle de tous les peuples du monde, ou Histoire des Hommes* (Paris, 1779).

3 Ibid., vol. I, pp. 50–51.

4 Ibid., vol. pp. lxviii, 227.

5 F.-.R. de Chateaubriand, *Le Génie du Christianisme* (Paris: Migneret, 1802), vol. I, pp. 143–4.

6 P. Leroux, *La Grive de Samarez*, ed. J.-P. Lacassagne (Paris: Klincksieck, 1979), vol. II, p. 447.

7 See L. Celier, *Fabre d'Olivet. Contribution à l'étude des aspects religieux du Romanticisme. Illuminisme – Théosophie* (Paris: Nizet, 1957), pp. 12–15.

8 *L'Invisible journal politique, littéraire et moral*, no. 7 (26 May 1797).

9 A. Fabre d'Olivet, *Lettres à Sophie sur l'histoire* (Paris, 1805), vol. I, pp. 206–84.

10 Ibid., vol. II, p. 7.

11 Vidal-Naquet, op. cit. (2007), p. 102.

12 A. Fabre d'Olivet, *Histoire philosophique du genre humain, ou L'homme considéré sous ses rapports religieux et politiques dans l'état social, à toutes les époques et chez les différents peuples de la terre, précédée d'une dissertation introductive sur les motifs et l'objet de cet ouvrage*, 2 vols (Paris, 1824).

13 Ibid., vol. I, p. 5. See Vidal-Naquet, op. cit. (2007), p. 102.

14 Fabre d'Olivet, op. cit. (1824), vol. I, p. 67 f.

15 Ibid., vol. I, p. 135 f.

16 Ibid., vol. I, pp. 190–2.

17 Ibid., vol. I, p. 308 f.

18 Ibid., vol. I, 195 f., 309 f.

19 Exodus 2.11–14.

20 Fabre d'Olivet, op. cit. (1824), vol. I, p. 308 f.

21 Ibid., vol. I, pp. 326–35.

22 Ibid., vol. I, p. 193.

23 Vidal-Naquet, op. cit. (2007), p. 105 f.

24 See G. Keynes (ed.), *Blake: Complete Writings with Variant Readings* (Oxford: Oxford University Press, 1979), pp. 578, 580.

25 W. Blake, *Jerusalem: The Emanation of The Giant Albion*, object 27 (Bentley 27, Erdman 27, Keynes 27), 'To the Jews'.

26 Ibid., object 86 (Bentley 86, Erdman 86, Keynes 86); object 91 (Bentley 91, Erdman 91, Keynes 91).

27 Ibid., object 49 (Bentley 49, Erdman 49, Keynes 49).

28 Ibid., object 36 (Bentley 36, Erdman 32, Keynes 36).

29 *America a Prophecy*, object 12 (Bentley 12, Erdman 10, Keynes 10).

30 M. Holley, 'Blake's Atlantis', *Colby Quarterly*, no. 30 (1994), p. 109.

31 N. Leask, *British Romantic Writers and the East: Anxieties of Empire* (Cambridge: Cambridge University Press, 2004), p. 107. Cf. J. Malik, *Perspectives of Mutual Encounters in South Asian History, 1760–1860* (Leiden: Brill, 2000); A. Gilroy, *Romantic Geographies: Discourses of Travel, 1775–1844* (Manchester: Manchester University Press, 2000).

32 See p. 130.

33 The Greek mythological tradition here is complex and contradictory (which often suits theories like this): the White Isle, aka the Islands of the Blessed, was often located in the western stream of Oceanus, although some later Greek writers associate the White Isle with an island near the mouth of the Danube, and place Islands of the Blessed in the Atlantic Ocean. See Homer, *Odyssey* 24.12 ff.; Arctinus of Miletus, *Aethiopis* fragment 1; Apollodorus, *Epitome* 5.5; Pausanias 3.19.11–13; Antoninus Liberalis, *Metamorphoses* 27; Servius, *On Virgil Eclogues* 7.61.

34 See Leask, op. cit., p. 213.

35 *Asiatic Researches*, no. 11 (1810), pp. 4, 48, 53, 69, 74, 80, 89. See A. Gilroy, *Romantic Geographies: Discourses of Travel, 1775–1844* (Manchester: Manchester University Press, 2000).

36 Leask, op. cit., p. 107.

37 F. Wilford, 'An Essay on Sacred Isles in the West', *Asiatic Review*, no. 8 (1805), p. 251. See U. App, *The Birth of Orientalism* (Philadelphia, PA: University of Pennsylvania Press, 2010), p. 335.

CHAPTER 12

1 See p. 171f.

2 F. W. H. A. Humboldt, *Personal narrative of travels to the equinoctial regions of the New Continent during the years 1799–1804* (London: Longman, Hurst, Rees, Orme and Brown, 1814), vol. I, p, 201. Madrepores are types of coral.

3 See p. 361, n. 40.

4 See F. M. Cross, 'The Phoenician inscription from Brazil: A nineteenth-century forgery', *Orientalia*, no. XXXVII (1968), pp. 437–60; C. H. Gordon, 'The authenticity of the Phoenician text from Parahyba', *Orientalia*, no. XXXVII (1968), pp. 75–80; C. H. Gordon, 'Reply to Professor Cross', *Orientalia*, no. XXXVII (1968), pp. 461–3; C. H. Gordon, *Before Columbus: Links Between the Old World and Ancient America* (New York: Crown, 1971), pp. 120–7; C. H. Gordon, *Riddles in History* (New York: Crown, 1974), pp. 71–92; M. F. Doran, 'Phoenician contact with America?', *Anthropological Journal of Canada*, vol. XII, no. 2 (1974), pp. 16–24; R. H. Fritze, *Invented Knowledge: False History, Fake Science and Pseudo-Religions* (London: Reaktion Books, 2009), pp. 83–8.

5 T.-H. Martin, *Etudes sur le Timée de Platon* (Paris: Ladrange, 1841), vol. 1, pp. 257–333.

6 Ibid., p. 257.

7 Ibid., p. 281.

8 Ibid., pp. 330–2.

9 Ibid., p. 333.

10 Vidal-Naquet, op. cit. (2007), p. 14.

11 See, for example, http://www.crystalinks.com/mayanism.html [accessed 14 January 2017].

12 C.-E. Brasseur de Bourbourg, *Grammaire élémentaire de la langue quichée* (Paris: Bertrand, 1862).

13 See p. 170f.

14 C.-E. Brasseur de Bourbourg, *Manuscrit Troano. Études sur le système graphique et la langue des Mayas* (Paris: Imp. impér., 1869–70), published under the name of the Commission scientifique du Mexique.

15 C.-E. Brasseur de Bourbourg, and J.-F. Waldeck, *Monuments anciens du Mexique. Palenqué et autres ruines de l'ancienne civilisation du Mexique. Collection de vues, has-reliefs, morceaux d'architecture, etc.* (Paris: Bertrand, 1866). See also C.-E. Brasseur de Bourbourg, *Recherches sur les ruines de Palenque et les origines de la civilisation du Mexique* (Paris: Bertrand, 1866).

16 C.-E. Brasseur de Bourbourg, *Quatre Lettres sur le Méxique: exposition absolue du système hiéroglyphique mexicain, la fin de l'âge de pierre: d'après le Teo-Amoxtli et autres documents mexicains, etc.* (Paris: Durand et Pedone, 1868).

17 See, for example, Mythology.net Editors (2014), 'Mu', http://mythology.net/others/concepts/mu/# [accessed 14 January 2017].

18 See https://en.oxforddictionaries.com/word-of-the-year/word-of-the-year–2016 [accessed 14 January 2017].

19 Matthew 27.46.

20 J. Verne, *Vingt mille lieues sous les mers* (Paris: Hetzel, 1871). The illustrations are by Alphonse de Neuville and Édouard Riou.

21 Fritze, op. cit., p. 34.

22 See M. Ridge, *Ignatius Donnelly: Portrait of a Politician* (Chicago: University of Chicago Press, 1962); R. G. Kennedy, 'The Wild Jackass of the Prairie: The Heroism of Ignatius Donnelly', in *Rediscovering America* (Boston: Houghton Mifflin), 1990.

23 S. H. Holbrook, *Lost Men of American History* (New York, Macmillan, 1946), p. 271.

24 See de Camp, op. cit., p. 37.

25 I. Donnelly, *Atlantis: The Antediluvian World* (New York: Harper and Brothers, 1882).

26 I. Donnelly, *Ragnarok: The Age of Fire and Gravel* (New York: Appleton, 1883).
27 See, for example, http://www.livescience.com/40311-pleistocene-epoch.html [accessed 14 January 2017].
28 I. Donnelly, *The Great Cryptogram: Francis Bacon's Cipher in the So-called Shakespeare Plays* (New York and London: Peale, 1888).
29 E. Boisgilbert (pseud.), *Caesar's Column: A Story of the Twentieth Century* (Chicago: Schulte, 1891).
30 Donnelly, op. cit. (1882), p. 3.
31 Ibid., p. 1 f.
32 See Ridge, op. cit., p. 198. This style of presentation, which allows scope for considerable rhetorical flourishes, is often favoured by writers after Donnelly. See, for example, Peter Tompkins' introduction to Otto Muck, *The Secret of Atlantis* (London: Collins, 1978), pp. vii–xi.
33 De Camp, op. cit., p. 42.
34 W. M. F. Petrie, *Seventy Years in Archaeology* (London: Low, 1931), p. 34 f.
35 This has been effectively done by a number of writers. See, for example, de Camp, op. cit.; P. Jordan, *The Atlantis Syndrome* (Stroud: Sutton Publishing, 2001); E. S. Ramage (ed.), *Atlantis: Fact or Fiction?* (Bloomington, IN and London: Indiana University Press, 1978). The following discussion owes much to Ramage, pp. 33–6.
36 Donnelly, op. cit. (1882), p. 111.
37 Ibid., pp. 230–8.
38 Ibid., p. 157 f.
39 See Ridge, op. cit., p. 201 f.
40 Fritze, op. cit., p. 37.
41 The process is well explained by the Geological Society at https://www.geolsoc.org.uk/Plate-Tectonics/Chap3-Plate-Margins/Divergent/Mid-Atlantic-Ridge [accessed 15 January 2017].
42 See M. Allaby, in *A Dictionary of Geology and Earth Sciences*, fourth edition, s.v. 'Tachylyte', http://oxfordindex.oup.com/view/10.1093/acref/9780199653065.013.8358 [accessed 25 January 2017].
43 See de Camp, op. cit., pp. 47–54; S. Ramaswamy, *The Lost Land of Lemuria; Fabulous Geographies, Catastrophic Histories* (Berkeley, CA: University of California Press, 2004), pp. 19–52.
44 Donnelly, op. cit. (1882), p. 497.

Chapter 13

1 See, for example, Papamarinopoulos, op. cit. (2007); Papamarinopoulos, op. cit. (2010).
2 H. P. Blavatsky, *Isis Unveiled, A Master-Key to the Mysteries of Ancient and Modern Science and Theology* (Pasadena, CA: Theosophical University Press, 1877).
3 Richard Hodgson, quoted in P. Washington, *Madame Blavatsky's Baboon: A History of the Mystics, Mediums, and Misfits Who Brought Spiritualism to America* (New York: Schocken, 1995), p. 83.
4 H. P. Blavatsky, *The Secret Doctrine, The Synthesis of Science, Religion, and Philosophy* (Pasadena, CA: Theosophical University Press, 1888).
5 See S. Williams, *Fantastic Archaeology: The Wild Side of North American Prehistory* (Philadelphia, PA: University of Philadelphia Press, 1991), pp. 140–5; de Camp, op. cit., pp. 54–70.

NOTES

6 Blavatsky, op. cit. (1888), vol. II, pp. 86–108.
7 Ibid., vol. II, pp. 109–30.
8 Ibid., vol. II, pp. 131–85.
9 Ibid., vol. II, pp. 191–250.
10 W. Scott-Elliot, *The Story of Atlantis* (1896) and *The Lost Lemuria* (1904), later combined as *The Story of Atlantis & The Lost Lemuria* (London: Theosophical Publishing House, 1925).
11 W. Scott-Elliot, *The Story of Atlantis* (London: Theosophical Publishing Society, 1896), p. 18.
12 Scott-Elliot, op. cit. (1896), p. 41.
13 Tompkins, op. cit., p. xi.
14 See, for example, http://www.akashicsecrets.com/akashic-records [accessed 15 April 2017].
15 E. E. Cayce, *Edgar Cayce on Atlantis* (New York: Hawthorn, 1968), p. 26 f.
16 Virgil, *Aeneid* 6.724 ff., trans. C. Day Lewis, in *The Eclogues, Georgics and Aeneid of Virgil* (Oxford: Oxford University Press, 1966).
17 See W. Stein, *Atlantis Opposing Views* (San Diego, CA: Greenhaven, 1989).
18 Virgil, *Aeneid* 6.735 ff.
19 See, for example, http://www.genetics.org.uk/Home.aspx [accessed 19 January 2017].
20 See, for example, R. J. Bain, 'Pleistocene Beach Rock in a Subtidal-Beach-Dune Sequence, Quarry A', in *Pleistocene and Holocene Carbonate Environments on San Salvador Island, Bahamas: San Salvador Island, Bahamas, July 2–7, 1989*, eds H. A. Curran, R. J. Bain, J. L. Carew, J. E. Mylroie, J. W. Teeter and B. White (Washington, DC: American Geophysical Union, 1989).
21 E. S. Ramage, 'Perspectives ancient and modern', in E. S. Ramage (ed.), *Atlantis: Fact or Fiction?* (Bloomington, IN and London: Indiana University Press, 1978), p. 36.
22 De Camp, op. cit., p. 91. Spence, op. cit. (1924).
23 L. Spence, *Atlantis in America* (London: Benn, 1925); L. Spence, *The History of Atlantis* (London: Rider, 1927).
24 Spence, op. cit. (1924), p. 75.
25 See, for example, http://humanorigins.si.edu/evidence/human-fossils/fossils/cro-magnon-1 [accessed 19 January 2017].
26 Spence, op. cit. (1924), p. 85.
27 Ibid., p. 88.
28 Ibid., p. 80.
29 Spence, op. cit. (1925), p. 66, repeated verbatim in Spence, op. cit. (1927), p. 151.
30 Spence, op. cit. (1927), p. 2.
31 Ibid.
32 R. N. R. B. in *Geographical Journal*, vol. 64, no. 2 (1924), p. 181 f.
33 See http://pseudoarchaeology.org/whatis.html [accessed 21 January 2017]; http://anthropology.msu.edu/anp203h-ss14/2014/03/30/ancient-aliens-and-pseudoarchaeology [accessed 21 January 2017].
34 Dust-jacket notes to O. Muck, *The Secret of Atlantis* (London: Collins, 1978).
35 This is not to say that mainstream archaeology is free of this – it isn't – but the analysis of bias continually helps to improve archaeological theory and practice.
36 Pseudoarchaeology supporters routinely accuse genuine archaeologists of 'only doing it for the money', but no mainstream archaeologist can match the multi-million sales figures of, say, Erich von Däniken or Graham Hancock.

37 An example might be if I said, 'There is a litter of 10-metre high invisible liver and white spaniel puppies living under the trees at the end of my garden, but sadly no type of scientific equipment can detect them.' I might not be lying – this might be true – but the statement is deliberately framed so that can't be falsified in any way. We would need much better evidence to take it seriously. See B. Bennett, *Logically Fallacious: The Ultimate Collection of Over 300 Logical Fallacies* (Ebookit.com, 2012).

38 See, for example, G. G. Fagan (ed.), *Archaeological Fantasies: How Pseudoarchaeology Misrepresents the Past and Misleads the Public* (London and New York: Routledge, 2006).

39 G. Orwell, *Nineteen Eighty-Four* (New York: Harcourt Brace, 1949), p. 53.

40 K. G. Zschaetzsch, *Atlantis die Urheimat der Arier mit eine Karte* (Berlin: Arier-Verlag, 1922).

41 Jordanes, *Getica* 4.25.

42 Zschaetzsch, op. cit., p. 94.

43 E, Kiss, *Die letzte Königin von Atlantis: ein Roman aus der Zeit um 12000 vor Christi Geburt* (Leipzig: Koehler & Amelang, 1931). See also, for example, J. Beresford, 'The Nazis and the search for Atlantis', *Minerva: The International Review of Ancient Art & Archaeology* (May/June 2011), pp. 46–9.

44 Virgil, *Georgics* 1.30.

45 Kiss, op. cit., p. 31.

46 A. Herrmann, *Unsere Ahnen und Atlantis: Nordische Seeherrschaft von Skandinavien bis Nordafrika* (Berlin: Klinkhardt und Biermann, 1934).

47 Ibid., pp. 144–53.

48 Ibid., pp. 144–50.

49 See K. Anderson, *Hitler and the Occult* (Amherst, NY: Prometheus, 1995).

50 See pp. 191, 204.

51 See H. L. Cayce (ed.), *Edgar Cayce on Atlantis* (New York: Warner, 1968), pp. 24–72. See pp. 252ff.

52 See W. J. McCann, '"Volk und Germanentum": The presentation of the past in Nazi Germany', in P. Gathercole and D. Lowenthal (eds), *The Politics of the Past* (London: Unwin Hyman, 1990), p. 79.

53 W. J. McCann, 'The National Socialist perversion of archaeology', *World Archaeological Bulletin*, no. 2 (1988), p. 52.

54 H. Arendt, *The Origins of Totalitarianism* (New York: Harcourt, Brace and Co., 1951), p. 474.

55 Voltaire, *Questions sur les miracles* (1765), trans. N. L. Torrey, in *Les Philosophes: The Philosophers of the Enlightenment and Modern Democracy*, ed. N. L. Torrey (New York: Capricorn, 1960), pp. 277–8.

CHAPTER 14

1 Plato, *Republic* 522c–32a.

2 Fritze, op. cit., p. 185.

3 De Camp, op. cit., p. 89.

4 I. Velikovsky, *Worlds in Collision* (Garden City, NY: Doubleday, 1950).

5 I. Velikovsky, *Ages in Chaos* (Garden City, NY: Doubleday, 1952).

6 I. Velikovsky, *Earth in Upheaval* (Garden City, NY: Doubleday, 1955).

7 W. Whiston, *A New Theory of the Earth, From its Original, to the Consummation of All Things, Where the Creation of the World in Six Days, the Universal Deluge, And*

the General Conflagration, As laid down in the Holy Scriptures, Are Shewn to be perfectly agreeable to Reason and Philosophy (London: Tooke, 1696).

8 Velikovsky, op. cit. (1955), pp. 274–7.

9 See, for instance, http://abob.libs.uga.edu/bobk/vdtopten.html [accessed 21 January 2017].

10 Velikovsky, op. cit. (1950), p. 37.

11 Joshua 10.11–14.

12 Velikovsky, op. cit. (1950), p. 63.

13 See p. 231.

14 From the 1985 Tedlock translation.

15 Velikovsky, op. cit. (1950), p. 116. His chapter 6 is titled 'A Collective Amnesia'.

16 See T. Palmer, *Perilous Planet Earth: Catastrophes and Catastrophism through the Ages* (Cambridge: Cambridge University Press, 2003), pp. 114–24, 133–60, 215–51.

17 L. Ellenberger, 'A lesson from Velikovsky', an expanded version of a letter that appeared in *Skeptical Inquirer*, vol. X, no. 4 (1986), pp. 380–81, http://(bob.libs.uga.edu/bobk/vlesson.html [accessed 22 January 2017].

18 D. Hume, *An Enquiry concerning Human Understanding* (1748), ch. 10.4.

19 M. Truzzi, 'On the extraordinary: An attempt at clarification', *Zetetic Scholar*, vol. I, no. 1 (1978), p. 11.

20 In an article commissioned, but not published, by *Illustrated Magazine* in 1952.

21 C. Sagan, 'Encyclopaedia Galactica', *Cosmos*, Episode 12 (14 December 1980).

22 A. E. Eddington, 'The borderland of astronomy and geology', *Smithsonian Reports* (1923), pp. 195–202.

23 H. A. Brown, *Popular Awakening Concerning the Impending Flood. Lithographed manuscript copy of a proposed illustrated book, copyright 1948, with corrections and additions inserted by the author to 1951* (Ann Arbor, MI: Edwards, 1951).

24 K. A. Pauly, 'The cause of Great Ice Ages', *Scientific Monthly* (August 1952). See also J. White, *Pole Shift: Predictions and Prophecies of the Ultimate Disaster* (New York: Doubleday, 1980).

25 C. H. Hapgood and J. H. Campbell, *The Earth's Shifting Crust: A Key to Some Basic Problems of Earth Science* (New York: Pantheon, 1958).

26 Ibid., p. 14.

27 Ibid.

28 Ibid., p. 1.

29 P. Reid, '2012: Magnetic pole reversal happens all the (geologic) time', https://www.nasa.gov/topics/earth/features/2012-poleReversal.html (30 November 2011) [accessed 21 January 2017].

30 See *The Path of the Pole* (Philadelphia, PA: Chilton, 1970), a more or less revised version of *The Earth's Shifting Crust*.

31 C. H. Hapgood, *Maps of the Ancient Sea Kings: Evidence of Advanced Civilization in the Ice Age* (Philadelphia, PA: Chilton, 1966).

32 See Brotton, op. cit. (2015), pp. 90–3.

33 See, for example, https://www.uwgb.edu/dutchs/PSEUDOSC/PiriRies.HTM [accessed 21 January 2017; https://badarchaeology.wordpress.com/tag/maps [accessed 21 January 2017].

34 See p. 171.

35 See, for example, Brotton, op. cit. (2012), pp. 234 ff.; Brooke-Hitching, op. cit., pp. 134 f., 224 ff.

36 See D. C. Jolly, 'Was Antarctica mapped by the ancients?', *Skeptical Inquirer*, no. XI (1986), p. 38.

37 See P. James and N. Thorpe, *Ancient Mysteries* (New York: Ballantine, 1999), pp. 73–5.

38 R. and R. Flem-Ath, *When the Sky Fell: In Search of Atlantis* (London: Weidenfeld & Nicolson, 1995).

39 R. Flem-Ath and C. Wilson, *The Atlantis Blueprint: Unlocking the Ancient Mysteries of a Long-Lost Civilization* (London: Little, Brown, 2000).

40 Flem-Ath, op. cit. (1995), p. xv.

41 Ibid., pp. 94 ff.

42 See p. 191.

43 See http://www.atlascoelestis.com/Haci%201559%20base.htm [accessed 21 January 2017].

44 See p. 191.

45 Flem-Ath, op. cit. (1995), pp. 134–5.

46 Ibid., p. 150.

47 Conversation quoted in Adams, op. cit., p. 89.

48 Ibid., p. 91.

49 Ibid.

50 G. Hancock, *Fingerprints of the Gods: A Quest for the Beginning and the End* (London: Heinemann, 1995).

51 See, for example, M. Brass, 'Tracing Graham Hancock's shifting cataclysm', *Skeptical Inquirer*, vol. 26, no. 4 (2002), http://www.csicop.org/si/show/tracing_graham_hancockrsquos_shifting_cataclysm [accessed 21 January 2017].

52 *Washington Times* (30 December 2015).

53 G. Hancock, *Magicians of the Gods: The Forgotten Wisdom of Earth's Lost Civilization* (New York: Thomas Dunne Books/St Martin's Press, 2015).

54 https://grahamhancock.com/magicians [accessed 24 August 2016].

55 https://grahamhancock.com/magicians [accessed 24 August 2016].

56 Interview by Rupert Hawksley, *Telegraph* (4 October 2015).

57 https://grahamhancock.com/magicians [accessed 24 August 2016].

58 Interview by Rupert Hawksley, *Telegraph* (4 October 2015).

59 First published in German as *Erinnerungen an die Zukunft: Ungelöste Rätsel der Vergangenheit* (Düsseldorf: Econ, 1968).

60 Fritze, op. cit., p. 207.

61 A projection in which a region of the earth is projected onto a plane tangential to the surface. See http://gisgeography.com/azimuthal-projection-orthographic-stereographic-gnomonic [accessed 15 April 2017].

62 A projection in which you wrap a cylinder around a globe and then unravel it. See http://gisgeography.com/cylindrical-projection [accessed 15 April 2017].

63 E. von Däniken, *Odyssey of the Gods: The Alien History of Ancient Greece* (London: Vega 1998), p. 145.

64 Ibid., p. 146.

65 Ibid., p. 146.

66 *Critias* 115c.

67 Von Däniken, op. cit. (1998), p. 147.

68 Ibid., p. 147.

69 Ibid., p. 98.

70 E. Zangger, *The Flood from Heaven: Deciphering the Atlantis Legend* (London: Sidgwick & Jackson, 1992).

71 Ibid., p. 14.

72 See Kershaw, op. cit. (2010), pp. 47 ff.

73 E. Zangger, 'Plato's Atlantis account – a distorted recollection of the Trojan War', *Oxford Journal of Archaeology*, vol. 12, no. 1 (1993), pp. 77–87.

74 T. Bryce, *The Trojans and Their Neighbours* (London and New York: Routledge, 2006), p. 193.

75 De Camp, op. cit., p. 80.

CHAPTER 15

1 Homer, *Odyssey* 19.172–9, trans. E. V. Rieu, *Homer, The Odyssey* (Harmondsworth: Penguin Classics, 1946).

2 For Cretan mythology, see Kershaw, op. cit. (2007), pp. 275–95.

3 Our first literary works to mention the Minoan thalassocracy (sea-empire) come from Herodotus (3.122.2) and Thucydides (1.4) in fifth-century BC Athens, and the written tradition about Minos' expedition against Athens to avenge Androgeus is only as old as the third-century BC Atthidographer Philochorus (*FGrHist* 328 F17). So the Minoan thalassocracy might be a fifth-century BC Athenian invention, although there could be an older oral tradition behind it. See https://classical-studies.org/annual-meeting/147/abstract/athenian-thalassocracy-minos%E2%80%99-sea-power-archaic-and-non-athenian#sthash.ecqqqLDr.dpuf [accessed 16 April 2017].

4 Bacchylides, *Dithyramb* 17.92 ff., trans. A. Miller, in S. M. Trzaskoma, R. Scott Smith and S. Brunet (eds), *Anthology of Classical Myth* (Indianapolis, IN: Hackett, 2004), p. 72.

5 There is another tradition in which he wears a wreath, which lights up the darkness in the Labyrinth. Ariadne wore it until she was deserted by Theseus and rescued by Dionysus, when it became the constellation Corona.

6 A. J. Evans, *The Palace of Minos at Knossos*, vols I–IV with index volume (London: Macmillan, 1921–36).

7 Quoted in D. Powell, *The Villa Ariadne* (London: Hodder and Stoughton, 1973), p. 30.

8 See p. 384, n. 128.

9 This is pretty securely dated by archaeology, but subject to the usual academic caveats and disputes – scholars pretty much agree on the order of events, but not on the absolute chronology, thereby leaving both expert and non-expert alike facing a confusing picture in which, for instance, the Late Minoan period can start as early as 1600 BC (the 'conventional chronology') or as late as 1700 BC (the 'high' chronology').

10 ' "The Lost Continent" (From a correspondent)', *The Times* (19 February 1909).

11 The Minoans had excellent plumbing systems, just like the Atlanteans: cf. Plato, *Critias* 115c ff.

12 See Plato, *Critias* 119d–e.

13 *Timaeus* 25a.

14 J. V. Luce, *The End of Atlantis: New Light on an Old Legend*, New Aspects of Antiquity series (London: Thames & Hudson, 1969), pp. 46 ff., 176 ff.

15 Ibid., p. 35.

16 C. Gill, op. cit., pp. xi–xii.

17 See Kershaw, op. cit. (2010), pp. 27 ff.

18 See Luce, op. cit. (1969), p. 194.

19 See, for example, P. Y. Forsyth, *Thera in the Bronze Age* (New York: Lang, 1999); G. E. Vougioukalakis, *The Minoan Eruption of the Thera Volcano and the Aegean World* (Athens: Society for the Promotion of Studies on Prehistoric Thera, 2006).
20 Marinatos' ideas still get repeated, even now. BBC TV's *Timewatch*, 'Atlantis: The Evidence', directed by Natalie Maynes (2 June 2010), is a case in point: 'Historian Bettany Hughes unravels one of the most intriguing mysteries of all time. She presents a series of geological, archaeological and historical clues to show that the legend of Atlantis was inspired by a real historical event, the greatest natural disaster of the ancient world'.
21 S. Marinatos, *Some Words about the Legend of Atlantis*, translated from *Cretica Chronica* IV (1950) (Athens: Archaeological Deltion – No. 12 – of the General Direction of Antiquities and Restoration, second edition, 1971), pp. 195–213.
22 Ibid., pp. 14, 46.
23 Ibid., p. 46.
24 Ibid., p. 46.
25 L. Brisson, *Plato the Myth Maker* (Chicago: University of Chicago Press, 1998), pp. 21 ff. What follows is heavily derived from Brisson's discussion.
26 E. Benveniste, 'Formes et lens de mnaomaï', *Sprachgeschichte and Wortbedeutung. FestschriftAlbert Debrunner* (Berne: Francke, 1954), pp. 13–18.
27 Plato, *Timaeus* 23d; *Critias* 110a.
28 Plato, *Timaeus* 20e, 21a, 22a, 22b, 22e, 23a, 23b; *Critias* 110a.
29 Plato, *Timaeus* 21a, 22a, 22b; Brisson, op. cit. (1998), p. 21
30 See p. 33.
31 Plato, *Laws* 680d3, 682a8.
32 Plato, *Timaeus* 24a–b.
33 Ibid., 23a.
34 Brisson, op. cit. (1998), p. 22.
35 H. Fränkel, 'Die Zeitauffassung in der frügriechischen Literatur', in F. Tietze (ed.), *Wege und Formen frügriechischen Denken* (Munich: Beck, second edition, 1960), p. 2.
36 Nielsen, op. cit., p. 35.
37 *Republic* 382c–d, quoted on p. 360, n. 29.
38 Herodotus 1.147.4.
39 Apollonius Rhodius, *Argonautica* 4.1743 ff.
40 See, for example, A. B. Knapp and S. W. Manning, 'Crisis in context: The end of the Late Bronze Age in the Eastern Mediterranean', *American Journal of Archaeology*, vol. 120, no. 1 (2016), pp. 99–149.
41 W. L. Friedrich, B. Kromer, M. Friedrich, J. Heinemeier, T. Pfeiffer and S. Talamo, 'Santorini eruption radiocarbon dated to 1627–1600 BC', *Science*, no. 28 (April 2006), p. 548.
42 See J. Heinemeier, W. L. Friedrich, B. Kromer and C. Bronk Ramsey, 'The Minoan eruption of Santorini radiocarbon dated by an olive tree buried by the eruption', in D. A. Warburton (ed.), *Time's Up! Dating the Minoan Eruption of Santorini* (Athens: Danish Institute at Athens, 2009), pp. 285–93.
43 S. W. Manning et al., 'Dating the Thera (Santorini) eruption: Archaeological and scientific evidence supporting a high chronology', *Antiquity*, no. 88 (2014), pp. 1164–79.
44 C. Gill, op. cit., p. x.
45 G. Heiken and F. McCoy, 'Caldera development during the Minoan eruption, Thira, Cyclades, Greece', *Journal of Geophysical Research*, no. 89 (1984), p. 8448.

46 Fig. 7b, Heiken and McCoy, op. cit., p. 8450; Fig 7c, W. L. Friedrich et al.,
'Existence of a water-filled caldera prior to the Minoan eruption of Santorini,
Greece', *Naturwissenschaften*, no. 75 (1988), pp. 567–9; Fig 7d, T. H. Druitt and V.
Francaviglia, 'An ancient caldera cliff line at Phira, and its significance for the
topography and geology of pre-Minoan Santorini', in D. A. Hardy (ed.), *Thera and
the Aegean World III: Earth Sciences* (London: The Thera Foundation, 1990), pp.
362–9; Fig 7e, U. Eriksen et al., 'The Stronghyle caldera: Geological, palaeonto-
logical and stable isotope evidence from radio carbon dated stromatolites from
Santorini', in Hardy, op. cit., pp. 139–50; Fig. 7f, Forsyth, op. cit., pp. 10 ff.
47 Dio Cassius, *Epitome of Book* 61.7.
48 C. Gill, op. cit., p. xii.

CHAPTER 16

1 C. Gill, op. cit., p. vii.
2 Thucydides 6.76.4.
3 See, for example, W. Welliver, *Character, Plot and Thought in Plato's Timaeus-
Critias* (Leiden: Brill, 1977), p. 56 f.
4 A. N. Kontaratos, 'Criteria for the search of Atlantis', in Papamarinopoulos, op.
cit. (2007), pp. 573–6.
5 See www.atlantis-scout.de [accessed 28 January 2017]; T. C. Franke, U. Hofmann,
U. Richter, C. M. Schoppe and S. M. Schoppe, 'The Atlantis Research Charter: A
defined position in the colourful world of Atlantis research', in Papamarinopoulos,
op. cit. (2010), pp. 637–43.
6 Ibid., p. 640.
7 Ibid., p. 641.
8 http://atlantipedia.ie/samples [accessed 28 January 2017].
9 http://atlantipedia.ie/samples/21st-century-location-theories [accessed 26 August
2016]. Adams, op. cit., provides an entertaining survey of a number of these.
10 Quoted on p. 360, n. 29.
11 Plato, *Timaeus* 26e.
12 See p. 309.
13 See, for example, *Timaeus* 22a ff., 24c–d; *Critias* 109b.
14 *Timaeus* 21c–d.
15 Hesiod, *Works and Days* 109 ff.
16 Hesiod, *Theogony* 215 f.
17 Homer, *Odyssey* 1.53 f.; Hesiod, *Theogony* 517 f., 746 ff.
18 Hesiod, *Theogony* 678 ff., trans., D. Wender, *Hesiod and Theognis* (Harmondsworth:
Penguin Classics, 1973).
19 *Timaeus* 81e–2b.
20 *Critias* 115c–d.
21 *Republic* 372e–3e.
22 As does C. Gill, op. cit., p. xvi.
23 Letter to Bishop Mandell Creighton, 5 April 1887, published in J. N. Figgis and R.
V. Laurence (eds), *Historical Essays and Studies* (London: Macmillan, 1907).
24 Plato, *Gorgias* 523, trans. W. Hamilton, *Plato: Gorgias* (Harmondsworth: Penguin
Classics, rev. edn, 1971).
25 Plato, *Republic* 377, trans. D. Lee, *Plato: The Republic* (Harmondsworth: Penguin
Classics, second edition [revised], 1987).

26 Plato, *Protagoras* 320, trans. W. C. K. Guthrie, *Plato: Protagoras and Meno* (Harmondsworth: Penguin Classics, 1956).

27 Plato, *Phaedrus* 275b4–5, trans. C. Rowe, *Plato: Phaedrus* (Harmondsworth: Penguin Classics, 2005).

28 Herodotus 2.45.

29 I am indebted to my student Dominic Windram from Oxford University's Greek Mythology Online course for drawing my attention to these lines.

30 Bryce, op. cit., p. 197.

31 Plato, *Republic* 382d, quoted on p. 360, n. 29.

Index

Acosta, Father José de, 173–8
Acropolis, 92–3
Adams, M·ark, 287
Aegeus, King, 297–8
Aegine, expulsion of Athenians, 52
Aegospotami, 58
Aelian, 109, 111–12
Aeschylus, 5, 111
  The Persians, 42
Agamemnon, King, 293
'Age of Cronos', 30
Alaric, 193
Albion, 220–3
Alcibiades, 45, 57
Alcman, 111
Alexander the Great, 38, 108, 112, 121,
  128–9, 147, 159, 179, 216
Alexandria, Library at, 129–30, 291,
  311–12
Amazons, 131–2
Amelius, 141–2, 145–6
Ammianus Marcellinus, 147–8
Ammi-saduqa, King, 336
Ampheres, 95
Amphipolis, 56
Anaxagoras, 44
Anaxilaïdes, 54
Antaeus, 15
Antigonus, 38
Antilia (Antillia), 160, 162, 171, 257–9
Antilles, 160, 167, 227
Antipater of Sidon, 34
Antipatros of Thessalonica, 34
Antonine Wall, 25
Apatouria festival, 67, 76
Apollodorus, 10, 18, 50, 111, 195, 334
Apollonius of Rhodes, 17, 311–12
Archedemus, 64
Archytas of Tarentum, 61, 64

Arendt, Hannah, 268
Arginousae, 58
Argos, 61
Ariadne, 299
Ariston, 49, 54
Aristophanes, 5
  Assembly Women, 120
  The Clouds, 56
Aristotle, 27, 30, 44, 51, 65, 108,
  114–17, 128, 135, 195, 283, 319
  Cosmas Indicopleustes and, 155–6
  influence on Columbus, 163
  Meteorology, 115
  On Marvellous Things Heard
    (Pseudo-Aristotle), 115–16, 167
  On the Heavens, 114–15
  Proclus and, 151–3
Arnobius of Sicca, 146–7
Artaxerxes, King, 63
Arthur, King, 158, 181, 294
Asclepius, 144
Atalante, 56, 135
Athena, 4, 17, 77, 89–90, 93, 125, 139,
  276
  associated with the moon, 144
  birth of, 68
  equated with Neïth, 127
  festival of, 68, 74, 321
Athens
  antediluvian, 3–4, 90–4, 322–3
  approach to democracy, 27–31
  archonship of Ameinias, 51–2
  archonship of Lysimachus, 51
  Corinthian War, 59, 61–2
  earthquakes, 55–6, 92–3
  equates with Atlantis, 212–13,
    319–23
  Five Thousand Legislators, 58
  invasion of Sicily, 57–8, 321–3

Lucanian War, 64
outbreak of plague, 45–8
Pentekontaetia, 42–5
rule of the Four Hundred, 58
Second Athenian Confederacy/
  League, 62–3
Social War, 63
Thirty Tyrants, 54–5, 59
see also Peloponnesian War; Persian
  Wars
Atlantic Ocean
  Carthaginian voyages, 167, 227–8
  chasmatiae, 148
  islands and debris theories, 206–9
  mid-Atlantic ridge, 245–6
  as 'Outside Sea', 130, 150, 153
  Phoenician voyages, 227–8
  as 'Sea of Darkness', 158–9
  as 'sea of dissimilarity', 153
Atlanticum (Plato), 139
Atlantipedia website, 326
Atlantis
  and allegory, 139–48, 329–30
  as 'ancient mother-city', 97, 292
  and Antarctica, 282–8
  and the Arctic, 204
  and Atlantic islands, 206–9
  and the Bible, 197–8
  and Britain, 224–5
  and bull sacrifice, 63, 104–5, 304,
    324
  capital city, 97–101
  city plan, 98
  continuing search for, 323–7
  and Crete/Santorini theory, 301–18
  decline and punishment, 105–7
  Egyptian influence, 120–7, 229
  equates with Athens, 212–13,
    319–23
  first appearance of, 3
  and historia, 117–20, 125–7, 142–3,
    154, 309, 320
  and Italy, 199–203
  meaning of, 3
  and medieval West, 157–60
  military arrangements, 103–4
  mythology, 94–7
  and Nazi ideology, 261, 264–70

  and occultism, 215–20, 248–57
  plain, 101–3
  Plato's geography of, 81
  and Plato's purpose, 319–23,
    327–33
  political structure, 104–5
  politicisation of, 171–82
  and Sweden, 191–5
  transmission of Plato's story, 75
  and Troy, 292–5
Atlantis Quarterly, 257
Atlantis Research Charter, 325–6
Atlas (first king of Atlantis), 3, 14,
  95–6, 105, 165–6, 258
Atle, King, 194
Auchincloss Brown, Hugh, 279
Autochthon, 95
Azaes, 96
Aztecs, 169, 231, 258–9
Aztlan, 169, 258, 292

Babylon, 33–6, 271, 321
  statue of Zeus, 34–5
Bacchylides, 298
Bacon, Sir Francis, 183–7, 239
Baer, F.-C., 198
Bailly, Jean-Sylvain, 204–6, 218, 267
Bartoli, Giuseppe, 212–13
Becanus, Johannes Goropius, 173
Beccario, Battista, 160
Belshazzar's Feast, 234
Benincasa, Grazioso, 160
Bianco, Andrea, 160
Blake, William, 220–4
Blavatsky, Madame, 248–52, 264
Bonnaud, Abbé Jacques-Julien, 198
Book of Daniel, 234
Book of Esdras, 168, 174, 176–7
Book of Ezekiel, 271
Book of Genesis, 189
Book of Revelation, 271
Boulanger, Nicolas Antoine, 209–12
Brahe, Tycho, 180
Brasseur de Bourbourg, Charles-
  Étienne, 171, 231–3, 275
Breasal, King, 171
Brisson, Luc, 309, 328
Britannia, 6, 20–6

Brunschwig, Jacques, 230
Buffon, Georges-Louis Leclers, Comte de, 209
Bull of Marathon, 297
Bura, 134–5, 148, 179–80
Buris, 135
Byzantine Empire, 154

Cadmus, 311
Calcidius, 157
Callimachus, 10, 312
Calypso, 6, 10, 134, 192, 303, 320
Cape Artemisium, battle of, 42
Careri, John Francis Gemelli, 201
Carli, Comte Gian Rinaldo, 199–203, 239, 272
Carthaginians, 13, 116, 167, 207, 227–8, 283
Cassandra, 312
catastrophism, 277, 279
Cayce, Edgar, 252–7, 327
Cecrops, 90
Cervantes de Salazar, Francisco, 161–2, 193, 308
Chacmool statues, 235
Charles V of Spain, 167
Charmides, 54, 57
Chateaubriand, Vicomte de, 215
Christina, 'Queen of the Swedes', 193
Cicero, 60, 67, 129
Cimon, 43
Claudius, Emperor, 23
Clearchus, 54
Cleisthenes, 31, 321
Cleito, 3, 95, 99, 142, 258–9
Clement of Alexandria, 138–9
Cleopatra, 121, 128, 130, 134, 294
Clymene, 3
Coatlicue (goddess), 258–9
Coleridge, Samuel Taylor, 224
Columbus, Christopher, 115, 162–3, 181, 282, 292
Columbus, Ferdinand, 163
comets, 20, 199–200, 202, 239, 272–3, 276–7, 289
Constantinople, fall of, 154-5
continental drift, 172, 226, 277

Copernicus, Nicolaus, 165
Cosmas Indicopleustes, 155–7, 168, 197–8
Crantor of Soli, 112, 117–20, 125–7, 136, 139, 143
Crates of Mallus, 172
Cratylus the Heraclitean, 50
Critias III, the Younger, 54–5, 57, 59
Critias (Plato)
    Acosta and, 173–4
    Bacon and, 187
    description of bull-hunting, 104, 300–1
    Ficino and, 160–2
    Flem-Aths and, 286
    Hancock and, 289
    Hellenistic readings of, 128–9, 136, 141
    remains unfinished, 28–9, 87, 107, 187, 328, 330
    and Santorini, 315
    and Stonehenge, 251
    and storytelling, 332
    studied by Byzantine scholars, 157
    summary, 85–107
    Theopompus and, 109–11
Croesus, King, 29
Cro-Magnon man, 258
Cumaean Sybil, 194
Cynicism, 128
Cyrene, 59–60
Cyrus, King, 36–8, 216

da Costa, Joaquim Alves, 228
Daedalus, 297, 299–300, 305
daemons, 140, 143–4
Dalberg-Acton, Sir John, 330
d'Alembert, Jean Le Rond, 196
Däniken, Erich von, 234, 290–2
D'Anville, Jean Baptiste, 206
D'Avezac, M., 160
Darius I, King, 31, 38–9, 321
Darwin, Charles, 180
Dee, Dr John, 180–1
Delian League, 43–4, 57
Delisle de Sales, 215–17
Delium, battle of, 56
Demetrius of Callatis, 56

dēmiourgos (Demiurge), 66, 85, 123, 154
Deucalion, 77, 92, 310, 334
Diaprepes, 96
Diderot, Denis, 195, 198
Dio Cassius, 317
Diocletian, Emperor, 146–7
Diodorus Siculus, 56, 123, 130–4, 167, 193, 308
Diogenes Laertius, 50–1, 59–60, 65, 124
Dion, 51, 64–5
Dionysius I of Syracuse, 61, 64
Dionysius II of Syracuse, 64
Diop, Cheikh Anta, 122–4
d'Olivet, Antoine Fabre, 209
Donnelly, Ignatius, 238–49, 255, 258, 264, 272
Drake, Sir Francis, 184
Dropides, 53, 74
Druids, 218, 221–3, 248, 251

earthquakes, 1, 82, 88, 113, 132, 152, 172, 185, 188–9, 251, 270, 273, 321, 324
 Athenian, 55–6, 92–3
 and destruction of Helice, 62–3, 134–5
 at Nicomedia, 147
 predicted by Cayce, 256–7
 and Santorini, 305, 307, 314
 and site of Troy, 293–4
 see also tsunamis
Ecbatana, 36–8, 321
Eddas, 192, 264
Eddington, A. E., 279
Einstein, Albert, 270, 281
Elasippus, 95
elephants, 115, 204
Eleusinian Mysteries, 57
Eliot, T. S., 332
Elizabeth I, Queen, 180–2
Ellenberger, Leroy, 278
Epaminondas, 63
Epic of Atrahasis, 336–7
Epic of Gilgamesh, 335–6
Epicureanism, 128
Eratosthenes, 10, 63

Erechtheus, 90
Erichthonius, 90
Erysichthon, 90
Erytheia, 5, 11–13, 20, 320
Euaimon, 95
Euclides, 50
Eudoxus of Cnidus, 193, 308
Euenor, 95
Euhemerus of Messene, 111, 132–3
Euremius, J., 198
Euripides, 5, 60
Eurytus, 59
Evans, Arthur, 299–300

Fabre d'Olivet, Antoine, 216–20
Favorinus, 52
Ficino, Marsilio, 160–2
Finaeus, 284
Finlay, Alexander G., 172
Flem-Ath, Rand and Rose, 285–8
Forbes, Edward, 180
Fracastoro, Girolamo, 165–6
Franke, Thorwald C., 325
Fréret, Nicolas, 205–6
Fritze, Ronald H., 290
Frost, K. T., 301

Gadeira, 12, 14, 95, 155
Gadeirus, 14, 95
Garvey, Marcus, 122
Gaul, 21–2, 24
Geoffrey of Monmouth, 158
Gibbon, Edward, 206
Gill, Christopher, 303, 313, 317
Gladstone, William, 245
Gorgias (Plato), 139, 331
goropism, 193–4
Gozo, 6, 10
Graves, Robert, 111
Grimm, Friedrich Melchior, Baron von, 211
Guanches, 207
Gustavus Adolphus, King of Sweden, 193

Hadji Ahmed map, 285
Hadrian's Wall, 25
Haeckel, Ernst, 246

Halicarnassus, 31, 38
Hancock, Graham, 288–90
Hapgood, Charles H., 279–86
Hecataeus of Abdera, 129
Hecataeus of Miletus, 32
Heliades, 20
Helice tsunami, 62–3, 134–5, 148,
    179–80, 321
Heliopolis, 60, 123–4, 137
Hellespont, bridging of, 41
Hephaestion, 38
Hephaestus, 4, 79, 89, 93, 144
Heracleides, 63
Heracles, 11–12, 14–16, 151, 311
Heraclitus, 119
Herculaneum, 60, 135, 306
Hermippus, 50
Hermocrates, 58, 72–4, 83, 87, 322–3,
    322–3
Hermocrates (Plato), 107
Hermodorus, 50
Hermogenes, 50
Herms, mutilation of, 57
Herodotus, 5, 15, 18–19, 31–8, 173,
    195, 266, 321, 331, 333
    description of Babylon, 33–6, 321
    description of Ecbatana, 36–7
    and *historia*, 117–20, 309, 320
    and Persian Wars, 39–40
    visit to Saïs, 31–2, 60, 121, 311
Herrera y Tordesilla, Antonio de, 162
Herrmann, Albert, 265–7
Hesiod, 4, 111, 195–6, 328, 334
Hesperia, 5, 14–17, 20, 320
Hesperides, 14–18, 111, 134, 159, 164,
    167, 240, 311, 328
Himmler, Heinrich, 266–7, 320
Hipparchus, 30, 172
Hippias (philosopher), 44
Hippias (son of Peisistratus), 30
Hippodamus of Miletus, 44
Hodgson, Richard, 249
Hofmann, Ulrich, 325
Homer, 4–10, 13–14, 62, 110, 140, 157,
    320, 328
    and Achaean wall, 113–14
    description of Crete, 296
    and Nazi ideology, 267

and Rudbeck's Swedish theory, 192,
    194–5
and *Twenty Thousand Leagues Under
    the Sea*, 235
and Velikovsky, 276
and Zangger's Atlantis–Troy theory,
    292–4
Hooker, J. D., 180
Horace, 25
Hörbiger, Hanns, 270–2
Huet, Pierre-Daniel, 197
Humboldt, Alexander von, 160, 226,
    237
Hume, David, 278
Hyades, 134
Hyperborea, 5, 17–20, 204, 250, 320

Iamblichus, 145–6, 149
Iapetus, 3
Ice Age, 239, 256, 279–80, 282–4,
    289
al-Idrisi, Ash-Sharif, 158–9
Incas, 199, 201, 264
Ionian Revolt, 38
Isidore of Seville, 158
Isis (goddess), 233
Isle of Brazil, 171
Isle of the Demons, 171
Isle of the Seven Cities, 171
Isles of the Blessed, 158, 224, 331
Isocrates, 51

Janiculum, 202
Janus, 194, 202
Japheth (son of Noah), 173, 192–4, 334
Jason and the Argonauts, 17, 194, 311
Jesus Christ, 134, 161, 194, 234, 256
Julius Caesar, 21, 216

Kalokairinos, Minos, 299
Keftiu, 300, 303–4, 314
King's Peace, 62
Kircher, Athanasius, 191, 207, 286–7
Kiss, Edmund, 265, 270
Knossos, 296, 299–300, 302–4, 313,
    317

La Peyrère, Isaac, 190–1

Laches (Plato), 56
Lamprocles, 56
Landa, Diego de, 170–1, 231, 233
las Casas, Bartolomé de, 161
Laurium, 39
Laws (Plato), 219
Le Plongeon, Augustus, 233–5, 248
Lemuria, 246, 250–1, 254
Leonidas, King, 42
Leucippe, 95
Leuctra, 63
Lévi-Strauss, Claude, 164
Lipsius, Justus, 179–80
Locris, 73
Longinus, 141–3, 146, 149
López de Gómara, Francisco, 169, 197
Lost Tribes of Israel, 168, 171, 227
Luce, J. V., 303
Lucian, 33, 130, 307
Lucian of Samosata, 118, 158
Lycophron, 312
Lysimachus, 51

Madoc, Prince, 181–2
magnetic polarity reversals, 281–2
Mallery, Arlington H., 282–3
Manetho, 129
Mappamundi, 158
Marathon, battle of, 38–9
Marcellus, 130, 150, 224
Marcianus of Heraclea, 130
Marinatos, Spyridon, 303, 305–8
Martin, Thomas-Henri, 213, 228–30, 238
Maximinus Thrax, Emperor, 146
Maya, 170–1, 231–5, 275, 292
Megara, 59
Mehmet II, Sultan, 155
Melos, 57, 59
Mercator, Gerardus, 284
Meropes, 110–11
Mestor, 96
Milky Way, 118
Miltiades, 38–9, 43
Minos, King, 296–300, 305
Minotaur, 297, 299
Mnemosyne, 87, 225
Mneseus, 95

Montaigne, Michel de, 178–9
Montesquieu, Baron, 196
Moo, Princess, 233
More, Thomas, 183
Mount Qaf, 204
Mounychia, 54
Mu, Land of, 233, 246, 255
Müller, Friedrich Max, 244

Nabonidus Chronicle, 37
Napoleon Bonaparte, 219
Neanthes, 51
Nectanebo I, pharaoh, 127
neo-Platonism, 128
Netto, Ladislau, 228
Neumayer, Melchior, 246
New Atlantis, see Bacon, Sir Francis
Newton, Sir Isaac, 195
Nicias, 56, 58
Nicomedia earthquake, 147
Nile flood, 127, 337–8
Niobe, 77, 310
Noah's flood, 155, 167–8, 202, 227, 272, 334–5
Numenius of Apamea, 139–41, 145

O'Connell, Tony, 326
Odyssey, see Homer
Ogygia, 5–7, 10, 20, 192, 204, 215, 303, 320
Olivier, Claude Matthieu, 198
Olympic Games, 33
oreikhalkon, 96, 99–100, 104, 321
Origen, 140–1, 145–6, 237
Orpheus, 17, 195
Ortelius, Abraham, 171–2, 226, 283
Orwell, George, 263
Ovid, 19
Oviedo y Valdés, Gonzalo Fernández de, 167, 227

Paraiba Stone, 228
Pareto, Bartolomeo, 160
Parmenides, 44, 50
Parmenides (Plato), 44
Pasiphae, 297
Pauly, Karl, 279
Peace of Callias, 43

Peace of Nikias, 56
Peckham, George, 182
Peisistratus, 30
Peloponnesian League, 43
Peloponnesian War, 45–6, 56–9, 61,
    135, 212, 309, 322
Pepys, Samuel, 195
Pericles, 43, 48, 51–2, 55
    Funeral Oration, 46–7
Perictione (Potone), 53–4
Persephone, islands sacred to, 130
Persian Wars, 31, 38–42, 61, 154, 309,
    322
Peter Martyr d'Anghiera, 164
Petrie, Flinders, 242
Pfeiffer, Tom, 313
Phaedo (Plato), 139–40, 151
Phaedrus (Plato), 124, 331
Phaethon, 19–20, 77, 118, 144, 275,
    320
Philip II of Macedon, 51, 63, 108, 128
Philip II of Spain, 172
Philo of Alexandria, 134–5
Philolaus, 59
Phoenicians, 40–1, 116, 122, 206,
    227–8, 241, 307, 311
Phoroneus, 77, 310
Pillars of Heracles, 11–12, 14, 81–2,
    88, 95, 115–16, 150–1, 153–4,
    167, 194, 209, 237, 285, 303,
    320, 323
Pindar, 5, 15
Piraeus, 39, 44–5, 61, 321
Piri Re'is map, 172, 282–3, 285, 291,
    311
Pizzigano, Zuane, 160
Plato
    and Academy, 51, 61, 65
    biography and ancestry, 49–65
    death and funeral, 65
    descent from Solon, 53–4
    and Egyptian influence, 120–7
    epitaph for Dion, 65
    purpose of Atlantis story, 319–23,
        327–33
    travels, 59–61, 64–5
    works, *see individual titles*
Platonic *Letters*, 60

Pleiades, 134
Pleistocene Beach Rock, 256
plenoxia, 330
Pliny the Elder, 13, 135–6, 167, 176,
    207, 265
Plotinus, 142–3, 146
Plutarch, 7, 28–8, 39, 60, 136–7, 158,
    193, 195, 207, 308
Poinsinet de Sivry, Louis, 211
pole shifts, 279–81, 283
Polybius, 37, 265
Pompeii, 13, 135
Pomponius Mela, 23
Porphyry of Tyre, 143–6, 149
Poseidon, 3–4, 7, 15, 94–5, 97,
    99–100, 104–5, 111, 113, 139,
    142, 147, 320
    and Cretan mythology, 297–8
    island sacred to, 130, 150
    and Nazi ideology, 267
    and Plato's ancestry, 52–4
    in Spence's theory, 259
    temple of Heliconian Poseidon,
        62–3, 321
Poseidonius of Apamea, 113, 129, 136
Postel, Guillaume, 170
Potidaea, 45
Pratinas, 111
Proclus, 112, 114, 117–20, 130, 139–42,
    145, 148–55
Prodicus, 44
Prometheus, 16, 139, 334
Protagoras, 44
Protagoras (Plato), 44, 139, 331
Prutz, Robert, 227
Psenophis of Heliopolis, 28, 137
Ptolemy, 25, 151, 172, 195
Ptolemy I Soter, 129
pyramids, 201–2, 243–4, 289
Pyrilampes, 54–5
Pyrrha, 77, 310, 334

Ram-fish, 111–12
Reinl, Harald, 290
Renan, Ernest, 228
Republic (Plato), 64, 67–8, 120–1, 123,
    139–40, 328, 330–1, 333
Richter, Ulf, 325

Roger II, King (of Sicily), 158
Romulus Augustulus, Emperor, 154
Roselli, Pedro, 160
Rousseau, Jean-Jacques, 197
Rowling, J. K., 327
Rudbeck, Olaüs, 192–5, 198–9, 203–4, 212, 217–18, 267, 285, 308
Russell, Bertrand, 278

Saint Augustine, 189
Saint Bartholomew, 186
Saint Brendan the Voyager, 157–8, 181
Saint Brendan's Isle, 171
Saint-Vincent, Jean Baptiste Bory de, 207, 209
Saïs, 31–2, 60, 77, 121, 129, 308, 311
    Stele of Saïs, 126–7
Santorini, eruption of, 305–18
Sarmiento de Gamboa, Pedro, 162, 172
Saturnus, 202
Sayre, G. M., 169
Scepticism, 128
Scharbau, Heinrich, 198
Scherie, 5, 8, 10, 20, 25, 267, 320
Schliemann, Heinrich, 245, 260
Schöner, Johannes, 284
Schoppe, Christian M., 325
Schoppe, Siegfried G., 325
Sclater, Philip, 246
Scott-Elliot, William, 251
Sechnupis of Heliopolis, 124
Seleucus, 38
Seneca, 135, 163, 265
Septimius Severus, Emperor, 137
Serranus (Jean de Serres), 168
Seven Sages of Greece, 27, 74
Seven Wonders of the Ancient World, 34
Severus, 149
Shakespeare, William, 164, 239, 263
Shelley, Percy Bysshe, 224
Sheshonq, pharaoh, 137
Sicily, Athenian invasion of, 57–8, 321–3
Silenus, 111
Smith, William, 283
Snider-Pellegrini, Antonio, 227

Socrates, 4, 31, 44–5, 50–1, 56–9, 151, 311, 330–1, 333
    and Plato's Atlantis, 27, 67, 69–72, 76, 82–4, 87, 114, 121, 125
    and purpose of Atlantis story, 327–8
Solomon, 155
Solon, 27–30, 31–2, 60, 333
    Cosmas Indicopleustes and, 155
    and Crete/Santorini theory, 303–5, 308–10, 318
    and Plato's ancestry, 53–4
    and Plato's Atlantis, 28–9, 74, 76–7, 79, 82–4, 90, 94, 113, 118, 129, 136–7, 178, 191, 211, 219, 228, 266, 271
    Robert Graves and, 111
    and unfinished Atlantis story, 28–9, 328
Sonchis of Saïs, 28, 137
Sophocles, 5
Sophroniscus, 56
Sparta, 38, 41–3, 55
    see also Peloponnesian War
Spence, Lewis, 257–61, 264
Speusippus, 54
Sphinx, the, 256, 289
Spitsbergen, 204, 218, 248
Sprague de Camp, 242, 294
Statesman (Plato), 110
stēlais, 126–7
Steno, Nicolas, 189–90
Stesichorus, 12
Stoicism, 128, 179
Stonehenge, 251, 267, 309
Strabo, 6, 12–14, 18, 22–3, 56, 60, 113–14, 124, 129, 265
Strato of Lampascus, 208
Suleiman I ('the Magnificent'), Sultan, 282
supernovae, 180
Swan, John, 188
syphilis, 165–6
Syracuse, 57–8, 61, 64, 322
Syrianus the Great, 148

Tacitus, 23, 25, 195
Tarrant, Harold, 126, 137

Tarshish, 173
Ten Plagues of Egypt, 273
Terra Australis Incognita, 172, 284
Tertullian, 137–8, 146
Thebes, 61–3
Themistocles, 39, 42
Theodorus the mathematician, 59
Theophrastus, 135, 208
Theopompus of Chios, 51, 108–12, 115, 172
Thermopylae, battle of, 42
Theseus, 90, 297–9
Thespis, 111
Thonis-Heracleion, 126
Thrasylus, 54
Thucydides, 10, 31–2, 44–8, 321–2
Timaeus (philosopher), 155
Timaeus (Plato)
    Acosta and, 173–4
    and allegory, 142
    Egyptian influence, 120–1, 123–5, 229
    Ficino and, 160–2
    Flem-Aths and, 286
    Hancock and, 288
    Hellenistic readings, 128–9, 134–7
    Martin and, 228–30
    and physical health, 330
    Proclus and, 112–13, 118, 149, 154
    and storytelling, 332
    studied by Byzantine scholars, 157
    summary, 65–86
    Theopompus and, 109–11
    Velikovsky and, 275–6
Tiryns, 293
Titanomachy, 329
Tournefort, Joseph Pitton de, 207–8
Troano Codex, 231–3, 275

Trojan War, 31, 113–14, 147, 293
Truzzi, Marcello, 278
tsunamis, 56, 152, 273
    and destruction of Helice, 62–3, 134–5, 148, 179–80
    and eruption of Santorini, 305, 307, 313
Twenty Thousand Leagues Under the Sea, see Verne, Jules

Ultima Thule, 265
uniformitarianism, 277
Uranus, 132–3
Ussher, Bishop James, 189

Velikovsky, Immanuel, 272–9
Verne, Jules, 235–9
Vidal-Naquet, Pierre, 134, 167, 206, 217, 220, 230
Virgil, 165, 252–3, 265
Voltaire, 204, 206, 268

Waldeck, Jean-Frédéric, 232
Wegener, Alfred L, 245
Whiston, William, 272
Wilford, Captain Francis, 224–5
Wilson, Colin, 285
World Ice Theory, 270–1
Wyatt, T., 68

Xanthippe, 56
Xenophon, 37, 55
Xerxes, King, 39–42, 147, 321
Zangger, Eberhard, 292–6
Zeno of Elea, 44
Zenobia, Queen (of Palmyra), 142
Zschaetzsch, Karl Georg, 264–5, 272